Critical Acclaim for the First Edition

The following statements are what others who have read the first edition of *The Information Systems Security Officer's Guide: Establishing and Managing an Information Protection Program* have said:

If you are looking to grow as a security professional, this book can definitely help you. Regardless of if you're just getting started in the industry or if you have 20 years under your belt, you will learn something from this author. It discusses everything from marketing yourself, getting hired, planning, hiring staff, performing risk management, classifying your information, doing metrics analysis and of course how to deal with people and politics in your "ISSO" position. A definite must have for anyone looking to manage an Information Security program for an organization.—Scott C. Sanchez, CISSP, New York, NY, USA

I read this book for an Internet Security course and I was very intrigued with its handling of the subject matter. As the title suggests, it is a guide for an ISSO's job. It gives clear insight as to what you should be focusing on and how you should expect to handle your day to day job and also how important it is to get the entire company involved in your efforts. I enjoyed this book very much.— Arthur E. Gousby III, Hoboken, NJ, USA

This guide is a very comprehensive introduction to everything an information system security officer should know, plan and do. It contains valuable information for personal marketing. It is an easy understandable book with lots of factual information—my favourite tutorial of the year.—Lilian Hages, Germany

I have found the Information Systems Security Officer's Guide by Dr. Gerald Kovacich provides many gems of wisdom, not only valuable to me as a former ISSO, but also in my role as a business continuity planning (BCP) professional. For example, I've struggled with how to facilitate BCP communication and interaction among our mission-critical organizations. Making the BCP charter consistent with the company's Strategic, Tactical and Annual Plans, as Dr. Kovacich suggested, has provided the needed common thread of BCP motivation for rapid deployment. Most importantly from a personal perspective, the idea of the ISSO Portfolio in the chapter titled "How to Market Yourself as an ISSO" is worth its weight in gold! By following Dr. Kovacich's advice, I was able to effectively compete for and win my current global BCP management job.—Robert L. McCord, Senior Manager, Worldwide Business Continuity Programs, Ingram Micro Inc., California, USA

Having both a law enforcement and private sector background, I appreciated the premise of Dr. Kovacich's book as it related to the Information Security Officer's duties and challenges. His approach will enable the reader to better understand the corporate environment concerning, not only the management process involved in protecting information, but also the importance of communicating and interacting with the organization in a way that people feel motivated to develop and maintain a successful and effective InfoSec program. The book discusses important management tenets and procedures which demonstrates the author's insight and experience in dealing with "real world" InfoSec issues. This book is easy reading and provides a clear understanding of the information security functions by taking the reader through the business and management environment and at the same time stressing a very important point that is often overlooked, i.e., an awareness and expectation that change is constant. I've recommended this book to those who are currently in the information security business and anyone who is attempting to pursue a career in this field. This book would be an ideal supplement to a variety of college courses and/or seminars pertaining to business and information technology.—Jerry Swick, WorldCom Network Security Operations Center, Investigative Services, Los Angeles, California, USA

Greater than I expected. Well thought-out and organized; written in simple, clear language; good advice and guidelines for the new ISSO; excellent examples of using management techniques and tools for establishing an effective InfoSec program; forward looking, especially the chapter on 21st Century Challenges for the ISSO. This is a one-of-a-kind book for the InfoSec professional and a must reading by all people interested in an InfoSec career. Even the experienced ISSO can find great value in this book. If an ISSO followed the guidance offered, success is almost a certainty. A book that should be adopted for required study in business management, computer science, and information security courses.—Motomu Akashi, Security Manager and Software Engineer, Ford Aerospace Corporation, Western Development Labs (Retired), Palo Alto, California, USA

Shows good research done prior to writing. * Written in easy to understand terms. * Very well organized. * Contains highly factual information. * Accurately portrays the ISSO position. * A must for any person responsible for developing and maintaining corporate Information Systems security processes. * This guide is the best on the market •oday.—J. Ervin, former Automated Information Systems Security Supervisor, Northrop Grumman Corporation, Palmdale, California, USA

Companies are paying closer attention to information security management issues. Those who don't have policies and procedures are putting them together, and those that already have them know they need constant management. The world needs knowledgeable infosecurity managers, but experience is hard to come by. If you're one of those trying to get a foot in the door, even if you already have a nonmanagement InfoSec job, you can use all the advice you can get. *Information Systems Security Officer's Guide* may be just what you need to get started.—*Information Security Magazine* book review by David J. Bianco, October 2002

The Information Systems Security Officer's Guide

Other Books Authored or Coauthored by Dr. Gerald L. Kovacich

- *Information Systems Security Officer's Guide: Establishing and Managing an Information Protection Program*, 1st ed. (Czech translation also available.)
- *I-Way Robbery: Crime on the Internet.* (Japanese translation also available.)
- *High-Technology Crime Investigator's Handbook: Working in the Global Information Environment*
- *Netspionage: The Global Threat to Information*
- *Information Assurance: Surviving in the Information Environment*
- *Global Information Warfare: How Businesses, Governments, and Others Achieve Global Objectives and Attain Competitive Advantages*
- *The Manager's Handbook for Corporate Security: Establishing and Managing a Successful Assets Protection Program*

THE INFORMATION SYSTEMS SECURITY OFFICER'S GUIDE

Establishing and Managing an Information Protection Program

Second Edition

Dr. Gerald L. Kovacich

BUTTERWORTH
HEINEMANN

An Imprint of Elsevier

Amsterdam • Boston • Heidelberg • London • New York • Oxford • Paris
San Diego • San Francisco • Singapore • Sydney • Tokyo

Butterworth–Heinemann is an imprint of Elsevier.

Library of Congress Cataloging-in-Publication Data
A catalog record for this book is available from the Library of Congress.

ISBN-13: 978-0-7506-7656-4   ISBN-10: 0-7506-7656-6

British Library Cataloguing-in-Publication Data
A catalogue record for this book is available from the British Library.

The publisher offers special discounts on bulk orders of this book.
For information, please contact:
Manager of Special Sales
Elsevier
200 Wheeler Road
Burlington, MA 01803
Tel: 781-313-4700
Fax: 781-313-4882

For information on all Butterworth–Heinemann publications available, contact our World Wide Web home page at: http://www.bh.com

10 9 8 7 6 5 4 3

Printed in the United States of America

To my son James, and daughters Leann and Christy:

May the world of your generations be a better place;

And may you do your part to make it so.

Table of Contents

Preface

Because of the popularity of the first edition of this "ISSO" book, the publishers asked me to do a Second Edition. When I agreed to write a second edition, I wanted to be sure not only that it would be brought up to date, but that it would continue to be a useful reference for you, the reader. Over the years since the book was first published, I have received comments and recommendations as to the book's content and what should be included in any new editions. I also solicited numerous information systems security (InfoSec) professionals for their comments. Based on everyone's input, this new edition was written.

The changes in this edition include:

*   An update of all chapters;
*   The rearrangement of the chapters based on InfoSec professionals' input into what they considered a more logical flow;
*   The dividing up of the chapters of this book into three major sections:

    Section I: The Working Environment of an ISSO;

    Section II: The Duties and Responsibilities of an ISSO; and

    Section III: The Global, Professional, and Personal Challenges of an ISSO.

*   Six new chapters:

    Chapter 3, Understanding Today's Threats to Information Assets;

    Chapter 11, High-Technology Crimes Investigative Support;

    Chapter 12, InfoSec in the Interest of National Security;

    Chapter 13, The Related World of Information Assurance, Information Operations, and Information Warfare;

    Chapter 14, The ISSO and Ethical Conduct; and

    Chapter 17, So, Are You Ready to Become an InfoSec Consultant?.

As with any book, sometimes the readers were critical of this book's first edition. That's fine if one can sit down and discuss InfoSec and ISSO responsibilities with the critics. After all, they have important points that could be considered when updating the book. However, that is usually not possible.

So, with all that said, let me state for the record what this book is *not*:

- It is not a book that is the "end all and be all" of ISSO and InfoSec functions, duties, and responsibilities. The rapid changes in information environments, high technology, etc., make such a book impossible.
- It is not a technical book and does not purport to be—it will not tell you how to install a firewall. The rationale is that there are many good books on the market that cover specific aspects of InfoSec, narrowly focused and very technical. It is expected that the ISSO will read these books as needed based on specific InfoSec needs of the ISSO.

In short, this book's goal is to provide a basic overview of the InfoSec professional's (ISSO) world, duties, responsibilities and challenges in the 21st century. It is a primer. It is about an ISSO who must establish and manage an InfoSec program for an international corporation, although all of the material is applicable to various work environments, such as government agencies or charitable organizations.

It was written because over the years many associates and I had to establish and manage such organizations and found no primer to guide us. So, over the past 40 years that I have been involved in various aspects of security, eventually focusing on InfoSec and its related functions in about 1980, I think I have developed a basic approach that has been successful. Others who have read this book, listened to my lectures based on what became this book, and whom I have mentored over the years have agreed with me.

So, if you are an InfoSec techie, engineer, or the like looking for the Holy Grail of information protection, that is not what this book is about. However, if you want an ISSO career, want to know what the ISSO profession is all about, and want to be able to build a foundation for a successful InfoSec program and organization, then yes, this book is for you.

This book was also written for non-InfoSec professionals in management positions, such as corporate security directors and business managers, who are responsible for overall government agency and business assets protection. These professionals should also know what the ISSO profession is all about and the basics of information assets protection.

This book can also be used as a textbook or "recommended reading" for university courses related to security and information systems security.

I hope you enjoy it. After reading it, please drop me an e-mail through my publisher and let me know:

- Any questions you may have;
- What you liked about it;
- More importantly, what you didn't like;

- Why you liked or disliked it;
- What ideas presented were most important to you;
- Your implementation of some of the ideas presented, and your result; and
- What I should write about or cover differently in the third edition.

After all, I want you to be able to use this book in the real world of the ISSO. All feedback is welcome. By the way, be sure to surf by my Web site for additional information that may be of use to you as an ISSO (http://www.shockwavewriters.com). Much of the information in this book and other related information is posted there. The information is free, there are no advertisements, and there is no tracking of who looked at what, when.

Thanks!
Jerry
Dr. Gerald L. Kovacich
ShockwaveWriters.Com
Whidbey Island, Washington, USA

*Acknowledgments
(Second Edition)*

To carry out a project such as this, it takes more than just the author. It takes friends, professional associates, and others who unselfishly give of their time and effort to help make my writing life easier and my books worth publishing.

To Chiang Hsiao-yun, researcher, analyst, critic, and wife who always provides support and who has had the patience of a saint for over 28 years.

I am also very grateful to a special group who has helped me over the years and again with such projects as this, including the following friends, associates, and colleagues:

- Motomu Akashi, my mentor and great sage;
- Bill Boni, a great coauthor and master of the management game we all must play in the profession, and now a Motorola Vice President for InfoSec;
- Don Evans, the "workhorse" of ISSA, and an InfoSec guru who is always ready to help;
- Ed Halibozek, security management guru of Northrop Grumman Corporation;
- Andy Jones, InfoSec and InfoWar professional now turned professor;
- Steve Lutz, global InfoSec consultant guru;
- John Quinn, master of the game of information collection, and unofficial book agent; and Winn Schwartau, a guy who has never been given the credit that he deserves for getting government and business folks thinking outside the bureaucratic box—the "Phoenix" of the trade.

To the staff and ISSO-2 project team of Butterworth–Heinemann of Mark Listewnik, Chris Nolin, Jennifer Rhuda, Kevin Sullivan, Julio Esperas, and Troy Lilly, thanks for the time, effort, and support in making ISSO-2, and my other BH books, a reality. Without your support and guidance this book truly could not have been written.

About the Author

Dr. Gerald L. Kovacich graduated from the University of Maryland with a bachelor's degree in history and politics, with emphasis in Asia; the University of Northern Colorado with a master's degree in social science with emphasis in public administration; Golden Gate University with a master's degree in telecommunications management; the DOD Language Institute (Chinese Mandarin); and August Vollmer University with a doctorate degree in criminology. He was also a Certified Fraud Examiner, Certified Protection Professional, and a Certified Information Systems Security Professional.

Dr. Kovacich has over 40 years of industrial security, investigations, information systems security, and information warfare experience in both the U.S. government as a special agent and business as a technologist and manager for numerous technology-based, international corporations as an ISSO, security, audit and investigations manager, and consultant to United States and foreign government agencies and corporations. He has also developed and managed several internationally based InfoSec programs for Fortune 500 corporations; and managed several information systems security organizations, including providing service and support for their information warfare products and services.

Dr. Kovacich has taught both graduate and undergraduate courses in criminal justice, technology crimes investigations, and security for Los Angeles City College, DeAnza College, Golden Gate University, and August Vollmer University. He has also lectured internationally and presented workshops on these topics for national and international conferences, as well as writing numerous published articles on high-tech crime investigations, information systems security, and information warfare, both nationally and internationally. He has written more than 100 security-related articles that have been published in various international magazines.

Dr. Kovacich currently spends his time on Whidbey Island, Washington. He continues to conduct research, write, consult, and lecture internationally on such topics as:

- Global and nation-state information systems security;
- Corporate information systems security;

- Corporate and government fraud;
- Corporate security;
- High-tech crime investigations;
- Information assurance;
- Proprietary information protection;
- Espionage, including Netspionage, economic, and industrial; and
- Information warfare—offensive and defensive.

He is also the founder of ShockwaveWriters.Com, an informal association of writers, researchers, and lecturers who concentrate on these topics.

Introduction

There are many debates as to where the information and information systems security (InfoSec) and the information systems security officer (ISSO) position fit in a company or government entity. Some believe it belongs in the information technology (IT) department, others say it belongs in the security department. Others believe it should report to the CEO, CIO, or some level of executive management other than the two mentioned.

The IT people may want control of the InfoSec function so that they can ensure that it does not hamper their IT functions. A corporate security manager may want the function to be sure these valuable assets, like other assets whose protection is the responsibility of the security department, are properly protected.

Four individuals, with different backgrounds and InfoSec responsibilities over the many years they have been in the business, share their views on InfoSec and the ISSO function. They are:

- *William "Bill" C. Boni*: Mr. Boni is the Vice President and Chief Information Security Officer, Motorola Information Protection Services (MIPS), Motorola Corporation.
- *Edward Halibozek*: Mr. Halibozek is the Corporate Director of Security, and IS Sector & Western Region Manager—Security, for a multi-billion-dollar, global corporation headquartered in Los Angeles, California, USA.
- *Andy Jones*: Mr. Jones was the business manager for the Secure e-Business department of QinetiQ, the privatized portion of Defense Evaluation and Research Agency (DERA), Malvern, United Kingdom. He is now a senior lecturer at the University of Glamorgan, Wales, United Kingdom.
- *Steve Lutz*: Mr. Lutz is the President, WaySecure, an information and information systems security international consulting specialist.

WILLIAM C. BONI

Information security is one of the fastest growing professions at this time. The combination of the terrorist attacks of September 11, 2001, and the increasingly critical role of information systems and technology in global business have contributed to that increase. As this book was being written, the Internet was subjected to an attack against the core infrastructure, terrorists and nation-states are reported to be honing their skills for future cyber attacks, and criminals are siphoning off profits from electronic commerce systems around the globe. There has never been a greater need nor greater appreciation of the need for capable, skilled information security professionals to guard the frontiers of businesses and nations.

Yet, as the importance of information security has increased, the field has become crowded with "instant experts." Many of those who now call themselves "experts" owe their current notoriety to some specific technical skill or to short periods of time in consulting or vendor organizations. Most who publish books and articles on information security have never held the accountability for protecting major organizations against the dizzying array of risks nor dealt with the harsh realities of doing so in the context of corporate cultures, politics, and the grind of daily operations.

In contrast, you hold in your hands a book containing the distilled wisdom of 40 years of practical experience from one of the original leaders in Information Security. Dr. Kovacich, "Jerry" to his many friends and admirers, has spent a lifetime developing and perfecting the materials that are the core content of this book. The original has held up over the years precisely because it is "technology independent." The assumption is that a reader has either attained already or can obtain from other books, courses, and seminars the technical skills to work in the information security field.

Therefore, if you are looking for technical solutions to the current or latest set of acronym challenges, then this is not the book you want to buy. However, if you are an information security professional seeking to understand what it takes to be successful as a manager and to become a leader in your organization and ultimately in the profession, then you have the right book.

Students considering their career options, as well as professionals in other but related fields such as information technology (IT), physical security, or IT audit, will also find the information presently so artfully by Dr. Kovacich to be of great value. Readers from all these backgrounds will find this book expands their knowledge of the many activities involved in establishing and sustaining an organization's information security program.

This updated and expanded edition builds upon the content that made the original volume one of the best-selling security books ever published. What the Guide does that is different, perhaps unique in the information security field, is to coach, mentor, and tutor the reader in the various managerial and operational skills that will assure a more successful and ultimately more satisfying career.

From my personal experience I can testify to the practical wisdom that is captured in these pages. I owe a significant part of my professional success and achievement to actually applying many of the methods and techniques described in the original Guide. Over the past six years I have recommended the previous edition to countless aspiring information security professionals, and note with satisfaction that many found the content to be key to their successful participation in the rapidly burgeoning information security profession.

Understand that a keen appreciation and lifelong commitment to information technology will be required for success as an information security practitioner. However much that background is necessary, it alone is not sufficient for professional success and personal satisfaction. Those who aspire to leadership and seek to become the managers, directors, and Vice Presidents of Information Security in the future will enjoy and learn much in the Guide that will support their success. I believe they will find, as I have, that Dr. Kovacich has provided them with knowledge that better prepares them for the challenges of managing these important responsibilities.

ED HALIBOZEK

Make no mistake about it. Information security is critical to the success of a business. Whether the enterprise is for-profit or not-for-profit, protecting information is an essential part of managing information and information systems. Modern companies, corporations, and governments, for their success and survival, are dependent upon information. Information that is created, processed, stored and shared. Yet the act of creating, processing, storing, and sharing information makes that same information vulnerable to loss, manipulation, theft, or destruction.

Whether information concerns a new product or technology, a proprietary process, a business plan, a customer or donor list, or military operations, information has value to its owner. That same information may also have value to competitors, criminals, or enemies. Some will take bold measures to obtain information. Others will rely on the failure of organizations to adequately protect their own sensitive and proprietary information making it easy for unauthorized collection and use. A few will seek to obtain information any way that they can, using legitimate or illegitimate means.

The very information that contributes to the viability and success of an enterprise, if unprotected and found in the possession of competitors or enemies, may cause the loss of a competitive edge, the embarrassment of exposure, or, in the event of military operations, may place war-fighters in "harm's way." Thus, protecting the availability, confidentiality, and integrity of information is an essential task.

In this book, Dr. Kovacich addresses the question "Is the position of an Information Systems Security Officer (ISSO) necessary?" Bluntly, unless your goal is failure, the answer is clearly "Yes." Protecting information is not an easy task. So much information resides on sophisticated and complicated information systems linked in local and wide area networks. To effectively and efficiently protect information and information systems requires the skills and dedication of a security professional: an ISSO.

The ISSO must be skilled in the disciplines of management, security, and information systems; must be capable of convincing others of the need to protect information; and must understand that protecting information is more about risk management than it is about risk avoidance. The ISSO needs to understand how information is used in the context of the world and business environment in which we operate. This includes understanding threats and where they come from, such as competitors, detractors, enemies, opportunists, and "bad guys."

A skilled ISSO is essential to any enterprise. However, an ISSO is not the only answer or solution. Understand that the ISSO is not an uebermensch. The ISSO alone cannot do everything that needs to be done to protect information. The ISSO must be capable of bringing together diverse persons with divergent interests in an effort to develop a protection profile for the enterprise. In this book, Dr. Kovacich provides the architecture to do just that. He provides a framework for establishing an effective information protection program.

Regarding the debate as to where an ISSO should report in the organization hierarchy . . . stop! Now is not the time for debate. Now is the time to act. Information security is serious business. The protection of information is just as serious as the management of information. In today's organizations most company information is processed, stored, displayed, and transmitted on and over information systems. Chief Information Officers (CIO) are skilled executives employed to ensure that information systems are effectively managed, meeting the needs of the enterprise and making information available to all users. Protecting this information and its availability, integrity, and confidentiality is just as important. A skilled executive is needed to accomplish this—a Chief Security Officer (CSO). The CSO is someone knowledgeable in matters of security, information protection, information systems, and business management. The CSO should be independent of the CIO and report directly to the CEO or COO. Separating the CIO function from the CSO function is important, as the need to protect information is often in conflict with the need to share and disseminate information. The ISSO should either report to the CSO or be the CSO.

Let's end the discussion on the need for information protection and the need for an ISSO. One would have to be a resident of Plato's Cave to not realize that information is critical to a business and requires protection. Let's shift our focus to understanding just what requires protection, how it should be protected, and from whom. Using this book by Dr. Kovacich is a very good beginning.

ANDY JONES

The role of the Information Systems Security Officer (ISSO) has never been of greater importance than in the environment in which we presently find ourselves and which we anticipate for the future.

As organizations and companies continue to become more dependent on information systems and connect to an ever wider group of partners that we have to rely on and "trust," the probability that they will encounter problems increases on an almost daily basis. In addition to this increasing reliance on systems that are increasingly interconnected, it is now an unfortunate reality that those people who would seek to do us harm increasingly have the knowledge and capability to do so.

For a number of years, the governments of a number of countries have been aware that there are some industries and systems that are essential to the well-being and maintenance of normal life within a country. These may include power production, telecommunications, water supply, food distribution, banking and the financial sector, and a whole range of other industries and have, together been tagged the Critical National Infrastructure (CNI). It is unfortunate for the ISSOs of these industries that in addition to all of the other risks that they must deal with, they now have to be concerned that they will be a target of attack by terrorists and others who wish to affect not their organization, but the government. This makes life a whole lot more difficult in a number of ways.

Some organizations are starting to better appreciate the implications of these developments and are recognizing that the role of the ISSO is not only increasingly important, but also increasingly difficult. Unfortunately, others have not taken the situation on board for the often repeated, endless set of reasons that have caused them to ignore it in the past. These include the lack of understanding of the underlying problems, a lack of skill to address them, insufficient resources, the "it won't happen to me" attitude, a lack of education and training, and a lack of direction from government.

The last of these has changed significantly in the recent past, and there is now a will by the governments of most developed countries to improve the security of information systems. This is particularly true of the United States, and huge investment has been made in "Homeland defense," with an apparently genuine drive by government to make information-dependent countries a safe place to live and trade.

One of the major problems that an organization faces in recognizing the need for an ISSO is based on the undeniable truth that in most cases, security is a costly drain on resources, in both financial and staff terms, that delivers no tangible return on the investment. If you are a member of the board of a company and have to make the choice between investing in a new plant that will reduce production costs and improve profitability, and investing in information security, which is likely to get your vote? This is often the decision that must be made, especially when the argument for "spend on information security" is based largely on the intangible and the unprovable. How do you prove that you are likely to be attacked or have security problems, when the evidence from past experience is that it has not been a problem before? How does the person presenting the argument for the information security investment convince a group of people who have probably never suffered the consequences of an information security breach that this is good value for money? If the members of the corporate board have been involved in a previous breach of information security, the investment argument will be received in a very different manner and by people who understand the value of it.

What is different about an ISSO from other types of security officers? Well, the short answer is that the ISSO is a hybrid that did not need to exist in the past. Security officers have traditionally gained their experience in the military or in government or public service (police or three-letter agencies) and they can tell you all about protecting tangible "things," whether they are objects or people. They are normally very good at it and the methods, tools, and techniques that they use have all been tested and refined over a long period of time.

Because the security of information systems cannot and must not be treated in isolation, the ISSO needs to have all of this knowledge and then, in addition, needs to be able to understand information systems and computers and the implications of their use. In this area, there is no collective pool of knowledge that has been gained over centuries by a large group of people. Information systems are, in historical terms, very young, and their maturity has taken them through so many evolutions in such a short time that there are very few computer professionals, let alone security specialists, who are able to keep pace with the changes and the diversity that have occurred. So the ISSO needs to have a wealth of knowledge and experience in security and in information technologies and has to be able to develop, implement, and manage policies that will protect the information resources of the organization in a dynamic environment.

A complication now arises. Where people will complain about physical security and will subvert it if it becomes too inconvenient and complain about the delays that the checking of passes and locked doors will cause, when you apply security to the information environment, a whole new set of problems is exposed.

The users of information systems have been exposed to and suffered from years of badly conceived and implemented information security that has caused inconvenience and prevented them from getting on with their job. It is a sad comment that, in the field of information security, the user of the system has often had more knowledge of the information technology than has the "security expert."

The bright side of the situation is that things are improving—the "information security experts" within organizations are gaining experience and the technologies that can help them to provide coherent security for systems are becoming available. The whole issue of threat and risk assessment is gaining credibility as methods are developed that give traceable routes to support the decisions that are made.

In the global context, while things proceed at a very slow pace, there are at least discussions on ways to harmonize the laws in different countries and groups of countries and the exchange of information between those who need it in order to maintain security.

It is easy for information security officers to become very insular and to look at the problems that they are facing in terms of only their organization—after all, these are busy, overworked people who are struggling just to keep pace with events and developments. This is a huge mistake and can only lead to disaster in the long term. We can no longer, for the most part, "conduct our business in isolation." The organizations that we work in have an ever-increasing need to communicate and to interconnect with other systems and organizations and in doing so, we have to be aware of the problems that such connections expose us to.

Learning from the best practice that has been developed in other organizations provides two benefits: The first is that it allows the knowledge of many to be applied to the problem of one; and the second is that it is one step down the line toward common standards and practices, which engenders confidence in others that the security that is being applied to your systems is of an acceptable standard (they can understand what you have done to make your systems secure and why you have done it!).

When the larger picture is examined, the responsibility that is placed on an information security officer is immense. The ISSO has a responsibility and a duty to the organization that the ISSO works for, but also has responsibility to partner organizations and others that may rely on the product of the organization. An example of this might be a power company, where the effect of a security breach might be the loss of availability of their systems. Unfortunately, the power supply company is networked to a number of other power suppliers to facilitate the balancing of power production to meet the customer needs. If one is affected, it may prove to be the weak link in the chain and allow the attacker to gain access to other power suppliers. There is also the issue of the customers—what impact will the loss of power supply have on their businesses? In turn, will it have an effect on their customers?

From the ISSO's point of view, life can only get worse. In some countries, laws are being introduced that place a legal obligation on organizations and their employees to take what is referred to as "reasonable" (or in some cases "appropriate") care of information that they have in their possession and also to take "effective measures" to protect the business, sometimes referred to as "due diligence."

How can ISSOs cope with doing the job of developing, implementing, and managing the security of the information while at the same time making sure that they understand the current risks and threats to their organization and the current technologies and techniques and the laws and best practice and standards? Well, no one ever said it would be easy. . . .

Gone forever are the good old days when we could operate with an island mentality and rely on the perimeter security of our organization to provide the first and main line of defense. The security perimeter is now almost meaningless with regard to our information, although it still has some benefits for the protection of physical assets. Now the routes into our organization are as much about the wires and fibers as they are about the roads and sidewalks. We can monitor physical access to our environment with a variety of technologies (CCTV, Access Control, pass entry systems) and we can also, fairly effectively, monitor what our staff is doing on our information systems (as long as we have the monitoring systems turned on and are watching them). We can put our security barriers up on the information systems (firewalls), but unless we deploy methods and tools to allow us to see what activity is taking place in our environment through systems such as intruder detection systems, we can not see what is happening in the area around our "virtual office." The nearest equivalent would be having the external doors locked, but not having any windows or cameras to let you see what is happening on the sidewalk outside the door (a potentially dangerous situation for when the door is opened, given that our door on an information system opens onto a sidewalk anywhere in the world).

It is also reasonable to suppose that, after the World Trade Center attacks, there is increased consciousness of the impact that a terrorist attack can have. It is a sad fact that in addition to the lives that were lost as a result of the outrage, a number of organizations that could and should have survived the incident did not, as they could not reinstate their business within the necessary period of time. Who was responsible for their demise? You could argue that it was the terrorists, but the reality is that it was actually their own lack of foresight and resilience and in some cases, just plain bad luck. If the organizations had all carried out risk assessments for their businesses in the environment in which they were operating, more would have taken steps to ensure that they had taken action on very old advice—have backups and store them in a safe place in another location, have contingency plans and practice them. As the ISSO, part of this is your responsibility—how are you going to ensure that your information is stored securely elsewhere and that you can recover it when you need to?

The life of an ISSO can never be an easy one—you are the voice of doom and authority within an organization that says "No" to users who want to do things that to their mind are quite reasonable. You are the one who acts as their conscience and highlights or investigates their sins, and you are the bearer of bad tidings to the board (you need more investment to keep the systems secure, or you have just had a security incident and are reporting the damage). You are the one who is responsible for the security of the "crown jewels" of the company. So why would you want to take on this role? Well, the answer is that it is one of the most satisfying and rewarding roles that you can imagine. It should never be boring, and there will usually not be the same problems to tax your intellect twice. It also allows you to use and develop skills in an area where you can make a difference and to contribute to a struggle that is becoming increasingly fast-moving and ruthless. It can be a hugely satisfying role, for those who can survive the apprenticeship and can accept the responsibility while maintaining a balanced view of the world.

STEVE LUTZ

The demand for Information Security consulting has been steadily increasing in the past 10 years, and for good reason. As everyone got on the technology bandwagon in the 1990s, the pressure increased to find innovative ways to deploy technology and increase productivity. The business community "discovered" the Internet and grand proclamations were made about the obsolescence of "brick and mortar" to be replaced by "e-commerce." While much of this was over-hyped, the race was on and "time to market" became one of the anthems of the new economy.

So in the frantic race to beat the competition, technology was deployed with little thought to security. Indeed, people had just enough time to get whatever it was working, let alone secure it in any meaningful fashion. And then *pow*, some security breach was discovered and it had to be fixed fast. In the rush to put the Web site or whatever together, no one budgeted for security, and there's nobody in-house with the expertise to handle it. Enter the information security consultant. Since it wasn't budgeted for in the first place, it's an out-of-cycle approval from management, and there you are trying to secure a system that has deep design flaws from a security perspective with an obscenely small budget. You explain that to really do it right, a complete redesign is in order. Yes, we understand and No, we can't do that. "It's a production system," "Our competition will kill us," "We don't have that kind of budget for security," and so on. With a sigh, you do the best you can to place some security Band-Aids on it and advise them to call you before the next design meeting for version 2.0. Guess what happens when v2.0 is released? Same thing.

This cycle repeated itself for pretty much the entire "dot-com" era with some exceptions. Some of the more forward-thinking companies hired consultants for security architecture and design work and saved themselves a whole lot of money and headaches. Still, the InfoSec consultants had more work than they could handle. (The same was probably true in the 1920s for radio engineers.) One good thing that came out of the 1990s was raised awareness of the role that Information Systems Security plays in a successful technology deployment. Oh, and there are now hundreds (thousands?) of companies offering security products for every conceivable problem.

Now that the party is over and technology has fallen back to being just another business tool, what will this mean for Information Systems Security consultants? Virtually all companies have cut back on their IT spending and are focusing on using what they've already overbought. Part of the hangover is that companies have had to lay off significant numbers of people across the board, including IT. Lean and mean, baby. Now it's time to take stock of what we did during the frenzy and see if there's anything we missed. Did we buy enough servers? Yes, we've got plenty. Networking? Yup, plenty of that. Web sites? Got 'em. There was something we missed, though. . . . What was it? Something critical. . . . Oh, yeah! That security thing. OK, get somebody on it. Oops, we laid them off. Hmm, can we hire someone? No way, there's a hiring freeze on. Well, we better call a consultant then.

And that's where we're at now. Information Systems Security consulting is doing quite well in these times and mainly for those reasons. A lot of what we're seeing is going back over everything and locking it down. That's great, but where is it going? I think that this will continue for some time during the economic downturn. At just about the time the retrofitting work is done, the economy will probably heat up again and companies will start buying IT again. When that happens, we InfoSec folks will be there to secure the next generation of information technology. Let's just hope everyone does it right the next time around, rather than rushing into every project just to get it out there fast.

Section I

The Working Environment of an ISSO

Section I (Chapters 1–4) provides an introduction into the ever-changing world in which today's information systems security officer (ISSO) must work. This section begins with an overview of the past and present world of nation-states, societies, high technology, criminal justice systems, the global marketplace, and the modern business and management environment.

The first section of this book then discusses some of today's threats to information and information systems. This section then culminates in the presentation of the establishment of a fictitious global corporation, the International Widget Corporation (IWC). IWC will be used as the employer of an ISSO who must establish and manage a successful and cost-effective information and information systems assets protections program, as well as manage an InfoSec organization.

1

Understanding the Information World Environment

The world is not merely the world. It is our world. It is not merely an industrial world. It is, above all things, a human world.—Agnes E. Meyer[1]

CHAPTER OBJECTIVE

The objective of this chapter, "Understanding the Information World Environment," is to provide a general overview of the changing information-dominated and information-dependent global environment in which the information systems security officer (ISSO) must work.

INTRODUCTION

We live in a world of information, known these days as an information environment (IE). Information that is pulled, pushed, dragged around the world through wireless, cable, optical fiber, and other assorted physical devices—and all of us along with it. We are dependent on information as individuals, companies, and government agencies. In fact, has that not always been the case? In days gone by, information was communicated by word of mouth, by drums, smoke signals, in writing carried by couriers on horseback, by telegraph, telephone, and now through the use of high technology.

The difference today is that in the "modern" countries of the world, we are more dependent on information and the high technology that allows us to communicate and do business, globally, at the speed of light. Today, more than ever, information—accurate information, and more of it,

---

[1] Agnes E. Meyer (1887–1970), U.S. journalist. *Out of These Roots*, Chapter 13 (1953). Meyer was concerned about the negative impact of technological progress on human happiness. From *The Columbia World of Quotations*. Copyright © 1996 Columbia University Press.

delivered faster—allows one an advantage. More than ever, this applies to companies, especially those involved in the global marketplace and in global competition.

Fast, accurate, and *complete* information provides the opportunity to gain a competitive advantage—assuming of course that the information is correctly acted upon in time to provide that advantage. The responsibility of the ISSO is to support this process by assisting in storing, processing, transmitting, and displaying that *fast, accurate,* and *complete* information in a secure manner. This support is necessary in order to assist in providing the company competitive advantage opportunities.

These opportunities to take advantage of information were summarized by Colonel John R. Boyd, United States Air Force, as a strategy based on the "OODA loop" (Observe–Orient–Decide–Act). The idea is to look at it from the viewpoint that whoever can be the quickest to move through this loop can gain a competitive advantage. Information has always been time dependent and probably is more so today then ever before. That is why it is crucial to be able to have a tighter (using less time) OODA loop than one's adversaries, whether they be a nation-state, a business, or an individual.

In addition, this advantage is created because the competitor becomes more confused and uncertain over events, and that may influence the competitor's judgement and decisions. In *Patterns of Conflict*, Boyd concluded that operating inside an opponent's OODA loop (see Figure 1.1) generates *uncertainty, doubt, mistrust, confusion, disorder, fear, panic, and chaos.*

Figure 1.1 is one example of the OODA loop where a company with a smaller OODA loop (inner circle) operates faster than the competition, shown by the large circle.

Figure 1.1   The OODA Loop Concept

CASE STUDY

In his book *Following the Equator*,[2] Mark Twain wrote about how one can take advantage if one has information before the competitor *and* knows how to act on that information. At the time of Twain's world travels, sharks populated the harbor of Sydney, Australia. The government paid a bounty on sharks. A young man was down on his luck and walking around the harbor when he met an old man who was a shark-fisher, who had not caught a shark all night. The old man asked the young man to try his luck. The young man caught a very large shark. As was the custom, the shark was disemboweled, as sometimes one found something of value. As it happened this young man did.

The young man went to the house of the richest wool-broker in Sydney and told him to buy the entire wool crop deliverable in 60 days. They formed a partnership based on what the young man found in the shark. It seems that the shark had eaten a German sailor in the Thames River. In the belly of the shark were found not only his remains, some buttons, and a memorandum book discussing the German's returning home to fight in the war, but also a copy of the *London Times* that had been printed only *10 days* before. At that time, news from London came by ship that took about 50 days. However, sharks traveled faster than the ships of that time. The *Times* stated that France had declared war on Germany, and wool prices had gone up 14% and were still rising. No other Australian wool brokers or wool producers would know that wool prices were skyrocketing for at least 50 days. By then the young man and his partner the wool broker would own all the wool, purchased at the "normal lower price," and could ship it to Europe for a very handsome profit.

This case study is an example of how accurate information received and acted upon within the competitor's OODA loop can give one a tremendous advantage in business. So, the old saying "information is power" is probably more true today than ever before, again providing that:

- The information is accurate,
- It is acted upon correctly, and
- It is acted upon before it is acted upon by your competitor.

---

[2] Twain, Mark, *Following the Equator*. P.F. Collier & Son, New York, 1992, pp. 109–116.

Information[3]

1. **knowledge:** *definite knowledge acquired or supplied about some-thing or somebody*
2. **gathered facts:** *the collected facts and data about a particular subject*
3. **making facts known:** *the communication of facts and knowledge*
4. **computer data:** *computer data that has been organized and pre-sented in a systematic fashion to clarify the underlying meaning*

Remember that if your company's information systems were the victim of a successful denial-of-service attack, important information could not get to the right people at the right time so that they could use that information to gain a competitive advantage.

Understanding Your Information-Driven Environment

As an ISSO, it is very easy to get caught up in high technology and view that as "your world." After all, in today's high-technology-driven and high-technology-dependent world, it is very easy to look at information and high technology as your working environment, what causes your problems, and where the solutions to your problems lie. However, the truth is that high technology is just a tool like any other tool. And as with any tool, it can be used as intended, abused, or used for illegal purposes—*by people.*

In today's information world environment that you must work in, it is much more than just high technology. You must understand this world and also us humans, as all these topics have a direct bearing on the protection of information and information systems. They include such things as:

- Global and national marketplaces;
- Global and nation-states' economies;
- International politics;
- World cultures and societies;
- International and national laws, treaties;
- Major languages of the world;
- Major religions;
- Business;

---

[3] Definition taken from Microsoft's *Encarta World English Dictionary* (see http://www.microsoft.com/encarta/).

- Human relations and psychology; and
- Governments of nation-states.

To be successful, the ISSO must have a varied background not only in such things as computer sciences but also in psychology, social science, geopolitical matters, international business, world history, economics, accounting, and finance. Also, the more foreign languages the ISSO knows, the better. Volumes have been written about each of these topics. It would behoove the ISSO to have a working understanding of each of these topics, as they all affect the ISSO's ability to successfully establish and manage a successful information protection program. There are few professions today that offer the challenges that face the ISSOs of government agencies and businesses all over the world.

ISSOs must understand the world in which they will work in order to be successful. In the past, this understanding was generally limited to the company or government agency in which the ISSO worked, and to their computer systems, which were isolated within the company. The ISSOs generally were only concerned with the events that took place within their respective countries, as what happened outside of that limited world usually did not affect their work. However, that was in the past.

> If you know the enemy and know yourself, you need not fear the result of a hundred battles. If you know yourself but not the enemy, for every victory gained you will also suffer a defeat. If you know neither the enemy nor yourself, you will succumb in every battle.—Sun Tzu

The environment of the ISSO that may affect the protection of information and information systems is now global in scope, and high technology is changing more rapidly with each passing year. This new global business environment and its associated high technology must be clearly understood by the ISSO. This is because it is all integrated into a driving force which will dictate what must be done to protect the information systems and the information that they store, process, display, and transmit. It will also determine how successful the ISSO's information systems security (InfoSec) program will be in providing protection at least cost to the business or government agency.[4]

Today's computer system environments are all based on the microprocessor. The microprocessors have become cheaper and more powerful

---

[4] Throughout this book, we will use the terms "business," "company," and "corporation" interchangeably. Although the information provided is very applicable to government agencies, nonprofit entities, and the like, these terms will not usually be used. The reader who is responsible for information and information protection within these other entities is kindly asked to just think of "company" et al. as describing a government agency or other entity as applicable.

at the same time. This is the primary cause for their proliferation through-out the world. One systems specialist has found that one megabyte of storage in 1975 cost $350; in 1985 it cost $30; and in 1995 it cost $1! Now, its costs are measured in pennies. If this rate continues, storage may soon be free. And as we all know, the storage of information is one of the key elements needing protection within the company or government agency. In fact, some computer manufacturers now offer free upgrades when you purchase one of their systems online.[5]

> Desktop Special Offers—Notebook Special Offers:
> - FREE Memory Upgrade—Online Only! With purchase of any new Dimension desktops. Ends Wednesday!
> - FREE Hard Drive Upgrade—Online Only! With online purchase of any new InspironTM 8200 or 4150 notebook. Ends Wednesday!
> - FREE 2nd Battery—Online Only! With purchase of new Inspiron 8200 notebooks. Ends Wednesday!

When we think of computers, we sometimes look at them as very complicated devices, when in fact they are not that difficult to understand. Computers are composed of the hardware, the physical pieces; the soft-ware, the instructions to the computer which can be altered; and the firmware, which are instructions embedded on a microprocessor. Together, they are used to process, store, display, and/or transmit information. Of course the more an ISSO knows about how hardware, firmware, and soft-ware work, the better position the ISSO will be in to protect those systems and the information they process, store, display, and/or transmit.

Computers have been around for some time. We continue to celebrate the "birthday" of the ENIAC, the world's first major computer system. The microcomputer, which is much more powerful than the ENIAC, has not been around that long.

In many of today's information-based nation-states, we have been able to network thousands of systems because of the rapid advances in high technology and cheap hardware. We have built the information systems of the nation-states' businesses and government agencies into major information infrastructures known as the National Information Infrastructures (NIIs). A standalone computer system (one with no exter-nal connections between it and other computers) today is relegated to a small minority of businesses and government agencies. We cannot func-tion in today's business world and in our government agencies without being connected to other information systems—both national and internationally.

The protection of information systems and the information that they process, store, display, and/or transmit is of vital concern in this infor-

---

[5] http://www.dell.com/us/en/dhs/default.htm?rpo=true

mation world. Many nation-states are already in the Information Age, with many other nation-states now entering that age, with yet many more close behind. This will complicate the information protection problems of the ISSO.

The ISSO must remember that the information protection program must be *service* and *support* oriented. This is of vital importance. The ISSO must understand that the information protection program, once it is too costly, outdated, and does not meet the service and support needs of the business or government agency, will be discarded or ignored. So, one of the ISSO's challenges is to facilitate the networking of systems nationally and internationally while protecting company information and systems.

In order to provide the cost-effective information protection program, the ISSO must continually keep up with high technology. The ISSO must continuously be familiar with technological changes in general and intimately familiar with the technology being planned for installation within their business or government agency.

The ISSO must understand how to apply information protection and integrate information protection into, around, and onto the new high technology. Failure to do so would leave the information and their systems vulnerable to attack. In that case, the ISSO would have a serious problem— possibly a job security problem—if a successful attack occurred due to the new-found vulnerability brought on by the newly implemented technology.

The ISSO could delay installation of the new high technology until a suitable information protection "umbrella" could be installed. However, in most businesses, this would be considered a career-limiting or career-ending move. In today's business world, the phrase "time is money" is truer than ever. In today's and tomorrow's highly technologically based environment, *innovation* and *flexibility* are key words for the ISSO to understand and apply to the company's or government agencies' information protection program.

Thus, the ISSO has very little choice but to support the installation of the new high technology and incorporate information protection as effectively and efficiently as possible. And one of the ways to successfully provide that service and support is to keep up with technological changes.

REVOLUTIONS AND EVOLUTIONS IN HIGH TECHNOLOGY

As was mentioned in previous paragraphs, one cannot address the issue of information protection without first addressing the changes brought on by high technology, and its impact on businesses, government agencies, societies, global, economic competition, and the world in general. High technology obviously has a major impact on information and information systems protection (InfoSec) and the ISSO's ability to successfully protect information.

High technology has many uses, and over the centuries it has driven how we humans work, live, and interact. In a speech televised on the program *BookTV* on April 4, 2002, Michael Eisner, Chairman and CEO, The Walt Disney Company, discussed the impact of technology on the world and used the following timeline of the beginnings of communications related "devices":

- 1455: Gutenberg Bible
- 1689: Newspapers
- 1741: Magazines
- 1892: Movies
- 1907: Radio broadcast
- 1927: TV
- 1975: Microsoft

All these forms of technology and communication systems, as well as companies, have had a major impact on our lives throughout history. They not only entertain us, but also provide us with information. Some of the information provided is sensitive information that a company or government agency may want to keep private and not release to the general public. Consider this as an ISSO: If that private, sensitive information communicated to the public is about your company, how that information is obtained may indicate a vulnerability in an information protection process. If so, you have a serious problem. The more free a society is, the more free the news media will be, and consequently, the more challenging your job to protect sensitive business information. However, with that said, remember that as an ISSO, your job is also to protect the privacy of individuals in your company.

> Some day, on the corporate balance sheet, there will be an entry which reads "Information"; for in most cases the information is more valuable than the hardware which processes it.—RADM Grace Murray Hopper, United States Navy

We've been using the terms *technology* and *high technology*, but what exactly do these two terms mean? In general, technology is described as a means to handle a technical problem. It can be a method, process, or thing. When we talk about high technology, what do we mean? Many definitions of high technology are vague and often interpreted and thought of based on the environment of the person defining it. Those of us in the world of the 21st-century ISSO think of high technology as basically computer-based systems. For our purposes, we will define technology and high technology as those things that are microprocessor based.

GLOBAL INFORMATION INFRASTRUCTURE (GII)

The importance of information protection continues to grow, as we become more and more dependent on high-technology systems. The networking of systems around the world is continuing to expand the Global Information Infrastructure (GII). Today, because of the microprocessor, its availability, power, and low cost, the world is "building" the GII. The GII is the massive international connections of world computers that are carrying business and personal communications as well as that of the social and government sectors of nation-states. Some say it could connect entire cultures, erase international borders, support "cyber-economies," establish new markets, and change our entire concept of international relations.

GII is based on the Internet and much of the growth of the Internet. The GII is not a formal project; rather, it is the result of thousands of individuals', corporations', and governments' need to communicate and conduct business by the most efficient and effective means possible.

The importance of information protection takes on added meaning because of the increased threats to the systems and the information they store, process, display, and transmit due to this expanded connectivity provided by the GII. After all, it will come as no surprise to you that there are people and nation-states in the world that consider your company and your country an adversary—the enemy. That being the case, they will do whatever they can to meet their own objectives—generally at the expense of your company or nation-state.

One example is the aggressive information infrastructure vision and plans of Malaysia. Malaysia not only wants to aggressively pursue the total integration of information systems in government, businesses, and schools throughout the country, but it also wants to establish a government that is "paperless"! Imagine the information protection problems associated with such endeavors. And of course, Malaysia wants to provide global access, e.g., the Internet, to its citizens, while still maintaining their basic culture and religious values. Quite a challenge for the 21st century, and one that unfortunately has been set back because of Malaysia's current economic environment.

Because of Malaysians' religious beliefs, Internet access to material considered pornographic or topics that violate their culture is not acceptable. One of their society's struggles, as with many nation-states, will be how to provide access to the world's information without causing some moral decay of their society. This will be a struggle for many countries, and it is believed that the ISSOs and their information protection programs will have a major impact on the society of such developing countries.

NATIONAL INFORMATION INFRASTRUCTURE (NII)

The National Information Infrastructure (NII) alluded to earlier is basically the network of computers upon which the nation-state and its people rely in this information–knowledge age. The NII is the high-technology, critical information infrastructure of a nation-state. The critical infrastructures, according to several nation-states, are generally defined as systems whose incapacity or destruction would have a debilitating impact on the defense or economic security of the nation-state. They include:

- Telecommunications,
- Electrical power systems,
- Gas and oil,
- Banking and finance,
- Transportation,
- Water supply systems,
- Government services, and
- Emergency services.

HOW DID WE GET FROM ADAM TO THE INTERNET?[6]

The use of the Tofflers' model of technological evolution provides a useful framework for discussing changes arising from the impact of the technology generally, and the Internet specifically. The model begins by describing the Agricultural Age that lasted from about the time of Adam until about 1745 in the United States.[7] Manual labor and a focus on accumulating a minimum food surplus to allow for governance characterized this long period. During this time, technological progress was very limited, slow, and laborious. The major lack of understanding of even the most basic concepts of science impeded progress. Warfare, although common, was generally short in duration and was often decided by major battles or campaigns lasting less than a year, with some exceptions such as the Hundred Years' War and the Crusades. Although large armies were possible (at one point the Roman Empire fielded more than 700,000 soldiers), there were limited and relatively ineffective methods for communicating and controlling more than a small percentage of these forces. Runners and horse-borne message couriers supplemented by flags and other visual media were the major methods of remote communication.

---

[6] This information was taken from the author's coauthored book, *Internet Robbery: Crime on the Internet*, also published by Butterworth–Heinemann.

[7] The time of the agricultural period varies by progress of individual nations.

The "Industrial Age," in the United States, lasted a much shorter time, only from approximately 1745 until about 1955.[8] The defining event of the Industrial Age was the introduction of the steam engine, which allowed mechanical equipment to replace muscle-powered efforts of both humans and animals. These devices introduced a new and much accelerated pace of technical innovation. During this 200-year period, there was a dramatic expansion of human knowledge and understanding of the basic principles of physical science. Enhanced agriculture allowed nations to accumulate huge food surpluses. Upon foundation of the food surplus, the nation-states increased their power, which was driven by mass production. Mass production of weapons and the mass slaughter of both combatants and noncombatants characterized the conflicts of this period.

Communications technology evolved from primitive signaling involving lanterns and reflected lights (heliograph) to supplement the continued use of human couriers, whether riding horses, trains, or waterborne craft. The inventions of the telegraph in the early 1800s followed in the late 1890s by the telephone and then by wireless radio in the early 1900s were essential evolutionary steps toward today's telecommunications infrastructure.

The "Information Age" in the United States, according to the Tofflers, began about 1955, which is the first year that the number of white-collar employees exceeded the number in blue-collar production jobs. This has been the era with the most explosive growth in human knowledge. More has been discovered in the past 50 years in both science and engineering than in the thousands of years of recorded human history. In the information age, knowledge is growing exponentially.

The pace of evolution in communications and other technologies accelerated during the early years of the Information Age with the advent of satellites, fiber-optic connections, and other high-speed and high-bandwidth telecommunications technologies.

It is in the context of this phenomenal growth of technology and human knowledge that the Internet arises as one of the mechanisms to facilitate sharing of information and as a medium which encourages global communications. According to the United States General Accounting Office, in a report to Congress,[9] the rapid developments of telecommunications infrastructure in the United States resulted in creation of three separate and frequently incompatible communications networks:

- Wire-based voice and data telephone networks;
- Cable-based video networks; and
- Wireless voice, data, and video networks.

---

[8] As with the Agricultural Age, dates vary for individual nations.
[9] "Information Superhighway: An Overview of Technology Challenges." GAO-AIMD 95-23, p. 12.

Birth of the Internet[10]

The global collection of networks which evolved in the late 20th century, and continue to evolve in the 21st century, to become the Internet represent what could be described as a "global nervous system" transmitting from anywhere to anywhere facts, opinions, and opportunity. However, when most security and law enforcement professionals think of the Internet, it seems to be something either vaguely sinister or of such complexity that it is difficult to understand. Popular culture, as manifested by Hollywood and network television programs, does little to dispel this impression of danger and out-of-control complexity.

The Internet arose out of projects sponsored by the Advanced Research Project Agency (ARPA) in the United States in the 1960s. It is perhaps one of the most exciting legacy developments of that era. Originally an effort to facilitate sharing of expensive computer resources and enhance military communications, over the 10 years from about 1988 until 1998 it rapidly evolved from its scientific and military roots into one of the premier commercial communications media. The Internet, which is described as a global meta-network, or network of networks,[11] provides the foundation upon which the global information superhighway will be built.

However, it was not until the early 1990s that Internet communication technologies became easily accessible to the average person. Prior to that time, Internet accesses required mastery of many arcane and difficult-to-remember programming language codes. However, the combination of declining microcomputer prices, enhanced microcomputer performance, and the advent of easy-to-use *browser*[12] software created the foundation for mass Internet activity. When these variables aligned with the developing global telecommunications infrastructure, they allowed a rare convergence of capability.

It has now become a simple matter for average people, even those who had trouble programming their VCRs, to obtain access to the global Internet, and with the access search the huge volume of information it contains. The most commonly accessed application on the Internet is the World Wide Web (Web). Originally developed in Switzerland, the Web was envisioned by its inventor as a way to help share information. The ability to find information concerning virtually any topic via search engines from among the rapidly growing array of Web servers is an amazing example of

---

[10] See the book *I-Way Robbery: Crime on the Internet*, published by Butterworth–Heinemann, 2000, and coauthored by Dr. Kovacich and William C. Boni, for more details about the Internet and criminal activities.

[11] *Ibid.*, p. 11.

[12] Software that simplifies the search and display of information supplied by the World Wide Web.

how the Internet increases the information available to nearly everyone. One gains some sense of how fast and pervasive the Internet has become as more TV, radio, and print advertisements direct prospective customers to visit their business or government agency Web sites.

An important fact to understand, and which is of supreme importance for security and law enforcement professionals, is that the Web is truly global in scope. Physical borders as well as geographical distance are almost meaningless in "cyberspace"; the distant target is as easily attacked as a local one. This is an important concept for security and law enforcement professionals to understand because it will affect their ability to successfully do their jobs. The annihilation of time and space makes the Internet an almost perfect environment for the Internet robbers. When finding a desired server located on the other side of the planet is as easy and convenient as calling directory assistance to find a local telephone number, Internet robbers have the potential to act in ways that we can only begin to imagine. The potential bonanza awaiting the Internet robber, who is undeterred by distance, borders, time, or season, is a chilling prospect for those who are responsible for safeguarding the assets of a business or government agency. As the ISSO, you have responsibility for deterring these miscreants, as well as helping security and law enforcement personnel investigate them.

"Future Shock"

With appreciation for the Tofflers' book *Future Shock*, the reaction of people and organizations to the dizzying pace of Internet progress has been mixed. Although some technologically sophisticated individuals and organizations have been very quick to exploit the potential of this new technology, many have been slower, adopting more of a wait-and-see posture. The rapid pace of evolution of the Internet does raise some questions as to how much a society can absorb, and how much can actually be used to benefit organizations in such a compressed time frame. Sometimes lost in the technological hype concerning the physical speed of Internet-enabled communications or the new technologies that are making it easier to display commercial content is the reality of the Internet's greatest impact: It provides unprecedented access to information. The access is unprecedented in terms of the total volume of information that is moving online and may be tapped for decision making.

It also is unprecedented when we consider the increasing percentage of the world's population that enjoys this access. More and more information moves online and becomes available to more and more people, causing fundamental changes in how we communicate, do business, and think of the world we live in. Consequently, there are also fundamental changes in how criminals and miscreants commit crimes.

Throughout much of human history, the educated elites of every culture have jealously guarded their knowledge. Access to knowledge, whether in written or spoken form, was often the source of the elite's privileged position and often allowed them to dominate or control the great uninformed masses of uneducated humanity—information was and is still a means to power. "Outsiders" were never granted accesses to the store of wisdom unless they were inducted into the privileged elite. Now, however, the average Internet traveler, wherever resident, with little more than a fast modem and a mediocre microcomputer, can access, analyze, and/or distribute information around the world on almost any topic.

Some pundits have concluded that we now live in an era where there are "no more secrets." By some estimates, early in this century there will be more information published and available online than has ever been accessible in all the libraries on earth. How this torrent of information will be managed to ensure that Internet robbers do not wreak havoc and dominate the Internet, or have power over others, is now (or should be) the primary objective of every security and law enforcement professional whose business or government agency travels the Internet.

Roadmap for the Internet

The Internet can be compared in some ways to a roadmap for a superhighway. Some basic examples will help explain it in common terms.

When multiple computers (whether microcomputers or larger) are linked together by various communications protocols to allow digital information to be transmitted and shared among the connected systems, they become a network. The combination of tens of thousands of organizational networks interconnected with high-capacity "backbone" data communications and the public telephone networks now constitutes the global Internet. However, there is a major difference in this environment that is important to consider for security and law enforcement professionals.

When the isolated by-ways of individual business or government agency networks become connected to the global Internet, they become an "off-ramp" accessible to other Internet travelers. The number and diversity of locations that provide Internet "on-ramps" is vast and growing. Today, one can access the Internet from public libraries, cyber-cafés in many cities around the world, even kiosks in some airports. These and other locations provide Internet on-ramps to anyone who has a legitimate account—or an Internet robber can hijack one from an authorized user.

Typically a business or government agency will use centrally controlled computers, called servers, to store the information and the sophisticated software applications used to manage and control its information flow. These systems could be equated to a superhighway interchange.

Commonly business and government agency networks are considered private property and the information they contain as proprietary for the exclusive use of the organization. These business and government agency networks are connected to large networks operated by Internet service providers (ISPs) such as UUNET, GTE, AOL, and AT&T, who provide the equivalent of toll roads and turnpikes—the highways for the flow of information.

The Internet: No Traffic Controls

The Internet challenges the security and law enforcement professional with an array of new and old responsibilities in a new environment. From the perspective of managing risks, this new access to information creates new kinds of dangers to businesses and government agencies. It also allows well-understood security issues to recur in new or unique ways. No longer can organizations assume they will obtain any security through obscurity, no matter where they are physically located. In other words, because there is an Internet off-ramp, they will be visible to Internet robbers. Everything from a nation's most critical defense secrets to business information is vulnerable to easy destruction, modification, and compromise by unauthorized Internet travelers.

Too often careless managers fail to take adequate measures to safeguard sensitive information, which results in premature disclosure with attendant adverse impact. The major part of the controllable risk arises from inadvertent disclosure to the ever-vigilant eyes of Internet robbers and others, such as competitive intelligence analysts with Internet access.

When the Internet was limited to scientists, academic researchers, and government employees, such a collaborative framework was probably a very cost-effective means of controlling the virtual world. However, in the early 1990s, for the first time there were more commercial sites than educational and governmental sites using the Internet. Since that time matters have become increasingly complex. The informal array of social sanctions and technical forums for cooperation is no longer capable of ensuring a modicum of civilized behavior.

What Has Been the Impact of the Internet?

It is apparent that the Internet has rapidly become a significant element in modern society, figuring in advertising, films, and television, even facilitating the rapid dissemination of investigative reports involving a U.S. president. The Internet has provided many additional information services, and they are all becoming easier to access. The two primary new avenues for increased volume of information access are the Web browser and net-enabled e-mail. This increased access to information has been principally an advantage for law-abiding citizens and legitimate businesses, but it also offers both hardened and prospective Internet robbers new, high-speed venues for perpetrating their crimes and schemes.

Almost everyone working in America has been exposed to some form of computer technology. From the front-line retail clerk at the local fast-food franchise, to the Wall Street analyst, to the farmer planning his crop rotations, individual work performance has been substantially enabled by the widespread proliferation of microcomputer technologies. But the macro impacts on organizations are in some ways less remarkable than they have been for individuals. Go to any good computer store, or better yet, if you have Internet access, browse the Web sites of major microcomputer manufacturers. You will discover a wide range of systems with memory, speed, and storage capabilities that would have been descriptive of large, mainframe-type computers in the early 1980s. For example, a large regional bank in Southern California in the late 1980s operated its electronic wire/funds transfer machine with only 48 MB of RAM and 120 MB of disk storage, and the system transferred billions of dollars nightly for the bank. Now the performance of an equivalent system is available to anyone with a few thousand dollars, and the nightly transactions run to the hundreds of billions.

In business, it has become in some ways a David versus Goliath world, where the advantages do not always accrue to the organization that can field the bigger battalions. Advanced information technology was once the province exclusively of governments, the military, universities, and large corporate entities. This is no longer true. Now anyone with a modest investment in hardware and software can acquire a powerful processor and attach it to the Internet. It should be obvious that criminals and those with criminal intentions also have access to powerful information technology. The question remains: How will they use it?

As we consider the potential for criminal actions directed against organizations, it is critically important to consider these factors. The same information technology we use to manage our organizations can and will be used by savvy Internet robbers to the detriment of governments, businesses, and others.

When powerful microcomputers are networked, the communication capabilities inherent in these arrangements multiply their value. A single microcomputer standing alone is little more than a sophisticated typewriter or calculating machine. The real power comes when individual machines link together to create networks which will allow the flow of information from one person to the entire world. As a case in point, consider the story of Russia's transition from Communism. When the military coup against Gorbachev occurred in the early 1990s, the military plotters seized control of all the classic means of communication: newspapers, telephones, and radio and TV stations. However, the anti-coup forces quickly drove their message on the Internet to get word to the outside world of the situation, and timely communications played a significant part in defeating an attempt by the most powerful military and police apparatus on earth to regain power over the Russian people.

The capabilities brought to the individual by the Internet are considerable and growing almost daily. One example is the ability to sign up for investment services from low-cost brokerages and stock market advisors and enjoy the kind of timely advice that for generations has been the perquisite of the rich and powerful classes. Grass-roots political organizing and civic action are also enabled. For example, in California, a concerned parent scanned into a database and posted on a Web page the details of the state's list of sexual predators/pedophiles, thus allowing average people to determine whether there was a registered sex offender residing in their neighborhood.

From shopping for homes and automobiles, where online services promise to eliminate the brokers' monopoly of information, to traffic, weather forecasts, and directions prior to trips, the Internet is providing more information to more people every day, and we are only at the beginning of that process! The major trend here is clear: There will be more information accessible to more people than has ever been possible in the past. How this information power will be used ultimately depends on the ethics and motives of the individual: Internet robbers can use such power negatively.

Organizational Impacts

The major benefits to organizations of the Internet and related technologies are significant and far ranging. In large part, the impacts may be characterized as dramatically lower costs for transmitting and sharing information. To appreciate how far we have come, before electronic mail became ubiquitous, it took as long as a week for first-class postal mail, derisively called "snail mail" by Internet aficionados, to travel from one coast of the United States to the other. Even the fax machine, which itself was a significant improvement over postal and overnight courier services, requires dedicated fax equipment and only operates from point to point. Contrast these with the capabilities of Internet e-mail. E-mail, which may transit the globe in seconds, allows the recipients to obtain the message when it is convenient; they need not be present to receive it. Through the use of digital attachments, e-mail can carry more information in a convenient compression of transmission times.

Whereas the innocent e-mail user sees only increased speed and volume of communication, security and law enforcement professionals must understand how damaging even one message could be to a business or government agency. A single e-mail message could contain the whole strategic business plan of the organization or the source code to a breakthrough product, and could be transmitted anywhere on earth in a nanosecond.

To show that this threat is much more than theoretical, consider the allegations involving two leading Silicon Valley software companies, A and B. Company A accused rival Company B of theft of trade secrets and proprietary source code. Company A's management alleged as one element in their complaint that a former Company A employee used his company-provided Internet access to transfer source code of key products to his own, personal account. The employee then tendered his resignation. Upon arrival at his home-based office, the now-former Company A employee allegedly downloaded the stolen source code to his home computer system. Employed as a programmer consultant by rival startup Company B, he reportedly used the purloined source code as the foundation for a remarkably similar product created at Company B.[13]

Another example is a former employee of Company X who was accused of transmitting the source code for a new digital device to rival Company Y. This scheme apparently was discovered only by accident when the highly confidential materials created such a long message that it caused the e-mail system to crash and allowed a system administrator to discover the purported scheme.

These two incidents are drawn from press reports in the media, and it is likely that they are only the very tip of the iceberg. In fact, many organizations do not have the security systems and technologies to detect similar incidents. Because of the adverse publicity and the prospect of a lengthy criminal justice process, even those businesses and government agencies that have been victimized by Internet robbers frequently do not report similar incidents to the proper authorities.

Using the Internet to Share Information

One of the truly remarkable developments in information technology has been the widespread use of the Web browser and related technology to deliver information both to internal employees and to the external customers of an organization. If e-mail could be described as a virtual duplication of the postal services into the global Internet environment, then Web servers can be thought of as kiosks or bulletin boards. On these "virtual bulletin boards," an organization can make accessible to target populations the information they need to make decisions and perform administrative, operational, or other functions. For example, one very common intranet (internal company Internet) application is to provide a central "forms page" where employees find the most current version to be downloaded and printed for everything from payroll deductions to medical reimburse-

---

[13] Although based on actual cases, the names have not been used because the cases are still being adjudicated through the criminal justice process.

ments. Another use is to front-end a database in which is stored information which must be accessible to a widely dispersed population of users or broad cross-section of Internet travelers.

> More Americans go online: Even as Internet usage, satisfaction levels rise, many consumers are still worried about security[14]: NEW YORK (CNN/Money)—Americans are using and enjoying the Internet more . . . even though they're still not entirely sure their personal information is secure. Sixty-one percent of all Americans go online at least once a month, compared with 59 percent at the end of 2001. . . . More than 35 percent of Internet users go online daily, while 15 percent go online several times a week. . . . More than 33 percent of the survey respondents said they'd never been online at all.

Currently the most common and growing destination for the Internet traveler is the business or government agency Web site. For the Internet traveler, Web sites are a combination of superhighway billboards, banks, shopping malls, rest stops, and even fast-food delivery services. All of these services as well as hundreds of others can be found located at the on- and off-ramps to the Internet.

These Web sites are used by businesses for advertising, public relations, and marketing, as well as to sell or deliver products or services to Internet travelers.

Web sites may contain and dispense government information concerning everything from how to prepare and submit forms, to descriptions of the most wanted criminal fugitives, to recruiting advertisements for future employees. Even the most secretive U.S. government agencies such as the Central Intelligence Agency, the National Security Agency, and others have established Web sites that provide useful information to Internet travelers.

The business and government agency Web sites are often the targets of miscreants, juvenile delinquents, and other Internet robbers. Successful attacks against these Web sites can be disruptive and destructive of the reputation of the sponsoring organization. Therefore the protection of the Web site should be an important part of the business or government agency plan for using this technology.

CHANGING CRIMINAL JUSTICE SYSTEMS

Thus far, it appears that information protection will increase in importance. If so, the world's criminal justice systems and processes undoubtedly will also be affected. The question is, will they change for the better

---

[14] See http://money.cnn.com/2002/10/16/news/internet_barometer/index.htm

or for the worse? If the United States is any indication, they will worsen. Why, in such a technologically advanced country? Ironically, technology brings with it rapid social change as well.

One may wonder what is the impact of the criminal justice system on the ISSO and Information protection. The answer is simple: The people who steal business or national secrets, damage, destroy, or modify information and systems, and commit other criminal acts are the main reasons why the ISSO and Information protection program exist. After all, if no one violated laws or company policies, and everyone protected information and systems, why would businesses or government agencies need an ISSO or an information protection program?

At some point in your career, you will become involved in a high-technology crime investigation, and thus will become actively involved in the criminal justice system. You must understand how that system operates, or you'll not only be at a disadvantage, but probably disappointed as well!

In the global marketplace that your company undoubtedly works in and is affected by, you as the ISSO must understand the international and foreign nation-state laws that have an impact on your business, especially those related to privacy and security. For example, your company may operate in a foreign country. If so, that country may not allow the encryption of transmissions through their country. If this is the case, do you violate that law, understanding its entire ramifications, in order to protect company secrets, or do you not encrypt and understand the risks of others reading the "company mail"?

As society embraces the Third Wave, as described by the Tofflers, it does not wait for the two prior waves' processes to catch up. Thus, one can see the trend of a disintegrating U.S. criminal justice system where crime increases faster than the criminal justice system can deal with it. More discretionary arrests, plea-bargaining prosecutions, overburdened court systems, and the release of convicted criminals from jails and prisons are indications of this change to a Third Wave society. We seem to be trying to use Second Wave criminal justice system processes and functions to handle Third Wave problems, and it doesn't seem to be working.

One of the disadvantages of being a leading technology-based country such as the United States is that one does not have the opportunity to learn from the mistakes of others who are more advanced. This is an extremely important point, especially when discussing the criminal justice system, because the criminal justice system is the primary system responsible for the prevention of crime and the promotion of social stability of a nation.

If a nation is to be strong economically to compete in the world, it must have stability in which businesses can operate and people can have a secure and peaceful life. Lack of security and peace leads to increases in crime. It follows that high-technology crimes would likely increase. In addition, without a good criminal justice system, frauds and other crimes not only will be more frequent, but also will sap the economic strength from the people, businesses, and the country.

We know that technology is increasing at a rapid rate. Computer-based technology has become a necessary and integral part of businesses, government agencies, and our personal lives. No longer can we efficiently function without the use of today's modern, computer-based technology.

As with any tool, computers, including telecommunication systems, can be a target or used as a tool of criminals, also known as techno-criminals. The threats to society, businesses, and government agencies by techno-criminals are increasing as our technology and our dependence on technology increase.

A 1997 *Computer Crime and Security Survey* conducted by the Computer Security Institute in cooperation with the FBI disclosed that computer crimes were increasing and reported losses totaling more than $100 million! Their 2002 survey[15] stated:

- Forty-four percent (223 respondents) were willing and/or able to quantify their financial losses. These 223 respondents reported $455,848,000 in financial losses.
- As in previous years, the most serious financial losses occurred through theft of proprietary information (26 respondents reported $170,827,000) and financial fraud (25 respondents reported $115,753,000).

The techno-criminals, vis-à-vis the world's criminal justice systems, are also faced with a system which provides them some measure of immunity to techno-crimes. For example, the attacks against U.S. computer systems are becoming more internationally oriented. Today's techno-criminal can attack any place in the world from any place in the world.

What is worse, because of our complicated communication systems, it is difficult to trace the attacks back to the attackers. Also, many countries' laws do not even address the issue of techno-crimes, making it almost impossible to prosecute anyone attacking a U.S. computer from outside the United States. And because of the political ramifications alone, extradition of these attackers to the United States, or any other country, for prosecution is a complicated and generally impossible task! After all, what nation-state wants to give up sovereignty over its citizens?

For the ISSO, it is imperative to understand the criminal justice systems of the United States and other countries where the company or government agency does business. The problems with the criminal justice systems, conflicts and changes, will continue to be an underlying force whose impact on information protection functions will extend into the 21st century.

---

[15] For additional information see http://www.gocsi.com

The change in society where white-collar crimes, frauds, are being perpetrated more and more through the use of computers and telecommunications systems seems to be an obvious result of the rapid changes in societies, and our reliance on information systems.

This is understandable, as alluded to earlier, because what once was done by paper and pencil has now been automated, e.g., accounting systems. Therefore, although today's criminals have the same motive as in the past, they must now operate in a new environment, a technological environment. If criminals want to steal money, they must use and attack information systems. To paraphrase an old-time bank robber: "Because that's where the money is!"

Since it appears that more crimes are being committed by using the computer as a tool to attack other computers, and that trend is likely to continue, the ISSO's responsibilities include an Information protection program which will assist in minimizing the opportunities for frauds and other crimes through the systems. If such crimes do occur, it is expected that the ISSO will play a vital role in the investigation, and in any disciplinary action or prosecution of the offenders—thus offering another challenge and opportunity to the ISSO profession.

THE HUMAN FACTOR

With all the talk of high technology, need for information protection, computer crimes, and the like, there is one important factor to remember. It is the human being who uses the tools for good or bad purposes, and it is the human being whom the ISSO often loses sight of when trying to protect information and high technology.

Yes, it is true that for the ISSO to be successful, the ISSO must understand not only information systems—computers and their associated networks—but also other forms of high technology, e.g., cellular phones, faxes, and pagers. However, one must never lose sight of the human element—usually the most neglected factor in information protection. To be sure, one talks about information protection awareness programs, but the human factor must be addressed in more detail and given more emphasis if the ISSO is to protect information.

QUESTIONS TO CONSIDER

Based on what you have read, consider the following questions and how you would reply to them:

- Can you think of information that would be of value to you as an ISSO that would allow you to act within the OODA loops of

those who want to attack your company's or government agency's systems?
- What information on the systems must be protected so that your company's competitors or others cannot obtain it to act within the OODA loop of your company?
- As an ISSO, do you see the extremely important role that you play in a corporation based on the "shark scenario"?
- Do you know how secure your information and the high-technology devices that store, process, display, and transmit that information are from internal and external attacks?
- Will the importance of information protection increase, decrease, or stay about the same as high technology and the world changes? (You may say that of course its importance will increase. However, don't be so sure.)

SUMMARY

As this chapter's quote states, we live in a *human* world. We sometimes forget that and look to technology—high technology—to solve our problems. As an ISSO, your working world revolves around high technology *and* people in a global IE. It is important to remember that high technology is a tool, a tool that can be—in fact, is—used for both good and bad purposes. It takes a human to use that tool. A human is the root of your information protection problems—the systemic problem. Never forget that. High technology can help you in protecting information from humans, but it is not THE ANSWER. Solving the human issues related to information protection must be considered an integral part of information protection.
   Remember also that:

- Technology is changing rapidly, and will continue to do so in the future.
- Changes in high technology and massive networks (intranets, the Internet, NIIs, and the GII) are changing the way countries, societies, and people in general communicate and interact, and how they view themselves and others—often leading to conflicts.
- The three periods of change, according to the Tofflers, are the Agricultural, Industrial, and Information periods.
- Understanding the periods of change, the reasons for the changes, and their impact on the world and information environments will assist in planning and maintaining a dynamic, effective, and efficient information protection program.
- The ISSO must understand high technology and its impact on society, the criminal justice system, and the ISSO's company or government agency in order to professionally establish and manage an information protection program.

2

Understanding the Business and Management Environment

> *. . . globalization has served to undermine the role of the nation-state as the sole determinant of a society's well-being.*—Henry Kissinger[1]

CHAPTER OBJECTIVE

The objective of this chapter, "Understanding the Business and Management Environment," is to provide the reader with a basic understanding and philosophy of information and information systems security (InfoSec) within the business environment, to include how to communicate with management in "their language."

THE CHANGING BUSINESS AND GOVERNMENT ENVIRONMENTS

Many of the changes in the world environment are the basis for the rapid shifts in the way we do business, both nationally and internationally. Businesses can, and do, adapt to these changes quite rapidly. However, in government agencies, these changes come more slowly, and sometimes threaten the agencies' very existence. For example, a day may come in the not too distant future when the post offices of the world will be unnecessary. E-mails may take the place of letters even for the poorest people of the world, as they will have access to Internet networks. As for packages, commercial firms such as DHL, FedEx, and UPS have already been providing that service for some time.

Clear examples of these changes are the "global marketplace," as well as business-to-business networks (b2b), electronic commerce, electronic business, and the like.

---

[1] Kissinger, Henry. Does *America Need a Foreign Policy: Toward a Diplomacy for 21st Century.* Simon & Schuster: New York, 2001.

Massive, growing networks such as the Internet, NIIs, and GII are adopted, and must continually be adapted, by businesses if they are to maintain a competitive advantage—or at least compete—in today's marketplace. As an ISSO, you must find ways to facilitate such growth in a secure and yet invisible manner. That is a challenge for all of us in the profession. As an ISSO, if you try to slow down this phenomenon, you will be run over by "progress" and will soon be updating your resume. Business comes first, and if you don't provide a professional InfoSec service that supports and enhances the business, what good are you? After all, business is about profits—and remember, you are a "parasite" on the profits of most companies, since your function is identified as an overhead cost.

As an overhead cost, you do not have direct, hands-on experience in building your company's widgets, for example. Yeah, yeah, yeah, we all have tried to explain that without InfoSec and us as professional ISSOs, companies can lose their business and their competitive edge through loss of trade secret information, etc. However, the bottom line is that it appears that most of today's business executives are in it for the short term, not the long term. Their concern is the "bottom line" for the next quarter to one year. They can easily terminate an InfoSec program and take their chances by having auditors audit for compliance with laws and policies and recommend InfoSec policies that information technology (IT) people can write. Then they can just buy insurance to cover any potential losses. So, as today's ISSO, you must do a better job of making yourself part of the "company team" and finding ways to provide value-added and integral services to the company.

In the private sector, telecommunications businesses have become Internet providers. As we look into the future, we see more and more people making use of the long-distance voice telephone capabilities of the Internet, at very little additional cost. Perhaps one day the need for a separate telephone in the home or office, as we now know it, will be a thing of the past.

Speaking of Internet service providers (ISPs), let's take a moment to look at this new business born out of the Internet and see how well it is supporting InfoSec and InfoSec standards.[2]

For some reason, one of the least talked about InfoSec related topics is InfoSec applied to ISPs. Well, it's about time there were more discussions on this topic and something done to enhance their InfoSec—and by the way, all you ISPs, please don't even mention self-policing! You had your shot at that and did little if anything to protect our information, our privacy!

---

[2] Previously written by the author under the name Shockwave Writer and published by Reed Elsevier in their magazine *Computer Fraud & Security* (2002), as the article "Internet Service Providers and InfoSec Standards."

First a little history of how we got to where we are: The Internet was born in the 1960s and arose out of projects sponsored by the Advanced Research Project Agency (ARPA) in the United States. It was originally a project to facilitate the sharing of computer resources and enhance military communications. As the Internet was maturing, there were conflicts between the "haves" who had the use of the Internet and the "have-nots" who did not. The haves were computer scientists, engineers, and some others. They argued that the Internet should not be made available to the public. Well, they lost that battle, especially after the business sector found out what a lucrative marketing and public relations tool the Internet could be for reaching potential customers, suppliers, etc. Thus, the ISPs were born.

From that time until now, the Internet has rapidly grown from an experimental research project and tool of the United States government and universities to the tool of everyone in the world with a computer. It is the premier global communications medium. With the subsequent development of search engines and of course, the World Wide Web (Web), the sharing of information has never been easier. For example, Google.com states that they search more than 3 billion Web pages!

Using the Google search engine, I searched for "Internet service providers" and got 1,330,000 hits in a search that took, according to Google, 0.20 seconds! Through a process of elimination, I then clicked on Google's Web Directory and got 16 ISP categories. I clicked on the Business category and got 49 categories, one of which was Internet and had 11,930 hits. Clicking on Access Providers, I got 721 hits. That led me to AOL (46); By Region (343); Cable (30); CompuServe (6); Cooperatives (6); Directories (17); DSL (121); Free Internet Access (18); Resources for ISPs (56); Reviews (41); Unix Shell Providers (72); and Wireless (41). Clicking By Region (343) I found Africa (8); Asia (9); Caribbean (1); Central America (5); Europe (41); Middle East (3); North America (263); Oceania (2); and South America (2).

In other words, there are many, many ISPs operating and connected all around the globe. We all should know by now that our e-mails don't go point-to-point, but hop around the Internet, where they can be gleaned by all those with the resources to read other people's mail, steal information in order to commit crimes such as identity theft, collect competitive intelligence information, etc.

So, what's the point? The point is that there are ISPs all over the world with few regulations and absolutely no InfoSec standards. So, some ISPs may do an admirable job of protecting our information passing through their systems while others may do nothing. Furthermore, as we learn more and more about Netspionage (computer-enabled business and government spying), we learn more and more about how our privacy and our information are open to others to read, capture, change, and otherwise misuse. In addition, with such programs as SORM in Russia, Internet monitoring in China and elsewhere, global Echelon, and the U.S. FBI's Carnivore (still Carnivore no matter how often they change the name to make it more "politically correct" or try to "hide" it from the public), we might as well take our most personal information, tattoo it on our bodies, and run naked in the streets for all to see. Although that may be a slight exaggeration, the point is we have no concept of how well ISPs are protecting our information.

Now, we are quickly expanding into the world of instant messaging (IM) through ISPs. After all, the more rapidly our world changes, the more rapidly we want to react and we want everything—*now*! IMICI.com's Web site stated that they expect more than 200 million users sending 2 trillion messages per year by 2004. They state that IM is the fastest growing Internet technology. Furthermore, it can be used to transfer files, send graphics, and unlike the telephone and normal e-mails, with IM one knows whether or not the person being contacted is there. Interesting ramifications—check to see if a person is on line; if not (after already setting up a masquerade or spoof), take over that person's identity and contact someone posing as the other—instantly. Of course there are perhaps hundreds, if not thousands, of examples of ISPs being penetrated or misused. Around November 1995, for example, *The Wall Street Journal* ran a story entitled "America Online to Warn Users about Bad E-mail." We all know about the basic issues of viruses and other malicious code also being sent via ISPs. So, the problem has existed for quite some time.

I asked a couple of trusted InfoSec professionals about a portion of this topic—a basic InfoSec requirement, audit records: Did they know of federal or state laws in the United States requiring ISPs to keep audit records of e-mails and/or of chat room sessions? One person who leads a major InfoSec effort for a billion (probably trillion)-dollar corporation said: "Nope, there have been attempts to do so that met with much opposition." Steve Lutz, an international InfoSec consulting leader who runs an ISP and the highly successful WaySecure (waysecure.com) consulting firm said:

> On the flip side of that, I have had great success in getting ISPs to turn over audit records, e-mails, etc., in the course of an investigation simply by asking. The problem is that the quantity and quality of data varied widely. Some of them had logging enabled on nearly every device with exceptional detail available. Others just had the basics (minimal logging) or even less. At the ISP I am president of, we have an elaborate logging system (including capturing ANI data on dial-in subscribers and correlating it to subsequent activities by that user (entity)) with the ability to generate a report of cross platform/network activities. The reason we developed such a paranoid system was that we formerly hosted the web and e-mail servers for *2600*, the hacker quarterly. We were barraged hourly with people from all over the world looking to break in and claim they had hacked the premier hacking web site . . . there have been several attempts to do so that failed. One of the

problems is that additional logging costs money (more disk space) and time (slower performance). The other is that (unlike telcos, radio stations, television stations, etc.) ISPs do not have to be licensed to operate. If they were, then the FCC could require minimum standards for security, privacy and log collection and retention. ISO 17799 would be a good place to start to look for guidance as to what would be considered "best practices" as it could then be applied worldwide.

Using an Internet search engine, I found others that were also concerned about InfoSec standards for ISPs. One such group (ftp://ftp.isi.edu/in-notes/rfc3013.txt) is looking into what should be the "Best Current Practices" for ISPs. They have an excellent document online and have invited readers to comment. This "Network Working Group" document, according to them, is to "raise awareness among ISPs of the community's expectations, and to provide the community with a framework for discussion of security expectations with current and prospective service providers." Suggest you check out this document and get involved in pushing for some standards across the entire spectrum of ISPs— everywhere in the world.

Let's close with a recent example in the United States which makes the need for InfoSec standards clear. In December 2000, the U.S. newspaper *The Detroit News*, and subsequently CourtTV (a U.S. cable television channel), discussed a murder case: The defendant "loved the nation's Internet because it allowed her to be different people. Prosecutors claim one of them turned out to be a killer. . . . In what is being dubbed the nation's first Internet-related murder, the chat-room regular is accused of sweet-talking her online lover into murdering her husband with a shotgun blast. . . ."

The investigation led to information from the killer's computer, but none was allegedly found on the defendant's computer. They of course used an ISP to communicate through the chat room and e-mails. Information about the case did not mention whether or not investigators tried to obtain records from the ISP. If they did and were successful, it certainly would have helped in the investigation. However, we don't know. For the sake of discussion, let's say that there was no evidence found on the killer's computer or the defendant's computer, nor were there any hardcopy documents related to the crime. In that case, the only evidence to corroborate other noncomputer evidence would come from the audit records of the ISP. Since no laws require the ISP to keep such records, or, if records are kept, how long they must be retained, it is quite possible the murderer and coconspirator would have literally gotten away with murder. If records were available and with a proper search warrant obtained by the investigators, they would have assisted in proving or disproving the allegations of murder, and thus help convict murderers or help ensure that innocent people are not convicted of crimes they did not commit.

So, as one can see from this simple example, ISP InfoSec standards and requirements can be used in life-or-death situations, a strong counterargument to the protests of the ISPs that they don't have the resources, etc., etc. We have heard those cries and complaints from others who hold our privacy and protection in their hands. Isn't it about time that all of us who use ISPs, probably a few hundred million by now, demand that they start doing what is ethically and morally the right thing to do?

The Internet and ISPs have matured enough that their customers—all of us—should demand such protection. After all, as Mr. Lutz pointed out, telcos, television networks, and radio stations, just to name a few, are monitored and regulated. They must meet certain standards. So, why not ISPs?

So, what do you think? Should ISPs be regulated? Should there be some minimum InfoSec standards or requirements that every ISP must meet? Let your ISP and politicians know what you think. After all, we are all in this together, not only as InfoSec professionals representing government agencies and corporations whose networks are connected to the Internet and thus ISPs, but also as Internet citizens.

ISPs must be required to meet certain InfoSec standards in order to ensure our privacy.

This issue is important to the ISSO because many of the verbal conversations that may take place through the Internet will be sensitive, proprietary business or government information. As the ISSO, you have the responsibility to ensure that these conversations can be carried on securely.

Anyone who is currently an ISSO and dealing with the problems of Internet's InfoSec knows that compounding that InfoSec problem with the use of verbal communications protection on the Internet would make one want to retire early! At the same time, it offers the ISSO new, unique challenges—and to a certain extent, maybe a little more job security.

One does not have to look far to also see the vital need for an InfoSec program in corporations and government agencies which also protects the privacy of individuals whose information is stored, processed, and transmitted by these systems.

UNDERSTANDING THE BUSINESS ENVIRONMENT

An InfoSec program and supporting organization is not the reason that a business or government agency exists. In the case of a business, the company usually provides a service or a product. The business has certain information or systems that are vital to performing its service and producing its product. The purpose of an InfoSec program, therefore, is to provide *service and support* to the business.

In order to meet the needs of its customers, both internal and external to the company, it is imperative for the ISSO to understand the company and the company's business. This includes the following:

- History
- Products
- Business environment
- Competition
- Long-range plans
- Short-range plans
- Cost of business
- Product value

These are important because the InfoSec program is not a product to be sold in the global marketplace; it does not bring in revenue. In fact, the costs of an InfoSec program, no matter how efficient and effective its operation, take profits away from the business—unless you can prove that the InfoSec program is a value-added service which financially supports the business, assisting in bringing in revenue.

In this globally competitive economy, there is increasing competition for market shares in the worldwide marketplace. It is important for the ISSO to understand this competition and what can be done by the ISSO through the InfoSec program to enhance business, increasing such things as profits, market shares, and income.

Kenichi Ohmae, in his book *The Mind of the Strategist*,[3] discusses product/service differentiation in the form of "the strategic three C's": the corporation, the customers, and the competition (Figure 2.1). Corporations and competitors are differentiated by costs. Customers differentiate between the corporation and competitors by value.

Customers will buy a product that they want (consider of value), if it is a quality product at the right price. Therefore, it is important that the InfoSec program add value to the product and do so at least cost, in order for the business to remain competitive in the marketplace. So, treat the InfoSec program as a product which adds value and minimizes costs. Since it is your product, market it and sell it!

MANAGEMENT RESPONSIBILITIES AND COMMUNICATING WITH MANAGEMENT

One of the biggest mistakes made by ISSOs is to assume that they "own" the systems and information. The ISSO must remember that the owners of

---

[3] Ohmae, Kenichi. *The Mind of the Strategist*. Penguin Books, Ltd., Middlesex, UK, 1982.

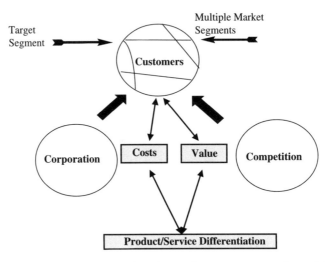

Figure 2.1   Business competition based on Ohmae's strategic three C's.

the business, whether it be private ownership or public ownership through the stockholders, make the decisions as to how the business is run. The stockholders do it through the elected members of the company's board of directors, who are the risk-takers. Their responsibilities include making decisions relative to company risks.

As an ISSO, you are there because the management believes you have the expertise they need to protect the business's information systems and the company's information.

All too often, the ISSO gets into the "tail wagging the dog" situation where the ISSO can't understand why management does not provide the ISSO with the support that is needed or wanted. The ISSO must keep in mind that if management did not provide at least some support, the company would not employ the ISSO!

When decisions are made to process, store, display, or transmit information that goes against the desires of the ISSO, many ISSOs take that personally. *Remember, it is not your information!* It belongs to the business owners.

Of course, depending on your responsibilities and the authority delegated to you by management, you will probably be responsible for making the majority of decisions that involve InfoSec. However, even with that responsibility and authority, the ISSO must gain the support and concurrence of others within the company.

When an InfoSec decision must be made and that decision is outside the purview of the ISSO, the ISSO must elevate the final decision to a higher level of management. Although each company's culture and policies will dictate when and how that process will be implemented, the ISSO should be sure to provide complete staff work on which the management can base the required decision. In other words, the person making the decision must be provided with all the necessary information on which to base the decision. If that information is not provided to upper management, the wrong decision could be made, which may jeopardize the protection of the company's information and/or systems, or may cause the company to incur unnecessary costs.

If you have done your homework—if you have assessed the risks to the information and systems, the protection alternatives, the costs involved, and the benefits involved, and you are in a position to make your recommendations accordingly—then you have done your job.

Before you bring a problem and decision to management, you, the ISSO, should be sure that you have addressed the problem by providing management with clear, concise information, using nontechnical language, on which they can base their decision. The following, as a minimum, should be included in that process:

- Identification of the problem
- Possible problem solutions, to include cost and benefits
- Recommended solution to the problem, and why
- Identification of who should fix the problem (it may not be an InfoSec issue, or it may be one outside your authority)
- Consequences of no decision (no action/no decision is always an option, and sometimes the right one)

Whether it is the responsibility of the ISSO to fix the problem or not, the ISSO should follow up. Once the problem is fixed, it is always good to contact the other personnel who were at the meeting where the problem was discussed and the decision made, and advise them either verbally or in writing when the corrective action is completed or the project is closed out.

An excellent gesture would be to send a letter of appreciation to those involved in fixing the problem, with appropriate copies to management. This is especially important if others fixed the problem outside your organization, or if staff outside your organization assisted you in fixing the problem.

It is the responsibility of the business management to make the final decision, unless of course they abdicate that responsibility to you. They, in turn, are held accountable to the owners of the business.

Remember that managers are usually only authorized to make decisions related to accepting InfoSec risks for the organizations under their authority. They should not be allowed by the business to make decisions that affect the entire company. If that appears to be occurring, you are obligated to ensure that the manager as well as upper management knows that information. This is of course a sensitive matter and must be handled that way.

A word of caution: Some managers will abdicate their management responsibility to the ISSO. As the ISSO, you may be flattered by such a gesture, but beware! You may also be getting set up to take the blame for the consequences. These consequences may be due to a decision that you may not have recommended—in fact, it may be a case where you were in total disagreement with management as to the correct course of action to be taken.

The responsibility of business management is a serious one. Under current laws in many nation-states, managers can be held personally responsible, and possibly liable, for any poor decisions that affect the value of the business. So, your responsibility as a service and support InfoSec professional is to give management the best advice you can. When their decision is made, do your job by supporting that decision and by ensuring that the information and systems are protected based on that decision.

There may be times when, in the opinion of the ISSO, management makes the wrong decision relative to protection of information. The ISSO then has several additional choices:

- Meet with the decision maker in private to try to convince that person of the consequences of the decision and why it may not be right;
- Appeal the decision to the next level of management;
- Quit the job; or
- Quit the company.

Another word of caution is needed here. Whether the decision is right or wrong, the ISSO should document that decision process. The documentation should answer the typical security/investigative questions of who, how, where, when, why, and what.

This is important, not from the standpoint of just another bureaucratic process, but to have a history of all actions taken that are related to InfoSec. Thus, when similar instances occur a year or more after the last decision, it can be used as a precedent. This not only helps in making subsequent decisions based on similar instances, but also helps ensure consistency in the application of InfoSec. Inconsistent InfoSec decisions lead to confusion, which leads to not following sound InfoSec policy and causes increased costs to the business. This process follows the process used by the legal community, where case law is used to argue a current illegal issue. Precedence is a logical process to follow—assuming that the decisions previously made were the correct ones, of course.

If it is subsequently shown that the last decision had unexpected, adverse consequences, then it will help the decision maker not to make the same mistake again—one would hope. People come and go, but a good historical file will ensure consistency and keep you from having to rely on the memories of people involved—assuming they are even still employed by the company.

For example, assume that a major decision had to be made concerning InfoSec, and the decision was determined to be that of management. You, as the ISSO, should do the following:

- Lead the effort to resolve the issue;
- Request a meeting;
- Ensure all the applicable personnel are invited; and
- Brief those at the meeting on the situation as stated above.

If you as the ISSO are to keep minutes of the meeting, the minutes should include:

- Why the meeting was held;
- When the meeting was held;
- Where the meeting was held;
- Who was at the meeting;
- What information was presented and discussed;
- What the decision was;
- How management made their decision; and
- Who made the decision.

Someone in management should sign the minutes of the meeting showing the results of the meeting—preferably the person who made the final decision. You will find that such decisions are usually verbal, and most managers do not want to sign any document that will place them at risk. So, how do you deal with such issues? There are several methods which can be used, all of which may cause your position as the ISSO to be questioned: "not a team player," "you don't understand the big picture," or "you are not a business person, so you don't understand the situation." By the way, having an MBA would definitely help in winning this argument.

Even though you have the best interest of the company at heart and it is the basis for your recommendation, and even though you consider yourself a dedicated and loyal employee, in the eyes of some in management you're not a team player. In other words, you are not on *their* team.

You will soon find that the position of the ISSO is sometimes a risky one. Even if you do the best professional job that can be done or has been done in the history of the ISSO profession, office politics must be considered. Such non-InfoSec situations will often cause many more problems than the ISSO will face in dealing with InfoSec issues, hackers, and the like.

If the you don't know about such things as "turf battles" and "protecting rice bowls," the local bookstore is the place to go. There, you will find numerous books that will explain how to work and survive in the "jungle" of office politics. You may know InfoSec, but if you don't know office politics, you may not survive—even with the best InfoSec program ever developed. Always remember: "It's a jungle out there!"

Why is it that way? There are many reasons, but for ISSOs the primary reason is that you *make* people do things that they do not consider part of their job. And if they don't follow the InfoSec policies and procedures, they could face disciplinary action. So, you, like corporate security personnel and auditors, are not always popular.

Obviously, as the ISSO, you want to eliminate or at least minimize that type of image—the "cop image." It is hard work, but you must constantly try to overcome the negativism that people tack onto the ISSO and InfoSec. Some ways of countering that negative image can be found throughout this book.

Many business meetings require that minutes be taken. If so, and if you are not responsible for taking the minutes, obtain a copy and ensure that your recommendations are noted in them, as well as who made what decisions. This is the best method of documenting what went on in the meeting.

If the minutes do not adequately describe what has taken place—if, for example, they lack details of what was presented, the potential risks, or who made the final decision (all crucial pieces of information)—then annotate the minutes. Attach any of your briefing charts, sign and date the minutes, then place them in a file in case you want to use them as a reference at a later date.

Another method which can be used, but is more confrontational, is to send a memo to the manager making the decision in which you document the InfoSec options, costs, benefits, and associated risks. You then conclude with a sentence that states, for example, "After assessing the risks I have concluded that the best course of action is option 2." Leave room for a date and the signature block of the manager you want to sign the document.

The document should be worded professionally and should be as nonintimidating to the manager as possible. Even so, in most cases, you may find that you won't get a signed copy returned to you if you send it in the company mail.

You should hand-carry this document to the manager and discuss it with that person. Imagine yourself in the manager's position. When you put your signature on such a document, there can be no mistake. You made the decision. If something goes wrong, that letter may document the fact that in retrospect it was a poor decision. No manager—no one—ever wants to be put in that position. Remember that the manager does not have to sign the InfoSec document. In fact, no matter how it is presented, you will find most managers will find some way *not* to sign the document if there is the slightest chance of being second-guessed later. In today's environment of "touchy-feely don't-hold-me-responsible" management, today's ISSOs are more challenged than ever before to get management to own up to their decisions.

Asking a manager to sign such a document, especially if you have voiced disagreement about the decision, should be a last resort. It should only be done if you feel so strongly about the decision that you are willing to put any possible raise or promotion, or even your employment, on the line. So, you'd better be right, and you'd better strongly believe that it is worth it. Also, as the ISSO, you must do this as an ISSO professional, a person of integrity and principles.

Even so, you may end up being right, but also right out of a job. Well, no one said that being an ISSO professional is easy.

CREATING A COMPETITIVE ADVANTAGE THROUGH INFOSEC

To ensure that the InfoSec program supports the company's business services and products, the ISSO must think of methods, philosophies, and processes that will help the company in gaining a competitive advantage. Such methods and philosophies should include a team approach. That is, have the company employees and especially management support your InfoSec program.

To help in that endeavor, you should strive to insert, in appropriate company policy documents, policies which can help support your efforts. The following are some examples that may be useful in incorporating into company policy documents support for your InfoSec program and your quest to assist the company in gaining a competitive advantage through InfoSec:

- Managers will ensure a compliant InfoSec program within their organization.
- Managers will develop our customers' trust that their sensitive information will be effectively protected while under our control.
- Managers will employ cost-effective InfoSec systems and strive to help keep the price of our company's services and products as low as possible relative to our competitors.
- Managers will help keep the company's overhead down through effective loss prevention and assets protection processes.
- Managers will minimize the adverse impact of our InfoSec controls on the efficiency of the company's operational functions by working with the InfoSec staff to find the most cost-effective ways of protecting our information assets.
- Managers will proactively find ways to securely and efficiently provide the company's services and products.

THE ISSO AS A BUSINESS MANAGER

The role of the ISSO in managing an InfoSec program is somewhat different from the role of the ISSO as a manager of the company.

All company managers have some role to play that applies regardless of the manager's area of responsibility. This also applies to the ISSOs in management positions. The following items should be considered for implementation by the ISSO as a manager within the company:

- Comply with all company policies and procedures, including the intent of those policies and procedures.
- Take no action that will give the appearance of violating applicable company policies, procedures, or ethical standards.
- Implement applicable management control systems within the InfoSec organization to ensure the efficient use of resources and effective operations.
- Identify business practices, ethics, and security violations/infractions; conduct inquiries; assess potential damage; direct and take corrective action.
- Communicate with other departments to provide and receive information and guidance for mutual benefit.
- Plan, organize, direct, coordinate, control, report, assess, and refine business activities to achieve quality, cost, schedule, and performance objectives, while retaining responsibility for the results.
- Exercise due diligence to prevent fraud, waste, or abuse.
- Establish and maintain a self-audit process to identify problem areas and take corrective action to eliminate deficiencies.

These items, if made part of the ISSO's philosophy and goals, not only will benefit the company, but will assist the ISSO in professionally meeting the InfoSec duties and responsibilities as a valued member of the company's management team. Remember that the InfoSec program is a *company* program. That means you need help from everyone in the company to ensure its success.

SERVICE, SUPPORT, AND A BUSINESS ORIENTATION

In any business, the ISSO must strive to balance the required "user friendly" systems demands of management and users with those of InfoSec. After all, InfoSec, unless it can be proven to be "value-added," thus at least paying for itself, is a parasite on profits, or at least adversely impacts budgets. This will be a factor to consider as you, the ISSO, establish the company's InfoSec processes, programs, plans, projects, budgets, etc.

Remember, that the InfoSec program must be service and support oriented. This is of vital importance. The ISSO must understand that the InfoSec program, if it becomes too costly, outdated, or does not meet the service and support needs of the business or government agency, will be discarded or ignored. Each of these possibilities will eventually lead to the dismissal of the ISSO. (Additional information on this will be discussed throughout this book.)

The dismissal of any ISSO affects all ISSOs. The ISSO profession is damaged, as is our professional credibility and our opportunities to protect vital information for our internal and external customers. It is difficult enough, even in today's environment, to "sell" an InfoSec program. It makes our jobs as ISSOs harder when one of us fails. The failure of an ISSO could be a lesson learned for all ISSOs. Learn not only from your own failures, but also from those of others.

The word of an ISSO's dismissal and failures does get around within the industry and government agencies, making it much more difficult for the ISSO's replacement to develop a professional InfoSec program. You may be that replacement.

As the ISSO, you must constantly update your InfoSec program and its processes. You must continuously look at changes in society and technology, plan for those changes, and be prepared to address InfoSec ramifications of the installation of new technology into the business before it is installed. You must implement InfoSec measures *before* someone can take advantage of a system vulnerability.

So far, ISSOs for the most part have been in a reactive mode, with little time to be proactive and put InfoSec defenses in place before they are needed! How to do that will be discussed in the following chapters.

BUSINESS MANAGERS AND INFOSEC

Some ISSOs may want to talk "techie" to keep business managers in the dark about the "mysteries" of InfoSec. They think that it will make the ISSOs invaluable to the corporation and, therefore, always needed. That is illogical and also works against the ISSO. The more the managers and all employees understand about the concepts and philosophies of InfoSec, the more they will understand ISSO decisions—and also the more supportive they will be.

Corporate management's knowledge may also challenge an ISSO, causing him or her to rethink some decisions and the logic that led to them. That's good, except for those ISSOs who do not want to excel and accept such a challenge—in other words, the lazy and unprofessional people in ISSO positions. However, in the long run, such criticisms and recommendations are good for the corporation. Why? Because it means that management is actually looking at InfoSec and becoming, as they should, a part of the information and information systems protection team. As an ISSO, you should know that the more input you get and the more interested corporate management and employees are in InfoSec, the better your InfoSec program will become, and the better it will meet the needs of the corporation. It is true that you will probably spend more time in discussions with corporate management, but that is really a good thing. In the long run, your job, if you do it right, will actually be easier.

It should come as no surprise to company managers that they are responsible for the protection of company assets. In today's information-dependent and information-based companies, it should also come as no surprise that these assets include information. These are facts of business life today and are probably concurred in by 99.9% of the company managers that one could survey. I would say 100%, except that there are always some managers (many of us have met them in our careers) who just don't seem to get it. So, let's allot the 0.1% to those managers that just don't get it.

So, if most company managers agree with that premise, why do so many either battle to negate information and information systems protection (InfoSec) instead of supporting InfoSec? Maybe they don't care for anything beyond their paychecks and bonuses. It seems today that there are many of those. It is ironic, but it seems in many companies around the world today that the truly company-loyal people are mostly the "regular employees" and not the managers. Employees are out there working hard and doing their best to help the company succeed. They have a loyalty—though somewhat less than in earlier years—to the company that it seems most of today's managers do not.

Today's managers either are so self-centered that they only care about their careers—you see, managers have "careers," while employees have "jobs"—or are ignorant as to their responsibilities. Let us assume ignorance is their problem. Perhaps they have been promoted into management but no one has ever explained their assets protection responsibilities. That may be because their boss did not know—it was not explained to him or her. Maybe it is because the managers try to avoid that responsibility by hiring someone to provide InfoSec. Thus the problem is delegated to someone else. Therefore, when things go wrong, it is not the company manager's fault; it is the fault of those hired to protect the assets.

Then what can be done about it? Whatever the reason, it is up to the company managers to know their responsibilities and the InfoSec professionals to politely remind them of those responsibilities. As the saying goes, "You can delegate authority but not abdicate your responsibilities."

If you are a company manager reading this, other than a security professional of some kind, congratulations! You are one of the few who are interested in InfoSec. May your career rise above the stars. For you others out there, it is assumed you have some responsibility for InfoSec or InfoSec-related tasks such as fraud prevention or other asset protection. If so, you should provide your company managers information that politely and professionally explains to them that they have some very basic and direct InfoSec responsibilities. Lay out those responsibilities to them as part of some awareness e-mail, on an internal company Web page or newsletter—whatever communication form works best in your environment.

The first things that company managers should be made aware (or reminded) of is that they do have a responsibility for protecting company assets—and some of the most important of those assets are sensitive information and information systems within their organization.

Company managers should understand the basics of InfoSec. It is not rocket science. It is common sense. They should know that the purpose of InfoSec is to do the following:

- Minimize the probability of a successful attack on the company's information;
- Minimize the damage if an attack occurs; and
- Provide a method to quickly recover in the event of a successful attack.

The three basic principles that are the foundation of InfoSec are:

- Access control,
- Individual accountability, and
- Audit trails.

These are rather basic and should be easy enough for company managers not versed in InfoSec to understand. Once managers understand the InfoSec purpose and the three basic principles, the InfoSec professional must be able to explain the concepts in detail and how they apply to the individual company managers. Obviously, there is not sufficient space in this entire book to adequately cover that topic. Furthermore, I hoped that, as an ISSO responsible for InfoSec within your company, you do understand these concepts and can easily explain them to company managers. If not—well, that is too scary a thought to contemplate.

What Company Managers Should Ask of Their InfoSec Professionals

Company managers should also be sufficiently knowledgeable to ask intelligent questions about InfoSec-related matters, and ideally the company ISSO can answer them. Some questions company managers should ask, and some possible answers that the InfoSec can give and then explain in more detail, include the following:

- *Question*: How do you know you are actually under attack and not the victim of misconfigured systems? *Answer*: You may not know until it is too late; you may never know; you may know, but can't stop it.

- *Question*: What are the warning signs of potential or actual attacks? *Answer*: There may not be any.
- *Question*: Is it possible to know of pending attacks? *Answer*: Yes. No. Maybe—depending on conditions.
- *Question*: What can you do to set up an "imminent" attack warning system? *Answer*: Base it on history; on the latest techniques identified in CERTs; on target visibility; on your defenses; on your countermeasures; on your use of technology; and on vendor products.
- *Question*: What is the basis of deploying intrusion detection to assist in countering the attacks? *Answer*: What is normal activity? What is abnormal? One can compare activity against known attack methods and establish countermeasures; and one must have, as a minimum, an InfoSec policy, procedures, and awareness program.
- *Question*: What must be considered when deploying the intrusion detection system and processes? *Answer*: Any available tools should be adapted to your unique environment. The intrusion detection process must be always secure, operating, and "fool-proof." It must detect all anomalies and misuse; must have audit-based systems for history; must have real-time monitoring and warnings; and take immediate action based on each unique attack. Also, one must know what to do if attacked.
- *Question*: Any other things to consider? *Answer*: Audit entry ports, especially to critical areas; prioritize processes, shut down others; isolate the problem; and establish alternate routing paths.

What InfoSec Professionals Should Do

If the company managers are able to ask such questions and understand the answers and the details provided, the InfoSec professional has gone a long way to help protect their information and systems from attacks and external fraud. The ISSO has also gone a long way in gaining some basic, active support from company managers.

As part of the above, to be successful, the InfoSec professional should do at least the following:

- Collect information on attacks from all available sources;
- Develop and maintain a threat toolkit containing strategies, tactics, tools, and methodologies used to attack systems;
- Continuously maintain a current toolkit and methodologies that can threaten systems through attack methods;

- Model the capabilities of the potential intruders against real-time attacks;
- Collect information related to the corporation's information systems' vulnerabilities; and
- Establish systems simulating intruder attacks using threat tools in a simulations and testing environment;
- Establish defenses accordingly.

QUESTIONS TO CONSIDER

Based on what you have read, consider the following questions and how you would reply to them[4]:

- Do you understand the company where you have InfoSec responsibility—its history; what products and services it produces; its environment, culture, competition, and business plans; the impact of the InfoSec program on profits; and the like?
- Are you absolutely clear as to what management expects of you?
- Are you absolutely clear that management understands your InfoSec program?
- Is management clear as to what you expect from them, such as support?
- Do you have good communication channels with management?
- Are there managers who are against your InfoSec program, and if so, do you avoid them or try to understand their position and work with them?
- If not work with them, why not?
- Do you understand your business management responsibilities?
- Are you trying to make the InfoSec program a value-added function?
- If so, are you succeeding, and how do you know?
- Does management also think the InfoSec program is a value-added program, and if so, how do you know?

SUMMARY

As we begin this 21st century, an ISSO faces many more challenges than existed only a decade ago. The environment is faster, more technical, and much more challenging. The 21st-century ISSO must understand the global marketplace and the company's business environment much more than was necessary only a decade or so ago:

---

[4]Obviously, if you answer No to any of these questions, you have some additional work to do.

- ISSOs must understand their company's business, including its history, products, competition, plans, costs, and product value.
- ISSOs must understand business, management, and how to communicate with management in management's language—not in "computerese"!
- ISSOs must document major InfoSec decisions to provide a historical file that can be used in the future when considering similar situations.
- ISSOs must also think and act as business managers of the company.
- ISSOs must be service and support oriented.

Company managers must understand their assets protection responsibilities. That is especially important today, when information protection and crime prevention should be a major responsibility of every company manager. For it is only with that understanding, support, and action that companies can respond to attacks against them from competitors, nation-states, and techno-spies.

3

Understanding Today's Threats to Information Assets

If you know the enemy and know yourself, you need not fear the result of a hundred battles. If you know yourself but not the enemy, for every victory gained you will also suffer a defeat. If you know neither the enemy nor yourself, you will succumb in every battle.—Sun Tzu[1]

CHAPTER OBJECTIVE

"Understanding Today's Threats to Information Assets" discusses today's threats to the information and information systems of modern, global corporations and government agencies.

INTRODUCTION

It seems that since the beginning of time, as we human beings multiplied across this earth, there has been a division between the "haves" and the "have-nots." In the days of the hunter-gatherers, through the agricultural period, industrial period, and right into our information period approaching the knowledge age, there have always been people who threatened others. Some wanted food without hunting for it; others wanted material possessions of others without working for it; and others wanted power, fortune, and glory without earning it.

Throughout the ages, humans have used technology for good and for bad purposes:

- Fire can be used for cooking and heating, or it can be used to burn down someone's home or crops;
- Guns can be used to kill game and defend one's family, or they can be used to kill others and take what they own; and

---

[1] From Sun Tzu's *Art of War. The Oldest Military Treatise in the World.* Translated from the Chinese by Lionel Giles, 1910.

- Computers can be used to help find medical cures, or they can be used to break into other computers to destroy, modify, or steal others' information.

There are many examples of the utilization of all types of technology that can be used for good or bad purposes. However, they all have something in common. *People* are the driving force behind it all, and it is people as threat agents that the ISSO must always take into account when building a Corporate Information Assets Protection Program (CIAPP).

For our purposes, we will look at the various categories of threats to information and information systems in this our age of information. In order to discuss threats, we must look at them in the context of the overall triad of threats, vulnerabilities, and risks.

---

threat [thret] noun (plural threats)[2]

1.   declaration of intent to cause harm: the expression of a deliberate intention to cause harm or pain;
2.   indication of something bad: a sign or danger that something undesirable is going to happen;
3.   somebody or something likely to cause harm: a person, animal, or thing likely to cause harm or pain

---

Threats to our information and the systems that store, process, display, and transmit that information fall into two basic categories: manmade or natural occurrences that can cause adverse affects to systems and information when combined with specific vulnerabilities. For example:

- *Natural threats* include such things as fire, floods, hurricanes, and earthquakes.
- *Man-made threats* or threat-related matters include such things as unauthorized system access, hacker/cracker/phreaker programs, the perpetrators themselves, theft of systems or services, denial of services, and destruction of systems or information.

Vulnerabilities are defined basically as weaknesses that allow specific threats to cause adverse affects to systems and information. For example:

---

[2] *Encarta World English Dictionary* © & (P) 1999, Microsoft Corporation. All rights reserved. Developed for Microsoft by Bloomsbury Publishing Plc.

- Lack of current antivirus software;
- Lack of systems access controls; or
- Generally anything that weakens the security of the systems and the information they process, store, display, and transmit.

The chances that a specific threat can take advantage of a specific vulnerability to cause adverse affects to systems and information is known as *risk*. For example:

- If you live in a strong earthquake area, what are the chances that your systems will be damaged in the event of a strong earthquake?
- If you do not have audit trails on your system, how will you know if someone tries to penetrate your system, or worse yet, whether or not they succeed?

When one looks at the threats to information and their associated systems, the vulnerabilities of that protection system and their associated risks, one tries to assess or evaluate the level of risk to systems and their associated information. Assessments are usually done through a qualitative or quantitative analysis, or a combination of the two. It is the measurement of risks:

- *Qualitative analysis* usually uses the three categories of risk, that is, high, medium, and low. It is an "educated best guess" based primarily on opinions of knowledgeable others gathered through interviews, history, tests, and the experience of the person doing the assessment.
- *Quantitative analysis* usually uses statistical sampling based on mathematical computations determining the probability of an adverse occurrence based on historical data. It is still an "educated best guess," but primarily based on statistical results.

The proliferation in the use of computer and communications technologies over approximately the last 20 years has resulted in significant changes in the types of threats that are posed to the information environment that we have come to rely on. The way in which the threats that are posed to an information environment are measured has not advanced at the same rate as the technology has developed and as a result, has not yet transitioned from being an art to science.—Andy Jones[3]

---

[3] Andy Jones is a Senior Lecturer at the University of Glamorgan, Wales. Professor Jones has been kind enough to allow the extensive use of his master's thesis, "Identification of a Method for the Calculation of the Capability of Threat Agents in an Information Environment," in the writing of this chapter. Professor Jones is also the co-author, along with Dr. Kovacich and Perry Luzwick of the book, *Global Information Warfare*, published by Auerbach in June 2002.

This leads us to risk management. Risk management is defined as the total process of identifying, controlling, and eliminating or minimizing uncertain events that may affect system resources. It includes risk assessments; risk analyses, including cost-benefit analyses; target selection; implementation and testing; security evaluation of safeguards; and overall InfoSec review. The process of identifying InfoSec risks, determining their magnitude, and identifying areas needing safeguards is called risk assessment. In other words, you are assessing the risk of a particular target, such as a new software application's impact on the system's security processes, architecture, etc. The risk assessment process is subdivided into threats, vulnerabilities, and risks.

Analyses of the risks, the countermeasures to mitigate those risks, and the cost-benefits associated with those risks and countermeasures make up the risk analysis process. Basically, it is risk assessment with the cost and benefit factors added.

> If I want to wreak havoc on a society that, in some cases, has become complacent, I am going to attack your quality of life. —Curt Weldon, R-PA, U.S. House Armed Services Committee[4]

Types of Threats

As an ISSO, you must become extremely familiar with the types of threats that may adversely affect the information and associated systems—the information environment for which you are responsible—as well as the details of each threat. Furthermore, you must understand how to mitigate each threat. As mentioned earlier, threats include but are not limited to employees, terrorists, techno-fraudsters, Netspionage agents, information warriors, other miscreants, a combination of these, or such things as malicious software programs. These threats are often called threat agents.

Natural Threats

Natural threats, as the name implies, are acts of nature. Some may call them "acts of God"; however, that is a personal choice. Since we are discussing information and systems protection, we won't delve into discussing whether or not God plays a role in threatening our information and our systems.

Although natural threats may seem to be random acts, often historical records and interviews with experts will help the ISSO determine if any type of pattern can be identified. If so, the data can be analyzed and a determination can be made as to the extent of risk based on the identi-

---

[4] Speaking at an InfoWar Conference in Washington, D.C., in September 1999.

fied pattern. Defensive measures can then be employed to mitigate that risk. For example, if one lives in a region where there are hurricanes or typhoons, one can talk to meteorologists and review historical records. That review can help the ISSO determine a pattern and thus determine the amount of risk based on that specific threat. The ISSO would, for example, want to know:

- How often a hurricane or typhoon strikes the area;
- What were the maximum, minimum, and average wind speeds, damage, and rainfall associated with such storms;
- What time of year they usually occur; and
- What the impact in the past has been to the company's facilities and information systems.

Such information on this type of threat can assist the ISSO in mitigating the threats at least cost, based on how much risk the company's management would want to assume. By the way, as an ISSO, remember that you are the in-house consultant on such matters. Risk taking and risk-taking decisions are the purview of company management. As an ISSO, you provide them expert opinion and recommendations, but under no circumstances should you make the final risk decision. That is why they "make the big bucks." Risk management decisions may be pushed on you; however, don't fall for that ploy, as it is management's way of getting out of their company responsibilities. Furthermore, if something occurs, based on the risk accepted, that damages the protection of company information and systems, at least management knew the risks.

You will find that management is averse to taking risks but will do so to save money—usually to the detriment of InfoSec. Make no mistake, you probably will still be blamed even if they do not take your recommendation; therefore, it is imperative that such decisions be formally documented and the risks acknowledged in writing by the manager assuming the risks. You may still lose your job if something fails; however, your chances of winning a "wrongful discharge" lawsuit may be enhanced. Such is the life of an ISSO.

The other natural threats based on the physical locations of your company's information systems, such as fire and earthquakes, can be dealt with in a similar manner.

Andy Jones, a security and assets protection expert looks at natural threats and accidents as follows[5]:

---

[5] Andy Jones is a Senior Lecturer at the University of Glamorgan, Wales. Professor Jones has been kind enough to allow the extensive use of his master's thesis, "Identification of a Method for the Calculation of the Capability of Threat Agents in an Information Environment," in the writing of this chapter. Professor Jones is also the coauthor, along with Dr. Kovacich and Perry Luzwick, of the book *Global Information Warfare*, published by Auerbach in June 2002.

For this group of threat agents, which includes fire, wind, water, earthquake, and accidental damage, each element will need to be considered in isolation as they have only tenuous links to each other and the main area of commonality is that they are not planned or directed.

- *Fire.* The likelihood of a direct effect on a system from fire is easily calculable and there is considerable experience and documented case histories in the insurance industry of underwriting this type of event.
- *Wind.* The possibility of damage from wind is largely geographically dependent, as some locations are far more prone to wind damage than others. Again there is considerable experience and documented case histories in the insurance industry of underwriting this type of event.
- *Water.* The likelihood of a direct effect on a system from water is easily calculable and there is considerable experience and documented case histories in the insurance industry of underwriting this type of event.
- *Earthquake.* The possibility of damage from an earthquake is also largely geographically dependent, but again there is considerable experience and documented case histories in the insurance industry of underwriting this type of event.
- *Accidents.* The threat to a system from accidental misuse or damage is very different from the other categories in this group, as it will be affected over time by the attitude and disposition of the staff in addition to the environment. What separates this from the malicious threats is the absence of malice or motivation. Again, this threat is well understood and the probability of such an event occurring can be reasonably predicted from actuarial data.

It is possible that more than one of these natural threats will affect a system at the same time or shortly after each other. An example of this might be an earthquake that is followed by a fire as a result of the disruption to the gas or electrical services that the initial event caused.

- *Natural Threat Agent.* The "threat agent" element expands into the types of agent that may be seen. These have, for convenience and because they can be dealt with in two very different ways, been subdivided into two different groups, the natural threat agents and the malicious threat agents (See Figure 3.1).

These are a relatively well-understood set of threats and there is actuarial history for the effects of Fire, Wind, Water, and Earthquake components that is based on long established experience within the insurance industry. For the last of components, accidental damage, there is also a wealth of information available with regard to the likelihood of an incident occurring in the physical domain (e.g., someone dropping a piece of equipment).

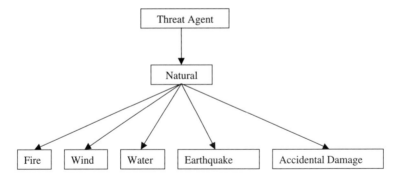

Figure 3.1   The components of the natural threat agents.

Unfortunately there is little or no documented information available for incidents that have occurred in the electronic environment, so little obvious benefit can be gained from any past experience in the domain.

Human Error—Accidents

As noted above, Professor Jones includes accidents under the "Natural" category. Surprisingly, many ISSOs don't consider the threats caused by human error: accidents. Being human, we naturally will make mistakes. So, does human error fall under the category of natural threats, and are we humans as users of systems to be categorized as natural threat agents? Or do we fall under the category of "manmade" threats? There is no law or rule that says that you as an ISSO must treat accidents as one, the other, both, or neither. However, human error is a threat to information and systems, and as such should undoubtedly be considered as such by an ISSO—and dealt with accordingly.

As an ISSO, you may look at such a threat as one that falls into the category of "sh*t happens," and there is no way to mitigate or plan for such occurrences. However, that is not true. Let's look at an example: Some employees install their own software, causing systems problems; modify group files; accidentally delete files; and do other things that affect information systems protection. Processes can be developed and put in place to mitigate such threats. For example, employees can be trained on installing software, or trained experts can be designated to do it for them.

So, yes accidents happen, but most accidents that are serious threats to the protection of information and systems can be mitigated. One or more studies or surveys taken over the years and lost in time (at least lost in time to the author) have indicated that human errors have a greater impact on information and systems protection than do manmade threats caused by purposeful attacks. As an ISSO, be sure to consider human error threats when developing a Corporate Information Assets Protection Program (CIAPP).

Manmade or Malicious Threats

Manmade or malicious threats take many forms, with new types of threats being identified on what it seems to be almost a weekly basis. However, these threats can all be categorized into general groupings. Again quoting Andy Jones's paper on threats:

> In order for a malicious threat to exist, there must be an agent that will implement the threat and that agent must have the motivation to carry it out, the capability and the opportunity to do so.

- *Capability.* The capability of an organization or an individual to mount an attack and to sustain it at an effective level will vary with the complexity, resources, and sophistication of both the attacking force and of the target. It may be sufficient for an attacker to mount an attack at any level in order to achieve their objective, but it may also require a high level of processing power over a long period to have a significant effect.
- *Motivation.* The motivation to carry out a malicious attack on a system could rise from any number of situations. Some commonly accepted motivational drivers are: political, secular, personal gain, religious, revenge, power, terrorism, curiosity, and the like.
- *Access.* In order for a threat agent to carry out an attack on an information system, they must have either physical access to the system (the threat agent gaining direct access to the system) or electronic access (via other networks). Without this, an attack cannot be initiated.
- *Catalyst.* A catalyst is required to cause a threat agent to select the target and the time at which the attack will be initiated. The catalyst could be something that affects either the target or the threat agent.
- *Inhibitors.* There are a number of factors (affectors) that will inhibit a threat agent from mounting an attack either on a specific target or at a specific time. Again, these may affect either the target or the threat agent. An example of this may be the perception that the target system is well protected and that any attempt to attack it will be quickly detected.
- *Amplifiers.* There are a number of factors (affectors) that will encourage a threat agent to mount an attack at a specific time against a particular target. Again, these may affect either the target or the threat agent. An example of this may be the perception that the target system is not well protected and that an attempt to attack it will not be detected.

System-Related Factors

In order for a threat agent to mount a successful attack on a system, there are at least two system-related factors that must be present.

The first is that there must be an exploitable vulnerability in the system for the threat agent to utilize in order to have an effect. For a vulnerability to be exploitable, it must be known (or there must be an expectation that it will be known) to the threat agent, and the threat agent must have sufficient access to the system to affect the attack. The vulnerability may exist in the hardware, the operating system software, or the applications software.

The second is that the target system must be important enough to the organization that its loss or degradation in its availability, confidentiality, or integrity would have an impact on the business process of the organization.

Relationship of Threat Elements

The potential for a threat agent to pose an actual threat to an information infrastructure will be influenced by a number of factors. In reality, for the threat agent to pose a real threat to an information infrastructure, the agent must posses a capability and must also be able to gain either physical or electronic access.

The potential impact of such a threat agent will be influenced by its level of capability. The threat agent will be inhibited by factors that hinder their ability to form a threat and will be strengthened by other factors. In addition, there will be some type of catalyst that will cause them to act, depending on their motivation. The components of "threat" that apply to a malicious threat and their interrelationships are detailed in Figure 3.2.

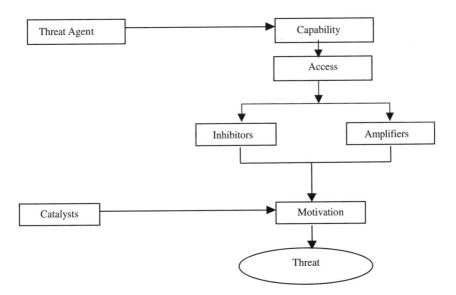

Figure 3.2   The threat components and their relationships.

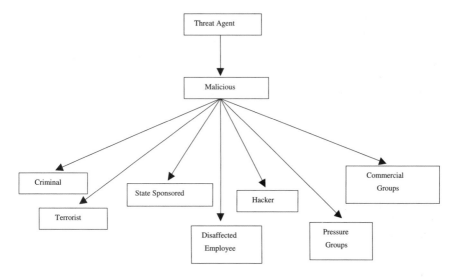

Figure 3.3   The components of the malicious threat agent.

Malicious Threat Agent

Malicious Threat Agents expand into at least seven components (See Figure 3.3).

A malicious threat agent can be generated from any number of groups. This is not meant to be an exhaustive list of potential sources or groupings of malicious threat agents, as these will change over time as technology, education, national and international politics, cultural, and a host of other factors have an effect.

Capability

In order for a malicious threat agent to be effective, they must have the capability to conduct and sustain an attack. The constituent elements of "capability" are detailed in Figure 3.4.

For a malicious threat agent to be able to carry out an attack, they must have the means and the necessary skills and methods to be successful. They must also, in some cases, have a sustainable depth of capability in order to achieve their aims.

Inhibitors

There are several factors that both inhibit and assist a malicious threat agent in perpetrating a successful attack. These have been labeled as inhibitors and amplifiers. The inhibitors are identified in Figure 3.5.

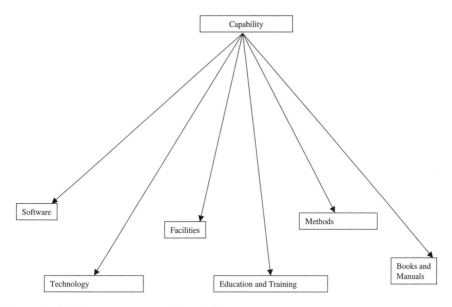

Figure 3.4 The components of capability.

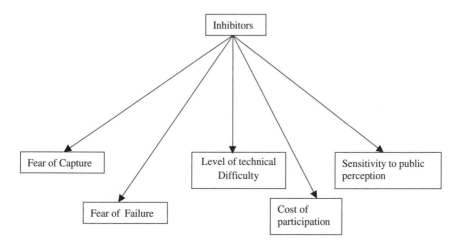

Figure 3.5 The components of inhibitors.

An inhibitor will either prevent a threat agent from carrying out a successful attack, minimize the impact that a successful attack will have, or reduce the inclination of a threat agent to initiate an attack. The fear of being captured as a result of conducting an attack may well act as a sufficient deterrent to the threat agent and cause it to decide not to carry out the attack. If the threat agent perceives that its peers, or indeed the public, will hold it in contempt for attempting the attack (for example if the target was a hospital or a charity), this may be sufficient to inhibit the attack. Also, if the level of technical difficulty that the threat agent encounters is sufficiently high, the threat agent may decide that the investment of effort required to carry out the attack is not worth it.

Amplifiers

The types of affectors that will amplify or increase the possibility of a successful attack are varied, but include factors such as peer pressure. In this amplifier, the threat agent desires to be well regarded by their peers. Their desire to gain the recognition and respect of their peers through the demonstration of their skills strengthens their resolve to carry out the attack. The level of education and skill that an agent possesses, or can gain access to, will improve the confidence of a threat agent and also increase the likelihood of success. Access to the information that the agent needs in order to mount an attack, in terms of information on the target, other relevant information systems, organizations or in terms of programming scripts and tools that can be run to conduct an attack, will also increase the possibility of a successful attack.

Catalysts

The causal factor in a threat agent deciding if and when to carry out an attack on an information system may be a result of an event, such as publicity for an organization with which the agent has a disagreement, or perhaps the start of an armed conflict between the agent's country and an opponent. Another factor may be the circumstances of the agent and any change (perhaps in location, social grouping, or employment status) may affect their ability or desire to carry out an attack.

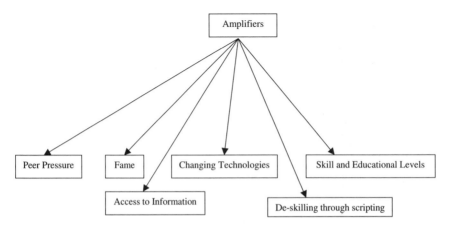

Figure 3.6   The components of amplifiers.

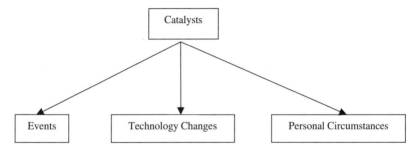

Figure 3.7   The components of catalysts.

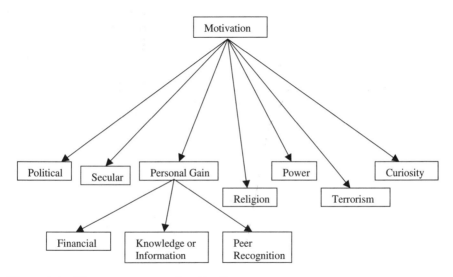

Figure 3.8   The components of motivation.

An attack may also be triggered by the advent of a new technology which makes what was previously not achievable a possibility. (See Figure 3.7.)

Motivation

The motivation of the threat agent is a subjective area that is influenced by a wide range of factors dependent on the grouping from which the threat agent originates. The components that are shown above are not intended to be a comprehensive list of motivational factors, but rather to give an indication of the range of drivers that may have an influence. In some cases a number of these drivers will act together to influence the threat agent. (See Figure 3.8.)

Malicious Threat Agent—State Sponsored

State sponsored malicious threats may take the form of denial of service attacks on financial systems or critical national infrastructures in order to modify public perception, or cause instability in the target country and prevent it from taking other actions. It may also take the form of espionage or industrial espionage[6]. A characteristic of this group is that it will be risk-averse and conservative in its actions, taking great efforts to evade identification.

Information on nation states is, in the main part readily available from open sources. The limiting factor in this is that by its nature, the information may be dated and the elements useful for the purposes of determining a nation's readiness to mount an attack may be limited.

For an attack sponsored by a nation state to be effective, it would require sufficient technology available to mount the attack, telecommunications, Internet connectivity, and power supplies to allow the attack to take place and be sustained, and sufficient personnel resources with adequate levels of education and skill to mount and maintain the attack. Each country will have specific cultural drivers.

A threat agent that is sponsored by a nation state may have the objective of preventing or reducing access to information systems (denial of service), manipulating or corrupting information (disinformation), or gaining access to information (espionage). The impact that each of these types of attack will have varies, and the likelihood of each must be considered separately.

Malicious Threat Agent—Terrorists

Terrorist activity may be linked to criminal activity and as a malicious threat agent, the terrorist may operate in both groups. Terrorism requires funding to be effective. Given that terrorists operate outside of the normal national and international laws, it is common for them to resort to criminal activity to generate funds to support their activities, in addition to any direct terrorist related action. Direct terrorist activities may include the publication of propaganda, communications, or attacks on systems to either influence the public, users, or owners of a system, or to prevent the system from operating. For example, this includes causing the electrical supply system in a city to fail and gaining the desired effect from the ensuing chaos.

Qualitative information on terrorist organizations is not readily available from open sources. While generic information from external sources is available, accurate and in-depth information is not normally available in a

---

[6] Espionage through the networks (network-enabled espionage) has become known as "Netspionage." See *Netspionage: The Global Threat to Information*, published by Butterworth–Heinemann, 2000, for a detailed look at this growing threat.

verifiable form except where it is released or disseminated from national resources that will probably be hostile to the terrorist organization.

For a terrorist sponsored attack to be effective, it would require sufficient technology available to mount the attack, telecommunications, Internet connectivity, and an adequate power supply to allow the attack to take place. If one of the required outcomes is a sustained attack, then they must also have sufficient depth of personnel resources with adequate levels of education and skill available to mount and maintain the attack. Each terrorist group will have specific drivers. These may be religious, cultural, ethnic, political, or any number of others.

A terrorist threat agent is most likely to have the objective of preventing or reducing access to information systems (denial of service), and this should be the area that is further investigated.

Malicious Threat Agent—Pressure Group

Pressure groups will tend to have a specific focus or cause that they support and wish to further the aims of. Recent history has shown that such groups, whether secular or religious, have learned they can achieve results by exerting influence on peripheral targets, rather than on a direct attack on the primary target.

Qualitative information on pressure groups is not, for the main part, readily available in the public domain from open sources. While generic information from external sources will be available, accurate and in-depth information is not normally available in a verifiable form, as these are not accountable organizations.

For an attack sponsored by a pressure group to be effective, it would require that the necessary technology was available to mount the attack. It is assumed there would be telecommunications, Internet connectivity, and an adequate power supply to allow the attack to take place. If the required outcome is a sustained attack, then the pressure group must also have sufficient personnel resources with adequate levels of skill available to mount and maintain the attack. Each pressure group will have specific drivers that may be religious, cultural, ethnic, political, or any number of others.

Due to the range of organizations that are included in this group and the fact that they have varying degrees of legitimacy and history, identifying specific sources of information for the various aspects of pressure groups cannot easily be documented. For detailed information on a specific pressure group, it would be necessary to look at the information sources that were specifically related to that group. Details that are available on a pressure group will vary over time as it becomes more or less active.

Pressure groups are affected by a wide range of factors that influence their motivation, ability, and likelihood of them carrying out an attack. A threat agent sponsored by a pressure group may have the objective of preventing or reducing access to information systems (denial of service), manipulating or corrupting information (disinformation), or gaining access to information ([industrial] espionage). The impact that each of these types of attack will have varies, and the likelihood of each must be considered separately in the light of the aims of the pressure group and its target.

Malicious Threat Agent—Commercial Group

A threat agent that acts on behalf of a commercial group will tend to have one of a small number of objectives. These will range from industrial espionage, to damaging the interests of competitors, to influencing small nation states. A characteristic of this group is that it will be risk averse and conservative in its actions, taking great efforts to evade identification. Qualitative information on the capability of a commercial organization to carry out an attack is not, for the main part, available in the public domain from open sources. While very specific and detailed information will be available on a number of aspects relating to the commercial concern, specific information with regard to its capability to pose an information threat will only be generated from analysis of the organization, or from information on past activity that becomes available.

For an attack sponsored by a commercial organization to be effective, it would require sufficient technology and available resources. It is assumed that there would be telecommunications, Internet connectivity, and an adequate power supply to allow the attack to take place. If the required outcome is a sustained attack, then the organization must also have sufficient personnel resources with adequate levels of skill available to mount and maintain the attack. The driver for a commercial organization to mount an information attack will be to gain a commercial advantage in the marketplace, either by gaining information on or from its competitors, or by reducing the ability of the competitor to operate efficiently in the marketplace.

Commercial groups are affected by a wide range of factors that influence their motivation, ability, and the likelihood of them carrying out an attack. A threat agent sponsored by a commercial group may have the objective of preventing or reducing access to information systems (denial of service), manipulating or corrupting information (disinformation), or gaining access to information ([industrial] espionage). The impact that each of these types of attack will have varies and the likelihood of each must be considered separately in the light of the perceived aims of the commercial group and its target.

Malicious Threat Agent—Criminal

Criminal activity that provides a threat to information systems will be a result of the criminal attempting to:

* Gain access to the system in order to defraud someone of resources (money or property),
* Prevent the detection or investigation of other criminal activity,
* Gain information that will enable them to commit other crimes,
* Gain access to personal information that will enable them to commit other crimes (identity theft, blackmail, stalking, harassment).

As the descriptor "criminal" covers a huge range of activities, from financial gain through to murder, drug smuggling, trafficking, and sex offences, it is not possible to define generic characteristics.

For the purposes of this discussion, the threat agent from a "criminal" group will tend to have one of a small number of objectives. These will range from industrial espionage, to damaging the interests of competitors, to influencing small nation states. A characteristic of this group is that it will be risk-averse and conservative in its actions, taking great efforts to evade identification.

For an attack sponsored by a criminal group to be effective, it would require available resources to mount the attack. This is not normally an issue for a criminal group as they tend to be "cash rich" and do not have to account for their funds. If the required outcome is a sustained attack, they must also have sufficient personnel resources with adequate levels of skill available to mount and maintain the attack. Each criminal group will have specific drivers, but these will predominately be financial or competitive gain.

Any form of useable information on the capability of a criminal organization to carry out an attack is not, for the main part, available in the public domain from open sources. Law enforcement and national intelligence agencies invest a vast effort on attempting to gather this type of information and have had only limited success. Some inference can be gathered over a period of time as the effect of the actions of a group become apparent.

For an attack sponsored by a criminal group to be effective, it would require that the technology and level of skill was available to mount the attack. It is assumed there would be telecommunications, Internet connectivity, and an adequate power supply to allow the attack to take place. If the required outcome is a sustained attack, then the organization must also have sufficient depth of personnel resources with adequate levels of skill available to mount and maintain the attack. The driver for a criminal group to mount an information attack will be for financial gain or influence. This may not be apparent from the form of an attack. For example the Cali Drug Cartel may mount an intelligence gathering attack to gain information on the movements of British Royal Naval shipping assets in the Caribbean. The purpose of gaining this information would be to enable them to avoid the ships and thus allow them to deliver the drugs to mainland USA and as a result make more profit.

Although it is difficult to deal separately with each of the factors that may contribute to the capability of a criminal group to pose a threat, considerable information is available from which the individual elements that are required can be extracted.

Criminal groups are affected by a wide range of factors that influence their motivation, ability, and likelihood of them carrying out an attack.

A threat agent sponsored by a criminal group may have the objective of preventing or reducing access to information systems (denial of service), manipulating or corrupting information (disinformation), or gaining access to information ([industrial] espionage). The impact that each of these types of attack will have varies, and the likelihood of each must be considered separately in the light of the perceived aims of the criminal group and its target.

Malicious Threat Agent—Hacker

Hackers' objectives will normally be to gain status from their peers by causing visible damage to a system "because they can." Other reasons for an attack may be to gain access to a system in order to utilize its resources, either for the processing capability or in order to cover other activities. Due to the basis of this group being a technical capability rather than a specific motive or pressure, the type of attack that may be mounted will not be based on the impact to the system owner but rather the real or perceived benefit to the perpetrator.

For an attack sponsored by a hacker or hacker group to be effective, it would require available resources to mount the attack. This is not normally an issue for a hacker group, as they have support from their peers. If the required outcome is a sustained attack, they must also have sufficient personnel resources with adequate levels of skill available to mount and maintain the attack. Each hacker group will have specific drivers, but these will predominately be for self-aggrandizement or revenge.

Any form of useable information on the capability of a hacker group to carry out an attack will, if it is available, be in the public domain from open sources. Law enforcement and national intelligence agencies attempt to gather information on these groups, but due to their transient nature, have had only limited success. Some inference can be gathered over a period of time as the effect of the actions of a hacker group become apparent.

For an attack sponsored by a hacker group to be effective, it would require an appropriate level of skill available to mount the attack. It is assumed that there would be telecommunications, Internet connectivity, suitable technology, and an adequate power supply to allow the attack to take place. The driver for a hacker group to mount an information attack varies, with the main drivers being anything from curiosity, to financial gain, to revenge.

It is difficult to deal separately with each of the factors that may contribute to the capability of a hacker or hacker group to pose a threat, however considerable information is available from which the individual elements that are required can be extracted:

Hacker groups are affected by a wide range of factors that will have an influence on their motivation and ability and the likelihood of them carrying out an attack.

A threat agent that is sponsored by a hacker group may have the objective of preventing or reducing access to information systems (denial of service), manipulating or corrupting information (disinformation), or of gaining access to information ([industrial] espionage). The impact that each of these types of attack will have varies, and the likelihood of each must be considered separately in the light of the perceived aims of the hacker or hacker group and the target.

Malicious Threat Agent—Disaffected Staff

In this scenario, a disaffected member of staff is seeking to cause damage to the image or structure of the organization, or to extract value in the form of funds or property of some value.

Indicators of potential disaffected staff can be isolated, as there are a number of identified case histories that can be used to identify significant common factors from these case histories.

Any form of useable information on the capability of a disaffected member of staff to carry out an attack will, if it has been made available by the employing organization, be in the public domain. Information that is held by law enforcement and national intelligence agencies is not likely to be made available in reasonable time as it will, potentially, be required for prosecution.

For an attack undertaken by a disaffected member of staff to be effective, it would require that they possess the appropriate level of skill. The drivers for a disaffected member of staff to mount an information attack will vary, with the main drivers being anything from financial gain to revenge.

Malicious Threat Agent—Subversive Organizations

A member of staff belonging to a subversive organization will not, in probability, be known to their employer. The membership of a subversive organization will become an issue when the aims and objectives of the employing organization are in conflict with those of the subversive organization, or when the subversive organization can further its own aims using the information, facilities, infrastructure, or influence that is provided by the employing organization.

Indicators of this type of threat agent will be difficult or impossible to identify, as the motivation of the perpetrator will not be clear and their membership of the subversive organization will be difficult to determine. It is clear that some organizations will be more prone to this type of threat agent (for example government departments, the judiciary and law enforcement) as these are the types of organization that can leverage significant influence and favor. A possible example of a subversive organization would be the Freemasons.

Any form of useable information on the effect of subversive or secretive organizations on an organization with regard to their ability to carry out an attack will, if it has been made available, be unlikely to be in the public domain. Information that is held by law enforcement and national intelligence agencies is not likely to be made available as it will have either been gathered either as part of an investigation for subsequent criminal prosecution, or will have been gathered as intelligence for reasons of national security.

For an attack that is undertaken by a subversive within an organization to be effective, it would require that they possess appropriate level of skill. The drivers for a subverted member of staff to mount an information attack will vary, with the main drivers being to gain influence or intelligence.

Perhaps the most widely known society that affects members of the law enforcement community in the United Kingdom is that of the Freemasons. Whilst there is no attempt to impugn the name of the society or of its members, there has, for a number of years, been concern in the law enforcement community in the UK, that members of its staff belong to this organization but do not, and in some cases, will not, declare their membership. There are around the world many more examples such as The Skull and Bones Society in the United States, which boasted among its leadership President George Bush, or the Illuminati.

In this case it is not the individual or group that poses the threat agent that is the most significant element, but instead it is the organization that is the target of their attention. The most likely reason for this type of threat agent to mount an attack on an organization would be to gain influence and power. As a result, it is most likely that the organization type that will be most likely to be affected by this type of threat agent will be one where the major currency is power or influence.

Threat Amplifiers

A threat amplifier is any factor that increases either the likelihood of an attack taking place or the likelihood of the attack being successful. The factors may be either real or imagined. Examples of amplifiers may be discussion amongst hackers of the discovery of a new method for penetrating the security of a particular system or the announcement of a breakthrough in research at a particular organization that attracts attention from competitors.

Threat amplifiers will be a mixture of transient and longer-term influences and as a result, the sources of information on these will be varied. There is an added dimension with these influencing factors in that some are real and some are perceived.

Of the factors that were identified, those that are detailed below were considered to be the most significant. Taking each of these factors in turn:

- *Peer Pressure.* A threat agent is more likely to carry out an attack if they feel that to do so will advance their prestige or status within their peer group. Particularly within hacking circles, elevated status and regard by other hackers will gain the individual access to information and resources that they did not have before, and will also achieve one of their aspirations of increased status within the community.
- *Fame.* In all social groupings, a proportion of the individuals will seek to be recognized for the actions that they have undertaken. These actions may have been good or bad, but the desire of the individual that has carried out the attack to be recognized for their skill and daring will be quite high.
- *Access to Information.* If an individual or group believes that they will gain access to useful information, either as a direct result of carrying out an attack or as an indirect benefit, they will, in some cases, be more

inclined to carry out the attack. This access to information may be the primary motivation for the attack or a secondary benefit.

- *Changing Technology.* Typically, the release of new technology is followed by its acceptance into common use, the discovery of weaknesses in the technology, and the exploitation of those weaknesses for illicit purposes.
- *De-Skilling through Scripting.* As new techniques to subvert the security of systems are understood, the more skilled attackers, most particularly from the hacking community, will write scripts that will automate the attack. As these become available to the less skilled users who could not carry out the attack without the automated tools, the number of people that could conduct an attack is increased.
- *Skill and Education Levels.* As the general level of education with regard to technology increases, the use of technology becomes almost ubiquitous, and as the skill level with regard to the use of new technologies increases, so too will the number of people who have the understanding of the technology and ways to carry out attacks increase.

Other Issues That Will Amplify the Threat to a System

- *Law Enforcement Activity.* If the laws within the target country or the country from which the threat agent is operating are perceived to be weak or not relevant (for example, using the theft of electricity to charge a person for a hacking offense), or if the laws that are being used have not been tested in the courts or have been tested and shown to be ineffective, or if the law enforcement community is seen to be reluctant in its application of the law, the perceived lack of law enforcement will act as an amplifying factor.
- *Target Vulnerability.* If the target that the threat agent has identified is perceived to be in a poorly protected state (for example if the system software is poorly maintained) or if it has vulnerabilities that come into effect through no fault of the system management, this may amplify the likelihood of the threat agent undertaking the attack.
- *Target Profile.* If the profile of the target is such that in comparison to similar organizations, it is more attractive to the threat agent, this will amplify the likelihood of an attack.
- *Public Perception.* if the perception of the public is against the organization that the target represents, then this will increase the likelihood of a threat agent carrying out an attack. An example of this would be Arab language web sites in the period after September 11, 2001.

Threat Inhibitors

A threat inhibitor will be any factor that decreases either the likelihood of an attack taking place or the likelihood of an attack being successful. The factors may be either real or imagined. Examples of inhibitors may be publicity relating to individuals being prosecuted or investigated for attempting to break into a system or a change in the state of the security of a system.

Threat inhibitors will, in a manner similar to threat amplifiers, be a mixture of transient and long-term influences and as a result, the sources of information on these will be varied. There is an added dimension with these influencing factors in that some are real and some are perceived. Examples of the type of factor that may inhibit the likelihood of an attack are detailed below.

Of the factors that were identified, those that are detailed below were considered to be the most significant. Taking each of these factors in turn:

- *Fear of Capture.* If the threat agent has the perception that, if they initiate an attack, they are likely to be identified and captured, this will act as a deterrent and will inhibit the perpetrator.
- *Fear of Failure.* If the threat agent believes that they are likely to fail in their attempt to conduct an attack, this may act to deter them from trying. This effect will be further enhanced if they are sensitive to the opinions of others and believe that the failure will become known to them.
- *Level of Technical Difficulty.* If the defenses of a target that has been identified by a threat agent [are] shown to be difficult to overcome, then this will, in most cases, reduce the likelihood of the threat agent attacking the system as the threat agent will search for a less challenging target. In some cases this may be inverted as the threat agent will attack the most difficult of targets to prove or demonstrate their skills and abilities.
- *Cost of Participation.* If the cost of undertaking the attack is too high, then this will inhibit the threat agent from initiating the attack. The cost may be in terms of finances or of the appropriate equipment or of time or information.
- *Sensitivity to Public Perception.* If the target that the threat agent has selected is one that would gain the threat agent disfavor in the eyes of the public, this may act as a deterrent. An example of this would be an attack on the military resources of your own country during a conflict or an attack on a respected charity. The sensitivity of the threat agent to the public feelings may inhibit the action.

Other Issues That May Inhibit the Threat to a System

- *Law Enforcement Activity.* If the laws within the target country of the country from which the threat agent is operating are strong and relevant laws that have been tested in the courts and shown to be effective and if the law enforcement community is seen to be aggressive in its application of the law, this will act as an inhibiting factor.
- *Target Vulnerability.* If the target that the threat agent has identified is perceived to be in a well protected state (for example if the system software is well maintained and any probes of the system are actively pursued) or if the system is thought to be protected by a variety of devices, this should inhibit the likelihood of the threat agent undertaking the attack.

- *Target Profile.* If the profile of the target is such that in comparison to similar organizations, it is less attractive to the threat agent, this will inhibit the likelihood of an attack.
- *Public Perception.* If the perception of the public is in favor of the organization that the target represents (for example a hospital or an animal rescue center), then this will reduce the likelihood of a threat agent carrying out an attack.
- *Peer Perception.* If the consensus of opinion of the peers of the threat agent is that the target would be "poor" for reasons of ease of access, resulting in no peer acknowledgement for a successful attack, or because the business of the target receives the support of the peer then this [decreases] the likelihood of an attack.

Threat Catalysts

Threat catalysts are those factors or actions that cause an attack to be initiated at the time and on the target that is selected. Again, the catalyst may be either real or perceived. Examples of catalysts are a change in the political relationship between two countries or the initiation of armed conflicts between two groups or an event that receives media attention and is, as a result, highlighted in the public awareness.

The main groupings of threat catalysts have been identified as:

- *Events.* An event may be related to the attacker or to the target, either directly or indirectly. An event that influences the threat agent might be a personal experience or exposure to news that triggers predetermined actions. An event that affects the target might be a declaration of war or the initiation of a conflict between two nation states or for a company, a research and development success that might change the value of the company.
- *Technology Changes.* A change in technology occurs at approximately nine-month intervals and as a result, new uses for technology become apparent and also shortcomings in the technologies that are in use become understood in the wider community. This constant technology churn can be the catalyst for a threat agent to carry out an attack as they see an opportunity developing.
- *Personal Circumstances.* A change in the personal circumstances of the threat agent may be as a result of exposure to information that affects their values or beliefs. Alternatively it might be as a result of the actions of others, such as them being fired from their job and as a result having time to conduct an attack and the motivation of revenge against the former employer. Another alternative may be an elevation in position or peer regard and a desire for them to demonstrate their skills.

The catalyst that will cause a threat agent to initiate an attack on a target will, by its nature, be a transient occurrence.

Threat Agent Motivators

The factors and influences that motivate a threat agent are diverse and may operate singly or in unison. Whilst a range of groupings of threat agent motivators can be easily generated, the reason that each of the factors would come into effect and the degree that it would influence the threat agent is subject to a large number of varying influences.

The primary groupings of threat agent motivators are detailed below, together with a general description, but no further analysis of this subject area will be undertaken as a part of the research in this paper. The main motivational factors are:

- *Political.* Where the motivation is for the advancement of a political cause, it may be because the threat agent wishes to further the cause of the political organization or further their own position within the political grouping. The outcome may be an attack on a political party's web site or the denial of service of a resource, particularly during the period running up to an election.
- *Secular.* If the motivation of the threat agent is to support their secular beliefs, it is possible that the level of action that they will be prepared to take is quite high. A person that is supporting their secular beliefs will be likely to pursue an attack to a final conclusion.
- *Personal Gain.* There are a number of aspects that have been grouped together under this general descriptor, as individuals are motivated by different rewards and gains. In this example, three types of gain have been identified. The first is financial gain, where the threat agent will gain money, goods or services as a result of carrying out the attack. This may be direct gain with the result being able to use stolen credit card numbers or it may be indirect gain through being paid to carry out the attack. The second type of gain is the acquisition of knowledge or information. In this area the benefit that the threat agent may seek is in the information itself or the knowledge that is gained in obtaining access to the information. The third type of personal gain is in the form of recognition by the threat agent's peers. This may result in the threat agent gaining status amongst their peers or gaining access to additional information or resources as a result of having demonstrated their abilities.
- *Religion.* This is one of the more regularly observed motivational factors. Religious conflicts are amongst the most common and as a result it is to be expected that this will be a major motivational factor for a threat agent. Given the number of conflicts that are occurring at any point in time and the profile of the varied religions and the ability of an attacker to identify not only the religious artifacts but also the assets of the adherents of that religion (in a number of cases, it is possible to tell from an individual's name what their religion is likely to be), attacks on these types of targets are common.
- *Power.* If an individual seeks to gain or to demonstrate that they have gained power, they may choose to demonstrate their capability through an attack on an information system.

- *Terrorism.* Cyber Terrorism has not yet been conclusively observed. The use of information systems by terrorists is, conversely, well proven. An example would be if a terrorist threat agent were to use their capability to further their cause by denying service to the enemy or by achieving a propaganda victory.
- *Curiosity.* This is a strong and difficult to quantify motive. As it is normally unfocussed and will only be directed at the target in question whilst the curiosity lasts, it is difficult to predict or to determine when the threat agent will have sated their curiosity.

Motivation

The elements that provide the motivation for an individual or a group to carry out an attack will be highly variable and subjective. Something that would provide motivation to one individual or group may not affect another similar group in the same way. The elements that have been identified below are general indicators only.

No attempt has been made to quantify or value the effect of the above factors on the threat agent as this is outside the scope of the project.

ISSO MUST UNDERSTAND THREAT AGENTS' MOTIVE–RATIONALIZATION–OPPORTUNITY

Professor Jones pointed out that motivation and opportunities play a major role in manmade threats. The topic of threat agents can be discussed and written about for volumes; however, the above provides the ISSO at least an overview of the topic. In order for the ISSO to be able to mount an adequate, cost-effective defense of company information and systems, the ISSO must understand all the threats against the company systems. Furthermore, the ISSO must also understand the minds of these miscreants. One must understand as much as possible how they think and why they act and react as they do. Remember that first and foremost it is the human factor involved in all these threats, and it is the human miscreants whom the ISSO must understand. This can not be overemphasized, especially since it is precisely the human factor and how the miscreants think that is usually lacking in the ISSO's quest to build a successful CIAPP.

The ISSO, though required to be knowledgeable in international politics, business, marketing, finance, managing, leadership, auditing, high technology, social science, psychology, and the like, must also have a good working knowledge of criminology. Being an ISSO is a very challenging job, and to be successful, one must have much more than just a background and experience in high technology. In fact, that is one of the major problems with many ISSOs. Their backgrounds are usually planted firmly in high technology, and they seek high-technology solutions to the InfoSec problems when in fact many are rooted more in the human factors associated with the threat agents.

Understanding the human factors is at least if not more important than understanding when and how to install information and systems protection mechanisms, such as a firewall.

The ISSO must first of all understand the threats and then use a holistic, systematic approach to finding a solution to mitigate the threats. Some threats may be completely eliminated; some may be mitigated to provide for the least amount of risk; while others—well, the ISSO can only hope and pray that the company systems will not be threatened by them. It seems that there are always some of those threats around.

According to the Association of Certified Fraud Examiners and members of the criminology profession, there are three requirements that are present when considering the human threat agent. They are the same regardless of the type of attack to be launched. The three requirements are:

- *Motive*: If one is not motivated to commit an attack on a system, one will not attack; therefore, one is not a threat.
- *Rationalization*: One must be able to rationalize the attack. For example, many devoutly religious people have committed crimes. If they were that religious, how could they do so when they also believe that they will go to hell and suffer eternal damnation for their crimes? They must rationalize in their minds that what they were to do was not in violation of God's law, or that God would forgive them. If they could not rationalize or justify it to themselves, they would not commit the crime. The rationalization need not be logical or make any sense to anyone else, but the attacker must believe it.
- *Opportunity*: The other part of this triad is opportunity. If one were motivated and could rationalize an attack, but knew there was no opportunity to successfully commit that attack or to commit that crime without getting caught, one won't commit the crime.

When discussing this triad, it is important to remember that as human beings we all would probably commit a crime under the "right" circumstances. An internal employee of the company may be a model employee; however, if the employee's circumstances changed for the worse, elements of the triad would come into play and an employee once not considered a threat becomes a threat. For example:

Suppose you had a family with kids growing up and getting ready for college; you had a mortgage, car payments, and the normal other bills; you had worked for a company for about 25 years; and you were about

54 years old. You were called into the boss's office one Friday and told that the company was downsizing and they were terminating your employment. However, because the company was terminating over 500 people, the federal law (in the U.S.) required that you be given 60 days' notice.

You knew that you would have difficulty finding another job, especially at your age, and besides, your skills were somewhat outdated, not in great demand. You didn't know how you would make it. You knew that the college money for the kids would have to be used to survive. You also knew that you'd have to sell one car, as you couldn't afford two. You were also concerned about other finances. In other words, in about 60 days, you knew that your entire world would be turned upside-down, and you didn't know how you would survive. Gloomy enough for you? It happens every day. Sometimes thousands of times!

For most people that would be enough to start them thinking somewhat negatively about the place where they work and the managers, company president, etc. However, to really push you over the edge, let's say the next morning you get up for work and read in the business section of the paper that company you work for was having greater sales than ever and had posted record profits. You read on to learn that because of that, the company president was getting a $2.5 million bonus and the executive managers were getting $1 million each for saving the company so much money over the years and for increasing sales and profits.

You are now motivated to get what you can from that company in the next 60 days. You deserve it. You gave them your "blood, sweat and tears" for 25 years, and they are where they are today partly because of you. And what did they give you? The boot! So now, you have the motive and the rationalization. Some people use violence, such as a post office worker who kills a manager who yelled at him. Others use fraud, theft, and whatever opportunity gives them; still others steal and sell sensitive company information and destroy or modify company information and systems.

The triad "bar" for some is higher than for others. However, it is now a matter of survival, a basic and extremely strong human trait. You and your family must survive. You are not about to have your house repossessed, as well as your car, and become one of the homeless out there. Add to that a little revenge, frustration, and hostility at not being able to find another job as day 60 approaches.

Yes, we all have our limits. As an ISSO, keep the triad in mind as you build the CIAPP. The culture and atmosphere of a company is important to know, and as the ISSO, you must be tuned into the changes caused by downsizing, restructuring, and the like, as they often create additional threat agents.

QUESTIONS TO CONSIDER

Based on what you have read, consider the following questions and how you would reply to them:

- Have you identified the natural threats to your company's information and systems?
- Have those threats been documented and processes put in place to mitigate them?
- Have you identified the manmade threats and the malicious code that can attack your information and systems?
- Have those threats been documented and processes put in place to mitigate them, for example, disaster recovery/contingency plans?
- Do you know the difference between risk management, risk assessment, and risk analysis?
- Do you have formal processes, policies, and procedures in place to use these risk management techniques?
- Have you identified your personal education and experience weaknesses that are associated with a complete understanding of the threats, such as malicious code and human factors?
- If not, why not?
- If so, what are you going to do about it?
- Does your CIAPP have contingency plans for terminating employees who, for example, are given 60 days' notice?
- When do you terminate an employee's access to sensitive information and systems?

  When the employee is given a 60-day notice?

  When they leave?

- Does it depend on their position in the company and their access?
- What is your definition of cyber-terrorism?
- Do you agree with the terrorist-related definitions cited above?
- If no, what are your definitions for each of those definitions that you do not agree with?
- Do you believe that a true cyber-terrorist attack will affect your corporation?
- If so, what plans do you have in place to mitigate it?

SUMMARY

Today's ISSO is faced with many threats. Where once the threats were primarily internal, because of interfaces to the Internet and other businesses' networks, the number of threats, and thus of threat agents, has grown exponentially. It appears that the internal threats are equally matched by the external threats—or exceed them.

Today's ISSO must understand these internal and external (e.g., global) threats to the company's information and systems. These threats can be categorized as natural and manmade. As a separate category or included in one or both of these categories, one must consider the threat of accidents and their adverse impact on information and systems protection. The new, emerging threat may be the threat of cyber-terrorism.

Note: Additional information on matters contained in this chapter is available on the Web site: http://www.shockwavewriters.com. Click on "Books," this book's cover icon, and then Chapter 3.

4

The International Widget Corporation (IWC)

*—Capitalism needs to function like a game of tug-of-war. Two opposing sides need to continually struggle for dominance, but at no time can either side be permitted to walk away with the rope.—*Pete Holiday[1]

CHAPTER OBJECTIVE

The objective of this chapter, "The International Widget Corporation (IWC)," is to establish and describe a fictitious international corporation in which the information systems security officer (ISSO) will work. This method is used to assist the new ISSO, or an experienced ISSO who is looking for some new ideas for an information protection program, by providing a more practical model to help learn how to build a corporate information assets protection program (CIAPP) for a corporation. In other words, this is more of a "real-life" approach using real scenarios. The scenarios and the actions taken are based on actual situations found in today's modern business environments.[2]

INTRODUCTION

The reader is encouraged to build a CIAPP based on IWC. This practice not only will assist in focusing on the "how-to's," but can also be used when building a personal interview portfolio (to be discussed in Chapter 16).

One word of caution: The approach used is provided in a simplistic form. Things are often more complex. However, the basics provided should assist the ISSO in the more complex environment.

---

[1] http://www.quoteland.com/topic.asp?CATEGORY_ID=18
[2] This chapter is based both on Chapter 3 of the first edition of this book and on Chapter 5 of this author's coauthored book (with Edward P. Halibozek), *The Manager's Handbook for Corporate Security: Establishing and Managing a Successful Assets Protection Program,* also published by Butterworth—Heinemann, 2003.

IWC BACKGROUND INFORMATION

The IWC ISSO must understand the business and processes of IWC if a quality, cost-effective, CIAPP is to be developed for IWC. Part of that process requires the ISSO to identify those key elements of IWC's history and business that must be considered in developing the IWC CIAPP as well as its organizational structure (see Figure 4.1).

Although information is an asset and its protection should rightly fall under the purview of the corporate security department that is responsible for the leadership role in corporate asset protection, many security departments neither want nor are prepared to take on such responsibility. It is hoped that someday they will be prepared, since information and information systems are corporate assets and should be protected in a holistic manner as with any other corporate asset. (*Note*: If the security professionals of the past had aggressively lived up to their assets protection responsibilities, this would be a moot point. Furthermore, we might not be experiencing the problems we are experiencing today, such as IT personnel being responsible for asset protection when the systemic problem of information and information systems protection is first and foremost a people issue.)

The following is a summary of IWC's business environment:

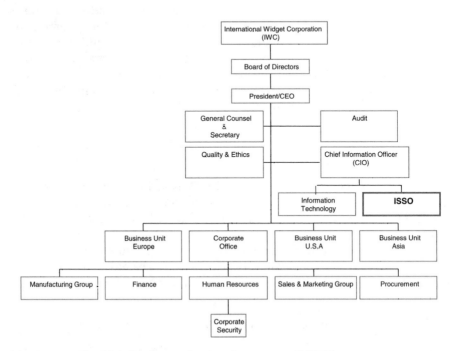

Figure 4.1   The high-level organizational structure of IWC.

- IWC is a high-technology corporation that makes high-technology widgets. In order to make these widgets, it uses a proprietary process that has evolved over the 5 years that IWC has been in business.

- The proprietary process is the key to IWC's success as a leader in the manufacturing of high-technology widgets. The process cost millions of dollars to develop, and protecting it is vital to IWC's survival.

- The manufacturing of widgets uses computers to control the robots in this manufacturing process. The use of robots has over the years drastically reduced costs by eliminating many of the human manufacturing jobs. This automated manufacturing process is the pride of IWC and one of its "crown jewels." Without this automation, the widgets could literally no longer be produced by IWC. This is not only because of cost factors, but also because the manufacturing requires such small tolerances that humans are not even capable of manufacturing today's widgets.

- IWC is in an extremely competitive global business environment. However, based on changes in technology that allow for a more efficient and effective operation through telecommunications and networks, it has found that it must network with its global customers and subcontractors.

- To provide for maximization of the high-technology widget process, it shares or interfaces its networks with its subcontractors, who must also use IWC's proprietary processes. The subcontractors, under contractual agreements, have promised not to use or share IWC's proprietary information with anyone. They have also agreed to protect that information in accordance with the security requirements of their contract with IWC. (*Note: All contracts that include the sharing of sensitive IWC information and/or networks should include security requirement specifications and address liability issues.*)

- Because of today's global marketplace, IWC has over the past several years expanded its operations to include some manufacturing plants, coupled with a small marketing and sales force, in Europe and Asia. This was done in order to take advantage of lower manufacturing and operational costs due to nation-states' incentives and the high cost of manufacturing in the United States. In addition, it has taken this approach to be able to take advantage of political considerations—for example, the corporation is looked upon as a local enterprise, thus gaining at least some political support to make marketing and selling easier in and from the countries where they are located.

- There currently is a small manufacturing plant in the Dublin, Ireland, area, and consideration is being given to opening up a plant outside of Prague, Czech Republic, within the next 1 to 2 years. Once that plant is operating as expected—with operating costs at least 25% less than those of the Dublin plant—the plan is to close the Dublin plant and use Prague as the European home manufacturing base.

- In order to also take advantage of the Asian market and the cheap labor and overhead costs in China, IWC has decided to move its Asian plant from Taiwan to China (PRC) within a year. The China plant will be located outside of Guangzhou. The decision to open the plant in China was hotly debated by the IWC executives. Before it will allow the plant to be opened in China, the Chinese government requires IWC to share its technology and do so as a joint partner with a Chinese firm known as Lucky Red Star. High-ranking members of the People's Liberation Army (PLA) own this firm. There is also a concern that this partnership will allow the PLA to use the widgets to support their military development. However, the United States government, and IWC, headquartered in Los Angeles, California, in the United States, approved of this move. Therefore, the IWC executive management did not concern itself with the issues related to technology transfer.
- The concern is that this joint venture involves sharing the "crown jewels," the proprietary processes of IWC. This information could subsequently be used to compete against IWC on a global basis, and with the Chinese government's support, the IWC executives were concerned that they might eventually be priced out of business. The executives decided that the business risks must be taken if IWC is to expand its sales throughout Asia and leverage the cheaper manufacturing costs in China and the Czech Republic. IWC will consider the elimination of the manufacturing plant within the United States sometime within the next 5 to 10 years, after the European and Asian operations have proved successful.

KEY ELEMENTS FOR THE ISSO TO CONSIDER

From the background information about IWC, noted above, the IWC ISSO should remember some key elements:

- IWC is a *high-technology corporation*: This means that it uses and is dependent on information and computer-based processes—a key factor that makes the information and information systems security portions of the IWC CIAPP of vital importance.
- IWC *uses a proprietary process*: This means that information relative to the proprietary process is the most valuable information within IWC, and it must be protected at all costs.
- *The proprietary process is the key to IWC's success and vital to company survival*: The number one priority of the CIAPP must be to ensure that this process receives the highest protection. It is therefore a priority for the ISSO to ensure that the current protection mechanisms are in place and are adequate.

- IWC is *in an extremely competitive global business*: To the ISSO, this means that the potential for industrial and economic espionage through the IWC networks (Netspionage)[3] is a factor to consider in establishing the CIAPP.
- IWC is *networked with its customers and subcontractors; subcontractors, must also use IWC's proprietary process, under contractual agreements*: When the ISSO builds the IWC CIAPP, the customers' and subcontractors' interfaces to sensitive IWC information and systems must be a key concern and adequately addressed.
- Because of today's global marketplace, IWC has over the past several years expanded its operations to include some *manufacturing plants, coupled with a small marketing and sales force in Europe and Asia*; the European and Asian plants must also be considered when developing the IWC CIAPP.
- Because of the foreign plants, *key executives will also be traveling extensively to the foreign locations.* Therefore, the threats posed by terrorists, corporate spies, and others must be taken into account when developing the CIAPP, as the executives will be carrying their notebook computers, cellular telephones, and PDAs containing sensitive IWC information as they travel. This protection must be coordinated with the IWC Director of Security, who has primary responsibility for executive protection.

GETTING TO KNOW IWC

Since the ISSO is new to IWC and the widget industry, the ISSO, in the first week of employment, will walk around the entire company, see how widgets are made, see what processes are used to make the widgets, and watch the process from beginning to end.

The ISSO wants to know as much as possible about the company. It is very important that the ISSO understand its inner workings. In fact, the ISSO, as an ISSO position applicant, researched and studied all available information about IWC and the widget industry before being interviewed and subsequently hired. Such knowledge proved very useful in the ISSO job interview process (see Chapter 16).

It is unfortunate, but many new ISSOs sit through the general in-briefing given to new employees and learn some general information about the company. They then go to their offices and start working, and they may not see how the company actually operates or makes widgets. They seldom see or meet the other people who have a role to play in hands-on protec-

---

[3] See also *Netspionage*, another Butterworth–Heinemann book coauthored by Dr. Kovacich and Bill Boni.

tion of the information and information systems—IWC's most vital assets, second only to the employees. These people include the people using automated systems on the factory floor, human resources personnel, quality control personnel, auditors, procurement personnel, contract personnel, in-house subcontractors, and other non-IWC employees.

When asked why they don't walk around the plant or understand the company processes, the normal reply from an ISSO is: "I don't have the time. I'm too busy 'putting out fires'!" The answer to that dilemma is take a time management course; manage your time better; and make the time! An ISSO can't provide a successful and cost-effective service- and support-oriented CIAPP if there is no understanding of the company, its culture, and how its products are made. If you want to spend your time "putting out fires," do it right and join the fire department—because you won't be a successful ISSO!

The ISSO should know:

- How the manufacturing processes operate;
- How manufacturing is supported by other company elements;
- How employees use IWC information and information systems;
- The problems they are having doing their jobs because of asset protection—InfoSec—constraints; and
- Whether or not they are even following the IWC asset protection policies and procedures related to IWC's sensitive information and information systems.

All the IWC assets protection policies and procedures neatly typed and placed in binders are ignored if they get in the way of employees doing their primary functions. The IWC ISSO must understand that one can't see this from the walled office or cubicle. The ISSO can only find this out by walking around the areas where the people are working and actually using IWC systems, and by talking to all levels of employees from corporate management to the system's custodians. In addition, the new ISSO should ensure that all members of the InfoSec staff do the same.

IWC'S BUSINESS PLANS

The ISSO must have an understanding of business and business competition on a global scale. Prior to developing a CIAPP, the ISSO must also read and understand the plans of IWC. These plans include the corporation's Strategic Business Plan, Tactical Business Plan, and Annual Business Plan. These plans are outlined at the executive management level and passed down to all IWC departments. The management of the departments then provide input into the plan outline. This information is then integrated at the executive management level. From there, they are passed

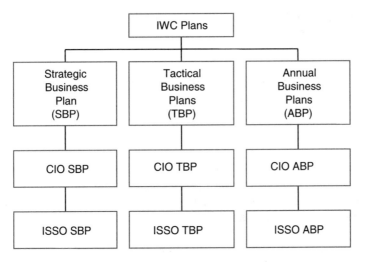

Figure 4.2 The structure of the IWC business plans.

down to the IWC departments, who will develop their own plans to support the overall IWC plans (see Figure 4.2).

Strategic Business Plan

IWC has developed a proprietary Strategic Business Plan (IWC SBP). The plan describes IWC's strategy for maintaining its competitive edge in the design, manufacturing, and sale of high-technology widgets. That plan sets the baseline and the direction that IWC will follow for the next 7 years. It is considered IWC's long-range plan. It was decided that any plan longer than 7 years was not feasible because of the rapidly changing environment brought on by technology, and IWC's competitive business environment.

The IWC SBP sets forth the following:

- The expected annual earnings for the next 7 years;
- The market-share percentage goals on an annual basis;
- The future process modernization projects based on expected technology changes of faster, cheaper, and more powerful computers, telecommunications systems, and robotics;
- IWC expansion goals; and
- IWC's acquisition of some current subcontractor and competitive companies.

The IWC SBP also calls for a mature CIAPP that can protect IWC's valuable assets, especially its proprietary information and processes, while allowing access to these assets by its international and national customers, subcontractors, and suppliers. In addition, it is expected that the CIAPP will be capable of supporting the secure integration of IWC processes and systems with others.

Key Elements of IWC's Strategic Business Plan that the ISSO Should Consider

The ISSO must ensure that the IWC SBP, which also resides on the IWC networks, is protected at a priority level second only to the proprietary processes.

Protection of this information is vital to the future of IWC. Its release to those without the need-to-know for the information could cause it to fall into the hands of IWC's competitors. If that happened, it would jeopardize IWC's competitive edge and its leadership position in the widget industry.

Another reason why the ISSO must understand the IWC SBP is that the CIAPP must include an information and information systems protection SBP that provides the strategies necessary to support the IWC SBP.

Tactical Business Plan

IWC also has a proprietary Tactical Business Plan (IWC TBP). The IWC TBP, which is a 3-year plan, sets more definitive goals, objectives, and tasks. The IWC TBP is the short-range plan that is used to support IWC's SBP. IWC's successful implementation and completion of its projects is a critical element in meeting IWC's goals and objectives.

The IWC TBP also calls for the *completion* of a CIAPP that can protect IWC's proprietary and sensitive information and systems while allowing access to them as needed under contractual agreements with national and international customers, subcontractors, and suppliers. In addition, it is expected to be able to integrate new, secure processes, etc., with *minimum* impact on schedules or costs.

Key Elements of IWC's Tactical Business Plan that the ISSO Should Consider

The IWC TBP must itself also be protected in much the same way as the IWC SBP; however, a less secure environment may be possible, since it is a support plan which provides the tactics to be used in support of the IWC SBP.

The ISSO must always remember that information is time-sensitive and the global marketplace is always dynamic. That is, its value is time-dependent and changes as global market conditions change. Therefore, the compromise of the IWC TBP would not cause as much damage to IWC as would the compromise of the IWC SBP. Thus, the protection requirements could be less, and also less costly. This is a key factor in protecting any information: *It should be protected using only those methods necessary, and only for the time period required, based on the value of that information over time.*

The ISSO must consider that the IWC CIAPP must contain processes to reevaluate the protection mechanisms used to protect IWC information and systems so that it is only protected for the period required.

As was true with the IWC SBP, the ISSO must understand the IWC TBP because an IWC information and systems protection TBP must be developed to integrate InfoSec services and support into the IWC TBP. The InfoSec TBP should identify the goals, objectives, and tactics necessary to support the IWC TBP.

A key point which should be not be overlooked can be found by comparing portions of the IWC SBP and the IWC TBP. The IWC SBP stated that, "In addition, it is expected that the CIAPP will be capable of supporting the integration of new customers, subcontractors, plants, processes, hardware, software, networks, etc., while maintaining the required level of information and information systems protection without impact on schedules or costs."

The IWC TBP also includes a similar statement: "In addition, it is expected that the CIAPP will be capable of supporting the integration of new customers, subcontractors, plants, processes, hardware, software, networks, etc., while maintaining the required level of information and information systems protection with minimal impact on schedules or costs."

The interpretation can be made that the ISSO has 3 years to establish a CIAPP with minimum impact on schedules and costs. After that 3-year period, it is expected that the CIAPP will *not* have an impact on schedules or costs. As the new ISSO, you must determine whether that goal of zero impact is possible. (*Hint*: There will always be some impact. The goal should be to minimize that impact.)

As the new ISSO, you should immediately bring this potential conflict to the attention of upper management for clarification and interpretation. The apparent conflict may have been caused by a poor choice of words. However, it may be that the IWC management meant what they said. It is then up to you as the IWC ISSO to meet that objective or have the sentence clarified and changed.

IWC's Annual Business Plan

IWC also has a proprietary Annual Business Plan (IWC ABP) that sets forth its goals and objectives for the year. The IWC ABP defines the specific projects to be implemented and completed by the end of the year. The successful completion of these projects will contribute to the success of IWC's Tactical Business Plan and Strategic Business Plan.

IWC's ABP called for the hiring of an ISSO to establish a CIAPP that can provide for the protection of IWC's valuable information and information systems assets, while allowing access to them by its customers, subcontractors, and suppliers. This obviously seems like an impossible challenge; however, it is not unusual for corporate executives to demand or require this.

The ISSO will also be responsible for forming and managing an InfoSec organization. The ISSO will report to the IWC Corporate Information Office (CIO) (see Figure 4.1, above). The ISSO must also develop a corporate security annual business plan. That plan must include goals, objectives, and projects that will support the goals and objectives of IWC's ABP.

IWC AND THE HISTORY OF ITS ISSO

At one time, IWC had only a professional physical security program made up of alarm systems, badge readers, and a guard force as the IWC asset protection program, while the information systems protection was an additional responsibility assigned to the IWC Information Technology Department. The IWC executives determined that they needed a professional ISSO and organization to meet their ever-increasing security requirements as they expand worldwide and mature as a corporation. Furthermore, they saw the need for a CIO to "get a handle" on all information processes and needs within IWC.

It should be noted that IWC's executive management agreed that an ISSO position should be established, and the ISSO hired should establish IWC's CIAPP and also establish and manage the InfoSec organization. However, there was not complete agreement as to where in IWC the ISSO reported.

Some members of IWC's executive management suggested the CIO, while others suggested that the ISSO report to the Executive Vice President of HR. They argued that placing the ISSO with the corporate security organization under HR was logical because it was mainly about people.

Other members of executive management recommended that the ISSO report to the Director of Auditing. However, the Director of Auditing advised that the auditing department was strictly responsible for determining IWC's compliance with applicable state, federal, and international laws, and company policies and procedures. The director felt that the auditors' limited scope and functions would adversely limit the ISSO in establishing and managing a CIAPP. In other words, like most auditors, they wouldn't want any part of that responsibility, since it is one that usually takes the blame anytime something goes wrong. The Director of Auditing also argued that it may be a conflict of interest for the ISSO to establish corporate InfoSec policies and procedures, albeit with management support and approval, while at the same time having another part of that organization (the audit group) determine not only compliance with the InfoSec policies and procedures, but also whether they were adequate.

The ISSO and the corporate security department was also considered for inclusion lower in the bureaucracy under the Information Technology Department (IT), since IWC was an information-based, high-technology-supported corporation whose major assets were computer-based. The reasoning was that the majority of assets that required protection were IT-supported. Furthermore, since as of this time, the InfoSec organization was under IT, it made sense to keep it all under IT. However, the Executive Vice President of IT objected and in fact offered to move the InfoSec organization under the corporate security department as long as IT was in the coordination loop for InfoSec matters that affected the IT department. That offer was tabled pending the hiring of the ISSO. They reasoned that the newly hired ISSO could meet with each department head to determine where the InfoSec organization would best fit in.

Also considered for the "home" of the ISSO and the InfoSec organization was the Finance Department or Legal Department, both reporting directly to the CEO. Both of these were not considered "practical" by the Vice President of Finance, the Director of the Legal Department, and the CEO.

A survey was taken of other corporations similar to IWC and it was determined that the majority of the InfoSec organizations in those corporations were part of the IT departments. Subsequently, at IWC an executive was hired and a newly formed department was established and led by a CIO. This new department was established because executive management concurred with the recommendations of a consultant that IWC's information must be managed in a holistic manner and sensitive information must be protected regardless of its environment—on a computer, hardcopy, transmitted by fax, telephone, PDA, or the like. Therefore, at IWC someone should be in an executive position in order to "get their arms around" the entire information issue. Thus, it was finally decided that the ISSO position and organization should be established under the CIO. It seemed a logical place since the IT department was also under the CIO.

An ISSO was hired; however, because of the lack of progress in developing a CIAPP, and the loss of some valuable corporate assets, the ISSO was fired and the new ISSO was hired. The new ISSO, during the interview process and again after being hired, determined what caused the ISSO position to be formed and why it reported where it did in the IWC organizational structure. The new ISSO's understanding of how this position ended up where it did provides some clues as to the feeling and inner workings of IWC's management vis-à-vis the ISSO and the CIAPP. This information will be useful when the ISSO begins to establish IWC's CIAPP, and when the ISSO requests support from these corporate executives. It also provides the ISSO some insight into what type of support might be received from these executives. The circumstances surrounding the firing of the previous ISSO also helped the new ISSO understand what must now be considered the number one priority: the establishment of the baseline IWC CIAPP.

As an example of the use of this information, the fact that no major departments within IWC wanted the InfoSec responsibility could be leveraged. Those department heads may not mind supporting the ISSO and the CIAPP, but they do not want to have too much responsibility for that effort. This provides the ISSO the possibility of being a strong leader without concerns that the departments identified would want to absorb some of the InfoSec functions into their departments. Thus, a more centralized, ISSO-directed CIAPP can probably be established. As with any position within a corporation, office politics always plays a major role; so do the informal information channels, such as the flow of gossip. The ISSO, to be successful, must understand the game of office politics, power, and "back-channel" information flows.

Furthermore, it is clear that the Director of Auditing would support the CIAPP from a compliance audit standpoint, but would probably not want to join an IWC CIAPP team with the responsibility for writing the new InfoSec policies and procedures. As the ISSO, you must keep this in mind when you decide how to establish InfoSec policies and procedures, and what departments should be involved in what part of that development and "buy-in" process.

CIAPP PLANNING

The main philosophy running through the preceding paragraphs should be obvious: As a service and support organization, the IWC ISSO and InfoSec organization staff and the IWC CIAPP must include plans that support the business plans of the corporation.

The ISSO should be able to map each major business goal and objective of each plan to key security projects and functions. When writing the applicable InfoSec plans, the ISSO will also be able to see which functions are not being supported. That may or may not be a problem. However, the mapping will allow the ISSO to identify areas where required support to the plans has not been identified in the ISSO's plans. The ISSO can then add additional tasks where increased CIAPP support is needed. An additional benefit of following this procedure is to be able to show management how the CIAPP is supporting the business. When mapping the security plans to the business plans, the ISSO should summarize the goals, as they will be easier to map.

IWC'S DEPARTMENTS OF PRIMARY IMPORTANCE TO THE ISSO

Since the InfoSec organization is a service and support organization, all the IWC departments and personnel are important to the ISSO. However, there are several departments that the ISSO must work with closely and rely on to successfully provide that service and support. In addition, several are an integral part of helping to ensure that the CIAPP is successfully implemented and managed. At IWC, these departments are as follows:

- *Ethics Department*: This small organization reports to the CEO and is managed by a director. This organization is responsible for working with the training department to provide ethics training to the employees. In addition, it manages the IWC Ethics Hotline. The Ethics Hotline was established to receive complaints and conduct inquiries into allegations of wrong-doing, such as unethical conduct, by employees or others who may be associated with IWC. The complainants may remain anonymous if they so choose. If they provide their names, that information is kept IWC-Private. If an allegation is received that requires more detailed inquiry where possibly evidence, more in-depth interviews, and interrogations are required, the Ethics Director provides that information to the Security Department's Manager of Investigations, who works directly for the Security Director and who conducts the inquiries and reports the results back to the Director of Ethics, who is defined as the internal customer for such matters. The Director of Ethics chairs a monthly ethics meeting whose members include the ISSO's representative, the Manager of Investigations, a legal representative, a Human Resources representative, and the Manager of Audits. The ISSO is to be called on to support these investigations and inquiries through technical support, such as computer forensics.
- *Audit Department*: IWC's Audit Department is similar to other corporate audit departments. The auditors in this department conduct audits to ensure that IWC is operating, and that its employees are performing their duties, in accordance with applicable federal, state, and local laws, as well as corporate policies and procedures. The audit manager and the ISSO share information of mutual interest, such as audit findings related to the lack of protection of information and systems.
- *Legal Department*: This department is responsible for performing all duties commonly associated with any corporation's legal department, such as providing advice and assistance to the ISSO as requested or deemed appropriate.
- *Employee Relations, Human Resources Department*: As its name implies, this organization within the Human Resources Department

deals with employee issues, such as employees' complaints about managers, and provides guidance to managers relating to employee discipline.

Within the structure of IWC, you will find that it is no different from most other corporations. The corporate environment (or corporate office) differs from that of a business unit. The corporate environment has a strategic outlook, managing the overall business performance and strategy of the company. The focus is on strategic direction of the enterprise, making the company profitable and producing shareholder value. A corporate office generally does not develop and deliver products and services. That is done by its business units, although they maybe colocated, as some are at IWC.

In support of its vision, the corporate office will establish the overall strategy for the company, determining the type and scope of business. The corporate office will also develop policy, provide performance and compliance oversight, and exercise its fiduciary obligations to the board of directors and the shareholders. The corporate office usually does not get involved in the daily operations of a business unit. However, there are exceptions or conditions such as poor performance where the corporate office will intervene in the operation of a business unit.

A business unit functions much differently than a corporate office. They operate in an environment where goods and services are designed, developed, produced, and delivered. It is a tactical operation in support of the company business strategy. The day-to-day focus is on getting the product out. Typically, many different business units operate independently of each other and report to a corporate office (see Figure 4.1, above). Each business unit has different strategic objectives that fit into the overall company strategy.

IWC, like every company, regardless of size, has its own special culture. Some companies encourage competition between business units. Here rivalries as well as aggressive behavior are encouraged and rewarded. In other companies, teamwork is encouraged.

Social scientists tell us that cultures are built upon behavioral "norms" which are defined as a set of expectations as to how people will behave in a given situation.[4]

The culture of a company can differ between the corporate environment and the operations environment just as much as it differs between companies. Subcultures within an organization exist which may differ significantly from the larger organization. Understanding the company culture is essential for success.

---

[4] Golin, Mark, Bricklin, Mark, and Diamond, David, *Secrets of Executive Success*. Rodale Press, Emmaus, PA, 1991.

Although assigned under the CIO, at IWC's corporate office, the ISSO has information and information systems protection authority within all corporate and business units of IWC.

IWC VISION, MISSION, AND QUALITY STATEMENTS

IWC requires certain management, although sometimes bureaucratic, tasks to be performed by all those in IWC management. Like many of today's modern corporations, IWC has developed vision, mission, and quality statements using a hierarchical process. IWC directed that the statements should link all levels in the management and organizational chain. The statements of the lower levels should be written and used to support the upper levels and vice versa.

Most employees seem to look upon such "statements" as just another management task that is somehow supposed to help all employees understand their jobs—or whatever. Such statements are often developed in "employee team meetings," printed, placed on walls, and soon forgotten. Confidentially, many managers feel the same way, and that is probably why managers present them as just another task to be performed by or with employees.

This is unfortunate. These statements are a good idea because they set a direction and philosophy for everyone at IWC, at all organizational levels. If the statements are presented with the right attitude, they can be used to focus the employees on objectives and give them a better understanding of why they are there doing what they are doing. The following are IWC's vision, mission, and quality statements:

Vision Statement

In many of today's businesses, management develops a vision statement. The vision statement is usually a short paragraph that attempts to set the strategic goal, objective, or direction of the company. IWC has a vision statement and requires all organizations to have statements based on the IWC corporate statements.

What is a vision? A vision statement is a short statement that:

- Is clear, concise and understandable by the employees;
- Is connected to ethics, values, and behaviors;
- States where IWC wants to be (long term);
- Sets the tone; and
- Sets the direction for IWC.

IWC's Vision Statement: IWC's vision is to maintain its competitive advantage in the global marketplace by providing widgets to our customers when they want them, where they want them, and at a fair price.

Mission Statement

Mission statements are declarations of the purpose of a business or government agency.

IWC's Mission Statement: Design, manufacture, and sell high-quality widgets, thereby expanding their global market shares while continuing to improve processes in order to meet customers' expectations.

Quality Statement

Quality is what adds value to a corporation's products and services. It is what your internal and external customers expect from you.

IWC Quality Statement: To provide quality widgets to our customers with zero defects by building it right the first time.

QUESTIONS TO CONSIDER

Based on what you have read, consider the following questions and how you would reply to them:

- Where do you think the ISSO position and InfoSec organization should report at IWC or within your company?
- Why?
- Have you read your company's business plans?
- Have you integrated your InfoSec organization plans to support the successful accomplishment of the company goals?
- If not, why not?
- If so, how do you measure your success in that support?
- Do you have a CIAPP?
- Is the CIAPP current?
- Do you have a process in place to keep it current?
- Do you have a process in place to ensure it is working at least cost and impact to the company's business?
- In support of the IWC vision, mission, and quality statements, what would you write as the IWC ISSO to support them or those of your company?
- Are the statements realistic?
- Are the statements known by your staff?

- Are the statements useful, or do they exist only because management said to write them?
- Are the statements one of the basic foundation pillars of the CIAPP?
- If not, why not?

SUMMARY

The fictitious corporation, IWC, can be used by the reader to build a CIAPP or improve a CIAPP for a corporation. Most corporations set their goals and objectives in planning documents such as strategic, tactical, and annual business plans. These plans are key documents for the ISSO to read and use to determine the corporation's future directions.

These plans are also key documents that the ISSO may be able to use to determine what is expected from the ISSO and the CIAPP. The plans should also be used as the basis for writing service and support assets protection plans, as separate documents or as sections which are integrated into the identified corporate planning documents.

The decision process of the IWC executive management in determining in which department the ISSO and the corporate security organization belongs provides some key information which should be used by the ISSO in establishing the CIAPP and organization. It helps identify potential "power plays" by managers and provides a glimpse of the corporate political environment.

The ISSO must look at IWC from a global perspective and consider political, technological, economic, criminal, terrorist, and other events around the world. This broad scope is required when developing a CIAPP for IWC that will meet the worldwide needs of the IWC, now and into the future.

Section II

The Duties and Responsibilities of an ISSO

After gaining a basic understanding of the external world with all its many threats to information and information systems—all of which have a direct bearing on the ISSO and the ISSO's job—Section II provides a more internal, business focus on the world of the ISSO.

This section of the book provides a look at the duties and responsibilities of an ISSO employed at the International Widget Corporation (IWC).

Section II begins with the identification of the position, duties, and responsibilities of the IWC ISSO. It progresses through a discussion of:

- Establishing and managing a Corporate Information Assets Protection Program (CIAPP);
- Strategic, tactical, and annual InfoSec and business planning;

- Developing and managing an InfoSec organization and its functions;
- Measuring InfoSec costs, failures, and successes through metrics management;
- Supporting the IWC security department's investigative staff; and
- An overview of InfoSec in a nation-state's national security environment.

5

The ISSO's Position, Duties, and Responsibilities

Responsible, who wants to be responsible? Whenever something bad happens, it's always, who's responsible for this?—Jerry Seinfeld[1]

CHAPTER OBJECTIVE

The objective of this chapter, "The ISSO's Position, Duties, and Responsibilities," is to define the role that the ISSO will play in a corporation or government agency. In this case, it is the role of the ISSO for IWC. The duties and responsibilities of an ISSO vary depending on the place of employment. However, in this case, we are assuming the ISSO has the *perfect* position because it is one all ISSOs should strive to attain in order to "do it right the first time."

INTRODUCTION

The position of the ISSO has evolved over the years. We began with only physical security, as after all, the ENIAC and others did not connect to the world. A guard, a paper authorized personnel access list, an alarm, and such were all that were needed in those early days. But as the computer evolved over time, so did the profession of the ISSO.

The security profession at that time was primarily made up of retired or former law enforcement or military personnel, who had no interest in computer security. They knew physical security, investigations, and personnel security. This new thing called a computer was best left to the computer scientists and engineers.

As systems evolved, so did the departments responsible for their support. Departments that were once engineering departments perhaps

---

[1] *Reader's Digest*, October 2002, p. 73.

became information resource management departments and later became known as information technology (IT) departments. The protection of this new technology stayed with the IT people. However, the computer security positions within the IT departments also evolved.

As the microprocessor and its related technology developed, the once-separated telecommunications and computer staffs began their integration. Consequently, the computer security profession began to also consider the protection of information as it flowed through telecommunications links. As the Internet evolved, the need for protecting information as it was displayed, such as on Web sites, also became an important task for those responsible for protecting the hardware, software, and firmware.

Information and related systems are some of a business's most valuable assets, probably second only to the employees. In fact, though no one in management within a business would ever prioritize assets to place information and systems above the employees—at least not publicly—people can always be replaced, and replaced at less cost and adverse impact to the business, than trade secrets and information networks. However, that will probably remain an unspoken issue because of the sensitive nature of valuing machines over humans.

When we think about it, though, information really is businesses' number one asset. After all, employees can be terminated, even replaced by computers, and the business survives. In fact, profits may even increase because of lower labor costs. However, eliminate an intranet, and the business incurs additional costs and possibly losses.

Today, the ISSO position is generally still part of the IT department's function. Now, the ISSO is responsible for the protection of information and the systems that store, process, transmit, and display that information. The ISSO profession has matured into a separate profession, and in most large to medium companies, it is more than a part-time job or additional responsibility these days. In smaller businesses it remains mostly a part-time job or is outsourced with other security-related functions.

Information systems of various types, such as cellular phones, notebook computers, PDAs, and fax machines, are all used to process, store, transmit, and display information. These devices are becoming more and more integrated into one device. Couple this phenomenon with the hard copies being produced, and one finds that information may be protected on an intranet but leaked through a cellular phone or printed on paper and then taken out of the business's facilities.

CASE STUDY

Cellular phones are becoming smaller and smaller. Digital cameras are also being installed into these cellular phones. Since management wants their employees to have the latest high-technology devices that help support the business in the most efficient and effective way possible, employees are issued cellular phones. The cellular phones with digital cameras integrated into them allow employees to digitally send photographs as part of their business communications processes. It also provides the opportunity for the employee to photograph sensitive documents, facilities, and such, and send them directly to unauthorized sources. Thus, there is now another method of performing "Netspionage" (network-enabled espionage). As an ISSO, do you have policies, etc., in place to mitigate this new threat?

The ISSO position must evolve to be responsible not only for protecting information and systems related to, or the responsibility of, the IT department, but also for protecting all of the business's information assets. It is ridiculous to have the business security profession responsible for the security of company assets, to include hard-copy documents, people, and facilities, and leave the protection of automated information and systems essentially to IT people. These positions must be integrated to provide a holistic asset protection approach. This may be accomplished through the evolution of the ISSO professional into more than a "computer protector" and the security manager into more than a physical security manager.

The ISSO position is evolving, but no real, permanent "home" has been identified for the ISSO position. We do see signs of this changing as this evolution continues from guard, computer scientist, engineer, IT specialist, computer security specialist, to ISSO, with some indications of change to Corporate Information Assurance Officer (CIAO) or Corporate Information Security Officer (CISO). In some cases, the evolution of the profession has already led to making the ISSO also responsible for physical security. This was the case with Howard Schmidt when he was at Microsoft. He started out as the Director of Information Security, was promoted to Chief Information Security Officer, and then was given the additional responsibilities of physical security, executive protection, and all investigations as Microsoft's Chief Security Officer.

Some like Bill Boni are also helping to lead the way in changing the profession. As Motorola's Corporate Information Security Officer (CISO), he is now the Vice President of Motorola's Information Protection Services. He is responsible for the company's overall program to protect critical digital proprietary information, intellectual property, and trade secrets. He also directs the people, processes, and technology programs that safeguard the company's global network, computer systems, and electronic business initiatives. Mr. Boni reports to Motorola's Chief Information Officer (CIO).

Still, the evolution must continue until all information and systems are integrated into a total business assets protection profession. This requires the combining of business (corporate) security, for example, physical security, personnel security, and the ISSO responsibilities. It is the best way to safeguard all business assets in a holistic and cost-effective manner.

THE ISSO IN THE INTERNATIONAL WIDGET CORPORATION (IWC)

At IWC, the ISSO reports to the Corporate Information Officer (CIO), who reports to the Corporate Executive Officer (CEO). The ISSO is in an extremely important position as a corporate leader and as the in-house consultant on Corporate Information Assets Protection Program (CIAPP) matters. The ISSO also represents IWC to the outside world on information and systems security protection matters. If you are chosen as the new IWC ISSO, you should have determined the history of that position:

* When was it established?
* Why?
* What is expected of you as the ISSO?
* What are your responsibilities and duties?
* What are you accountable for?
* What happened to the last one? (You want to know so you can understand the political environment in which you will be working.)

As you begin your new job as the IWC ISSO, you must clearly determine what is expected of you. Again, this information should have been asked during your interview process for two reasons:

* So you know what you were getting into by accepting the ISSO position with IWC; and so you could better prepare for the position with a more detailed CIAPP prior to beginning your first day at work.

You need a detailed plan prior to beginning your employment at IWC because you will be behind schedule from the moment you walk into IWC. That's because putting together a CIAPP from the start is a tremendous project. The ISSO has to determine the answers to the following:

* What is important and requires protection?
* What is being protected?
* In what manner?

- Is a staff needed?
- If so, how many?
- With what qualifications, for what positions?
- What are the tasks to be performed?
- What are the mandatory, best practices, and optional requirements to be met?
- What processes and functions are necessary to meet those requirements?
- What are the necessary budget allocations?
- What metrics management techniques are required?

and the list goes on.

On top of all that is the need to learn about IWC, the culture, normal corporate policies and procedures, and all the learning that comes with just joining a company. As the new IWC ISSO, you can't afford to waste any time in your 12- to 14-hour days. You must understand and learn your new environment, the key players, and the issues that must be addressed first. Often, ISSOs tend to isolate themselves from the rest of the corporation and consider it almost a "me against them" mentality. In today's corporations this will get you nowhere but possibly out the corporate door. As an ISSO, you and your staff must integrate your functions into the corporate mainstream and integrate yourselves into the processes of the business. "Teaming" with others in the corporation is the only way to succeed in today's information-based, information-supported, and information-dependent modern corporations.

The IWC ISSO must eventually get into a proactive mode to be successful: that is, identifying problems and solutions *before* they come to the attention of management. InfoSec-related problems will undoubtedly get management's attention when they adversely affect costs and/or schedules. Adverse impacts on costs and schedules run contrary to the CIAPP goal, objectives, etc.

When an ISSO is in the position of constantly *putting out fires*, the proactive CIAPP battle is lost. If that battle is lost, the results are adverse impacts on costs and schedules. The goal of a cost-effective CIAPP cannot be attained.

As IWC's ISSO, you have been told that you are expected to establish and manage a CIAPP program that works and one that is not a burden on IWC. You are told to establish a program that you believe is necessary to get the job done. You have the full support of management because they have come to realize how important their information and systems are to IWC maintaining its competitive advantage in the global marketplace. This honeymoon will last about 6 months. So, you must take advantage of it. To do so, you must have a fast start and then pick up speed.

Based on the "blank management check" and your prior experience (or for the inexperienced ISSO, the information gained reading this book), you have evaluated the IWC environment and have decided that the overall goal of IWC's CIAPP is to:

Administer an innovative CIAPP program that minimizes information protection risks at least impact to costs and schedules, while meeting all of IWC's and customers' reasonable expectations.

If that is what is expected of you, then that is your primary goal. Everything you do as the IWC ISSO should be focused and directed toward meeting that goal. That includes incorporating that philosophy into your:

- CIAPP Strategic Plan;
- CIAPP Tactical Plan; and
- CIAPP Annual Plan.

IWC ISSO DUTIES AND RESPONSIBILITIES

As IWC's ISSO, you have certain duties and responsibilities. These include the following:

- *Managing people*, which includes:

    Building a reputation of professional integrity;

    Maintaining excellent business relationships;

    Dealing with changes;

    Communicating;

    Developing people;

    Influencing people in a positive way;

    Building a teamwork environment; and

    Developing people through performance management, such as directing and helping CIAPP staff to be results-oriented.

- *Managing the business of CIAPP*, which consists of:

    A commitment to results;

    Being customer/supplier focused;

    Taking responsibility for making decisions;

    Developing and managing resource allocations, such as budgets;

    Planning and organizing;

    Being a problem-solver;

    Thinking strategically;

    Using sound business judgment; and

    Accepting personal accountability and ownership.

- *Managing CIAPP processes*, which includes:
  Project planning and implementation;
  Persistence of quality in everything;
  Maintaining a systems perspective; and
  Maintaining current job knowledge.

GOALS AND OBJECTIVES

Remember that your primary goal is to administer an innovative CIAPP *that minimizes information protection risks at least impact to costs and schedules, while meeting all of IWC's and customers' reasonable expectations.*
You must have as your objectives at least the following:

- Enhance the quality, efficiency, and effectiveness of the CIAPP.
- Identify potential problem areas and strive to mitigate them before they adversely affect processes, and especially before IWC management and/or customers identify them.
- Enhance the company's ability to attract customers because of the ability to efficiently and effectively protect their information.
- Establish and manage the InfoSec organization as the leader in the widget industry.

LEADERSHIP POSITION

As the ISSO, you will be in a leadership position. In that position, it is extremely important that you understand what a leader is, and how a leader is to act.
According to the definition of *leadership* found in numerous dictionaries and management books, it basically means the position or guidance of a leader, the ability to lead, the leader of a group; a person that leads; or the directing, commanding, or guiding head, as of a group or activity.
As an InfoSec *leader*, you must set the example: create and foster an "information protection consciousness" within the company.
As a *corporate leader*, you must communicate the company's community involvement; eliminate unnecessary expenses; inspire corporate pride; and find ways to increase profitability.
As a *team leader*, you must encourage teamwork; communicate clear direction; create a CIAPP environment conducive to teaming; and treat others as peers and team members, not as competitors.
As a *personal leader*, you must improve your leadership skills; accept and learn from constructive criticism; take ownership and responsibility for decisions; make decisions in a timely manner; and demonstrate self-confidence.

PROVIDING CIAPP SERVICE AND SUPPORT

As the ISSO and leader of a CIAPP service and support organization, you must be especially tuned to the needs, wants, and desires of your customers, both internal (those within the company) and external (those who are outside the company and are usually the company's customers).

To provide service and support to your external customers, you must:

- Identify their information protection needs;
- Meet their reasonable expectations;
- Show by example that you can meet their expectations;
- Treat customer satisfaction as priority 1;
- Encourage feedback and listen;
- Understand their needs and expectations;
- Treat customer requirements as an important part of the job;
- Establish measures to ensure customer satisfaction; and
- Provide honest feedback to customers.

To provide service and support to your internal customers, you must:

- Support their business needs;
- Add value to their services;
- Minimize security impact to current processes; and
- Follow the same guidelines as for external customers.

As the IWC ISSO, you will also be dealing with suppliers of CIAPP products. These suppliers or vendors are valuable allies because they can explain to you the many new CIAPP-related problems being discovered, and how their products mitigate those problems. In addition, they can keep you up-to-date on the latest news within the ISSO profession and about the latest InfoSec tools available. Furthermore, you can make yourself available to beta test new InfoSec products and provide feedback so the final products will meet your needs.

In dealing with suppliers of CIAPP-related products, you should do the following[2]:

- Advise them of your needs and what types of products can help you.
- Assist them in understanding your requirements and products that you want from them, including what modifications they must make to their products before you are willing to purchase them.
- Direct them in the support and assistance they are to provide you.
- Respect them as team members.
- Value their contributions.

---

[2] We will also discuss cost-effective ways to keep current in the ISSO profession in a later chapter. This is another way of doing it.

- Require quality products and high standards of performance from them.
- Recognize their needs also.

USE TEAM CONCEPTS

It is important that the IWC ISSO understand that IWC's CIAPP is a company program. To be successful, the ISSO cannot operate independently, but as a team leader, with a team of others who also have a vested interest in the protection of the company's information and information systems.

It is important to remember that if the CIAPP and/or InfoSec functions are divided among two or more organizations (e.g., other asset protection such as physical security of hardware under the Security Department), there will naturally be a tendency for less communication and coordination. The ISSO must be sensitive to this division of functions and must ensure that even more communication and coordination occurs between all the departments concerned.

The CIAPP must be sold to the management and staff of IWC. If it is presented as a law that must be followed or else, then it will be doomed to failure. The ISSO will never have enough staff to monitor everyone all the time, and that's what will be needed. For as soon as the ISSO's back is turned, the employees will go back to doing it the way they want to do it. Everyone must do it the "right CIAPP way" because they know it is the best way and in their own interests, as well as in the interest of IWC.

In IWC, as in many companies today, success can only be achieved through continuous interdepartmental communication and cooperation, and through forming specialists from various organizations into integrated project teams to solve company problems. The ISSO should keep that in mind. Teaming and success go together in today's modern corporation.

VISION, MISSION, AND QUALITY STATEMENTS

Many of today's modern corporations have developed vision, mission, and quality statements using a hierarchical process. The statements, if used, should link all levels in the management and organizational chain. The statements of the lower levels should be written and used to support the upper levels and vice versa (see Figure 5.1).

The following examples can be used by the ISSO to develop such statements, if they are necessary. And as you can already guess, they are required at IWC.

Vision Statements

In many of today's businesses, management develops a vision statement. As stated earlier in this book, the vision statement is usually a short para-

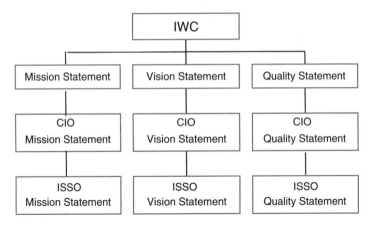

Figure 5.1   The integrated structure of IWC's vision, mission, and quality statements, indicating how they are to support each other.

graph that attempts to set the strategic goal, objective, or direction of the company.

IWC has a vision statement and requires all organizations to have statements based on the IWC corporate statements. Remember that a vision statement is a short statement that:

- Is clear, concise and understandable by the employees;
- Is connected to ethics, values, and behaviors;
- States where IWC wants to be (long term);
- Sets the tone; and
- Sets the direction for IWC.

IWC's Vision Statement: *IWC's vision is to maintain its competitive advantage in the global marketplace by providing widgets to our customers when they want them, where they want them, and at a fair price.*

IWC's CIO's Vision Statement[3]: *In partnership with our customers, provide a competitive advantage for the IWC widget by continuous maximization of available technology and innovative information management concepts to enhance productivity and cost-effectively support increased production of IWC widgets.*

CIAPP Vision Statement: *Provide the most efficient and effective CIAPP program for IWC, which adds value to IWC products and services, as a recognized leader in the widget industry.*

---

[3]If you recall, the ISSO reports to the CIO.

Mission Statements

Remember that mission statements are declarations of the purpose of a business or government agency.

IWC Mission Statement: *Design, manufacture and sell high-quality widgets, thereby expanding their global market shares while continuing to improve processes in order to meet customers' expectations.*

IWC's CIO Mission Statement: *The mission of IWC's Corporate Information Office is to efficiently and effectively manage IWC's information and provide low-cost, productivity-enhanced, technology-based services that will assist IWC in maintaining its competitive advantage in the marketplace.*

CIAPP Mission Statement: *Administer an innovative CIAPP program which minimizes information protection risks at least impact to cost and schedule, while meeting all of IWC's and customers' information and information systems assets requirements.*

Quality Statement

Remember that quality is what adds value to your company's products and services. It is what your internal and external customers expect from you.

IWC Quality Statement: *To provide quality widgets to our customers with zero defects by building it right the first time.*

IWC's CIO Quality Statement: *To provide quality information management services and systems support while enhancing the productivity opportunities of the IWC work force.*

CIAPP Quality Statement: *Consistently provide quality CIAPP professional services and support that meet the customers' requirements and reasonable expectations, in concert with good business practices and company guidelines.*[4]

INFORMATION SYSTEMS PROTECTION PRINCIPLES

The ISSO's duties and responsibilities are many and sometimes quite complex and conflicting. However, as the IWC ISSO, you must never lose sight of the three basic CIAPP principles:

---

[4]You will find that the same themes of service, support, cost-effectiveness, customer expectations, etc., continuously run through this book. It is hoped that the constant reinforcement will cause the reader to continuously think of these themes when establishing and managing a CIAPP.

- Access control;
- Individual accountability; and
- Audit trails.

This triad of CIAPP must be incorporated into the IWC CIAPP. For just as a three-legged stool requires three strong and level legs to be useful, the CIAPP requires these three strong principles. Without all three, the CIAPP will topple just as a two-legged stool will topple.

PROJECT AND RISK MANAGEMENT PROCESSES

Two basic processes that are an integral part of a CIAPP are project management and risk management concepts.

Project Management

As the CIAPP manager and leader for IWC you will also provide oversight on CIAPP-related projects which are being worked by members of your staff.

The criteria for a project are as follows: Formal projects, along with project management charts, will be initiated where improvements or other changes will be accomplished and where that effort has an objective, has beginning and ending dates, and will take longer than 30 days to complete.

If the project will be accomplished in less than 30 days, a formal project management process is not needed. The rationale for this is that projects of short duration are not worth the cost (in terms of time needed to complete the project plan, charts, etc.) of such a formal process.

Risk Management

To be cost-effective, the ISSO must apply risk management concepts and identify:

- Threats to the information and information systems of IWC;
- Vulnerabilities (information systems' weaknesses);
- Risks; and
- Countermeasures to mitigate those risks in a cost-effective way.

ISSO AND CIAPP ORGANIZATIONAL RESPONSIBILITIES

As the IWC ISSO, you will be managing and leading a CIAPP organization. You will be responsible for developing, implementing, maintaining, and administering a company-wide CIAPP program.

You have evaluated the IWC environment and found that a centralized CIAPP is required to cost-effectively *jump-start* the CIAPP and its associated processes. Your evaluation of what is needed led you to consider the following CIAPP-related functions for development[5]:

- Management of all functions and work which are routinely accomplished during the course of conducting the organization's business in accordance with IWC's policies and procedures.
- System access administration and controls, including the direct use and control of systems' access software, monitoring their use, and identifying access violations.
- Access violation analyses to identify patterns and trends that may indicate an increased risk to systems or information.
- Computer crime and abuse inquiries where there are indications of intent to damage, destroy, modify, or release to unauthorized people information of value to the company. (*Note*: This function was coordinated and agreed to by the Director of Security as long as his investigative organization manager was kept apprised of the inquiries and copies of all reports sent to that manager.)
- Disaster recovery/contingency planning, which includes directing the development and coordination of a company-wide program to mitigate the possibility of loss of systems and information, and ensure their rapid recovery in the event of an emergency or disaster.
- An awareness program established and administered to all system users to make them aware of the information systems protection policies and procedures that must be followed to adequately protect systems and information.
- Evaluation of systems' hardware, firmware, and software for impact on the security systems and information.
- Where applicable, conduction of risk assessments, with the results reported to management for risk decisions.
- Conduction of systems' compliance inspections, tests, and evaluations to ensure that all users and systems are in compliance with IWC's CIAPP policies and procedures.

IWC ISSO's Formal Duties and Responsibilities

Based on the above and in concert with the executive management of IWC, the ISSO has developed and received approval for formally establishing the following charter of IWC ISSO responsibilities:

---

[5] As previously mentioned, IWC is the ideal company for an ISSO, and therefore, we are developing an ideal CIAPP and organization.

Summary of the Purpose of the IWC ISSO Position

Develop, implement, maintain, and administer an overall, IWC-wide CIAPP to include all plans, policies, procedures, assessments, and authorizations necessary to ensure the protection of customer, subcontractor, and IWC information from compromise, destruction, and/or unauthorized manipulation while being processed, stored and/or transmitted by IWC's information systems.

Accountabilities

- Identify all government, customers, and IWC CIAPP requirements necessary for the protection of all information processed, stored and/or transmitted by IWC's information systems; interpret those requirements; and develop, implement and administer IWC plans, policies, and procedures necessary to ensure compliance.
- Evaluate all hardware, firmware, and software for impact on the security of the information systems; direct and ensure their modification if requirements are not met; and authorize their purchase and use within IWC and applicable subcontractor locations.
- Establish and administer the technical security countermeasures program to support IWC requirements.
- Establish and administer a security test and evaluation program to ensure that all of IWC's and applicable subcontractors' information systems are operating in accordance with their contracts.
- Identify, evaluate, and authorize for use all information systems and other hardware within IWC and at applicable subcontractor locations to ensure compliance with red/black engineering[6] where proprietary and other sensitive information is processed.
- Direct the use of, and monitor, IWC's information systems access control software systems; analyze all systems' security infractions/ violations and report the results to management and Human Resources personnel for review and appropriate action.
- Identify information systems business practices and security violations/infractions; conduct inquiries; assess potential damage; direct and monitor IWC management's corrective action; and implement/recommend corrective/preventive action.
- Establish and direct an IWC-wide telecommunications security working group.

---

[6] For IWC, red/black engineering means the methods used to separate those data lines that require special protection because of the sensitivity of the information which flows through them from those lines that do not require enhanced protection. One of the main concerns with such lines running together is the chance that emanations will transfer between the lines, thus exposing "protected" information to compromise.

- Develop, implement, and administer a risk assessment program; provide analyses to management; modify IWC and subcontractor requirements accordingly to ensure a least-cost CIAPP program.
- Establish and administer a CIAPP awareness program for all IWC information systems users, to include customers and subcontractor users, and ensure they are cognizant of information systems threats, and of security policies and procedures necessary for the protection of information systems.
- Direct and coordinate an IWC-wide information systems emergency/disaster recovery/contingency planning program to ensure the rapid recovery of information systems in the event of an emergency or disaster.
- Direct the development, acquisition, implementation, and administration of CIAPP software systems.
- Represent IWC on all CIAPP matters with customers, government agencies, suppliers, and other outside entities.
- Provide advice, guidance, and assistance to IWC management relative to CIAPP matters.
- Perform common management accountabilities in accordance with IWC's management policies and procedures.

QUESTIONS TO CONSIDER

Based on what you have read, consider the following questions and how you would reply to them:

- If you could define your title and your reporting level within a corporation, what would it be and why?
- Do you believe that all assets protection functions should be under one leader within a corporation?
- If so, what would that person's title be?
- If not, why not?
- As an ISSO, do you know what is expected of you?
- Do you have a strategic, tactical, and annual InfoSec (CIAPP) plan that supports the corporate plans?
- Do you have vision, mission, and quality statements?
- If so, are they something that you actually use in planning or just in meeting management requirements?
- If you are not using them, why not?
- Do you use formal project management processes and techniques?
- If so, how and when?
- Do you use formal risk management processes and techniques?
- If so, when and how?

- If you could change your ISSO duties and responsibilities, how would you change them and why?

SUMMARY[7]

The role of today's ISSO has evolved over time and will continue to evolve. The ISSO profession offers many challenges to anyone who wants to match wits with global hackers, criminals, terrorists, and other miscreants. In a business environment such as that of a global corporation, the ISSO has specific responsibilities. As an ISSO, you should understand the following:

- The ISSO position is a leadership position within a company.
- The recently hired ISSO must know what is expected of the company's new ISSO and should have a clear understanding of those expectations before taking the position.
- The three primary responsibilities of an ISSO are: (1) managing people; (2) managing the CIAPP; and (3) managing CIAPP processes.
- The ISSO must set forth clear goals and objectives.
- The ISSO in the leadership role must be a company leader, team leader, and personal leader.
- The ISSO must provide CIAPP service and support using team concepts.
- The ISSO should develop vision, mission, and quality statements as guides to developing a successful CIAPP.
- The ISSO should strive to administer a CIAPP where all the major InfoSec functions are under the responsibility of the ISSO.

---

[7]Much of the information in this chapter provides details that could be used to fill in the details of the ISSO's portfolio.

6

The InfoSec Strategic, Tactical, and Annual Plans

Though this be madness, yet there is method in't.—William Shakespeare[1]

CHAPTER OBJECTIVE

The objective of this chapter, "The InfoSec Strategic, Tactical, and Annual Plans," is to establish the Strategic, Tactical, and Annual plans for the InfoSec organization. These plans will also set the direction for IWC's CIAPP while integrating the InfoSec plans into IWC's plans, thus indicating that the CIAPP program is an integral part of IWC.

INTRODUCTION

The saying "Ya gotta have a plan" definitely applies to successfully accomplishing the duties and responsibilities of an ISSO. Without strategic, tactical, and annual plans, the ISSO would be spending all of every day running from crisis to crisis and haphazardly trying to protect information and information systems for IWC. In addition, these plans are the cost-effective method of providing a secure information environment for IWC.

There will always be crises to contend with; however, even most crises can be planned for so that when they occur, an emergency plan can be implemented. The plan will provide at least guidance and an outline of what to do—not only what to do, but when and how to do it rapidly and effectively. Let's face it: Most crises can be identified, and we are already accustomed to doing so through our disaster recovery and contingency planning for such events as fires, typhoons, and earthquakes. We should do the same for other events that would be classified as an emergency, such as, but of course not limited to, the following:

---

[1] William Shakespeare (1564–1616), English poet and playwright. Polonius, *Hamlet* (1601), Act 2, Scene 2.

- Web site attack and defacement;
- Denial of service attack;
- Worm or virus attack; and
- Other malicious attacks or accidents.

As an ISSO, when you learn of a new type of attack, check your emergency-contingency plans and determine whether the latest type of attack would be addressed by one of those plans. If so, great! If not, then it's time to develop another plan or update a current plan. By the way, as you should already know:

- These plans must be developed with input from various departments such as auditors, legal, and IT in a project team environment;
- They must be kept current; and
- They must be tested often to ensure that the identified emergency response team is trained and can operate effectively and efficiently.

As with the Corporate Information Assets Protection Program (CIAPP), all plans should be placed online with read access for all employees. It will also be easier to keep the plans current, and through the intranet Web site or through e-mail, everyone can be notified of the changes to the plans. The ISSO should also have a project to ensure that information and systems protection policies and procedures are kept online for read access by all employees. The ISSO should consider, as much as possible, having a paperless CIAPP and InfoSec organization.

At IWC, all information and systems protection plans are considered subsets of the CIAPP, as are all projects that are used to build the secure information environment.

IWC'S INFOSEC STRATEGIC PLAN

In order to be successful, the IWC ISSO must have an Information Systems Security Strategic Plan (ISSSP). That plan should be integrated, or at least compatible, with IWC's Strategic Business Plan. It is this plan that sets the long-term direction, goals, and objectives for information protection as stated in the CIAPP, vision, mission, and quality statements.

IWC's Strategic Business Plan sets forth the following information:

- The expected annual earnings for the next 7 years;
- The market-share percentage goals on an annual basis;
- The future process modernization projects based on expected technology changes of faster, cheaper, and more powerful computers, telecommunications systems, and robotics;
- IWC expansion goals; and

- IWC's acquisition of some current subcontractor and competitive companies.

The IWC ISSSP is the basic document on which to build the IWC CIAPP with a goal of building a comprehensive information protection environment at least cost and impact to the company.

When developing the ISSSP, the ISSO must ensure that the following basic, InfoSec principles are included, either specifically or in principle (since it is part of the InfoSec strategy):

- Minimize the probability of an information security vulnerability;
- Minimize the damage if a vulnerability is exploited; and
- Provide a method to recover efficiently and effectively from the damage.

Let's assume that the IWC Strategic Business Plan called for a mature InfoSec program known as the CIAPP (within the next 7 years) which:

- Can protect IWC's information while allowing access to its networks by its international and national customers, subcontractors, and suppliers; and
- Can support the integration of new hardware, software, networks, etc., while maintaining the required level of InfoSec without affecting schedules or costs.

The InfoSec Strategic Plan Objective

The objectives of the ISSSP are to:

- Minimize risks to systems and information;
- Minimize impact to costs;
- Minimize impact to schedules;
- Assist in meeting contractual requirements;
- Assist in meeting noncontractual requirements;
- Build a comprehensive systems security environment;
- Respond flexibly to changing needs;
- Support multiple customers' information protection needs;
- Incorporate new technologies as soon as needed;
- Assist in attracting new customers; and
- Maximize the use of available resources.

The majority of men meet with failure because of their lack of persistence in creating new plans to take the place of those which fail.—Napoleon Hill

ISSSP and Team Concepts, Communication, and Coordination

To have a successful CIAPP, the strategy calls for one that also deals with the office politics' aspects of the IWC environment. A key element, which was stated earlier in this book, is to remember that the information and information systems belong to IWC, and not to the ISSO. Therefore, cooperation and coordination are a must!

Many functional organizations have an interest in the ISSSP and other CIAPP-related plans; therefore, the plans should be discussed with other team members such as the auditors, security personnel, human resources personnel, legal, and others deemed appropriate.

The ISSSP should also be discussed with and input requested from key members of the user community and IWC managers. After all, what you do affects what they do! It is a great way to get communication and interaction going. This will lead to a better plan and one that has broad-based support.

Their input and their understanding of what the IWC ISSO is trying to accomplish will assist in ensuring IWC-wide support for the CIAPP. For only with this kind of communication and interaction can the ISSO's IWC CIAPP succeed.

ISSSP Planning Considerations

The ISSSP planning considerations must also include the following:

- Good business practices;
- Quality management;
- Innovative ideas;
- An InfoSec Vision Statement;
- An InfoSec Mission Statement;
- An InfoSec Quality Statement; and
- Providing channels of open communications with others such as the auditors, systems personnel, security personnel, users, and management.

All these factors must be considered when developing a CIAPP strategy and documenting that strategy in the IWC ISSSP.

The IWC process flow of plans begins with the IWC Strategic Business Plan through the IWC Annual Business Plan. Each of the plans' goals and objectives must be able to support each other: top-down and bottom-up (Figure 6.1).

Once this process is understood, then the next step is to map the IWC ISSSP into the IWC Strategic Business Plan goals and objectives.

Figure 6.1 The logical process flow of plans and InfoSec plans' integration into the IWC flow.

Mapping IWC's InfoSec Strategic Plan to the IWC Strategic Business Plan

IWC's strategy identified the annual earnings for the next 7 years as well as market-share percentage goals. This clearly underscores the need for a CIAPP that will be cost-effective.

As was previously mentioned, InfoSec is a "parasite" on the profits of IWC if it cannot be shown to be a value-added function (one that is needed to support the bottom line). Therefore, the CIAPP strategy must be efficient (cheap) and effective (good). If that can be accomplished, the CIAPP will be in a position to support the IWC's strategy relative to earnings and market share.

Mapping these points (Figure 6.2) can help the ISSO visualize a strategy prior to documenting that strategy in the InfoSec Strategic Plan. The mapping will also assist the ISSO in focusing on the strategies that support the IWC strategies.[2]

---

[2]For those readers who are inclined to argue the technical definitions of terms, I concede that the definition of terms varies between corporations and those used here may not nicely fit into the definitions used by the corporation or government agency of the reader. However, the reader should not lose sight of the process being discussed. That is the important aspect of this chapter.

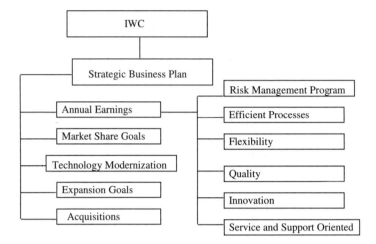

Figure 6.2   A sample mapping of an IWC strategic goal to the ISSSP goals.

Writing the InfoSec Strategic Plan

Writing the ISSSP will come much more easily once the mapping is completed. Once that is accomplished, the ISSO will write the ISSSP following the standard IWC format for plan writing.

The IWC format was determined to be as follows:

1. Executive Summary
2. Table of Contents
3. Introduction
4. Vision Statement
5. Mission Statement
6. Quality Statement
7. InfoSec Strategic Goals
8. How the InfoSec Strategies Support IWC Strategies
9. Mapping Charts
10. Conclusion

IWC'S INFOSEC TACTICAL PLAN

A tactical plan is a short-range plan (3-year plan) which supports the IWC CIAPP and InfoSec functional goals and objectives (Figure 6.3). The InfoSec Tactical Plan (ITP) should:

- Identify and define, in more detail, the vision of a comprehensive InfoSec environment, as stated in the ISSSP;

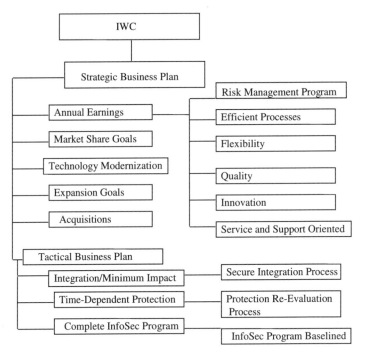

Figure 6.3   An example of mapping from the IWC Strategic Business Plan through the ITP in support of the IWC Tactical Business Plan.

- Identify and define the current IWC InfoSec environment; and
- Identify the process to be used to determine the differences between the two.

Once that is accomplished, the ISSO can identify projects to progress from the current IWC InfoSec environment to where it should be, as stated in the ISSSP. In the ITP, it is also important to keep in mind:

- The company's business direction;
- The customers' direction; and
- The direction of technology.

Once that is established, the individual projects can be identified and implemented, beginning with the InfoSec Annual Plan (IAP).

The IWC Tactical Business Plan stated, "In addition, it is expected to be able to integrate new hardware, software, networks, etc., with *minimum* impact on schedules or costs." Therefore, it will be necessary to establish a project with the objective of developing a process to accomplish that goal.

The ISSO must then also consider that the IWC CIAPP must contain processes to reevaluate the mechanisms used to protect information so that it is only protected for the period required. Therefore, a project must be established to accomplish that goal.

The IWC Tactical Business Plan also called for the *completion* of an InfoSec program that can protect IWC's information while allowing access to its networks by its international and national customers, subcontractors, and suppliers. Therefore, another project that must be developed is one that can accomplish this goal.

Writing the InfoSec Tactical Plan

Writing the ITP should be somewhat easier based on the experience gained in mapping the goals for the ISSSP and ITP and writing the ISSSP. Once that is accomplished, the ISSO will write the ITP following the standard IWC format for plan writing.

The IWC format was determined to be as follows:

1. Executive Summary
2. Table of Contents
3. Introduction
4. InfoSec Strategic Goals
5. How the InfoSec Tactics Support the ISSSP
6. How the InfoSec Tactics Support IWC Tactics
7. Mapping Charts
8. Conclusion

IWC'S INFOSEC ANNUAL PLAN

The ISSO must also develop an InfoSec Annual Plan (IAP) to support the IWC ISSSP and ITP. The plan must include goals, objectives, and projects that will support the goals and objectives of IWC's Annual Business Plan.

IWC's InfoSec Annual Plan (IAP) is to be used to identify and implement projects to accomplish the goals and objectives as stated in the ISSSP and ITP.

Remember, the InfoSec Program requires the following:

- Project management techniques;
- Gantt charts (Schedule);
- Identified beginning date for each project;
- Identified ending date for each project;
- An objective for each project;
- Costs tracking and budget; and
- Identification of the responsible project lead.

InfoSec Annual Plan Projects

The initial and major project of the IWC ISSO's first IAP is to begin to identify the current IWC InfoSec environment. In order to gain an understanding of the current IWC environment, culture, and philosophy, the following projects are to be established:

1. Project Title: IWC InfoSec Organization

    *   *Project Lead*: ISSO
    *   *Objective*: Establish a CIAPP support organization.
    *   *Start Date*: January 1, 2003
    *   *End Date*: July 1, 2003

2. Project Title: CIAPP Policies and Procedures Review

    *   *Project Lead*: ISSO
    *   *Objective*: Identify and review all CIAPP-related IWC documentation, and establish a process to ensure applicability and currency.
    *   *Start Date*: February 1, 2003
    *   *End Date*: April 1, 2003

3. Project Title: InfoSec Team

    *   *Project Lead*: ISSO
    *   *Objective*: Establish an IWC CIAPP Working Group to assist in establishing and supporting an InfoSec program.
    *   *Start Date*: January 1, 2003
    *   *End Date*: February 1, 2003

4. Project Title: IWC Proprietary Process Protection

    *   *Project Lead*: InfoSec Organization Systems Security Engineer
    *   *Objective*: Identification, assessment, and protection of IWC proprietary processes.
    *   *Start Date*: April 15, 2003
    *   *End Date*: September 1, 2003

5. Project Title: InfoSec Organizational Functions

    *   *Project Lead*: ISSO
    *   *Objective*: Identify and establish InfoSec organizational functions and their associated processes and work instructions.
    *   *Start Date*: January 15, 2003
    *   *End Date*: July 1, 2003

6. Project Title: InfoSec Support to IT Changes

    *   *Project Lead*: InfoSec Organization Systems Security Engineer
    *   *Objective*: Establish a process to provide service and support to integrate InfoSec as changes are made in the IT environment.

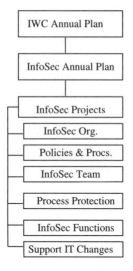

Figure 6.4   Mapping of IAP projects to the IWC Annual Business Plan.

- *Start Date*: March 15, 2003
- *End Date*: October 1, 2003

Mapping the IWC IAP to the IWC Annual Business Plan

As was previously shown, mapping the IWC CIAPP and the InfoSec Annual Plan to the IWC Annual Business Plan can be easily accomplished. However, in this case, the IWC Annual Plan objectives were not indicated or used to map the IAP.[3]

Writing the InfoSec Annual Plan

As noted earlier, writing of the plans must follow the IWC format. The IWC IAP is no exception, and the following format is required:

1. Executive Summary
2. Table of Contents
3. Introduction
4. InfoSec Annual Goals
5. InfoSec Projects

---

[3] The reader probably understands this process by now and can easily use this mapping method.

6.   How the InfoSec Projects Support IWC's Annual Plan Goals
7.   Mapping Charts
8.   Conclusion

MAPPING ISSSP, ITP, AND IAP TO PROJECTS USING A MATRIX

Another approach to mapping is using a matrix. This method can be used in a number of ways, and at various levels, such as IWC Strategic Business Plan to ISSSP. In the example provided in Figure 6.5, some mappings are intentionally left blank to show how easy it is to identify those items that map to others, and more importantly, those that don't!

This method can identify "holes" in your plans that must be addressed.

QUESTIONS TO CONSIDER

Based on what you have read, consider the following questions and how you would reply to them:

- Does your company have plans that can be considered to be strategic, tactical, or annual, for example, long-range, short-range plans?
- Have you read them?
- If not, how do you know you are providing adequate service and support to the company?
- Do you have strategic, tactical, and annual plans that support the company's business plans?

Projects	ISSSP	ITP	IAP
InfoSec Org.	X	X	X
Policies & Procs.			X
InfoSec Team			X
Process Protection	X		X
InfoSec Functions		X	X
Support IT Changes		X	X

Figure 6.5   Matrix mapping, which can also be used to show the relationship—or lack of a relationship—between items.

- If so, are they current?
- How do you know?
- Do you have a process in place to keep them current?
- If not, why not?
- If you do have such plans, do you have a process in place and flow-charted to show how the plans, your information and systems protection functions, projects, risk management strategy, cost–benefit philosophy, and such are integrated into your CIAPP that supports the company's plans?
- If not, why not?

SUMMARY

Planning is a vitally important and cost-effective way to establish a corporate information and information systems assets protection environment. It will help focus on tasks that will effectively and efficiently meet the planning goals and objectives of a CIAPP. As part of that planning, the ISSO should consider the following points:

- The IWC InfoSec Strategic, Tactical, and Annual Plans must be mapped and integrated into the IWC Strategic, Tactical and Annual Business Plans.
- The CIAPP-related plans must incorporate the InfoSec Vision, Mission, and Quality Statements, and their philosophies and concepts.
- The CIAPP-related plans must identify strategies, goals, objectives, and projects that support each other and the IWC plans.
- By mapping the goals of the IWC plans with those of the CIAPP-related plans, the required information fusion can take place and can be graphically represented.
- Mapping will make it easier for the ISSO to write the applicable InfoSec plans.
- The InfoSec Annual Plan generally consists of projects that are the building blocks of the CIAPP following the strategies and tactics of the ISSSP and ITP.

7

Establishing a CIAPP and InfoSec Organization

We trained hard, but it seemed every time we were beginning to form up into teams, we would be reorganized. I was to learn later in life that we tend to meet any new situation by reorganizing—Petronius Arbiter[1]

CHAPTER OBJECTIVE

The objective of this chapter, "Establishing a CIAPP and InfoSec Organization," is to describe how to establish a corporate information assets protection program and its associated organization.

INTRODUCTION

IWC's information and information systems are some of IWC's most vital assets. These valuable assets must be consistently protected by all IWC employees, contracted personnel, associate companies, subcontractors, and in fact everyone who has authorized access to these assets. They must be protected regardless of the information environment (IE), whether through faxes, telephones, cellular phones, local area networks, Internet e-mails, hard copies, scanners, personal digital assistants—any device which processes, transmits, displays, or stores IWC's sensitive information. By *sensitive* we mean all information that has been determined to require protection. That determination is based on basic, common business sense—for example, a marketing plan for next year's product must be protected, and it doesn't take a risk assessment to determine that—as well as the use of risk management techniques. Some information must also be protected because there are laws that make that information protection a requirement—for example, private information about employees.

---

[1] Petronius Arbiter (27–66), Roman satirist. *Satyricon* (1st century) as quoted in Microsoft's Encarta World.

In order to provide that consistent protection, those individuals who have authorized access to the information and information systems must therefore do the following:

- Be provided with guidance;
- Understand how to apply information asset protection;
- Understand why such information asset protection is required; and
- Understand IWC policy regarding that protection.

IWC's executive management had decided that a policy document was needed. So, the IWC ISSO was hired primarily to fulfill that requirement as stated in the IWC plans, such as the IWC Strategic Business Plan.

CORPORATE INFORMATION ASSETS PROTECTION PROGRAM (CIAPP)[2]

The ISSO knew that to successfully protect IWC's information-related assets there must be formal guidelines and directions provided to the IWC employees. There must also be some formal processes that are used to ensure that the IWC information assets are protected effectively and efficiently—in other words, "cheap and good." It was obvious to IWC's management and the ISSO that to do otherwise would cause employees to protect these information-related assets as they saw fit, or not protect them at all. Such was almost the case now, and the ISSO knew that there was an urgent need to quickly establish a CIAPP.

The CIAPP would be developed taking into consideration or incorporating the following:

- Reasons for the CIAPP;
- IWC vision, mission, and quality statements;
- Information and systems legal, ethical, and best business practices;
- IWC's strategic, tactical, and annual business plans;
- Information and systems protection strategic, tactical, and annual business plans;
- IWC's overall information assets protection plans, policies, and procedures as directed by the IWC Corporate Security Office;
- InfoSec vision, mission, and quality statements;
- Current CIAPP-related and InfoSec policies;
- Current CIAPP-related and InfoSec procedures; and

---

[2] Some of the information from this section was modified from Dr. Kovacich's coauthored book with Edward P. Halibozek, *The Manager's Handbook for Corporate Security: Establishing and Managing a Successful Information Assets Protection Program*, published by Butterworth–Heinemann, 2003.

- Other topics as deemed appropriate once the ISSO and the ISSO project team have established the baseline.

The CIAPP cannot be developed in a vacuum if it is to work. The input of others is a necessity: The CIAPP, if not done correctly, may have an adverse impact on the business of IWC. Remember that the ISSO's InfoSec functional organization must be a service- and support-driven organization. As part of that endeavor, the CIAPP must support the IWC business plans. It then follows that the plans call for certain actions to protect IWC's vital information and information systems assets.

Remember what is being discussed here are the plans, processes, policies, and procedures (P^4) that are established, implemented, and maintained as applying to all IWC departments (P^4 because as each of the "P's" is added to the others, protection baseline increases exponentially). This should not be confused with the ISSO's InfoSec organization's plans, policies, and procedures, such as work instructions and processes that apply strictly within that InfoSec organization.

As the ISSO, one of your first tasks is to obtain a copy of the IWC CIAPP that was to be established by the prior ISSO. You may find that:

1. There is no such document;
2. The current one is not really current at all and needs updating; or
3. To your shock and amazement, the IWC CIAPP is current and an excellent document.

Of the three options, which would you prefer and why? Actually, there are benefits to all of the options but they are listed in our preferred order. Does it seem strange that one would not opt for option 3? The one you choose will probably be based on where you are coming from and where you are going (your education and experience). OK, no more riddles.

Option 1 has some benefits. If there is no such document as the IWC CIAPP by any name, one can "do it right the first time" and develop one that meets the needs of IWC using your own tried and true methods. However, the less experience you have, the more difficult it will be to do it right the first time. If you are new to the IWC ISSO position, it may be doubly difficult and a real problem. No, not a problem, because you are now in a high management position. These are not called problems. They are called *challenges*.

Having an IWC CIAPP that has been approved by those who must approve it (executive management) has some benefits, of course. "Approve it?" you say. "Why does anyone have to approve it? I am the ISSO, the security professional, the expert in the business. I know what I am doing. I don't need any non-security people out there playing amateur information systems security expert." Great! That may have worked in the past, maybe in the times of the hunter-gatherers—but not now.

Here's the issue: As the ISSO, you are going to establish a CIAPP that will affect everyone and everything in IWC in one form or another, since information systems permeate all levels of IWC and IWC cannot function without them. You are new to IWC and really don't have a good handle on how information assets protection policies and procedures affect the IWC business of making widgets. You may have a great way to protect a certain, sensitive IWC information-related asset, but find that if it were implemented it would slow down production. That is not a good idea in the competitive, fast-paced, global marketplace in which IWC competes for business. That may get you a warning first, but then you'll be fired (as was the case of the last ISSO?); or it may increase costs in other ways (slowing down production is a cost matter also).

Option 2 also has some very good advantages, especially for the ISSO who has less experience in the profession and/or less experience at IWC. The advantage is that you have a framework on which to build, essentially changing it to how you envision the final baseline. However, as with option 1, some caution is advised. Option 2 allows you, as the new ISSO, the opportunity to see what executive management has authorized to date. In other words, you know how much "protection" the executive management of IWC will allow at what expense to productivity, costs, etc.

This is important also because if you increase security, you must provide sound, convincing *business* reasons why that should happen. In this cause, you have an edge because of the previous loss of IWC information assets, which caused the firing of the former ISSO. In addition, the CEO is supportive in that the Strategic Business Plan (SBP) and Tactical Business Plan (TBP) both have CIAPP goals, and those plans had to be approved by the CEO prior to implementation. Thus, the CIAPP already has high visibility and at least some executive management support. However, that honeymoon may not last long if you require protection mechanisms that aren't backed by sound business sense.

Option 3 is great if you are new to the ISSO position and/or lack confidence or experience in CIAPP development. However, caution is also needed here, because information assets were lost and the former ISSO fired. You must get answers for the following questions:

- Did the information assets protection processes as set forth in the CIAPP leave a vulnerability that allowed the threat agent to take advantage of it?
- Was the CIAPP not the issue—did some one or some group fail to follow proper procedures?
- Was the ISSO just not the right person for the job at IWC? (If this is the case, find out why so you don't make the same mistake, assuming you want to work for IWC for more than a year or two.)

As the new ISSO, you should find the answers to these questions, then determine how the CIAPP can be enhanced to mitigate future attacks. The benefit of a current CIAPP is that it has received the concurrence of executive management—but remember, it may be a bad plan. After all, what does executive management know of CIAPP matters except what the ISSO tells them, aside from the "common sense" knowledge?

Let us assume that no IWC CIAPP is in existence. So, the ISSO must start from the beginning. Actually, that is not entirely true. As an experienced ISSO, the IWC ISSO has brought knowledge and experience to the IWC ISSO position. In addition, there are always some sort of information and information systems protection policies and guidelines available. It may be just a matter of gathering them all together for analysis as part of establishing the CIAPP baseline.

In addition, the ISSO has swapped and collected CIAPP plans from other InfoSec professionals over the years that may prove useful. Several words of caution:

- Never take another's CIAPP (or any documents) without approval of his or her appropriate corporate authority. Such plans may be considered and marked as corporate-confidential, corporate-private, corporate-proprietary, or the like. There is an ethics issue here.
- Furthermore, the other CIAPPs may be outdated or may not meet the needs of IWC, perhaps because of technology changes, different corporate cultures, or environments.

Using formal project management techniques, the ISSO decides to establish an information and systems protection program project team (CIAPP PT) and selects a project lead, leads the team, or has the group select their own project lead. If the ISSO's InfoSec organization has one or more specialists in information assets protection policies and procedures, then one of those specialists would be the natural one to head up the project team. Other team members should include those within the InfoSec organization who are responsible for each of the InfoSec functions of the InfoSec organization.

These team members would not be used full-time on the project, but would represent the InfoSec functions and provide input as deemed appropriate by the CIAPP project team leader. The ISSO decided to use only specialists from the InfoSec organization at this time to speed up the draft of the baseline CIAPP's primary document—that which contains the requirements, and P^4. To do otherwise—to add auditors, IT staff, human relations specialists, legal staff, etc.—would invariably cause too much time discussing such matters as policies as too restrictive or not restrictive enough, leading to a slowdown or committee paralysis. The ISSO determined that coordination would be done upon establishment of the initial draft document.

Let's now assume there is a plan in place with outdated portions. The ISSO, who has already read the document and does not agree with some of the requirements in it, and who sees other requirements that are obviously lacking, should first meet with the specialist currently responsible for the CIAPP and that person's manager (the assumption is that there are some InfoSec staff already employed and that someone in the current InfoSec organization has responsibility for the CIAPP—or equivalent plan or program). The main purpose of the meeting would be to determine why it is not current and discuss the rationale for all the requirements stated in the document. It may be that some portions were deleted because of executive management objections. These must be identified, because it is of little use to update the CIAPP if it is to meet resistance and rejection when it is briefed to and coordinated with executive management.

If the ISSO determines that there was resistance and disapproval of some aspects of the CIAPP, then the ISSO should look at that issue first. The approach the ISSO will use is to establish another InfoSec project team, which will conduct a limited risk assessment related to the identified issues: management's rejection of some much-needed information assets protection requirements. The risk assessment is limited to a specific objective: determining the risks to a specific asset, the costs of mitigating that risk, or the rationale for the requirement. It is also limited in time. For each of these issues where different information assets and departments have been involved, such as manufacturing and marketing, a separate, limited risk assessment will be conducted.

The results of the limited risk assessments will then be provided as part of a formal briefing to the Vice President of that particular department, and a copy of the report will be given to the IWC Corporate Information Officer (CIO). The copy to the CIO (the ISSO's boss) will be given just to ensure that the CIO is in the communications loop, and because a copy will be available for use when briefing the CEO and the executive management team on the new CIAPP and its changes. The limited assessment will be part of the backup documentation for the briefing. The ISSO reasons that a copy to the CEO would not be a good idea at this time, because then the ISSO would have to explain what it is and why the CEO has it.

The CEO does not currently understand how the new ISSO operates, and now is no time to take away from the priority CIAPP project management to provide a "for your information" report to the CEO. Some ISSOs may think that such things help the ISSO gain visibility and show the "great" things that the ISSO and InfoSec staff are accomplishing. However, it may have the opposite affect, as the CEO would ask questions:

- Why do I have this?
- What is it?

- What am I to do with it?
- Do I have to make a decision now based on it?

What is your reply as the ISSO? "Oh, I just thought you would enjoy reading it because I know you are not that busy; you don't have better things to do; my stuff is so much more important than what you do to run IWC; and no, you don't have any action items that come from this. I just want to show you what a great job I'm doing." That *will* work in getting you recognized—but for all the wrong reasons and in the wrong way.

The limited risk assessment will state the risks, the mitigation factors, and the estimated costs of the increased protection of that particular asset or set of information assets. If the Vice President of that department, who is also the person immediately responsible for the protection of that information asset or assets, does not concur with the increased protection, then the Vice President must formerly accept the risks in writing on the last page of the report and send it back to the ISSO.

The acceptance of risk statement reads as follows: *I have reviewed the findings of the limited risk assessment conducted by members of the IWC InfoSec staff. I understand the potential loss of, or damage to, IWC information assets under my care that may occur if additional protective processes are not put in place. I accept that risk.*

You will probably find that most people will be unwilling to sign such a document, or will try to delay signing and hope the issue is forgotten. The ISSO can never let that happen. To resolve that issue, a reply of concurrence or nonconcurrence will be set forth in the document with a suspense date. If none is forthcoming by that date, the report states that additional safeguards will be put into effect no later than a specific date because of the failure of the action person to sign the document. A non-reply is taken as a concurrence.

Often the executive will try to find a way out of the dilemma and "negotiations" will take place where various options will be examined, other than those already stated in the report. The ISSO cannot say no to such a request: To do so would allow the executive to say that the ISSO was not being cooperative, was not a team player, had a "take it or leave it" attitude. At the same time, this negotiation cannot go on indefinitely. If a roadblock is reached, then the executive and the ISSO should agree that the matter be discussed at a meeting with the CIO and/or CEO.

The IWC CIO would probably be wondering if there was some other way out of it. The CIO thinks: Here this ISSO hasn't even been in the job a month, and already I'm getting involved in conflicts. The CIO does not like becoming involved in conflicts.

As a side note, no matter what final decision is made, the ISSO's performance review and probably merit raise may be affected because the

ISSO was not able to resolve the issue (even though the fault was that of others). The ISSO could have resolved the issue by just allowing the other vice presidents or managers to have it their way. However, the ISSO knows that also contributed to the previous ISSO being fired. It is a no-win situation, but that's life as an ISSO. For the ISSO to do otherwise is unprofessional and an ethics issue.

IWC CIAPP—Requirements

In developing a CIAPP, one must first look at requirements that drive the formation of policies, which lead to procedures, which turn into processes to be followed by all those having authorized access to the IWC information and information systems assets.

Requirements, also known as InfoSec *drivers* are those laws, regulations, common business practices, ethics, and the like on which the policies are based (Figure 7.1). The policies are needed to comply with the requirements; the procedures are required to implement the policy; and the processes are steps that are followed to support the procedures.

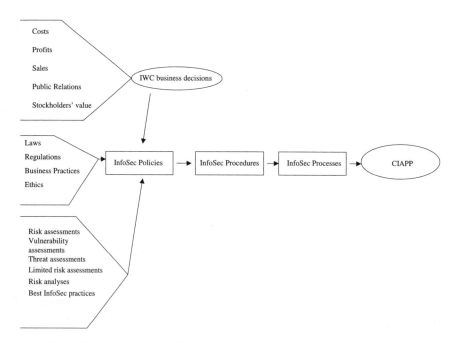

Figure 7.1   The flow of some of the requirements as drivers through to the CIAPP processes.

IWC CIAPP—Information Assets Protection Policies

When discussing information assets protection policy, we define it as a codified set of principles that are directive in nature and that provide the baseline for the protection of corporate information assets.

It is always the best policy to speak the truth, unless, of course, you are an exceptionally good liar.—Jerome K. Jerome

The corporate information assets protection policies are a series of policies that deal with the protection of various information assets categories within IWC. These policies make up a major portion of the CIAPP, as they are the protection "rules." They are the first building blocks of the IWC information assets protection environment. Information assets protection policies are the foundation for a CIAPP. It is crucial that they:

- Cover all information assets that must be protected;
- Cover all aspects of information assets protection;
- Do not have any loopholes that could contribute to vulnerabilities;
- Be clearly written;
- Be concise;
- Take into account the costs of protection;
- Take into account the benefits of protection;
- Take into account the associated risks to the information assets;
- Are coordinated with executive management and others as applicable;
- Are concurred in by executive management and others as applicable;
- Are *actively* supported by executive management and all employees; and
- Include a process to ensure that they are kept current at all times.

One cannot state these requirements too strongly. They are the key to a successful CIAPP. If it is not stated in writing, it does not exist. After the information assets protection policies are established and approved in accordance with IWC requirements (executive management approval for all policies that affect the entire corporation), the information contained in the policies must be given to all corporate employees. This will be done through the IWC CIAPP Education and Awareness Training Program (CIAPP-EATP).

A key process that the ISSO must establish is one that will maintain all information assets protection policies in a current state. Because this is a crucial function, the ISSO has assigned one staff member full-time to ensure that the policies are current at all times and ensure that when changes are considered, they are properly coordinated, and the information dispensed to all employees as soon as possible. After all, the changes may just be procedural, or they may mitigate a risk to some valuable IWC information assets.

The ISSO's focal point for information assets protection policies is the central InfoSec person to collect information that adversely affects the protection of information and information systems. That adverse information is analyzed by the focal point, with help from others as needed, to determine if policies must be added or modified to help mitigate the adverse effects—vulnerabilities—identified. If so, such changes are done based on a cost-benefits approach to mitigating the identified vulnerabilities.

For the position of an information assets protection policy specialist, the ISSO has chosen a person already employed by Human Resources. This was done after interviews and looking at the experiences of the InfoSec staff. None of the InfoSec staff were qualified or interested in such a position: The InfoSec staff saw it as being a "non-techie paper shuffler" job. The ISSO purposely looked for a qualified employee within IWC, since that person would already be familiar with IWC culture and processes—basically, how things were done at IWC.

The ISSO was able to get this new position approved by the Human Resources Department (HR) and rated at a sufficiently high position level to attract the best candidates. The ISSO's rationale was to rate all new positions at as high a level as possible, so the ISSO could attract the best candidates in IWC or outside IWC. Such a position would be seen as a promotion by many in IWC. This was not an easy task, but the ISSO had experience in working with HR specialists. The task was not as difficult as it might have been—and once had been for the ISSO.

The person hired had worked in an HR office whose duties included writing HR policy and procedures documents, coordinating document approvals, and maintaining the IWC documentation library. The individual responded to an IWC "vacant position" announcement that was available to all employees through the online HR network.

The job description for the *Information Assets Protection Policy Specialist* was developed by the ISSO based on past experiences. The person was not actively recruited within HR, as this violated IWC policy—people cannot actively try to "steal" employees from one another. As well as violating corporate policy, it is unethical.

One person who responded to the vacancy announcement had 2 years of experience at IWC and had a bachelor's degree in journalism, but no InfoSec or information assets protection experience. The ISSO wanted someone who could write and coordinate policies and procedures as the first priority and could secondarily learn about InfoSec-related matters. The incentive was that the position was a promotion from the person's previously held position, and the person would be the lead in this function, rather than "just another employee" in the HR organization[3].

At IWC, the ISSO developed an administrative document architecture where there is an overall information assets protection policy document followed by the other assets protection policy documents. The IWC overall policy document (IWC Information Assets Protection Policy Document 500-1, also known as IAPPD 500-1) begins with a letter from the IWC CEO to show employees that this program was supported by the CEO:

To: All IWC Employees

Subject: Protecting IWC's Information Assets to Maintain Our Competitive Edge

We are a leading international corporation in the manufacturing and sales of widgets. Today, we compete around the world in the global marketplace of fierce competition. In order to maintain a leadership position and grow, we depend first and foremost on all of you and provide you the resources to help you do your jobs to the best of your ability. You are vital to our success.

It is the policy of IWC to protect all our vital assets that are the key to our success, and among those are our information-related assets. These include information, automated manufacturing tools, technology, information and systems driven processes, hardware, software, and firmware that we all rely upon to be successful. You and these other vital IWC information assets must be able to work in a safe environment, and our resources must be protected from loss, compromise, or other adverse effects that affect our ability to compete in the marketplace.

It is also IWC policy to depend on all of you to do your part to protect these valuable information-related assets in these volatile times.

The protection of our information assets can only be accomplished through an effective and efficient information assets protection program. We have begun an aggressive effort to build such a program.

This directive is the roadmap to our corporate information assets protection program (CIAPP) and the continued success of IWC. In order for the CIAPP to be successful, you must give it your full support. Your support is vital to ensure that IWC continues to grow and maintain its leadership role in the widget industry.

(Signed by the IWC President and CEO)

---

[3] You may wonder why we go into such detail as to who is hired to do what or how it is done at IWC. The reason is to provide, as nearly as possible, real-world experiences to the reader. Such information helps the reader by providing information that can be applied in real corporations; it also develops an overall knowledge of establishing and managing a corporate information assets protection program. In this case, an ISSO may look for someone to write policies by first looking for someone who knows security, when in fact it is more important to hire someone who can write policy. What to write will come from many sources. The policy specialist will not operate in a vacuum. How to write in clear and concise terms without ambiguities is the key.

It is crucial that the CEO lead the way in the support of the protection of IWC information assets. To get the preceding statement published, the ISSO relied on the policy InfoSec staff member to draft a statement for the CEO to sign. The ISSO reasoned that it is always better to write a draft for someone to ensure that what is published meets the needs of the CIAPP and IWC. The statement was drafted after reviewing numerous other documents and speeches made by the CEO to ensure that the words and format used were consistent with what the CEO normally signed.

The draft was edited by the ISSO and then coordinated by the ISSO with the Director of Corporate Security, since this had to do with IWC assets. The Director of Security had no issues with the policy and in fact was happy that the ISSO was aggressively moving forward on this matter. In addition, the Director of Security believed that the ISSO pushing forward would eventually benefit the Security Department. Furthermore, if the ISSO ran into trouble with executive management, the Director could see how far the ISSO was able to go in meeting the information assets protection objectives. He likened the ISSO to a lead scout going through IWC's executive management minefield. It would help the Director to politically choose his ground. After all, the Director was "old school." He didn't care much for computers, and he had no problem letting the ISSO take on the InfoSec matters while the Director concentrated on more "mundane" security matters while awaiting his time for retirement in another 4 or 5 years.

Because the draft was going to the CEO, it was also reviewed and edited by the ISSO's boss, the CIO. It was then sent to the CEO's public relations staff and legal staff for editing and subsequently presented to the CEO by the ISSO accompanied by the CIO, who was always concerned when the ISSO was involved in anything that brought CEO visibility to any aspects of the CIO's department.

The ISSO accomplished another objective toward building a CIAPP for IWC. The letter signed by the CEO was just one part of it. The ISSO also got support from the CEO to aggressively attack the vulnerabilities problems, because the CEO did not object to the assessment approach briefed by the ISSO as part of the CIAPP philosophy. That "hidden agenda" was used to initiate a more proactive effort that the Director of Audits and the ISSO had agreed to prior to the ISSO's meeting with the CEO. This tacit approval allowed the ISSO to establish a more proactive and aggressive CIAPP. All this may seem a little devious but not unethical—or is it? Do the results outweigh the tactics used to gain those results? You be the judge.

The information assets protection policy document had a coordination note attached that showed all those who had seen the document (CEOs rarely sign anything relating to corporate business without input from the staff). If the ISSO had just made an appointment with the CEO and asked for concurrence on the document, the ISSO would undoubtedly be asked if the CIO had seen it, had it been coordinated with his (CSO's) staff, etc.

The ISSO would have said no, wasting the CEO's time and the ISSO's time. The CEO would never sign off on the document without CEO staff input. The whole incident would make the ISSO look foolish and unprofessional, and perhaps a little insecure, as though the CEO did not trust the ISSO.

One key factor is missing here. Do you know what it is? Would the CEO have signed the document without seeing the draft policy directive, IAPPD 500-1? The answer is probably yes. This is because the ISSO ensured that the letter was written without alluding to or identifying any "attached policy document," or any other document for that matter. Why is this important? It is important because this document is timeless and can be used as a standalone document. The ISSO thought that it could also be attached to any information assets protection policy directive, and would help enforce the policy directive because anyone would assume that the CEO's signed document is supporting the policy directive to which it is attached.

The fact is, it is probably true that the CEO would support the policy directive: That directive could not have been published and implemented without following the IWC directive publishing process. This process as stated in IWC directive, HRD 5-17, includes directions as to proper coordination with applicable departments that would be affected by the directive.

The next day, the ISSO happened to be in discussion with the InfoSec policy specialist around the coffeepot. They discussed the CEO's approval of the document, and the ISSO thanked the specialist for a great job.[4] The specialist said "Thanks" and also said, "You know, of course, that it is IWC policy that letters, regardless of who signs them, have no more than a 90-day lifespan? That policy was put in place because many executives and other managers were writing policy 'letters' to circumvent the coordination process for directives. So, these policy letters proliferated at IWC. No one knew what was current and what wasn't, and many failed to follow the letters because 'they didn't work for that person' (the person who signed the letters). So, the letters were ignored. The last thing that IWC needed was a bunch of letter policies flowing around and being ignored. That left the entire IWC atmosphere full of conflicts, some chaos, and an attitude of flouting any rules that one didn't like. In fact, that contributed to our loss of information assets, the firing of managers, including your predecessor. So, you don't want to end up starting that mess all over again. Do you?"

The ISSO didn't know that and was glad that the right person had been hired for the information assets protection policy specialist position.

---

[4] It is easy to take for granted the work of the staff. As an ISSO you should be sensitive to that and never forget to say thanks once in a while. It doesn't take a lot of effort, and it pays great dividends. Just like you, employees like to know they are appreciated.

It's funny how things sometimes work out better than expected. An "InfoSec techie" in that position would probably not have known that valuable piece of information.

The ISSO thought about what the information assets protection policy specialist had said. The ISSO wanted to keep to a minimum any objections to the information assets policy directives.

So, the ISSO directed that a copy of the CEO's signed document be attached to any information assets protection policy document the ISSO was trying to get though the coordination process, published, and implemented. The ISSO also included a note on the coordination sheet that states: *The attached document is an implementation document to meet the IWC information assets protection program requirements as stated in the CEO's document.* The ISSO was very satisfied at this approach, and also directed that the CEO's letter be changed to a formal directive and so instructed the InfoSec policy specialist. That directive, the ISSO reasoned, should not require any coordination because the CEO had already signed it. This was the case, and the CEO's letter became IWC's IAPPD 500-1. Therefore, all other policy directives flowed from that overall directive— the CEO's memo-directive.

The ISSO directed that a project, with the InfoSec policy specialist as the project lead, be established and implemented. The objective was to bring all information assets protection policy directives up to date. This would require all IWC policy directives related to information assets protection to be reviewed, updated, coordinated, republished, and placed online, and all briefings, training, and other processes be updated accordingly. The ISSO also directed that the project lead should prioritize the directives based on a review with the following prioritized schedule:

- Directives that did not currently exist but must be developed to address the protection of various information assets; and
- Directives that were the most outdated (continuing to those that were the least outdated).

The ISSO reasoned that outdated directives were better than no information asset policy directives, because where some were needed and did not exist, the information assets were more vulnerable. Although the missing directives would take the longest to get implemented, they were the most important. The ISSO also directed the information assets protection policy project team, with the policy specialist as the project lead, to do as much as possible in parallel. Those requiring the least amount of work could be done faster, and every updated directive was another victory in the war to protect corporate information assets.

War? The choice of words was used in all seriousness. The ISSO and the staff must get on a "war footing" and not treat their professional duties as some 9-to-5 job. Corporate information assets are being attacked from inside and outside corporations, from within the home nation-state, and from competitors and nation-states from around the world on a 24/7 basis. IWC was no exception, and in fact because of its leadership role in the widget industry, it was probably more at risk than some other corporations.

The ISSO directed that all policy directives be limited to specific issues. The ISSO reasoned that to develop one large policy directive that covers all aspects of IWC's information assets protection needs was not a good idea. Do you agree? Before answering, think about it from an employee's perspective. The employee has a job do to as a specialist in a chosen profession. Employees are not, nor do they want to be, InfoSec specialists. To assist them in at least complying with the CIAPP, the "KISS principle" (Keep It Simple, Stupid) should always be applied.

An employee who wants to do the right thing and comply with all the IWC directives and information assets protection directives is part of the group. Let's say the employee works in a marketing group. If there were just one large policy document, the employee would look at this monster and might be intimated by its size. The employee does not need to know about many of the information assets' protection requirements—for example, those that pertain to the manufacturing environment. Yes, one could do keyword searches if the documents are online, but in all probability, pertinent information would be scattered throughout the document. With the capability of putting documents online and maintaining them online, it is easy in today's word processing environment to just cut and paste applicable portions of other information assets protection documents that apply to more multiple information environments.

Many employees have lost patience trying to read through such large—and boring—documents. Let's face it, even InfoSec professionals get bored reading InfoSec documents. Ironically, some InfoSec personnel never read the entire series of InfoSec-related documents unless they have to, or unless someone embarrasses them by pointing out that they (InfoSec personnel) are violating their own InfoSec rules!

Topic-oriented information assets protection policy documents can be developed, coordinated, and implemented faster. In addition, employees can easily determine which directive to search for guidance without reading volumes. Also, one large directive would be almost constantly in a state of change because of various aspects requiring changes at different times.

The ISSO directed that as a minimum, individual information assets policy directives were to be established providing guidance for the protection of the following corporate information assets[5]:

---

[5] Of course this list is just a sample, as the topics would be based on the corporation, the corporate culture, and the methods used for publishing and implementing directives with each corporation.

- Overall information assets protection (CEO's signed letter);
- Information valuation, marking, storing, distribution, and destruction;
- Information processed, displayed, stored, and transmitted by information systems on the IWC's intranet;
- IWC's private branch exchange (PBX) and voice mail;
- Cellular phones, PDAs, and pagers;
- Fax machines;
- Teleconferencing;
- Printers and scanners;
- Automated manufacturing;
- E-mail;
- Vital, automated records; and
- Violations of information assets protection policies, procedures, and processes.

IWC CIAPP Requirements and Policy Directive

The IWC CIAPP directives followed the standard format for IWC policies and included the following:

1. *Introduction Section,* which includes some history of the need for InfoSec at IWC;
2. *Purpose Section,* which describes why the document exists;
3. *Scope Section,* which defines the breadth of the Directive;
4. *Responsibilities,* which defines and identifies the responsibilities at all levels to include executive management, organizational managers, systems custodians, IT personnel, and users. The Directive will also include the requirements for customers', subcontractors', and vendors' access to IWC systems and information.
5. *Requirements Section,* which includes the requirements for:

   A. Identifying the value of the information;
   B. Access to the IWC systems;
   C. Access to specific applications and files;
   D. Audit trails and their review;
   E. Reporting responsibilities and action to be taken in the event of an indication of a possible violation;
   F. Minimum protection requirements for the hardware, firmware, and software.[6]

The physical security aspects of the requirements would have been coordinated with the applicable Security Department managers, since they have the responsibility for the physical security of IWC assets. The ISSO's rationale was that physical security should be addressed in this document, because it a basic protection process. The Director of Security agreed and approved that process.

G. Requirements for InfoSec procedures at an IWC department and lower level.

Physical Security and CIAPP Policy

The physical security functions for the most part fall under the Security Department. It was agreed by the Director of Security and the ISSO that the physical security program, as it related to InfoSec, was to remain under the purview of the Security Department; however, those aspects related to the InfoSec would be coordinated with the ISSO or the ISSO's designated representative.

The Technical Countermeasures Program relating to emanations of systems' signals or covert signals which may be placed in IWC's sensitive processing areas had been initially placed under the purview of the ISSO; however, the Director of Security apparently became concerned because the systems permeate throughout IWC, which appeared to give the ISSO a great deal of authority.

The ISSO's authority, which the Director equated to *power*, for physical security related to systems facilities was relinquished by the ISSO. The ISSO's rationale was:

* It showed the executive management and the Director of Security that the ISSO was interested in getting the job done right and not who had the authority to do it;
* This move, coupled with the InfoSec procedures responsibility place on IWC management, gave clear indications to everyone that the ISSO was interested in getting the job done in a cooperative effort where InfoSec responsibilities belonged to everyone in a true teaming effort; and
* It took a heavy responsibility off the shoulders of the ISSO. The ISSO was no longer responsible for the physical security aspects; thus, the ISSO's attention could be directed to more technical aspects of the InfoSec program—those more enjoyable to the ISSO.

The agreement reached by the ISSO and Director of Security was for the Security Department to be responsible for:

* Physical access controls to information systems throughout IWC;
* Physical access control badge readers to areas containing sensitive information processing activities;
* Physical disconnects of all systems processing information so sensitive that the information could not be processed outside specified areas;
* Review, analyses, and action related to physical access controls' audit trails; and
* Physical access control of all visitors, vendors, subcontractors, customers, and maintenance personnel, and the escorting of such personnel into sensitive, information processing areas.

IWC CIAPP—Information Assets Protection Procedures

Over the years, the ISSO has had experience in several corporations. The ISSO learned that the best way to provide an updated CIAPP is to begin at the highest level and work down. This form of information assets protection evaluation, analysis, and improvements is based on the fact that information assets protection is driven *and must be supported* from the top down. Therefore, the ISSO began with the overall IWC assets protection requirements (drivers), followed by the information assets protection policies. Once they were in place, those related procedures that were already in place were analyzed, and projects established to update them and develop new ones where needed.

Each information assets protection policy requires compliance by those identified in the policy directives. Each of these directives requires one or more procedures to be established so that there is a standard method used to support and implement the policies, including their spirit and intent. The information assets protection directives previously discussed require procedures to be established in order to comply with those directives. For example, what procedures should be used to determine the classification to be given a piece of information: IWC trade secret, IWC sensitive, IWC proprietary? Some procedures may be written for everyone in IWC to follow, while various departments may write others based on their unique information environments.

There are various opinions as to how best to go about developing procedures. One continues to get to a more detailed level as one goes from requirements (drivers) to policies to procedures. The main issue is this: If the ISSO establishes a specific procedure to comply with a specific policy which in turn assists in meeting the IWC goals as stated in the SBP, TBP, and ABP, the procedures may not be practical in one or two of the IWC departments. The department head may so state, and may ask for a waiver saying that they can still comply if they have a different procedure that takes into account their unique working information environment. There may be more than one department with similar complaints. So, how does the ISSO ensure that people are following proper information assets protection procedures to comply with the information assets protection policies?

The ISSO has found that the best way to do this at IWC is to require that the individual departments establish, implement, and maintain their own set of information assets protection procedures that comply with the policies. This has several benefits:

- Having each department write their own procedures helps enforce the philosophy that information assets protection is everyone's responsibility.

- There will be fewer complaints and requests for waivers because one or more of the IWC departments cannot comply with the procedures as written by the ISSO's InfoSec staff. This benefits the ISSO, as tracking waivers may turn into a nightmare—who has what waivers, why, and for how long.
- The departments can develop procedures that meet their unique conditions and because of that, the procedures should be more cost-effective.
- The ISSO and InfoSec staff will save time and effort in writing and maintaining information assets protection procedures. To be blunt—it's the departments' problem. However, the ISSO has offered to make InfoSec staff available to answer questions and to provide advice as to what should be in the procedures' documents. This was done in the spirit of providing service and support to the IWC employees. The liaison contact for the ISSO would of course be the InfoSec policy specialist.

The question then arose as to how the ISSO could be sure that the procedures written by each department meet the spirit and intent of the policies. Two methods were identified:

- The InfoSec staff as part of their risk management processes would conduct limited risk assessment surveys, and as part of those surveys, the procedures would be reviewed. The limited risk assessments would indicate how well the procedures in place help protect IWC information assets under the control of each department or sub-organization.
- IWC's audit staff would compare the procedures with the policies during their routine audits. The Director of Audits agreed to conduct such reviews, since that department is responsible for auditing for compliance with federal, state, and local laws and regulations and IWC policies and procedures anyway. It also helped that since the ISSO's arrival, the ISSO and Director met and agreed to monthly meetings to share information of mutual concern. The ISSO learned long ago that InfoSec personnel have very few true supporters in helping them to get the job done, but auditors were one of them.

Procedures, along with their related processes, are the heart of a CIAPP because they provide the step-by-step approach for employees as to how to do their work and also ensure the protection of corporate information assets. And if the departments write their own procedures, they become actively involved as valuable team members in the process of protecting IWC's valuable information assets.

ISSO THOUGHT PROCESS IN ESTABLISHING THE INFOSEC ORGANIZATION

The ISSO also knew that a staff of InfoSec specialists would be required because of the large size and geographical locations of IWC systems and associated facilities. What the ISSO had to determine was how many specialists, what types, and how the ISSO's organization should be structured. Although there was a group of InfoSec specialists that made up the IWC InfoSec organization that the ISSO inherited, they were disorganized and had been sort of "thrown together" by the previous ISSO, who was not employed long enough to get around to properly organizing the group.

The IWC ISSO must, in parallel to establishing a CIAPP baseline, also begin the task of establishing a CIAPP-related InfoSec organization. The ISSO decided that the sole purpose of the organization was to lead and support the CIAPP. Therefore, the ISSO intended to provide an "umbilical cord" between the CIAPP and the ISSO's InfoSec organization. After all, without some form of CIAPP, no InfoSec organization would be necessary. In doing so, the ISSO needed to understand:

- The limits of authority;
- The amount of budget available; and
- The impact of establishing a CIAPP program on IWC—the culture change.

The ISSO must also determine how to find qualified people who could build and maintain a cost-effective CIAPP. The staff must also be able to develop into an InfoSec team where everyone acts and is treated as professionals. The IWC ISSO wanted a group of InfoSec professionals who were very talented, yet could leave their egos at the door when they came to work (not an easy task for very talented people).

The ISSO also had to consider that building an *empire* and a massive, bureaucratic organization would not only give the wrong impression to IWC management, but would also be costly. Furthermore, the ISSO must build an efficient and effective InfoSec organization, as required by IWC and as stated in the numerous plans. After all, wasn't that one of the implied conditions of employment?

Building a bureaucracy leads to cumbersome processes, which leads to slow decision cycles, which causes the CIAPP to have an adverse impact on costs and schedules, which leads to a CIAPP that does not provide the services and support needed by the company. This snowballing effect, once started, will be difficult to stop. And if stopped, it requires twice as long to rebuild the service and support reputation of the ISSO, the InfoSec staff, and the CIAPP.

In developing the CIAPP organization, the ISSO also had to bear in mind all that was discussed with IWC management and what was promised. These included:

- IWC's history, business, and the competitive environment;
- Mission, vision, and quality statements;
- IWC and CIAPP plans; and
- The need for developing a CIAPP as quickly as possible, for the work will not wait until the ISSO is fully prepared.

Determining the Need for InfoSec Subordinate Organizations

The ISSO must determine whether or not subordinate InfoSec organizations are needed. If so, a functional work breakdown structure must be developed to determine how many subordinate organizations are needed and what functions should be integrated into what subordinate organizations.

The IWC ISSO reviewed the ISSO's charter and CIAPP focus previously agreed to by the ISSO and executive management. That charter included the following CIAPP functions:

- Requirements, policies, procedures, and plans;
- Hardware, firmware, and software InfoSec evaluations;
- Technical security countermeasures (function subsequently transferred to the Security Department);
- InfoSec tests and evaluations;
- Information system processing approvals;
- Access control;
- Non-compliance inquiries;
- Telecommunications security;
- Risk management;
- Awareness and training; and
- Disaster recovery/contingency planning.

The ISSO analyzed the plans, functions, number of systems, number of users; and determined that two subordinate organizations would be needed to provide the minimum CIAPP professional services and support.

Actually, the ISSO thought of dividing the functions into three organizations, but the need for one of those was borderline. Also, having three suborganizations might give the wrong impression to others in IWC (one must always remember perceptions and appearances when building a CIAPP and organization). It would also provide another level of administrative overhead burden that would not be cost-effective. The ISSO reasoned that the two subordinate organizations would suffice for now;

the organizations could be reevaluated at the end of the first year's operation.

The ISSO decided to brief the Corporate Information Officer (the boss) on the plan. The CIO thought it was reasonable, but wondered how the ISSO would handle the off-site locations in the United States, Europe, and Asia.

As with any good plan, nothing ever runs completely as expected. Being an honest and straightforward ISSO, the only logical comeback was "Huh?" The CIO went on to explain that their global locations are manufacturing sites making final or subassemblies of the widgets, shipping them to the main plant or global customers, as applicable.

The ISSO asked the CIO how other organizations handled the off-site. The CIO explained that they have smaller, satellite offices to provide the service and support needed at that location. The ISSO determined that before deciding on the need for a satellite office, the problem should be further evaluated. The ISSO explained to the CIO that the evaluation would be conducted within a week and a decision made at that time.

The ISSO subsequently determined that in order to provide quality services and support to the off-site locations, small InfoSec organizations with dedicated staff should be in place at all facilities. This would replace the current staff, who as an additional duty, assigned by on-site facility executive managers, had to serve as part-time InfoSec persons. This decision was based on several considerations:

- Conversations with managers of other organizations, who had satellite offices at the off-site location, relative to how they handled the problem;
- Conversations with managers of other organizations, who did *not* have satellite offices at the off-site location, as to how they handled the service and support requirements;
- Conversations with off-site facility executive managers;
- An analysis of the off-site locations' information systems configurations and processing;
- Information flow processes; and
- The CIAPP needs of each location.

Based on the analysis, the ISSO determined that CIAPP satellite offices were indeed necessary, but some functions could be supported from the corporate office, such as risk management, policy development, and requirements.

The ISSO informed the CIO of the decision and the basis for the decision, emphasizing its cost-effectiveness. The CIO agreed based on the business logic shown by the ISSO, the minimal number of InfoSec staff needed, and what the CIO sensed as the ISSO's strong commitment to CIAPP using a least-cost/minimum risk approach.

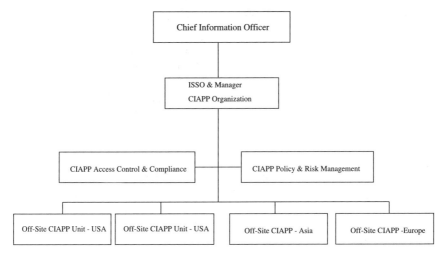

Figure 7.2   The primary structure of the CIAPP organization.

The number of people in any working group tends to increase regardless of the amount of work to be done.—Cyril Northcote Parkinson[7]

Developing the CIAPP Organization Structure

Based on the ISSO's analyses, the ISSO established the CIAPP organization—at least on paper (Figure 7.2).

The ISSO found that establishing the CIAPP organization to date had been the easy part. Now came the bureaucracy of coordinating and gaining approval of the CIAPP organization from the designated organizations, such as organizational planning, human resources, and facilities; as well as completing theirs and other organizations' forms.[8]

A word of caution to the ISSO: Some *service and support* organizations are more interested in proper completion of the administrative bureaucracy than in helping their internal customers. Just grin and bear it. You can't change it, except over time, and now is not the time. The priority is getting the CIAPP and the InfoSec organization off the ground. Concentrate on that priority.

---

[7] Cyril Northcote Parkinson (1909–1993), British political scientist, historian, and writer. Parkinson's Law (1958), as quoted in Microsoft's *Encarta World.*

[8] Since each corporation has a somewhat different *forms bureaucracy,* no attempt will be made here to complete any forms. Those readers who have to make any changes in an organization can appreciate the maze the ISSO must now go through.

Developing the CIAPP Subordinate Organizations

The ISSO determined that the subordinate organizations must also have charters that identify the CIAPP functions that are to be performed by the staff of those organizations. The ISSO further determined that to recruit managers for the subordinate organizations was premature. The ISSO reasoned that what was needed first was professional InfoSec personnel who could begin the actual CIAPP work. The ISSO would manage all the organizations until such time as the workload and cost-effectiveness considerations determined that a subordinate manager or managers were needed. Based on the work to be performed, and the analyses discussed above, the ISSO developed the charters for the subordinate organizations. In the interim, the ISSO used a matrix management approach with the off-site facility managers who were responsible to the CIO for overall information and information systems management

Responsibilities of CIAPP Subordinate Organizations

CIAPP Access Control and Compliance Subordinate Organization

The ISSO is the acting manager of the CIAPP Access Control and Compliance (IACC) subordinate organization

The following is the summary of the position:

Provide the management, direction, and conduct analyses required to protect information processed on IWC information systems, from unauthorized access, disclosure, misuse, modification, manipulation, or destruction; as well as implement and maintain appropriate information and information systems access controls; conduct noncompliance inquiries; and maintain violations tracking systems[9] (Figure 7.3).

Detailed accountabilities include:

1. Implement, administer, and maintain user access control systems by providing controls, processes, and procedures to prevent the unauthorized access, modification, disclosure, misuse, manipulation, or destruction of IWC information.

2. Monitor user access control systems to provide for the identification, inquiry, and reporting of access control violations. Analyze system access controls violations' data and trends to determine potential systems' security weaknesses and report to management.

3. Conduct inquiries into CIAPP violations/incidents and related CIAPP business practices, IWC policies, and procedures. Identify the expo-

---

[9]The ISSO decided that the priority of CIAPP was the TCI systems and information at their facilities. The sticky problem of dealing with non-TCI CIAPP issues, such as subcontractors and customers, would have to wait. The ISSO reasoned that if TCI had a successful, professional program, it would be easier to gain the cooperation of the outside corporations.

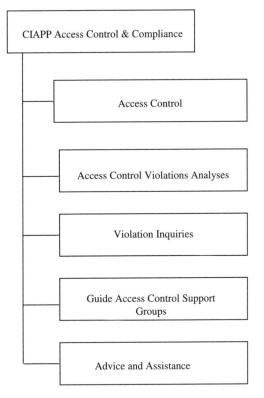

Figure 7.3 A CIAPP Access Control and Compliance subordinate organization and its primary functions.

sures/compromises created, and recommend to management corrective and preventive actions.

4. Direct, monitor, and guide the CIAPP activities of the IWC's access controls support groups and systems to ensure adequate implementation of access control systems in meeting CIAPP requirements.

5. Establish and manage an information systems defensive system, including firewalls and related intrusion detection systems.

6. Provide advice and assistance in the interpretation and implementation of CIAPP policies and procedures, contractual CIAPP requirements, and related documents.

CIAPP Policy and Risk Management

The ISSO is the acting manager of the CIAPP Policy and Risk Management subordinate organization.

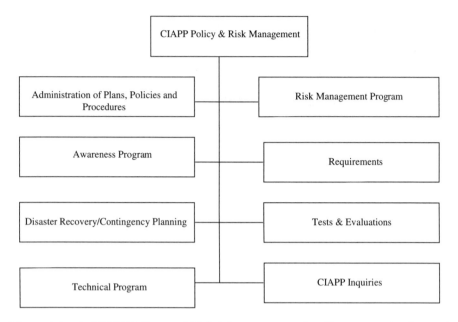

Figure 7.4 A CIAPP Policy and Risk Management subordinate organization and its primary functions.

The following is the summary of the position:

Provide the management, direction, and develop, implement, and maintain CIAPP policies and procedures; awareness; disaster recovery and contingency planning; CIAPP system life cycle processes; InfoSec tests and evaluations; risk management, and CIAPP technical security and related programs to protect IWC systems and information (Figure 7.4).

Detailed accountabilities include:

1. Identify all CIAPP requirements needed and develop IWC policies and procedures necessary to ensure conformance to those requirements.
2. Evaluate all hardware, software, and firmware to ensure conformance to CIAPP policies and procedures, recommend modifications when not in conformance, and approve them when in conformance.
3. Establish and administer an InfoSec Tests and Evaluations Program to ensure compliance with systems' security documentation and applicable CIAPP requirements.
4. Establish, implement, and maintain a CIAPP Technical Program to identify all electronic threats and mitigate those threats in a cost-effective manner.

5. Establish and maintain a CIAPP Awareness Program to ensure that IWC management and users are cognizant of CIAPP policies, procedures, and requirements for the protection of systems and information, and their related threats.
6. Develop, implement, and administer a Risk Management Program to identify and assess threats, vulnerabilities, and risks associated with the information for which IWC has responsibility and recommend cost-effective modifications to the CIAPP Program, systems, and processes.
7. Establish and maintain a Disaster Recovery/Contingency Planning Program that will mitigate CIAPP, IWC information, and systems' losses and ensure the successful recovery of the information and systems with minimal impact on IWC.

Off-Site CIAPP Organizations

The ISSO is also the acting manager of the Off-Site CIAPP subordinate organizations. However, the ISSO has also determined that it will be necessary to appoint a person as a supervisor to manage the day-to-day operations of the off-site CIAPP program. At the same time, there are not enough personnel, as stated by HR, to appoint a manager at the off-site locations. However, the supervisor has authority to make decisions related to that activity, with several exceptions. The supervisor cannot counsel the CIAPP staff, evaluate their performance (except to provide input to the CIAPP manager), make new CIAPP policy, or manage budgets.

The following is the summary of the position:

Implement, maintain, and administer a CIAPP program for IWC resources at the off-site location; and take the action necessary to ensure compliance with the CIAPP requirements, policies, and procedures to protect IWC information from compromise, destruction, and/or unauthorized manipulation.[10]

Detailed accountabilities include:

1. Implement and administer IWC plans, policies, and procedures necessary to ensure compliance with stated IWC CIAPP requirements for the protection of all information processed, stored, and/or transmitted on IWC information systems.

---

[10] Because of its off-site location, this position requires CIAPP functions to be performed which are similar to or the same as most functions noted for the entire CIAPP organization.

2.   Administer an InfoSec Tests and Evaluations Program to ensure that all IWC information systems are operated in accordance with appropriate CIAPP requirements and contract specifications.
3.   Administer and monitor the local use of IWC information systems access control software systems, analyze all infractions/violations, and document and report the results of questionable user activity for CIAPP inquiries.
4.   Identify information systems' business practice irregularities and security violations/infractions; conduct detailed inquiries; assess potential damage; monitor IWC management's corrective action; and recommend preventive measures to preclude recurrences.
5.   Administer a CIAPP Education and Training Awareness Program for all IWC managers and users of IWC information systems to ensure they are cognizant of information systems' threats and are aware of the CIAPP policies/procedures necessary for the protection of information and information systems.
6.   Represent the CIAPP Manager relative to all applicable IWC CIAPP matters as they apply to personnel, resources, and operations at the off-site location.
7.   Provide advice, guidance, and assistance to management, system users, and systems' custodians relative to CIAPP matters.
8.   Perform other functions as designated or delegated by the CIAPP Manager.

InfoSec Job Descriptions

After establishing and gaining final approval for the InfoSec organization, and while trying to begin establishing a formal, centralized CIAPP, the ISSO determined it was now time to begin hiring some InfoSec professionals.

However, before that could be accomplished and in accordance with IWC organizational development and Human Resources requirements, an InfoSec job family must first be established. After all, IWC, being a high-tech, modern corporation, requires that employees be assigned to career families to support their career development program as directed by the Human Resources Department. And, unfortunately, it seems that InfoSec functions have never been a formal part of IWC. Therefore, there are no job families that seem to meet the needs of the CIAPP functions.

The ISSO and the Human Resources person discussed the matter and agreed that the ISSO would write the InfoSec functional job family descriptions. The ISSO was told that they must be generic, so they are flexible enough to support several InfoSec job functions within each level of the job family. The Human Resources person advised the ISSO that this is necessary to ensure the flexibility needed for recruiting, hiring, and the subsequent career development of the InfoSec professionals. Also, it would streamline the process and ensure that the number of InfoSec job family positions' descriptions could be kept to a minimum, thus also decreasing bureaucracy and paperwork.

At the conclusion of the meeting, the Human Resources person provided the ISSO with the job descriptions for the security, auditor, and information technology job family. Also provided were several forms that must be completed when submitting the InfoSec job family descriptions, as well as forms to be used for documenting each job family description by grade level.

Armed with the challenges of this new onslaught of bureaucratic paper, and bidding adieu to the smiling Human Resources person, the ISSO headed back to the office to begin the task of writing IWC's InfoSec job family as sample-descriptions (while wondering when there would be time to do *real* CIAPP work).

After reviewing the provided job descriptions and reading the paperwork needed to make this all happen, the ISSO wrote and provided the Human Resources person with the function descriptions of the InfoSec job family! After several iterations and compromises, and approvals through a chain of organizational staffs, the job family was approved.

InfoSec Job Family Functional Descriptions

The following detailed InfoSec job family functional descriptions were developed and approved by the applicable IWC departments:

1. Systems Security Administrator

Position Summary: Provide all technical administrative support for the InfoSec organization.

Duties and Responsibilities:

1. filing,
2. typing reports, and other word processing projects,
3. developing related spreadsheets, data bases, and text/graphic presentations

Qualifications: High school diploma, 1 year of security administration or 2 years of clerical experience. Must type at least 60 words per minute.

2. System Security Analyst Associate

Position Summary: Assist and support InfoSec staff in ensuring all applicable IWC CIAPP requirements are met.

Duties and Responsibilities

1. Support the implementation and administration of InfoSec software systems.
2. Provide advice, guidance, and assistance to system users relative to CIAPP matters.
3. Identify current CIAPP and InfoSec functional processes and assist in the development of automated tools to support those functions.
4. Assist in the analysis of manual CIAPP and InfoSec functions, and provide input to recommendations and reports of the analyses to the ISSO.
5. Maintain, modify, and enhance automated InfoSec functional systems of InfoSec tests and evaluations, risk assessments, software/hardware evaluations, access control, and other related systems.
6. Collect, compile, and generate CIAPP functional informational reports and briefing packages for presentation to customers and management.
7. Perform other functions as assigned by the ISSO and InfoSec management.

Position requires being assigned to perform duties in one or more of the following areas:

*   *Access Controls*—Maintain basic user access control systems by providing processes and procedures to prevent unauthorized access or the destruction of information.
*   *Access Controls/Technical Access Control Software*—Assist access controls support groups and systems by providing software tools and guidance to ensure adequate implementation of access control systems in meeting CIAPP requirements, as well as defensive systems such as firewalls and related intrusion detection systems.
*   *Access Controls/Violations Analysis*—Monitor the use of IWC access control software systems; identify all systems CIAPP infractions/violations; document and report the results of questionable user and system activity for CIAPP inquiries.
*   *InfoSec Tests and Evaluation/CIAPP System Documentation*— Conduct InfoSec tests and evaluations on standalone (nonnetworked) systems to ensure that the systems are processing in accordance with applicable CIAPP-approved procedures.

Qualifications: This position normally requires a bachelor's degree in an InfoSec-related profession.

3. System Security Analyst

Position Summary: Identify, schedule, administer, and perform assigned technical InfoSec analysis functions to ensure all applicable requirements are met.

Duties and Responsibilities

1. Represent CIAPP to other organizations on select CIAPP-related matters.
2. Provide advice, guidance, and assistance to managers, system users, and system custodians relative to CIAPP matters.
3. Provide general advice and assistance in the interpretation of CIAPP requirements.
4. Identify all CIAPP requirements necessary for the protection of all information processed, stored, and/or transmitted by the information systems; develop and implement plans, policies, and procedures necessary to ensure compliance.
5. Identify current CIAPP functional processes and develop automated tools to support those functions.
6. Analyze manual CIAPP functions, and provide recommendations and reports of the analyses to InfoSec management.
7. Maintain, modify, and enhance automated CIAPP functional systems of InfoSec tests and evaluations, risk assessments, software/hardware evaluations, access control, and other related systems.
8. Collect, compile, and generate CIAPP functional informational reports and briefing packages for presentation to customers and management.
9. Perform other functions as assigned by InfoSec management.

Position requires being assigned to perform duties in the following areas:

- *Access Controls/Technical Access Control Software*—Administer and maintain user access control systems by providing controls, processes, and procedures to prevent the unauthorized access, modification, disclosure, misuse, manipulation, or destruction of IWC information; as well as defensive systems such as firewalls and related intrusion detection systems.
- *Access Controls/Violations Analysis*—Administer and monitor the use of IWC access control software systems; analyze all systems CIAPP infractions/violations; document and report the results of questionable user and system activity for CIAPP inquiries.
- *Noncompliance Inquiry*—Identify and analyze CIAPP business practice irregularities and CIAPP violations/infractions; conduct detailed inquiries; assess potential damage; monitor corrective action; and recommend preventive, cost-effective measures to preclude recurrences.
- *Risk Assessment*—Perform limited risk assessments of CIAPP systems and processes; determine their threats, vulnerabilities, and risks; and recommend cost-effective risk mitigation solutions.

- *InfoSec Tests and Evaluation/CIAPP System Documentation*—Schedule and conduct CIAPP tests and evaluations on standalone (non-networked) systems to ensure that the systems are processing in accordance with applicable CIAPP-approved procedures.

Qualifications

This classification normally requires a bachelor's degree in an InfoSec-related profession and at least 2 years of practical experience.

4. System Security Analyst Senior

Position Summary: Identify, evaluate, conduct, schedule, and lead technical InfoSec analysis functions to ensure that all applicable IWC CIAPP requirements are met.

Duties and Responsibilities

1. Provide technical analysis of CIAPP requirements necessary for the protection of all information processed, stored, and/or transmitted by systems; interpret those requirements; and translate, implement, and administer Division plans, policies, and procedures necessary to ensure compliance.
2. Represent CIAPP on security matters with other entities as assigned.
3. Provide advice, guidance, and assistance to senior management, systems' managers, and system users and custodians relative to CIAPP matters.
4. Perform other functions as assigned by InfoSec Management.

Position requires being assigned to perform duties in the following areas:

- *Access Controls/Technical Access Control Software*—Implement, administer, and maintain systems' user access control systems through the use of controls, processes, and procedures to prevent their unauthorized access, modification, disclosure, misuse, manipulation, and/or destruction; as well as defensive systems such as firewalls and related intrusion detection systems.
- *Access Controls/Violations Analysis*—Coordinate, administer, and monitor the use of systems' access control systems; analyze systems' security infractions/violations employing statistical and trend analyses and report the results.
- *CIAPP Awareness*—Prepare, schedule, and present CIAPP awareness briefings to systems' managers, custodians, and users. Act as focal point for dissemination of CIAPP information through all forms of media.

- *Disaster Recovery*—Coordinate and ensure compliance with system disaster recovery/contingency plans to ensure the rapid recovery of system in the event of an emergency or disaster.
- *Hardware and Software CIAPP Evaluations*—Evaluate all hardware, firmware, and software for impact on the CIAPP of the systems; monitor and ensure their modification if requirements are not met; and authorize their purchase and use within IWC.
- *Noncompliance Inquiry*—Identify and conduct technical analyses of CIAPP business practices and violations/infractions; plan, coordinate, and conduct detailed inquiries; assess potential damage; and develop and implement corrective action plans.
- *Risk Assessments*—Conduct limited InfoSec technical risk assessments; prepare reports of the results for presentation to management.
- *InfoSec Tests and Evaluations/CIAPP Documentation*—Schedule and conduct InfoSec tests and evaluations to ensure that all the applicable systems are operating in accordance with CIAPP requirements.
- *Technical Countermeasures*—Conduct technical surveys and determine necessary countermeasures related to physical information leakage; conduct sound attenuation tests to ensure that information processing systems do not emanate information beyond IWC's zone of control.

Qualifications: This classification normally requires a bachelor's degree in an InfoSec-related profession and 4 years of practical, related experience.

5. System Security Analyst Specialist

Position Summary: Act as technical CIAPP advisor, focal point, and lead to ensure all CIAPP functions are meeting IWC requirements, as well as develop and administer applicable programs.
Duties and Responsibilities:

1. Act as technical advisor for CIAPP requirements necessary for the protection of all information processed, stored, and/or transmitted by systems; interpret those requirements; and translate, document, implement, and administer IWC CIAPP plans, policies, and procedures necessary to ensure compliance.
2. Represent CIAPP on security matters with other entities as assigned.
3. Provide advice, guidance, and assistance to senior management, IT managers, system users, and system custodians relative to CIAPP matters.
4. Perform other functions as assigned by InfoSec Management.

Position requires being assigned to perform duties in a combination of the following areas:

- *Access Controls/Technical Access Control Software*—Implement, administer, and maintain systems' user access control systems through the use of controls, processes, and procedures to prevent their unauthorized access, modification, disclosure, misuse, manipulation, and/or destruction, as well as defensive systems such as firewalls and related intrusion detection systems.
- *CIAPP Awareness*—Prepare, schedule, and present CIAPP awareness briefings to system managers, custodians, and users. Act as focal point for dissemination of CIAPP information through all forms of media.
- *Disaster Recovery*—Coordinate and ensure compliance with system disaster recovery/contingency plans to ensure the rapid recovery of systems in the event of an emergency or disaster.
- *Hardware and Software CIAPP Evaluations*—Evaluate all hardware, firmware, and software for impact on the CIAPP of the systems; monitor and ensure their modification if requirements are not met; and authorize their purchase and use within IWC.
- *Risk Assessments*—Conduct limited CIAPP technical risk assessments; prepare reports of the results for presentation to management.
- *InfoSec Tests and Evaluations/CIAPP Documentation*—Schedule and conduct InfoSec tests and evaluations to ensure that all the applicable systems are operating in accordance with CIAPP requirements.
- *Technical Countermeasures*—Conduct technical surveys and determine necessary countermeasures related to physical information leakage; conduct sound attenuation tests to ensure that information processing systems do not emanate information beyond IWC's zone of control.

Qualifications
This classification normally requires a bachelor's degree in a CIAPP-related profession, and 6 years of CIAPP experience.

6. System Security Engineer

Position Summary: Act as a technical systems management consultant, focal point, and project lead for CIAPP functions and programs developed to ensure IWC requirements are met.
Duties and Responsibilities:

1. Act as a lead in the identification of government, customers, and IWC CIAPP requirements necessary for the protection of information

processed, stored, and/or transmitted by IWC's systems; interpret those requirements; and develop, implement, and administer IWC CIAPP plans, policies, and procedures necessary to ensure compliance.

2. Represent the CIAPP Office, when applicable, on CIAPP matters as well as serve as IWC's liaison with customers, government agencies, suppliers, and other outside entities.

3. Provide advice, guidance, and assistance to senior and executive management, IWC's subcontractors, and government entities relative to CIAPP matters.

4. Provide technical consultation, guidance, and assistance to management, systems' users; and CIAPP software systems by providing controls, processes, and procedures.

5. Establish, direct, coordinate, and maintain a Disaster Recovery/Contingency Program for IWC that will mitigate systems and information losses and ensure the successful recovery of the system and information with minimal impact on IWC.

6. Act as lead for the technical evaluation and testing of hardware, firmware, and software for impact on the security of the systems; direct and ensure their modification if requirements are not met; authorize their purchase and use within IWC, and approve them when in conformance.

7. Develop or direct the development of original techniques, procedures, and utilities for conducting CIAPP risk assessments; schedule and conduct CIAPP risk assessments and report results to management.

8. Direct and/or lead others in conducting technical CIAPP countermeasure surveys to support CIAPP requirements and report findings.

9. Direct and administer InfoSec tests and evaluations programs to ensure that the applicable systems are operating in accordance with CIAPP requirements.

10. Provide technical consultation and assistance in identifying, evaluating, and documenting use of systems and other related equipment to ensure compliance with communications requirements.

11. Investigate methods and procedures related to the CIAPP aspects of microcomputers, local area networks, mainframes, and their associated connectivity and communications.

12. Identify and participate in evaluation of microcomputer and local-area network CIAPP implementations, including antivirus and disaster recovery/contingency planning functions.

13. Perform development and maintenance activities on CIAPP-related databases.

14. Recommend and obtain approval for procedural changes to effect CIAPP implementations with emphasis on least-cost/minimum risk.

15. Lead and direct InfoSec personnel in the conduct of systems CIAPP audits.
16. Participate in the development and promulgation of CIAPP information for general awareness.
17. Perform other functions as assigned by the InfoSec Manager.

Position requires being assigned to perform duties in a combination of the following areas:

•   *Supervisor, Project Leader*—Provide assistance, advice, guidance and act as technical specialist relative to all InfoSec technical functions.

Qualifications: This classification normally requires a bachelor's degree in an InfoSec-related profession and a minimum of 10 years of CIAPP-related experience.

Recruiting InfoSec Professionals

Once the ISSO had gotten the InfoSec organizational structure, and the InfoSec job family functional descriptions both approved, the next task was to begin recruiting and hiring qualified InfoSec professionals.

Hold it! Not so fast! The ISSO must first determine the following:

•   How many InfoSec professionals are needed?
•   What functions will they perform?
•   How many are needed in each function?
•   How many are needed in what pay code?
•   How many should be recruited for the off-site location?
•   Does the off-site location or main plant have the highest priority?

The ISSO must plan for the gradual hiring of personnel to meet the CIAPP and InfoSec organizational needs based on a prioritized listing of functions. Obviously, a mixture of personnel should be considered. One or two high-level personnel should be hired to begin establishing the basic CIAPP and InfoSec processes. Personnel who meet the qualifications of a System Security Engineer should be hired immediately. At least two should be hired. One would be the project lead to begin the process of establishing the formal functions of one of the InfoSec subordinate organizations while the other would do the same for the other InfoSec organization. At the same time, the access control function positions should be filled as they represent the key CIAPP mechanism of access control.

Functions such as risk management, noncompliance inquiry, and the awareness program could come later. The rationale used by the ISSO for this decision was that CIAPP policies had not been established, so there was nothing on which to base noncompliance inquiries or an awareness program. The next position to be filled, after the two Systems Security Engineers and access control personnel, was the position of the emergency planning, disaster recovery planning, and contingency planning specialist.

The ISSO reasoned that while access controls were being tightened up and analyzed, the engineers were beginning to build the process for each function, with much of the access control process development being done with the assistance of the access control administrators. In the event of a disaster, the systems must be up and operational in as short a time period as possible. This is crucial to the well-being of IWC.

Unfortunately, the type of individual the ISSO would ideally want to employ is not usually readily available. In addition, IWC's policy is one of "promote from within" whenever possible. So, although a *more* qualified individual may be available from outside IWC, the ISSO may have to transfer a less qualified individual currently employed within IWC, because that person does meet the minimum requirements for the position—at least as interpreted by the Human Resources personnel.

The ISSO soon began to realize that compromise and coordination were a *must* if there was to be even a slight chance of succeeding in building the IWC CIAPP. Based on a self-evaluation, the ISSO decided to find as many people as possible within IWC who were willing to transfer and who met the minimum requirements for a CIAPP position. The ISSO soon learned why the job descriptions approved through the Human Resources Department include words such as "normally" and "equivalent." The ISSO naively thought that those words would assist in bringing in InfoSec professionals. It never entered the ISSO's mind that others could also use the position descriptions to help recruit personnel—some who just barely would meet the minimum requirements!

For the ISSO who is quickly trying to build a CIAPP and InfoSec organization, the compromises on staff selection may help or they may hurt. In either case, it is important to quickly begin the hiring process.

Identifying In-House InfoSec Candidates

Those individuals within IWC organizations who have been providing access control as either a full or part-time position for their department's local area networks (LAN) may be good access control candidates.

The IT Department may also be a place to "recruit" (make personnel aware of the positions available) InfoSec candidates. The Audit and InfoSec organizations may also provide a place to find InfoSec candidates.

A word of caution to the ISSO: Most managers do not take kindly to recruiting of their employees, as it means they will be short-handed until they can find replacements. In addition, the ISSO should beware of individuals whom the managers recommend. These may just be the people that the manager has been trying to find some way to get rid of for some time!

The ISSO has enough problems building a CIAPP, establishing and managing an InfoSec organization, handling the day-to-day CIAPP problems, attending endless meetings, trying to hire a professional CIAPP staff, having to transfer personnel who don't meet the ISSO's expectations, to then be saddled with an employee recommended by another manager who turns out to be a "difficult" employee.

A difficult employee will occupy more of the ISSO's time than three other staff members combined. It seemed that the IWC IT Department has a penchant for this. So, *beware of geeks bearing gifts!*

Identifying Outside InfoSec Candidates

There are many sources that can be used to recruit talented InfoSec professionals, many limited only by imagination and budget (especially budget!). Regardless of how or where you recruit, the recruitment must be coordinated with the Human Resources staff.

In order to recruit InfoSec personnel, the Controller must validate and approve (on another form, of course) that there is budget set aside for the InfoSec organization to hire staff.

Then once that hurdle is jumped, the Human Resources personnel must validate that you have completed the necessary form describing the position you want to hire against, the minimum qualifications, and the pay range for that position. Luckily, all the ISSO has to do in this case is basically transcribe the general position description onto the new Human Resources form used for recruiting candidates and advertising the positions.

Just as the IWC ISSO thought that the door was now flung wide open to recruit InfoSec professionals, one of the Human Resources personnel walked up to the ISSO and mentioned how boring the Human Resources job was, and that it would be nice to transfer to another, more exciting organization—and the InfoSec job seems to be a very exciting one. Experience? Well, of course the person is proficient is *using* a computer! Another often-found problem is the manager or staff member who has a cousin just graduating from college who would be perfect for the InfoSec position.

The ISSO soon began to realize that building and managing an outstanding, state-of-the-art CIAPP and an InfoSec organization staffed by talented InfoSec professionals might become more of a dream than a reality.

Once the ISSO was able to fend off these and similar charges, the recruitment effort within and outside IWC could start in earnest! Among the ways to recruit InfoSec professionals are through:

- Local advertisement in trade journals, newspapers, etc.;
- Hiring a consulting firm to find the right people;

- Passing the word among colleagues;
- Asking InfoSec associations to pass the word; and
- Using the Internet to advertise the position.

With a few InfoSec personnel on board, the ISSO could begin to work on the CIAPP and also begin work on developing the baseline processes and functions with the InfoSec organization.

QUESTIONS TO CONSIDER

Based on what you have read, consider the following questions and how you would reply to them:

- Do you have a formal, that is, documented CIAPP?
- If not, why not?
- What would you consider as the benefits of such a plan?
- What would you consider as the negatives of such a plan?
- Have you ever briefed executive management on InfoSec-related matters?
- Do you identify the costs of staffing and providing InfoSec functions using a cost–benefit–risk management process?
- If you were to develop a CIAPP for IWC, what would you do differently from what was stated in this chapter?
- If you could build and manage an InfoSec organization for IWC, how would the structure compare to the one cited in this chapter, and why?
- How would you manage the off-site locations—for example, would you manage them from the corporate office, or ask some off-site manager to matrix manage the staff for you?
- What other job descriptions would you add to the ones provided?
- What other duties and responsibilities would you add to the job descriptions provided in this chapter?
- Do you know how to successfully work with Human Resources staff to meet their requirements and also effectively and efficiently get your objectives accomplished?

SUMMARY

Once plans were in place, the ISSO could begin to develop an InfoSec organization to support the CIAPP. To do so, the ISSO must understand the following:

- Establishing an effective and efficient InfoSec organization and program requires a detailed analysis and integration of all the information that has been learned through the entire process of becoming an ISSO at IWC.

- Determining the need for InfoSec subordinate organizations requires detailed analysis of IWC's environment and an understanding of how to successfully apply resource allocation techniques to the InfoSec functions.
- Once the need for InfoSec subordinate organizations is determined, the ISSO must determine what functions go in what organizations.
- Establishing a formal InfoSec organization and InfoSec job family requires cooperation with Human Resources organizations and others; patience and understanding are mandatory.
- An ISSO who establishes a new organization for a corporation will be compelled to live within a less than ideal corporate world where forms and bureaucracies rule the day. To survive, the ISSO must understand how to use those processes efficiently and effectively in order to succeed.
- In most corporations, currently employed personnel who desire an InfoSec position, and who meet the minimum InfoSec requirements, must be hired before hiring an individual from the outside.
- Recruiting qualified InfoSec professionals can only be accomplished through widespread recruitment effort, using many marketing media; and successful advertisement is sometimes a matter of how much recruitment budget is available.

8

Determining and Establishing InfoSec Functions

Work is necessary for man. Man invented the alarm clock.—Pablo Picasso[1]

CHAPTER OBJECTIVE

We began this section of the book with an overview of the duties and responsibilities of the IWC ISSO, then discussed establishing a CIAPP and the related InfoSec organization. We will continue the trend to narrow the focus: This chapter describes a process to determine what InfoSec functions are needed to successfully establish a CIAPP and related organization, as well as how to incorporate those functions into the InfoSec organization's day-to-day level-of-effort work.

INTRODUCTION

There are many different ways to configure an InfoSec organization, and there are many ways to configure the InfoSec functions that are part of that organization. Many ISSOs begin establishing an InfoSec organization, or "inheriting" one, without looking at the need for the various functions and from where that need was derived. As stated earlier, all functions should be derived from at least one or more of the following requirements (drivers):

* Laws;
* Regulations;
* Best business practices;
* Best InfoSec practices;
* Ethics;

---

[1] Attributed to Pablo Picasso (1881–1973), Spanish painter and sculptor. Microsoft's *Encarta Dictionary.*

- Privacy needs; and
- IWC policies.

When developing or reorganizing a CIAPP-driven InfoSec organization, one can consider one of three basic structures as it relates to the InfoSec organization that the ISSO will manage and lead. The three basic options are:

- Centralized InfoSec under ISSO and InfoSec organization;
- Decentralized throughout the corporation; or
- A combination of the two.

One of the major factors in deciding what philosophy and approach to take is the culture of the corporation, as well as the charter of the ISSO spelling out the ISSO's duties and responsibilities. The ISSO must remember that the more centralized the organization, the more problems and work for the ISSO and staff. The old adage "If you want it done right, do it yourself" may work for some, but as an ISSO, that approach will bring you more stress than usual. In addition, you will definitely age exponentially. Developing and maintaining a protected information environment for IWC requires the support and active involvement of all IWC employees. Sometimes an ISSO forgets that and tries to take on the entire protection matter instead of leading a corporate team effort. Such an approach leads to more problems than solutions for developing and maintaining a protected information environment.

So, what should you do? The best approach seems to be a combination. For example, the IWC ISSO decided that the overall information and information systems protection logically should be centralized under the ISSO and InfoSec staff. After all, they have the experience and know-how to lead this IWC effort. However, at the same time, why get burdened down trying to write and maintain current InfoSec procedures that must be implemented by IWC departments to comply with those InfoSec policies? So, procedures written for compliance, as previously stated, will be the responsibility of the IWC departments. Their adequacy will be determined through audits, InfoSec tests and evaluations, noncompliance inquiries, and the like.

In addition, the IWC departments will be responsible for developing, implementing, and maintaining the processes that are an integral part of the procedures needed to comply with the CIAPP.

PROCESSES

The ISSO must also develop procedures, functions, and processes to comply with the CIAPP policies, as an organizational manager. In

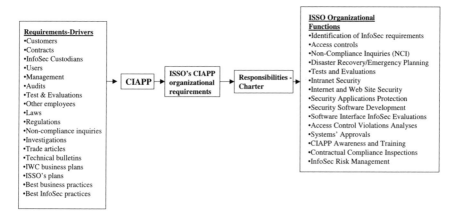

Figure 8.1   How the process flow from drivers to action items to functions can be viewed.

addition, the ISSO must lead the effort to develop functions that the InfoSec organization will perform in order to lead and support the IWC CIAPP.

The IWC ISSO decided that the best approach is through the drivers' (CIAPP–InfoSec requirements) baseline. So, based on the drivers, one is then able to develop a "needs" statement or statements. These can be set forth in various ways such as the vision, mission, and quality statements and incorporated into plans, for example, strategic, tactical, and annual as previously discussed. Regardless of how and in what form you state these needs for InfoSec, they must support IWC's plans, policies, objectives, and goals and must also eventually be tied to action items.

These action items are then analyzed and are implemented— for example, established as InfoSec functions that are then incorporated into the ISSO's InfoSec organization as its charter of responsibilities and accountabilities, as stated in the previous chapter. One step to look at is the process. A process is basically a "a series of actions directed toward a particular aim."[2] After the drivers and needs are identified, the ISSO must establish a process for meeting the identified requirements. The process is such a method and is basically the details of how a function is to be performed. One way of envisioning this process is noted in Figure 8.1.

The action items should be part of a formal project management program where, as stated earlier, you as the ISSO determine that there is a need for some sort of InfoSec action that will take time and must be

---

[2] *Encarta World English Dictionary* © & (P) 1999, Microsoft Corporation. All rights reserved. Developed for Microsoft by Bloomsbury Publishing Plc.

incorporated into the CIAPP or the InfoSec organization. Remember, the project plans have:

- Objectives to accomplish;
- Beginning and ending dates;
- Tasks identified and assigned;
- Personnel assigned to tasks;
- Budget allocated; and
- Time allocated for completing those tasks.

There are many InfoSec- and CIAPP-related functions; however, at IWC the ISSO determined that the functions identified in the ISSO's charter were the main functions that were driven by or related to the baseline CIAPP. Therefore, they are the basic functions that should be established, and a flow process description should be developed relative to how the functions should be performed. For example[3]:

- InfoSec requirements identification;
- InfoSec plans, policies, processes, and procedures;
- Awareness education and training;
- Access control;
- Evaluation of hardware, firmware, and software for impact on the security of the information systems;
- Security tests and evaluations;
- Noncompliance inquiries;
- Risk management; and
- Disaster recovery/contingency planning.

VALUING INFORMATION

Before addressing the InfoSec functions, the ISSO determined that to provide an effective CIAPP with least impact to cost and schedule, it is important to establish a process to determine the value of information.

The ISSO's reasoning is that no information should be protected any more than is necessary. The rationale used by the ISSO is as follows:

The value of information is time-dependent. In other words, information has value for only a certain period of time. Information relative to a new, unique IWC widget must be highly protected, and that includes the electronic drawings, diagrams, processes, etc. However, once the new widget is announced to the public, complete with photographs of the

---

[3] Others can be added, but using these basic examples gives the reader a good idea of what is needed.

widget, selling price, etc., much of the protected information no longer needs protection.

That information which once required protection to maintain the secrecy of this new widget can now be eliminated. This will save money for IWC because InfoSec and CIAPP costs are a *parasite on the profits* of IWC. Those costs must be reduced or eliminated as soon as possible. It is the constant task of the ISSO and staff to continuously look for methods to accomplish this objective.

How to Determine the Value of IWC Information

Determining the value of IWC's information is a very important task, but one that is seldom done with any systematic, logical approach by a company. However, the ISSO believed that in order to provide the program IWC required, this task should be undertaken.

The consequences of not properly classifying the IWC information could lead to overprotection, which is costly, or underprotection, which could lead to the loss of that information, and thus of profits.

To determine the value of information, the ISSO must first understand what is meant by *information* and what is meant by *value*. The ISSO must also know how to properly categorize and classify the information, and what guidelines are set forth by government agencies or businesses for determining the value and protection requirements of that information. In addition, how the information owners perceive the information and its value is crucial to classifying[4] it.

Why Is Determining Information Value Important?

If the information has value, it must be protected; protection is expensive. One should only protect that information which requires protection; only in the manner necessary based on the value of that information; and only for the period required.

The Value of Information

One might ask, "Does all the information of a company or government agency have value?" If you as the IWC ISSO were asked that question, what would be your response? The follow-on question would be "What information does *not* have value?" Is it that information which the receiver of

---

[4]In the context used here, the term *classify* has nothing to do with classification as it relates to national security information such as Confidential, Secret, and Top Secret.

the information determines has no value? When the originator of the information says so? Who determines whether information has value?

These are questions that the ISSO must ask—and answer—before trying to establish a process to set a value to any information. As you read through this material, think about the information where you work, how it is protected, why it is protected, etc.

The ISSO knows that a centralized approach would not work for valuing information, as every piece of information must be analyzed according to a specific criterion, identified according to a certain protective category, such as IWC Sensitive, and then marked and protected accordingly. The IWC ISSO knew that the best approach was to set the criteria and guidelines for the identification, marking, transmission, storage, and destruction of IWC information and have the information owners identify the information that they produce and, following the policy guidelines in the CIAPP, protect that information. Those criteria and requirements would be developed as part of the ISSO's project team that would also include various IWC department representatives, such as manufacturing, procurement, legal, security, finance, and planning.

The holder of the information may determine the value of the information. Each person places a value on the information in his or her possession. The information that is necessary to successfully complete a person's work is very valuable to that person; however, it may not be very valuable to anyone else. For example, to an accountant, the accounts payable records are very important, and without them, the accountants could not do their job. However, for the person manufacturing the company's product, that information has little or no value.

Ordinarily, the originator determines the value of the information, and that person categorizes or classifies that information, usually in accordance with the established guidelines.

Three Basic Categories of Information

Although there are no standard categories of information, most people agree that information can logically be categorized into three categories:

- Personal, private information;
- National security (both classified and unclassified) information (addressed in Chapter 12); and
- Business information.

Personal, private information is an individual matter, but also a matter for the government and businesses. People may want to keep private such information about themselves as their age, weight, address, cellular-phone number, salary, and likes and dislikes.

At the same time, many countries have laws that protect information under some type of "privacy act." In businesses and government agencies, it is a matter of policy to safeguard certain information about employees, such as their ages, addresses, and salaries. Therefore, this requirement (InfoSec driver) must be considered in developing the information value and protection policy and guidelines.

Although the information is personal to the individual, others may require that information. At the same time, they have an obligation to protect that information because it is considered to have value.

Business information also requires protection based on its value. At IWC, this information is sometimes categorized as follows:

- IWC Confidential;
- IWC Internal Use Only;
- IWC Private;
- IWC Sensitive;
- IWC Proprietary; and
- IWC Trade Secret.

The number of categories used will vary with each company; however, the fewer categories, the fewer problems in classifying information, and also, possibly, the fewer problems in the granularity of protection required. Again, this is a cost item consideration. The IWC ISSO has found that Private, Internal Use Only, and Proprietary would meet the needs of the IWC CIAPP.

This company information must be protected because it has value to the company. The degree of protection required is also dependent on the value of the information during a specific period of time.

Types of Valued Information

Generally, the types of information which have value to the business and which require protection include the following: All forms and types of financial, scientific, technical, economic, or engineering information including, but not limited to, data, plans, tools, mechanisms, compounds, formulas, designs, prototypes, processes, procedures, programs, codes, or commercial strategies, whether tangible or intangible, and whether stored, compiled, or memorialized physically, electronically, graphically, photographically, or in writing.

Examples of information requiring protection may include research, proposals, plans, manufacturing processes, pricing, and product.

Determining Information Value

Based on an understanding of information, its value, and some practical and philosophical thoughts on the topic as stated above, the ISSO must have some sense of what must be considered when determining the value of information.

When determining the value of information, the ISSO must determine what it cost to produce that information. Also to be considered is the cost in terms of damages caused to the company if it were to be released outside protected channels. Additional consideration must be given to the cost of maintaining and protecting that information. How these processes are combined determines the value of the information. Again, don't forget to factor in the time element.

There are two basic assumptions to consider in determining the value of information: (1) All information cost some type of resource(s) to produce, for example, money, hours, or use of equipment; and (2) not all information can cause damage if released outside protected channels.

If the information cost to produce (and all information does) and no damage is done if it is released, you must consider, "Does it still have value?" If it cost to produce the information, but it cannot cause damage if it is released outside protected channels, then why protect it?

The time factor is a key element in determining the value of information and cannot be overemphasized. Let's look at an example where information is not time dependent—or is it? There is a company picnic to take place on May 22, 2003. What is the value of the information before, on, or after that date? Does the information have value? To whom? When?

If you're looking forward to the company's annual picnic, as was your family, the information as to when and where it was to take place had some value to you. Suppose you found out about it the day after it happened. Your family was disappointed, they were angry at you for not knowing, you felt bad, etc. To the company, the information had "no value." However, the fact that the employee did not receive that information caused him to be disgruntled and blame the company for his latest family fight. Based on that, he decided to slow down his productivity for a week.

This is a simple illustration, but it indicates the value of information depending on who has and who does not have that information, as well as the time element. It also shows that what is thought to be information not worth a second thought may have repercussions costing more than the value of the information.

The following is another example: A new, secret, revolutionary widget built to compete in a very competitive marketplace is to enter the market on January 1, 2004. What is the value of that information on January 2, 2004?

Again, to stress the point, one must consider the cost to produce the information and the damage done if that information were released.

If it cost to produce and can cause damage if released, it must be protected. If it cost to produce, but cannot cause damage if released, then why protect it? At the same time, be sensitive to dissemination. Information, to have value, to be useful, must get to the right people at the right time.

Business Information Type and Examples

Types of *IWC Internal Use Only* information:

- Not generally known outside the company;
- Not generally known through product inspection;
- Possibly useful to a competitor; and
- Provides some business advantage over competitors.

Examples are the company telephone book; company policies and procedures; and company organizational charts.

Types of *IWC Private* information:

- Reveals technical or financial aspects of the company;
- Indicates company's future direction;
- Describes portions of the company business;
- Provides a competitive edge; and
- Identifies personal information of employees.

Examples are personnel medical records; salary information; cost data; short-term marketing plans; and dates for unannounced events.

Types of *IWC Sensitive* information:

- Provides significant competitive advantage;
- Could cause serious damage to the company; and
- Reveals long-term company direction.

Examples are critical company technologies; critical engineering processes; and critical cost data.

Questions to Ask When Determining Value

When determining the value of your information, you should, as a minimum, ask the following questions:

- How much does it cost to produce?
- How much does it cost to replace?
- What would happen if I no longer had that information?
- What would happen if my closest competitor had that information?

- Is protection of the information required by law, and if so, what would happen if I didn't protect it?

IWC INFOSEC FUNCTIONS PROCESS DEVELOPMENT

The ISSO has learned that the development of a new CIAPP requires the establishment of InfoSec functions for that program. Establishing a process for each function, as the first task, will assist in ensuring that the functions will begin in a logical, systematic way that will lead to a cost-effective CIAPP.

Requirements Identification Function

As previously stated, the ISSO has determined that the driver for any CIAPP-related function is the requirements for InfoSec function. The requirements are the reason for the CIAPP. This *need* is further identified and defined, and is subsequently met by the establishment of the InfoSec functions.

So, to begin the functions' process identification, it is important to understand where the requirements—where the need—comes from as seen from a slightly different perspective.[5] For IWC, it is as follows:

- A need for an InfoSec program (CIAPP) as stated by the IWC executive management to protect IWC's competitive edge, which is based on information systems and the information that they store, process, display, and transmit;
- Contractual requirements as specified in contracts with IWC customers, such as protecting customers' information;
- Contractual requirements as specified in contracts with IWC subcontractors, such as protecting subcontractors' information;
- Contractual requirements as specified in contracts with IWC vendors, such as protecting their information;
- IWC's desire to protect its information and systems from unauthorized access by customers and subcontractors, and vendors; and
- Federal, state and local laws which are applicable to IWC, such as requirements to protect the privacy rights of individuals and corpo-

---

[5] You may find that this driver–requirement, CIAPP–InfoSec functions topic is redundant. Ideally, it is, and you are beginning to get ingrained in your ISSO head that these are the basics that every ISSO should know and use as the baseline for leading and managing an information and systems protection program for a company or government agency. I hope that after reading this book, certain basic philosophies, such as the fact that InfoSec is a parasite on the profits, will be made an automatic part of any CIAPP type of program and InfoSec organizations you will lead and manage.

rations as they relate to the information stored, processed, and transmitted by IWC systems.

IWC ISSO'S INFOSEC FUNCTIONS

The ISSO has gone through the process previously noted to identify the baseline functions that are needed within the InfoSec organization in order to support the CIAPP, which as mentioned earlier supports IWC's business needs as stated in the IWC strategic, tactical, and annual business plans. The following paragraphs identify, describe, and discuss some of the functions identified by the IWC ISSO.

Awareness Program

The IWC ISSO decided to concentrate, as a high priority, on the IWC CIAPP Education Awareness and Training Program (CIAPP-EATP) as a major InfoSec organizational function and also as an integral part of the CIAPP. The CIAPP-EATP was needed to make the IWC users aware of the need as well as their responsibilities to protect IWC information and systems, as well as to gain the users' support in the protection of IWC information and systems.

The ISSO reasoned that once the IWC InfoSec policies of the CIAPP were developed and published, the employees must be made aware of them and also why they were necessary. For only with the full support and cooperation of the IWC employees could a successful CIAPP be established and maintained.

The Awareness Program process was broken into two major parts (Figure 8.2):

- Awareness Briefings; and
- Continuing Awareness Material.

Awareness Briefings

The awareness briefings included information relative to the need for information and systems protection; the impact of protecting and not protecting the systems and information; and an explanation of the IWC InfoSec Program.

The ISSO reasoned that the awareness material and briefings, when given as a general briefing could only be used for new employees. The general briefings failed to provide the specific information required by

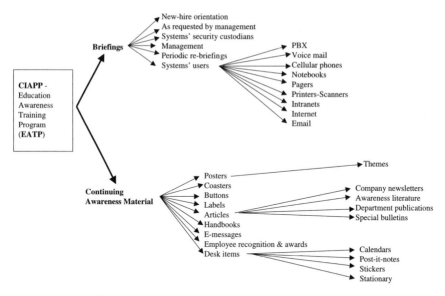

Figure 8.2 The flow process of IWC's CIAPP-EATP.

various groups of systems users. Thus, the awareness briefings were tailored to specific audiences as follows:

- All new hires, whether or not they used a system, the rationale being that they all handle information and come in contact with computer and telecommunication systems in one form or another;
- Managers;
- System users;
- Information Technology Department personnel;
- Engineers;
- Manufacturers;
- Accounting and Finance personnel;
- Procurement personnel;
- Human Resources personnel;
- Security and Audit personnel; and
- The system security custodians (those who would be given day-to-day responsibility to ensure that the systems and information were protected in accordance with the InfoSec policy and procedures).

A process was established to identify these personnel, input their profile information into a database, and, using a standard format, track their awareness briefing attendance, both their initial briefings and annual rebriefings. That information would also be used to provide them, through the IWC mail system, with awareness material.

Continuing Awareness Material

The ISSO, in concert with the Human Resources and Training staffs, decided that ensuring that employees were aware of their CIAPP responsibilities would require constant reminders. After all, information and systems protection is not the major function of most IWC employees. However, a way must be found to remind the employees that it is a *part* of their function.

It was decided that awareness material could be cost-effectively provided to the employees. This was accomplished by providing InfoSec material to the employees through:

- Annual calendars;
- Posters;
- Labels for systems and disks;
- Articles published in the IWC publications such as the weekly newsletter; and
- Logon notices and system broadcast messages, especially of InfoSec changes.

Although this CIAPP-EATP baseline was not all-inclusive, the ISSO believed that it was a good start that could be analyzed for cost-effective improvements at the end of the calendar year.

ACCESS CONTROL AND ACCESS CONTROL SYSTEMS

The ISSO determined that the access control and access control systems ranked as a high priority in establishing processes for the control of access to systems, as well as the access to the information stored, processed, and transmitted by those systems. Therefore, access controls were divided into two sections (see Figures 8.3 and 8.4):

- Access to systems; and
- Access to the information on the systems.

The ISSO reasoned that each department created and used the IWC systems and its information. Therefore, they should be responsible for controlling access to those systems and information.

The major systems such as IWC's wide-area network were owned and operated by the IT Department, while individual systems and LANs were owned and operated by the individual departments.

As part of the CIAPP, the IWC, in coordination with other departments' managers, established a process for all IWC employees who required access to the systems to perform their job functions. Such employees would

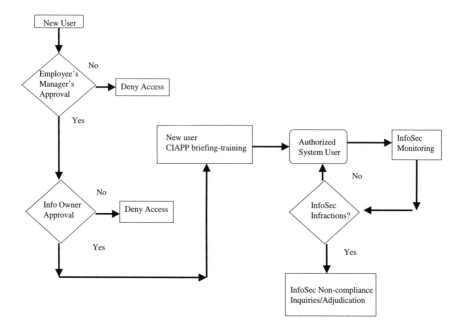

Figure 8.3   A baseline approach to information systems access control at IWC.

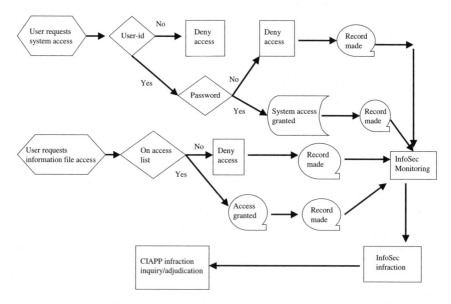

Figure 8.4   A baseline approach to information systems access control at IWC.

have to obtain system access approval from their manager and from the manager or designated representative of that system and/or information owner, such as for financial database access. The owners' approval was based on a justified need-for-access as stated by the employee's manager. If the system and/or information owners agreed, access was granted.

The ISSO had found, during the initial evaluation of the InfoSec of IWC, that departments had logically grouped their information into categories. They had done so to control access to their own files. This made it easy for the ISSO, because the managers of the departments agreed that once access to systems was granted by the system owners, access to the information on those systems should be approved by the owners of those groups of files, databases, etc.

Thus, the access control process included a justification by an employee's manager stating not only what systems and why they needed access to them, but also what information they required access to in order to perform their jobs.

For the most part, this was an easy and logical process. For example, in the Accounting Department, personnel generally had access to the groups of files and databases based on their job functions—accounts payable, accounts receivable, etc.

This access control process helped maintain an audit trail of who approved access to whom, and for what purposes. It also helped provide a separation of functions that are a vital component of any InfoSec program. For example, an accounts payable person should not also be the accounts receivable person and the invoice processing person. Such a system would allow one person too much control over a process that can be—and has been—used for committing fraud.

The benefits of the foregoing process to the ISSO were that it documented an informal process that for the most part had been in place, and it also placed InfoSec responsibilities for systems and information access exactly where it belonged, with the identified owners of the systems and information.

In one instance, an ISSO found that one manager did not want to take responsibility for a LAN in the department, and since others outside the department used the information, the manager did not want to take ownership of the information. The manager thought the IT Department should be the owner—after all, they were responsible for the maintenance of the system.

The ISSO in this case asked the manager if the ISSO could then be responsible as the owner of the systems and the information. The manager quickly agreed. The ISSO then told the manager that since it was now owned by the InfoSec organization, access would be denied to the systems and information to all those not in the InfoSec organization.

The manager objected, stating that the personnel in his organization needed access to those systems and their information in order to perform their job functions. After further discussion, the organizational manager agreed that his organization would appear to be the logical owners and subsequently accepted that responsibility.

Access Control Systems

The ISSO, in coordination with the IT, Security, and Audit Departments, determined that the access control systems (hardware and software) belonged to the same departments and organizations identified as system owners. However, the InfoSec personnel would establish the detailed procedures for the access control systems and the auditors would evaluate compliance with those procedures.

The system owners agreed to this process and also to appointing a primary and alternate system custodian who would be responsible for ensuring the IWC CIAPP policies and procedures were followed by all those who used the systems. In addition, the custodian would review the system audit trails, which were mandatory on all IWC systems.[6]

EVALUATION OF ALL HARDWARE, FIRMWARE, AND SOFTWARE

All new hardware, firmware, and software should be evaluated for its impact on the security of information and systems. This was determined to be necessary in joint agreement between the ISSO and the IT Department personnel, auditors, and security personnel.

In order to cost-effectively perform this function with minimal impact on cost and installation schedules, it was determined that a baseline checklist would be developed and that this checklist would be completed by the suppliers of the product, in concert with the InfoSec staff. Any items that adversely affected InfoSec would be evaluated based on a risk assessment, using the approved risk management and reporting process.

The process included completion of the baseline InfoSec checklist document, and a technical evaluation by InfoSec personnel in concert with IT personnel. If the item (hardware, software, etc.) was considered *risk-acceptable*, it was approved for purchase.

If the item was not risk-acceptable, the risk management process identified countermeasures. Although this process generally approves the

---

[6] At first the audit trails requirements were to be applied only to those IWC systems processing sensitive IWC information; however, it was quickly discovered that all the systems, because of their networking, fell under that category. IWC management agreed that the additional cost of such a requirement was beneficial to IWC based on the risks of loss of that information to internal or external threats.

purchase of almost all items, some items might have an unacceptable level of risk, but would still be accepted because of their value to the company. In those instances, special audit trails could be created to monitor the use of the item. In any case, the ISSO understood that it is always better to at least know that a system is vulnerable, than to not know the vulnerability existed until it was too late.

The ISSO identified the several potential processes relative to new, modified, or upgraded IWC systems' hardware, software, and firmware implementation where the protection of information and information systems could be subject to increased vulnerabilities (Figures 8.5, 8.6, and 8.7). The ISSO decided to form a project team to evaluate these and other processes. The project team would include ISSO's staff specialist as a project lead, as well as IT representatives, department representatives, procurement representative, contracts representative, and legal representative. These representatives were chosen for the following reasons:

- *IT*: They are responsible for the major systems, such as intranets and Internet interfaces.
- *Departments*: They are responsible for their own standalone systems, such as microcomputers, and for their own local area networks that are not connected outside the department.
- *Procurement*: They are responsible for ordering the hardware, software, and firmware.

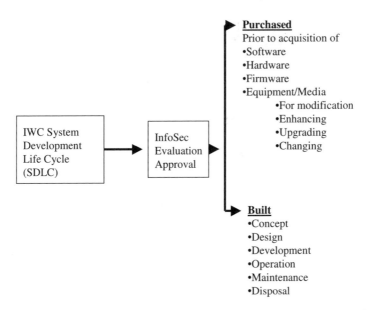

Figure 8.5 An overview of InfoSec input to a System Development Life Cycle (SDLC) process.

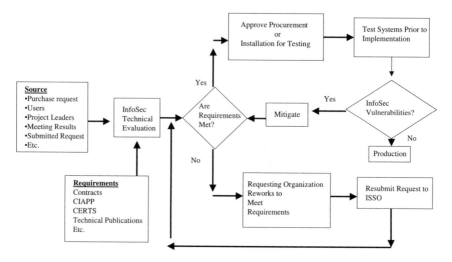

Figure 8.6   One view of the process of InfoSec technical evaluation and testing of a product for InfoSec vulnerabilities.

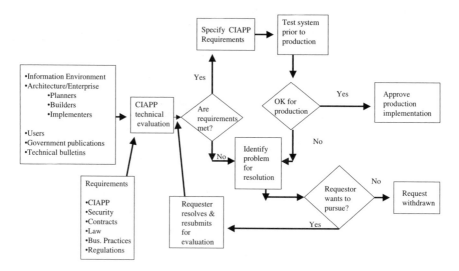

Figure 8.7   Another view of an InfoSec technical evaluation process.

- *Contracts*: They, based on ISSO coordination, include InfoSec-related specifications and clauses in the IWC contracts, such as software from a vendor certified free of malicious codes. Furthermore, if product is vulnerable or increases IWC systems' vulnerabilities, the contract may call for the vendor to patch the software or provide the source code for IWC programmers to patch the code.

- *Legal*: They are responsible for ensuring that all issues related to contracts and procurement matters mandating InfoSec criteria are stated in such a way as to ensure their enforcement through legal means.

RISK MANAGEMENT PROGRAM

The objective of IWC's risk management program is to *Maximize Security and Minimize Cost Through Risk Management.*

What Is Risk Management?

You may recall that the topic of risk management was discussed in Chapter 3. Because it is the baseline for all of the IWC ISSO's decisions relative to information and systems protection, the ISSO decided to formalize the function as an integral part of the CIAPP and the InfoSec organization.

The ISSO knew that for IWC employees, especially management, to understand the philosophy behind how InfoSec-related decisions were made, they should have some basic grasp of the risk management philosophy. Thus the ISSO directed that this topic be an integral part of the CIAPP and the CIAPP-EATP. The ISSO knew that in order to understand the risk management methodology, one must first understand what risk management means. The ISSO defined risk management as the total process of identifying, controlling, and eliminating or minimizing uncertain events that may affect system resources. It includes risk assessments; risk analyses, including cost–benefit analyses; target selection; implementation and test; security evaluation of safeguards; and overall InfoSec review.

The ISSO established as an objective of the risk management process *to provide the best protection of systems and the information they store, process, display, and/or transmit at least cost consistent with the value of the systems and the information.*

Risk Management Process

Remember that the CIAPP is an IWC program made up of professionals who provide service and support to their company. Therefore, the risk management process must be based on the needs of IWC customers.

Also, the ISSO wanted to be sure that the risk management concepts, program, and processes are informally and formally used in all aspects of the InfoSec program, including when and how to do awareness briefings and the impact of information systems security policies and procedures on the employees.

The following steps should be considered in the ISSO's process:

1. *Management interest*: Identify areas that are of major interest to executive management and customers; approach from a business point of view. So, the process should begin with interviews of your internal customers to determine what areas of InfoSec are adversely affecting their operations the most. Then, target those areas first as the starting point for the risk management program.
2. *Identify specific targets*: Software applications, hardware, telecommunications, electronic media storage, etc.
3. *Input sources*: Users, system administrators, auditors, security officers, technical journals, technical bulletins, CERT alerts (Internet), risk assessment application programs, etc.
4. *Identify potential threats*: Internal and external, natural or manmade.
5. *Identify vulnerabilities*: Through interviews, experience, history, testing.
6. *Identify risks*: Match threats to vulnerabilities with existing countermeasures, verify, and validate.
7. *Assess risks*: Acceptable or not acceptable, identify residual risk, then certify the process and gain approval. If the risks are not acceptable, then:

    - Identify countermeasures;
    - Identify each countermeasure's costs; and
    - Compare countermeasures, risks, and costs to mitigated risks.

Recommendations to Management

When the risk assessment is completed, the ISSO must make recommendations to management. Remember in making recommendations to think from a business point of view: cost, benefits, profits, public relations, etc.

Risk Management Reports

A briefing that includes a formal, written report is the vehicle to bring the risks to management's attention. The report should include identifying areas that need improvement; areas that are performing well; and recommended actions for improvement, including costs and benefits.

Remember that it is management's decision to either accept the risk or mitigate the risks, and how much to spend to do so. The ISSO is the specialist, the in-house consultant. It is management's responsibility to decide what to do. They may follow your recommendations, ignore them, or take some other action. In any case, the ISSO has provided the service and support required.

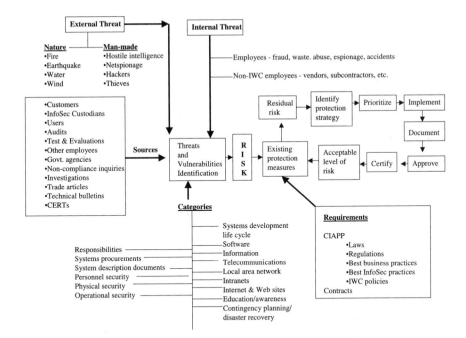

Figure 8.8   An overall risk management process.

If the decision is made that no action will be taken, there is still a benefit to conducting the analyses. The ISSO now has a better understanding of the environment, as well as an understanding of some of the vulnerabilities. This information will still help in managing an InfoSec program. The IWC ISSO developed a risk management process to be used as an overall baseline for implantation as part of the risk management philosophy for IWC (Figure 8.8).

SECURITY TESTS AND EVALUATIONS PROGRAM

The IWC ISSO saw the need for the Security Tests and Evaluations Program (ST&E) process once the IWC CIAPP processes of awareness, access control, and risk management were implemented.

The ST&E function's process was developed in order to incorporate testing and evaluating of total InfoSec processes, environments, hardware, software, and firmware, as a pro-active method to support risk assessments and the evaluations of the systems' components.

The ISSO believed that the auditors' compliance audits were more of a checklist process of ensuring compliance with IWC InfoSec policies and procedures. What was needed, the ISSO reasoned, was a process to actu-

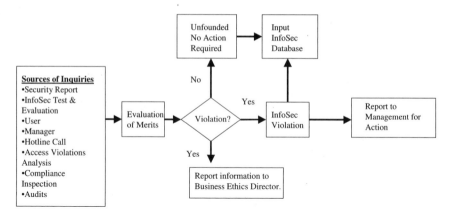

Figure 8.9   An overview of the NCI function.

ally test InfoSec processes, systems, etc., to determine whether they were meeting the InfoSec needs of IWC—regardless of whether or not they complied with the InfoSec policies and procedures.

For example, the ST&E would include periodically obtaining a userid on a system with various access privileges. The InfoSec staff member, using that identification, would violate that system and attempt to gain unauthorized access to various files, databases, and systems. That information was analyzed in concert with a comparison of the systems' audit trails, thus profiling the InfoSec of a system or network. Also, the ST&E would include a review of records and prior audit trail documents to help establish the "InfoSec environment" being tested and evaluated.

NONCOMPLIANCE INQUIRIES

Noncompliance inquiries (NCI) were identified as an ISSO responsibility and the process (Figures 8.9 and 8.10) developed by the InfoSec staff and coordinated with the audit and security management. The NCI process was as follows:

- Receive allegations of non-compliance by auditors, security personnel, managers, users, and generally anyone else.
- The allegation was evaluated and if not considered acceptable, filed.[7]

---

[7] The ISSO was sensitive to privacy issues and did not want to initiate an inquiry without substantiated information since someone may have a grudge against another and use the process to harass him or her.

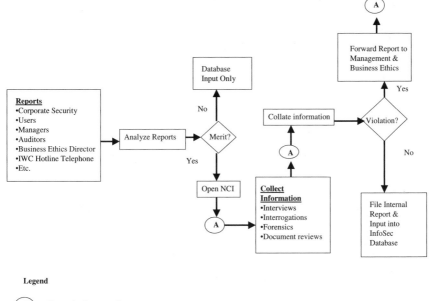

Legend

(A) = Determination to revoke user access

Figure 8.10 The NCI process where revocation of user access is a major consideration.

- If the allegation was substantiated, an inquiry was conducted. The inquiry included interviews, technical reviews, document reviews, etc.
- The information gathered was analyzed, collated, and provided in a formal report to management with copies to appropriate departments such as Security and Human Resources.
- The report was protected for reasons of privacy and also included recommendations and trend analyses to mitigate future occurrences.

CONTINGENCY AND EMERGENCY PLANNING AND DISASTER RECOVERY PROGRAM (CEP-DR)

A contingency planning and disaster recovery system is one of the least difficult programs to establish, and yet always seems to be a difficult task. With the change in information systems' environments and configurations—client–server, LAN, distributed processing, etc.—this problem may be getting worse.

Prior to discussing CEP-DR, it is important to understand why it is needed. It is really a very important aspect of an InfoSec program, and may even be its most vital part.

The ISSO must remember that the purpose of InfoSec is to:

- Minimize the probability of a security vulnerability;
- Minimize the damage if a vulnerability is exploited; and
- *Provide a method to recover efficiently and effectively from the damage.*

What Is It?

Contingency planning is making a plan for responding to emergencies, backup operations, and recovering after a disaster. It addresses what action will be taken to return to normal operations. Emergencies requiring action would include such natural events as floods and earthquakes, as well as human-caused acts such as fires, or hacker attacks causing denial of services.

Disaster recovery is the restoration of the information systems, facility, or other related assets following a significant disruption of services.

Why Do It?

Primarily users often ask the question, why is a CEP-DR program necessary? Everyone associated with using, protecting, and maintaining information systems and the information that they store, process, and/or transmit must understand the need for such a program:

- To assist in protecting vital information;
- To minimize adverse impact on productivity; and
- To support the business staying in business!

How Do You Do It?

Each CEP-DR program is unique to the environment, culture, and philosophy of each business or government agency. However, the basic program, regardless of business or agency, requires the development and maintenance of a CEP-DR plan. It must be periodically tested, problems identified and corrected, and processes changed to minimize the chances of adverse events happening again.

The CEP-DR Planning System

IWC's CEP-DR plan must be written based on the standard format used by IWC. The following generic format is offered for consideration:

1. *Purpose*: State the reason for the plan and its objective. This should be specific enough that it is clear to all that read it why it has been written.
2. *Scope*: State the scope and applicability of the plan. Does it include all systems, all locations, subcontractors?
3. *Assumptions*: State the priorities, the support promised, and the incidents to be included and excluded. For example, if your area does not have typhoons, will you assume that typhoons, as a potential disaster threat, will not be considered?
4. *Responsibilities*: State who is to be responsible for taking what actions. This should be stated clearly so everyone knows who is responsible for what. Consider a generic breakdown such as managers, systems administrators, users. Also, specific authority and responsibility should be listed by a person's title and not necessarily by that person's name. This approach will save time in updating the plan because of personnel changes.
5. *Strategy*: Discuss backup requirements and how often they should be accomplished based on classification of information; state how you will recover, etc.
6. *Personnel*: Maintain an accurate, complete, and current list of key CEP-DR personnel, including addresses, phone numbers, page numbers, and cellular-phone numbers. Be sure to establish an emergency prioritized, notification listing, and a listing of response teams members and how to contact them in an emergency.
7. *Information*: Maintain an on-site inventory listing and an off-site inventory listing; identify the rotation process to ensure a history and current inventory of files. Identify vital information. This information must come from the owner of that information and must be classified according to its importance, based on approved guidelines.
8. *Hardware*: Maintain an inventory listing, including supplier's name, serial number, and property identification number; ensure that emergency replacement contracts are in place; maintain hard copies of applicable documents on and off site.
9. *Software*: Identify and maintain backup operating systems and application systems software. This should include original software and at least one backup copy of each. Be sure to identify the version numbers, etc. In this way, you can compare what is listed in the plan with what is actually installed. It would not be a unique event if software backups were not kept current and compatible with the hardware. If this is the case, the systems might not be able to work together to process, store, and transmit much-needed information.
10. *Documentation*: All-important documentation should be identified, listed, inventoried, and maintained current in both on- and off-site locations.

11. *Telecommunications*: The identification and maintenance of telecommunications hardware and software listings are vital if you are operating in any type of network environment. Many systems today cannot operate in a standalone configuration; thus, the telecommunications lines, backups, schematics, etc., are of vital importance to getting back in operation within the time period required. As with other documentation, their identification, listing, etc., should be maintained at multiple on- and off-site locations. Be sure to identify all emergency requirements and all alternative communication methods.

12. *Supplies*: Supplies are often forgotten when establishing a CEP-DR plan, as they often take a back seat to hardware and software. However, listing and maintenance of vital supplies are required, including the name, address, telephone numbers, and contract information concerning suppliers. Be sure to store sufficient quantities at appropriate locations on and off site. If you don't think this is an important matter, try using a printer when its toner cartridge has dried out or is empty!

   Physical supplies for consideration should include plastic tarps to protect systems from water damage in the event of a fire where sprinkler systems are activated.

13. *Transportation and equipment* : If you have a disaster or emergency requiring the use of a backup facility or to obtain backup copies of software, etc., you obviously must have transportation and the applicable equipment (e.g., a dolly for hauling heavy items) to do the job. Therefore, you must plan for such things. List emergency transportation needs and sources; how you will obtain emergency transportation and equipment; and which routes and alternate routes to take to the off-site location. Be sure to include maps in the vehicles and also in the plan. Be sure there are fully charged, hand-held fire extinguishers available which will work on various types of fires, such as electrical, paper, or chemical.

14. *Processing locations*: Many businesses and agencies sign contractual agreements to ensure that they have an appropriate off-site location to be used in the event their facility is not capable of supporting their activities.

   Ensure that emergency processing agreements are in place that will provide you with priority service and support in the event of an emergency or disaster. Even then, you may have a difficult time using the facility if it is a massive disaster and others have also contracted for the facility.

   Be sure to periodically use the facility to ensure that you can process, store, and/or transmit information at that location. Don't forget to identify on-site locations that can be used or converted for use if the disaster is less than total.

15.   *Utilities*: Identify on-site and off-site emergency power needs and locations. Don't forget that these requirements change as facilities, equipment, and hardware change. Battery power and uninterruptable power might not be able to carry the load or might be too old to even work. They must be periodically tested. As with the printer cartridge supplies, systems without power are useless. Besides power, don't forget the air conditioning requirements. It would be important to know how long a system can process without air conditioning based on certain temperature and humidity readings.

16.   *Documentation*: Identify all related documentation; store it in multiple on- and off-site locations; and be sure to include the CEP-DR plan.

17.   *Other*: Miscellaneous items not covered above.

Test the Plan

Only through testing can the ISSO determine that a plan will work when required. Therefore, it must be periodically tested. It need not be tested all at once, because that would probably cause a loss of productivity by the employees which would not be cost-effective.

It is best to test the plan in increments, relying on all the pieces to fit together when all parts have been tested. Regardless of when and how you test the plan, which is a management decision, it must be tested. Probably the best way to determine how and what to test, and in what order, is to prioritize testing based on prioritized assets.

When testing, the scenarios used should be as realistic as possible. This should include emergency response; testing backup applications and systems; and recovery operations.

Through testing, document the problems and vulnerabilities identified. Determine why they occurred and establish formal projects to fix each problem. Additionally, make whatever cost-effective process changes are necessary to ensure that the same problem would not happen again, or that the chance of it happening is minimized.

The ISSO evaluated IWC organizational structure relative to IWC (Figure 8.11). After coordination with the Director of Security, a process was developed to integrate the ISSO and staff into the current CEP-DR process (Figure 8.12).

QUESTIONS TO CONSIDER

Based on what you have read, consider the following questions and how you would reply to them:

•   Do you believe that the basic requirements—drivers—discussed in this chapter are valid?

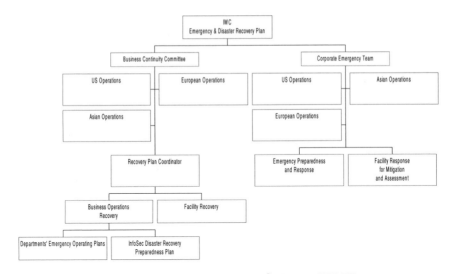

Figure 8.11   The IWC organization structure relating to CEP-DR.

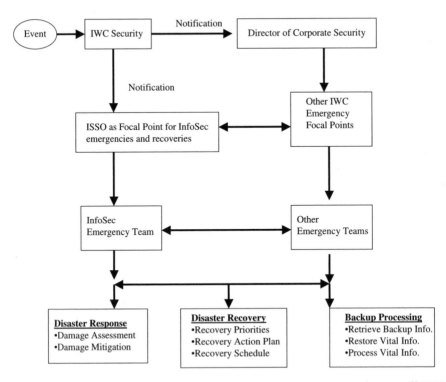

Figure 8.12   The basic process flow of the ISSO's integration into the overall IWC CEP-DR.

- Can you think of others that you would use as an ISSO?
- After the requirements are identified, in what order would you prioritize policies, procedures, plans, processes, functions, and processes?
- Why did you decide to prioritize each in the order noted?
- Do you have a process in place for valuing company information?
- If not, how do you know what to protect in a cost-effective manner?
- If you have such a process in place, is it current?
- Is it working?
- How do you know it is working cost-effectively?
- What are the functions that you as an ISSO believe are required to be a part of your InfoSec organization?
- Which ones are optional, and why?
- Which ones would never be authorized by management to be part of your InfoSec responsibilities?
- Do you use a formal, documented risk management philosophy?
- If not, how do you cost-effectively make InfoSec decisions?
- If so, is that philosophy shared with the employees so they can understand why certain InfoSec decisions are made?
- Are you an integral part of the company's CEP-DR processes?
- If not, should you be?
- If so, are you involved in testing the CEP-DR plans?
- After an emergency or disaster, are you involved in verifying and validating that all the security hardware, software, and firmware are operating in accordance with the CIAPP and security specifications?
- If not, how do you know they were even turned back on by IT personnel after the systems went offline and were brought back online again?

SUMMARY

It is crucial for an ISSO who is new to the corporation to evaluate the current InfoSec organizational structure, the staff, and their experience and education and ensure the organization is cost-effectively structured. The ISSO should consider the following points:

- Establishing the proper InfoSec functions in the right priority order is vital to establishing the InfoSec organization and CIAPP baseline.
- The InfoSec functional processes should generally follow the function descriptions noted in the ISSO's charter of responsibilities.
- Establishing a process to determine the categories of information identified by the general value of that information would assist in the development of a cost-effective CIAPP.
- Functions and processes should be developed based on requirements, such as laws and regulations.

- Flowcharts should be developed to help visualize the linkage between requirements; plans; vision, mission, and quality statements; policies; processes; and functions.

Note: Additional information on matters contained in this chapter is available on the Web site: http://www.shockwavewriters.com. Click on "Books," this book's cover icon, and then Chapter 8.

9

Establishing a Metrics Management System

Don't work harder—work smarter.—Ken Blanchard

CHAPTER OBJECTIVE

This chapter, "Establishing a Metrics Management System," is designed to provide basic guidance necessary for the development of a metrics methodology to understand what, why, when, and how InfoSec can be measured. Using the fictitious company (IWC) and functions that were previously described, a metrics system will be developed. It includes a discussion of how to use the metrics to brief management, justify budget, and use trend analyses to develop a more efficient and effective CIAPP.

INTRODUCTION

Some of the most common complaints ISSOs make are that management doesn't support them, and—as the famous comedian Rodney Dangerfield is known for saying—"I get no respect." Another complaint is that the cost and benefits of InfoSec cannot be measured.

As for the first two, you get support because you are being paid—and these days, more often than not, quite handsomely—and you have a budget that could have been part of corporate profits. Furthermore, respect is earned. Besides, if you want to be popular, you are definitely in the wrong profession.

One often hears management ask:

- "What is all this security costing me?"
- "Is it working?"
- "Can it be done at less cost?"
- "Why isn't it working?"

That last question often comes right after a successful denial of service attack or some other attacks on the corporate systems or Web sites. Of course, many ISSOs respond by saying that it can't be measured. That is often said out of the ISSO's ignorance of processes to measure costs or because the ISSO is too lazy to track costs.

The more difficult question to answer is, "What are the measurable benefits of a CIAPP and InfoSec functions that provide support under the CIAPP?" Of course, one could always use the well-worn-statement, "It can only be measured as a success or failure depending on whether or not there have been successful attacks against our systems." The truth is that many attacks go unnoticed, unreported by the users or IT people. Furthermore, separating attacks from "accidents" (human error) is usually not easy; however, metrics can help in the analyses.

What Is a Metric?

To begin to understand how to use metrics to support management of a CIAPP, it is important to understand what is meant by "metrics." For our purposes, a metric is defined as *a standard of measurement using quantitative, statistical, and/or mathematical analyses.*

What Is an InfoSec Metric?

An InfoSec metric is the application of quantitative, statistical, and/or mathematical analyses to measuring InfoSec functional trends and workload—in other words, tracking what each function is doing in terms of level of effort (LOE), costs, and productivity.

There are two basic ways of tracking costs and benefits. One is by using metrics relative to the day-to-day, routine operations of each InfoSec function. These metrics are called level of effort (LOE) and are the basic functions noted in the ISSO's charter of responsibilities and accountabilities. Examples would be daily analyses of audit trail records of a firewall; granting users access to systems; and conducting noncompliance inquiries. In more financial terms, these are the recurring costs.

The other way of tracking costs and benefits is through formal project plans. In other words, if the tasks being performed are not the normal LOE tasks, then they fall under projects. Remember that functions are never-ending, daily work, while projects have a beginning and ending date with a specific objective. In more financial terms, these are the nonrecurring costs.

So, in order to efficiently and effectively develop a metrics management program, it is important to establish that philosophy and way of doing business. Everything that an ISSO and staff do can be identified as fitting into one of these two categories: LOE or project.

What Is InfoSec Metrics Management?

InfoSec metrics management is the managing of a CIAPP and related InfoSec functions through the use of metrics. It can be used where managerial tasks must be supported for such purposes as backing the ISSO's position on budget matters, justifying the cost-effectiveness of decisions, or determining the impact of downsizing on providing InfoSec service and support to customers.

The primary process to collect metrics is as follows:

- Identify each InfoSec function[1];
- Determine what drives that function, such as labor (number of people or hours used), policies, procedures, and systems; and
- Establish a metrics collection process. The collection process may be as simple as filling out a log for later summarization and analysis. The use of a spreadsheet that can automatically incorporate InfoSec statistics into graphs is the preferred method. This will make it easier for the ISSO to use the metrics for supporting management decisions, briefings, etc.

The decision to establish a process to collect statistics relative to a particular InfoSec function should be decided by answering the following questions:

- Why should these statistics be collected?
- What specific statistics will be collected?
- How will these statistics be collected?
- When will these statistics be collected?
- Who will collect these statistics?
- Where (at what point in the function's process) will these statistics be collected?

By answering these questions for each proposed metric, the ISSO can better analyze whether or not a metrics collection process should be established for a particular function. This thought process will be useful in helping explain it to the InfoSec staff or management, if necessary. It will also help the ISSO decide whether or not the ISSO should continue maintaining that metric after a specific period of time. Since the IWC ISSO had

---

[1] It is assumed each function costs time, money, and use of equipment to perform.

begun with an analysis of InfoSec requirements (drivers) that led to identification of an ISSO charter that led to the identification of InfoSec functions with process flowcharts, the task of developing metrics will be much easier. That is because each step noted in the InfoSec functions' flowcharts can be a point of quantifying and qualifying costs of performing that specific function.

All metrics should be reviewed, evaluated, and reconsidered for continuation at the end of each year, or sooner—when a requirement changes, a function may also change. Remember that although the collection of the metrics information will help the ISSO better manage the InfoSec duties and responsibilities, a resource cost is incurred in the collection and maintenance of these metrics. These resources include:

- People who collect, input, process, print, and maintain the metrics for you;
- Time to collect, analyze and disseminate the information; and
- The hardware and software used to support that effort.

When using these metrics charts for management briefings, one must remember that the chart format and colors are sometimes dictated by management; however, which type of chart is best for analysis or presentation to management is probably up to the ISSO.

The ISSO should experiment with various types of line, bar, and pie charts. The charts should be kept simple and easy to understand. Remember the old saying, "A picture is worth a thousand words." The charts should need very little verbal explanation.

If the ISSO will use the charts for briefings, the briefing should only comment on the various trends. The reason for this is to clearly and concisely present the material, and not get bogged down in details which detract from the objective of the charts.

One way to determine whether the message of the charts is clear is to have someone look at each chart and describe what it tells him or her. If it is what the chart is supposed to portray, then no changes are needed. If not, the ISSO should then ask the viewer what the chart does seem to represent and what leads him or her to that conclusion. The ISSO must then go back to the chart and rework it until the message is clear and is exactly what the ISSO wants the chart to show. Each chart should have only one specific objective, and the ISSO should be able to state that objective in one sentence, such as "This chart's objective is to show that InfoSec support to IWC is being maintained without additional budget although the workload has increased 13%."

The following paragraphs identify some basic examples of InfoSec metrics that can be collected to assist an ISSO in managing a CIAPP and briefing the management on the CIAPP and the InfoSec organization. By the way, when establishing a briefing to management where the metrics

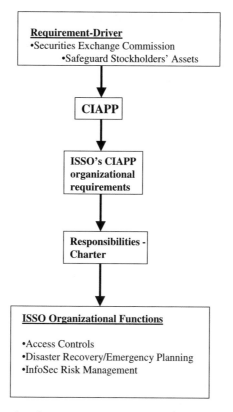

Figure 9.1 An example of tracing a requirement to a specific function.

charts will be used, a chart similar to Figure 8.1 (as shown in Chapter 8) should be used to start off the briefing. That chart tracks the requirements (drivers) which can be traced to each function. One may also want to provide more detailed charts tracking specific requirements to specific functions (Figure 9.1).

Of course, as the ISSO, you would want to get more specific and track to a more detailed level of granularity. In fact, the InfoSec staff responsible for leading a specific function should be tasked with developing this chart or charts. That way, the staff will know exactly why they are doing what they do. The next step would be for them to track their workflow, analyze it, and find more efficient ways to do the job. At the same time they would also look at current costs and cost-savings as more efficient ways are found to successfully accomplish their jobs.

The ISSO must remember that the use of metrics is a tool to support many of the ISSO's decisions and actions; however, it is not perfect. Therefore, the ISSO must make some assumptions relative to the statistical data to be collected. That's fine. The ISSO must remember that metrics is not rocket science, only a tool to help the ISSO take better-informed actions and make better-informed decisions. So, the ISSO should never get carried away with the hunt for "perfect statistics," or become so involved in metrics data collection that "paralysis by analysis" takes place.[2]

The spreadsheets and graphs used for metrics management can become very complicated with links to other spreadsheets, elaborate 3-D graphics, etc. That may work for some, but the ISSO should consider the KISS (Keep It Simple, Stupid) principle when collecting and maintaining metrics. This is especially true if the ISSO is just getting started and has no or very little experience with metrics. One may find that the project leads who are developing an "automated statistical collection" application are expending more hours developing the application—which never seems to work quite right—than it would take to manually collect and calculate the statistical information.

It is also important, from a managerial viewpoint, that all charts, statistics, and spreadsheets be done in a standard format. This is necessary so that they can be ready at all times for reviews and briefings to upper management. This standard is indicative of a professional organization and one that is operating as a focused team.

ISSOs who are new to the ISSO position, or management in general, may think that this is somewhat ridiculous. After all, what difference does it make as long as the information is as accurate as possible and provides the necessary information? This may be correct, but in the business environment, standards, consistency, and indications of teaming are always a concern of management. Your charts are indicative of those things.

The ISSO has a hard enough job getting and maintaining management support. The job should not be made more difficult than it has to be.

Another negative impact of nonconformance of format will be that the attendees will discuss the charts and not the information on them. Once "nonconformance to briefing charts standards" is discussed, management has already formed a negative bias. Thus, anything presented will make it more difficult to get the point across, gain the decision desired, and meet the established objective of the briefing.

It is better just to follow the established standards than to argue their validity. It is better to save energy for arguing for those things that are more important. After all, one can't win, and the ISSO does not want to be seen as "a non-team player" more than necessary.

Of course the number, type, collection methods, etc., that the ISSO will use will be dependent on the environment and the ISSO's ability to cost-effectively collect and maintain the metrics.

---

[2]Dr. Kovacich had used approximately 47 metrics charts at various times to assist in managing several large CIAPPs and InfoSec organizations.

METRICS 1: INFOSEC LOE DRIVERS—NUMBER OF USERS

There are two basic InfoSec LOE drivers within an organization, that is, those things that cause the InfoSec workload to be what it is, increasing or decreasing. The two basic drivers are:

- The number of systems which fall under the purview of the CIAPP and ISSO's overall responsibility for protection; and
- The number of users of those systems.

A question that must be asked is: Why are these metrics worth tracking? They are worth tracking because they drive the InfoSec workload—the LOE—which means they drive the number of hours that the InfoSec staff must expend in meeting their InfoSec responsibilities relative to those systems and users.

As the number of users on IWC networks changes or the number of systems changes, so does the workload; therefore, so does the number of staff required and the amount of budget required—time to do the job. For example, assume that IWC is downsizing—a common occurrence, which ISSOs will eventually face in their InfoSec careers. If the ISSO knows that IWC will downsize its workforce by 10%, and assuming that the workforce all use computers, which is not unusual in today's corporations, the workload should also decrease about 10%. This may cause the ISSO to also downsize (lay off staff) by approximately 10%.

However, the downsizing, whether it is more or less than the IWC average, should be based on the related InfoSec workload. The InfoSec drivers are metrics that can help the ISSO determine the impact of the IWC downsizing on the CIAPP and InfoSec organization. The metrics associated with that effort can also justify downsizing decisions to IWC management—to include possibly downsizing by 5% or 12% instead of 10%. For example, more layoffs may mean more CIAPP-related infractions, which means an increase in noncompliance inquiries, and thus an increase in the workload. Massive layoffs would also mean more work for those who are responsible for deaccessing employees from the systems prior to employment terminations. The metrics can show this work increase and make a case to management for not laying off InfoSec staff until after the other major layoffs have occurred.

Charting LOE through Number of System Users

As an ISSO, you decided that it would be a good idea to use the driver's metric that is used for tracking the number of system users. You have gone through the analytical process to make that decision based on answering the why, what, how, when, who, and where questions.

Why Should These Statistics Be Collected?

The driver's metric which tracks the number of system users for which the ISSO has InfoSec responsibility is used to assist in detailing the needed head-count budget for supporting those users. As an example, the following functions are charted based on the number of IWC system users (Figure 9.2):

- Access control violations;
- Noncompliance inquiries; and
- Awareness briefings.

What Specific Statistics Will Be Collected?

- Total users by location and systems; and
- Total systems by location and type.

How Will These Statistics Be Collected?

- The total number of users will be determined by totaling the number of userids on each network system and adding to it the number of standalone systems. It is assumed that each standalone system has only one user.
- Standalone microcomputers and networked systems (which will count as one system) will be identified and totaled using the

Total Users of IWC Networks World-Wide - 2002

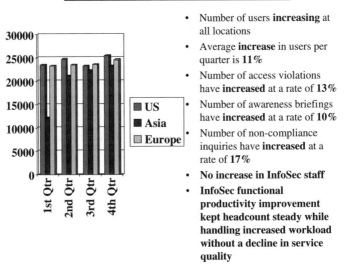

- Number of users **increasing** at all locations
- Average **increase** in users per quarter is **11%**
- Number of access violations have **increased** at a rate of **13%**
- Number of awareness briefings have **increased** at a rate of **10%**
- Number of non-compliance inquiries have **increased** at a rate of **17%**
- **No increase in InfoSec staff**
- **InfoSec functional productivity improvement kept headcount steady while handling increased workload without a decline in service quality**

Figure 9.2 Use of a metrics chart to show how the ISSO and staff are performing their jobs in an efficient manner without a loss of quality service and support.

approved system documentation on file within the InfoSec organization on the approved systems database. At IWC, all systems processing sensitive IWC information, falling within the categories
previously identified at IWC for identifying information by its value,
must be approved by the ISSO (designated InfoSec staff members).
Therefore, data collection is available through InfoSec organization's
records.

When Will These Statistics Be Collected?

The statistics will be compiled on the first business day of each month and
incorporated into the Metrics 1, InfoSec Drivers graph, maintained on the
InfoSec department's administrative microcomputer.

Who Will Collect These Statistics?

The statistics will be collected, inputted, and maintained by the project
leaders responsible for each InfoSec function, such as system accesses and
system approvals.

Where (at What Point in the Function's Process) Will These Statistics Be Collected?

The collection of statistics will be based on the information available and
on file in the InfoSec organization through close of business on the last
business day of the month.

Of course the number of system users affects all InfoSec functions;
however, Figure 9.2 is just an example of how the ISSO may want to depict
the InfoSec workload. Follow-on charts would show the workload relative
to the other InfoSec functions that are affected. The bold fonts are used to
highlight important facts that the ISSO wants to emphasize—management's eyes are naturally drawn to bold fonts.

Significance of the System Users Chart

The number of system users is also a driver of InfoSec workload because
the InfoSec functions' level of effort (LOE) and some projects are based on
the number of users. They include the following:

* The InfoSec staff provides access controls for users;
* The number of noncompliance inquiries will probably increase based
  on the increased number of users;
* The number of noncompliance inquiries may actually increase when
  IWC downsizes because of more hostility among the employees (a
  metrics charts showing caseload may help in defending ISSO staff

from more drastic layoffs than may have been required by management);

- The time to review audit trail records will increase as a result of more activity because of more users; and
- The number of awareness briefings and processing of additional awareness material will increase as a result of an increase in users.

Remember that as an ISSO you are also an InfoSec "salesperson" and must effectively advertise and market information and systems protection to IWC personnel. The chart noted in Figure 9.2 and similar charts can be used by the ISSO for the following:

- Justify the need for more budget and other resources;
- Indicate that the CIAPP is operating more efficiently because the budget and other resources have not increased although the number of systems has increased; and
- Help justify why budget and other resources cannot be decreased.

The "Total Users of IWC Networks World-Wide—2002" chart (Figure 9.2) is one of many that can be used to brief management on systems' users, and also for the ISSO to use internally to manage the InfoSec organization. A similar chart (Figure 9.3), related to Figure 9.2 and showing InfoSec LOE systems, is also useful for briefing management for example, on head count and budget matters.

When deciding to develop metrics charts to track workload, efficiency, costs, etc., of that function, always start at the highest level and then develop charts at lower levels (in more detail) that support the overall

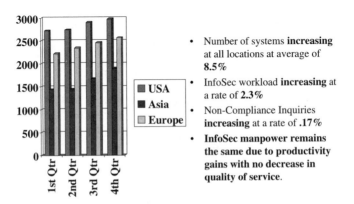

Figure 9.3   The number of IWC systems, a main InfoSec budget driver.

chart. This is done for several purposes. The ISSO may have limited time to brief a specific audience, and if it is an executive management briefing, the time will be shorter, as usually their attention span is short when it comes to InfoSec matters. So, the "top-down" approach will probably work best. If you have time to brief in more detail, the charts are available. If executive management has a question relative to some level of detail, then the other charts can be used to support the ISSO statements and/or position in reply to the question of the audience. Other systems' users-related charts flow from the main chart (Figure 9.4).

Granting Users Access to Systems

A major InfoSec service and support function is to add new users to systems and to provide them new access privileges as directed by their management and information owners.

As part of that service and support effort, the ISSO wants to ensure that these users are given access as quickly as possible, because without their access or new access privileges, the users cannot perform their jobs.

If users cannot gain expeditious access, then the CIAPP is costing IWC in terms of lost productivity of IWC employees or even possibly lost revenue in other forms.

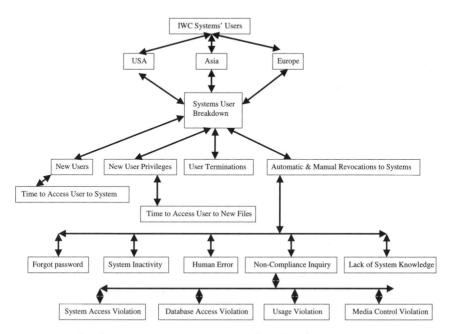

Figure 9.4 The flow of metrics charts related to the system users chart (Figure 9.2). Each box identifies a potential additional metric chart.

The ISSO, in coordination with the InfoSec staff responsible for the access control function, evaluated the access control process and determined that users should be given access within 24 hours of receipt of a request from management.

The ISSO decided to track this process because of its high visibility. Nothing can damage the reputation of the ISSO and staff faster than a hostile manager whose employees cannot get systems access to be able to do their work, leading, for example, to increased costs due to lost department productivity caused by the slowness of accessing employees to systems. In order to develop a metrics chart, one should first create a flowchart of the function. Then the ISSO can identify statistical collection points for metrics management charts (Figure 9.4).

Anything worth doing does not have to be done perfectly—at first.—Ken Blanchard

EXAMPLES OF OTHER METRICS CHARTS

There are numerous metrics charts that can be developed to support the various needs of the ISSO. The following are examples of some of those charts.[3]

The ISSO may also use this information when budget cuts are required. The chart can be shown to management and modified to show what would happen if the staff were cut one person, two people, etc. In other words, the average users' initial access to systems in terms of turnaround time would increase. Management may or may not want to live with those consequences. The cost can be quantified by taking the average hourly wage of the employee, identifying how much productivity time is lost with access coming within 1 business day, and comparing that to time lost if access, because an access control person has been laid off, takes 2 business days.

For example, an employee earns $15 an hour. The employee shows up at the desk of an access controller at the start of the business day, 8 A.M. That employee is authorized system access by 8 A.M. the next day. This loss of at least 8 hours of productivity at $15 an hour would be the normal cost of the InfoSec function of access control, or $120 per employee. However, if the access were not authorized until the day after, the costs per employee would be $240.

The chart can show the ISSO where staff cuts can be made and still meet the expected goals. The ISSO can also use this information when

---

[3]The reader should try developing other metrics charts and also, using the examples, determine how they could be used to support ISSO requirements; to determine successes and failures of the CIAPP; and to support briefings.

deciding to reallocate resources (transfer a person) to another function where the goals are not being met, and where the fastest way to meet the goal is to add head count. A word of caution here—adding or decreasing head count is usually considered a fast, simple solution. However, it is not always the answer.

> Sometimes when the numbers look right the decision is still wrong!—Ken Blanchard and Norman Vincent Peale

Many project leaders and ISSOs have found over the years that projects and level-of-effort problems are not always solved by assigning more bodies to solving the problem. One should first look at the process and at systemic problems. This is usually a more cost-effective approach to solving these types of problems. For example, using the example of the newly hired employee getting first-time system access, suppose a way was found to cut that time down to 1 hour. The costs saving would be from the normal $120 to $15, or a saving of $105 per new employee. Such charts can be used for management briefings and will show specifically how the ISSO and staff are lowering InfoSec costs, at least for that particular InfoSec function.

Samples of Noncompliance Inquiry Charts

Examples of this kind of chart are given in Figures 9.5 through 9.7.[4] These charts typically show infractions by individual departments (Figure 9.7). That means each department's vice president will internally compare his or her department against the others, thereby causing a covert competition to begin. Vice presidents do not want their departments to look bad, and because of their competitive nature, the vice-presidents will push to have a "zero" for each month. Each will want to know exactly what the individual NCIs were for. The ISSO must be prepared to answer them—using individual charts per department. Is this a lot of work? Yes. However, the benefits are that each department's vice-president will be pushing to have zero noncompliance inquiries conducted, which means the vice presidents will be overt supporters of the CIAPP and will push their staff to follow the CIAPP.

It also often leads to the ISSO joining the staff meetings of the departments' vice presidents and presenting the individual analyses of each department and sub-department. The ISSO should also then be in a position to explain what can be done to minimize these infractions, as well as minimize the loss of productivity, and thus dollars, caused by each

---

[4] Although these and all charts are published in this book in black and white, it is assumed that the ISSO's charts would be in color.

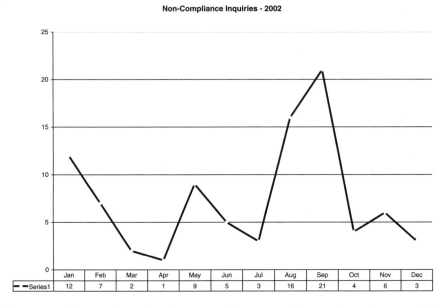

Figure 9.5   The total number of noncompliance inquiries conducted by month for the year 2002.

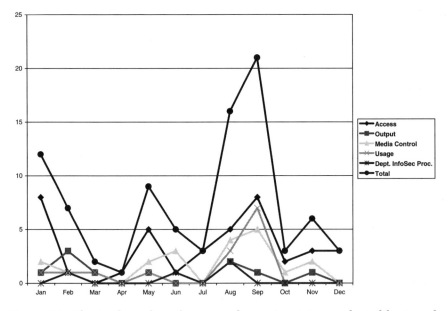

Figure 9.6   The total number of noncompliance inquiries conducted by type for the year 2002.

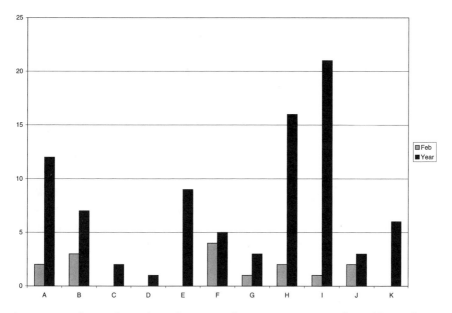

Figure 9.7   The total number of noncompliance inquiries conducted by each IWC department for the month of February, and the total of all departments for the period January and February 2002.

infraction. Showing the cost in lost productivity in hours per noncompliance inquiry will have a major impact on the staff. This can then also be linked to losses in terms of budget using an average IWC salary or hourly wage, which can often be gotten from the Finance or Human Relations staff.

The ISSO should also take to these briefings one or more of the InfoSec staff who have some responsibility for the information presented. This lets the staff members see how their work affects IWC department personnel. It also helps them become part of the entire process of working the InfoSec issues—and it is an opportunity for the ISSO to show confidence and support for InfoSec staff. By no means should they be used as a scapegoat or allowed to be the target of abuse by managers defensively rationalizing that a noncompliance inquiry was groundless, should not have been conducted, or the like. The ISSO should at all times take the blame and give the credit to InfoSec staff members. Furthermore, the ISSO must keep the focus of the meeting on the material being briefed and must discuss the numbers. The meeting should never be allowed to become a "finger-pointing" and inquiring report critique. This is not often easy to do as the department managers try to defend themselves. The meeting objective and ground rules for discussion should be stated in advance by the ISSO if the vice president does not so state.

The primary use of a chart like the one in Figure 9.8 is for the ISSO to understand the workload of one of the InfoSec functions. By looking at the number of inquiries opened, closed, and pending per month, the ISSO can, for example, determine whether the staff member conducting the inquiry requires additional staff support. The turnaround time of these inquiries is important—the sooner an inquiry is completed, the sooner, the employee's manager, in concert with IWC Human relations staff, can take whatever action is deemed appropriate. This is crucial if the person may be subject to termination or if the employee's system access had been suspended pending completion of the inquiry and the adjudication process.

As with all metrics charts, a decision must also be made whether to collect the data monthly, quarterly, semiannually, annually, or somewhere in between. The time period will depend on several factors. These include, but are not limited to:

- What they will be used for, such as monthly or annual executive briefings;
- Budget justifications;
- InfoSec staff functions resource allocations; and
- The objectives of each chart.

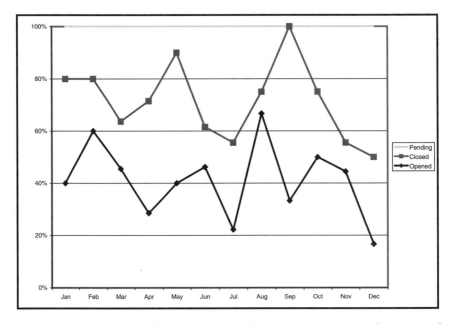

Figure 9.8 The total number of noncompliance inquiries opened per month, closed per month, and pending per month.

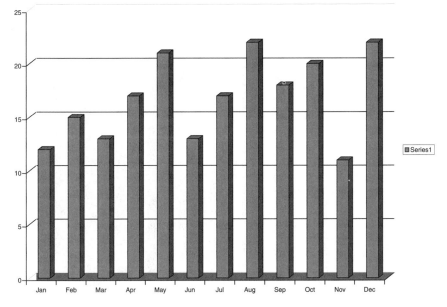

Figure 9.9   The average time spent in hours per noncompliance inquiry.

A subchart of this chart may be the average time spent, in hours, per type of inquiry (Figure 9.9). Once the time elements are known, they can be equated to productivity gains and losses, as well as budget, such as money, equipment, and staff.

InfoSec Tests and Evaluations

The ISSO decides to establish a process that will provide guidelines on the need, establishment, and implementation of metrics charts. The ISSO uses an InfoSec function to develop the process—the methodology—with the following results:

- IWC InfoSec will conduct security tests and evaluations (ST&E) as prescribed by IWC InfoSec policies and procedures.
- Results of IWC InfoSec ST&E will be charted.
- Each chart will be evaluated to determine whether a pattern/trend exists.
- Patterns/trends will be evaluated to determine how effectively a function is being performed.
- Results and recommendations will be presented, in accordance with InfoSec policies and procedures, to the applicable managers.

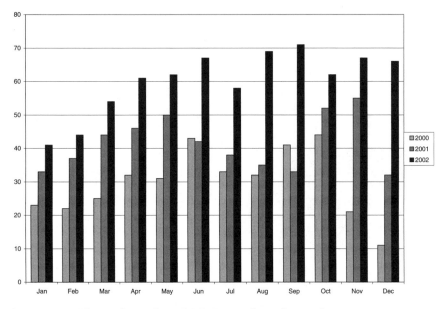

Figure 9.10 The total number of ST&Es conducted over the past 3 years.

Another InfoSec function that provides opportunities for using metrics management techniques is the function of InfoSec ST&E. The charts in Figures 9.10 through 9.12 are samples of metrics management charts that may be of use to an ISSO.[5]

Figure 9.10 is a useful chart in that it shows an increase in workload over time that can be compared with staffing for that function over time. The ISSO may consider a reallocation of staff because of the increased workload. Also to be considered is whether or not to change the ST&E process. One consideration is to conduct fewer ST&Es. If one does that, it would be important to monitor the number of noncompliance inquiries, as they may go up. For example, fewer ST&Es may result in increased systems vulnerabilities, which may in turn lead to more successful attacks, and thus to more noncompliance inquiries. Another factor the ISSO may consider is doing more ST&Es using automated InfoSec software to replace some currently manual testing.

One can also consider providing training to IWC department staff so they can do their own ST&Es and provide reports to the ISSO. This is usually not a good idea, as the objectivity of the testing may be question-

---

[5] For those readers trying to match numbers between charts and subcharts, you might as well know now that the numbers for each chart are arbitrarily assigned and do not reflect any consistency throughout. They are given as samples only. If you are looking for "real" numbers, you are missing the point of this chapter—the process and thinking behind metrics management of InfoSec functions.

able. For example, they may find vulnerabilities but not report them, because they do not want to incur the costs in time and budget to mitigate the risks identified by these vulnerabilities. In addition, as far the IWC as a whole is concerned, one is only passing on the costs in terms of allocation of resources to conduct the ST&Es to another department and not decreasing overall IWC CIAPP costs.

Remember that IWC is a global corporation with plants and offices on three continents. Since the ISSO has overall CIAPP and InfoSec functional responsibility for all locations, a process must be put in place for metrics management at all locations. The CIAPP-InfoSec functional leads at all the locations would provide the statistics and charts for their locations (Figure 9.11).

These statistics would be indicators in establishing InfoSec functional resource allocations based on the "worst" locations (Figure 9.12).

The issue that will often come up when designing charts is what type of charts to use—bar, line, pie, etc. The choice should be to use the format that meets the chart's objective in the most concise and clear way.

An ISSO sometimes comes across numbers that are out of balance with each other, e.g. 135 satisfactory ST&E ratings, 13 marginal. If the chart

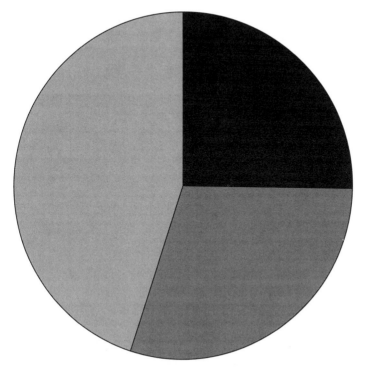

Figure 9.11   The number of ST&Es conducted per location in 2002.

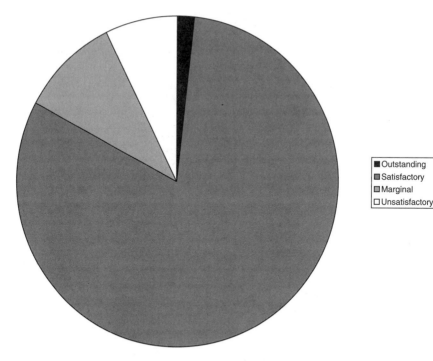

Figure 9.12 The ratings (Outstanding, Satisfactory, Marginal, Unsatisfactory) of ST&Es conducted within the corporate office in the year 2002.

chosen were a line chart or a bar chart, the smaller number would be so dwarfed as to be unreadable. In this case, the pie chart may be the solution.

The other solution may be to label each point in the chart with its number. For example, the bar or line designating 13 marginal ratings would have the number 13 over that point in the chart. This may give the perception that the marginal ratings were somewhat meaningless. However, as an ISSO, you are aware that is not the case, and in fact, indicates increased vulnerabilities to successful attack on those systems. The pie chart, on the other hand, shows that the number is small, but it at least appears large on the graph. The audience will see that number as being at least more significant than the same number shown on a line or bar chart.

InfoSec Education and Awareness Training

The CIAPP's InfoSec Education and Awareness Training Program (EATP) is one of the major baselines of the CIAPP. It follows that it is an integral part of the ISSO's InfoSec organization. It doesn't matter whether briefings, training and such are given by an InfoSec staff member, the IWC Training Office, the Director of Security's security training personnel, Human Resources new-hire briefings, or a combination of any of these organizations. It is a CIAPP, and therefore an InfoSec cost, and it should be metrics-managed.

For the purposes of this chapter on metrics management, let us assume that one of the ISSO's InfoSec staff is responsible for the EATP. At least two major metrics charts should be maintained (Figures 9.13 and 9.14).

Let's assume that to be somewhat cost-effective, the goal is to have at least 15 employees on average attend each briefing. That being the case, this metrics chart or another like it would show not only the number of briefings and the total attendees, but also the average number of attendees per briefing. In addition, a straight line could be included at 15 so that the average attendees per briefing can easily be compared against the goal of 15 employees per briefing. Lost? OK, let make it easy. See Figure 9.14.

If the goal was not being reached, as the ISSO, you might want to discuss the matter with your InfoSec leader for the EATP. Certainly if the goal is not being met, you can't and obviously shouldn't ignore it. There is nothing worse than setting a goal, metrics managing to attain that goal, and then ignoring it when it is not being met. Furthermore, as an ISSO you shouldn't just wait until the end of the year to attempt to correct the

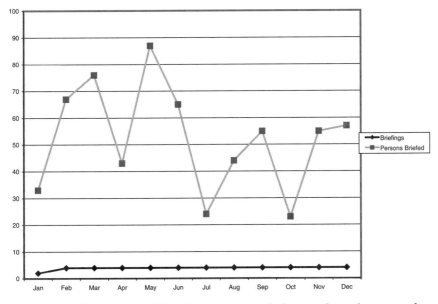

Figure 9.13 The number of briefings given and the number of personnel per briefing.

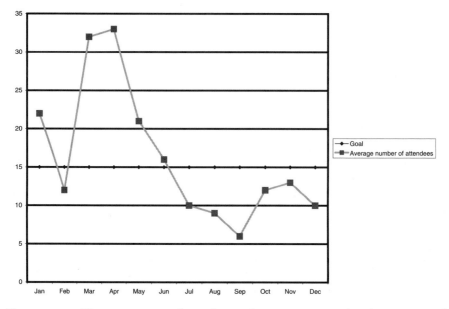

Figure 9.14   The average number of attendees per SEATP briefing measured against the goal of at least 15 personnel per briefing.

matter in discussion with your EATP lead, and then zap that person in his or her year-end performance evaluation.

Let us assume that employees must attend an annual briefing relative to the CIAPP and their duties and responsibilities. Assume that they prepare to attend the briefing and walk to the briefing room, and that it takes 15 minutes. They attend a 1-hour briefing and return to their place of work for a total time of 90 minutes. At an average employment rate of $15 per hour, each employee's time (and lost productivity, since they are not performing the work for which they were hired) for the annual briefing is $22.50. Let's also suppose that IWC employs 100,000 people worldwide and all of them must attend the annual briefing. That means that the annual briefing program, excluding the time the InfoSec specialist takes in preparing the updated material each year and other expenses, costs an astounding $2,250,000!

Figure 9.15 shows one type of category; however, there are others. For example, the ISSO may want to track the number of personnel briefed by such categories as InfoSec systems custodians, general users, subcontractors, Asian offices, European office, and U.S. offices.

One can argue that the briefings are necessary, they save money in the long run because valuable IWC is protected, and all that. However, that does not change the fact that this is a rather costly program. In fact, there is no indication that the cost–benefits have ever been validated. Yet, every

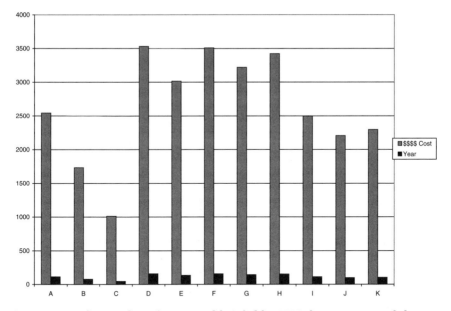

Figure 9.15   The number of personnel briefed by IWC departments and the costs of the briefings in each department, such as lost productivity equated to dollars of time.

ISSO knows that employee awareness of the threats, vulnerabilities, and risks to information and information systems is an absolute necessity. So, what can be done to lower the cost of such a program?

Using the project team approach the ISSO should establish a project team to look at the costs, benefits, and risks of not having an annual briefing and other methods for providing awareness to employees. Possibly the use of e-mails, online briefings, and other electronic means could eliminate the need for the employees to physically attend a briefing. Possibly briefings could be eliminated or online bulletins used.

Cost Avoidance Metrics

As an ISSO, you may want to use the metrics management approach to be able to quantify the savings of some of your decisions. For example, when analyzing your budget and expenditures, you note that a major budget item is travel costs for your staff. This is logical, because staff, as well as you, must travel to the various IWC offices to conduct InfoSec tests and evaluations.

Again, using the project management approach, you lead a project team of yourself, staff members, and a representative from the Contract

Office and Travel Office. Your goal is to find ways to cut travel costs while still meeting all the CIAPP and your charter responsibilities. A representative from the Contract Office will advise the project team on contractual obligations and way in which they can be met with less travel, but without violating the terms of the contracts. The Travel Office will give advice on ways to cut travel costs. For example, because many trips are known well in advance, flights and hotels can also be booked in advance.

The project team came up with some valid changes in the processes the InfoSec staff uses as part of their travel budget. Figure 9.16 was developed to track the savings based on the process changes.

Metrics Management and Downsizing

All ISSOs at one time or another in their careers face the need to downsize— that is, lay off, fire, or terminate—InfoSec staff. However, if you are operating at peak efficiency and have not built any excess staff into meeting your charter responsibilities, you may be able to make a case for not terminating staff, or terminating fewer personnel.

Many managers, and ISSOs are no exception, tend to forget that they are hired to do a job, and that job is not to build an "empire" or bureaucracy. The key to success is getting the job done efficiently and effec-

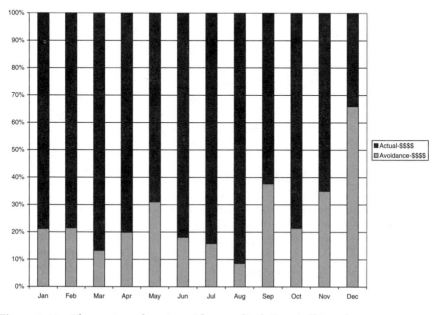

Figure 9.16 The costs and cost avoidance of InfoSec staff travel.

tively—as we said before, good and cheap. Besides, the more staff members and the larger the budget you have, the more people problems you will have and the harder the financial people will try to take some of your budget. So you are constantly battling to maintain your large budget.

If, on the other hand, you have a small staff and a smaller budget, you have a better chance of protecting what you have, because it is the minimum needed to get the job done. That approach coupled with metrics management techniques and periodic briefings to executive management will help you continue to get the job done as you deem appropriate, even though other organizations are losing staff.

Let's look at some figures showing various ways of presenting information based on metrics management's data collection efforts:

The LOE versus project support chart in Figure 9.17 clearly shows that the InfoSec organization has been supporting the projects of other IWC departments and that the workload is not "nice-to-have" projects. These are projects that require the support of the ISSO and InfoSec staff. It also shows that the ISSO and staff are an integral part of major IWC projects and are functioning as part of their service and support duties.

Taking this chart as an example, similar charts can then be developed using the same template but showing the workload per function versus budgeted hours for each function, such as SEATP and ST&E.

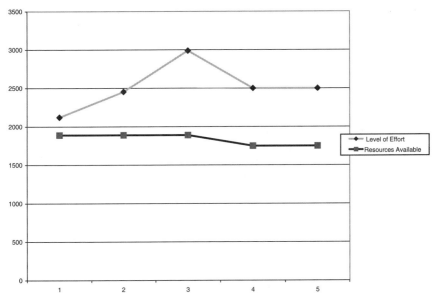

Figure 9.17 A 5-year period tracking the level of effort in hours of work of the InfoSec staff per year, per individual, compared to the hours of work that must be accomplished to support the IWC departments.

Another chart that is important for briefing management is one that shows the LOE versus the hours available for the InfoSec staff (Figure 9.18). The difference between LOE and time available can be shown to be part of a briefing on work backlog or used to show the difference is overtime being worked. A subchart may show details on the amount of backlog and its impact on the cost of doing business. It can also show the overtime costs being paid, and perhaps a comparison of that cost with the cost of hiring one or more additional staff. Seeing this comparison would help in making decisions as to which is cheaper, paying overtime or hiring more staff.

These charts must also be accompanied by others showing productivity and drivers of workload, as in some of the charts shown earlier. This is necessary because management will ask why you must do the things you do, and why must you do them in the way you are doing them. This quest for productivity and efficiency gains will be a constant chore for the ISSO. It is a challenge, but one that can be supported by metrics charts.

Layoffs are a fact of life in business, and metrics charts can help the ISSO justify head count and work, as shown by some of these charts. Other charts may also help, such as that shown in Figure 9.19. The chart can show measurement in terms of head count or hours that are equivalent to head count.

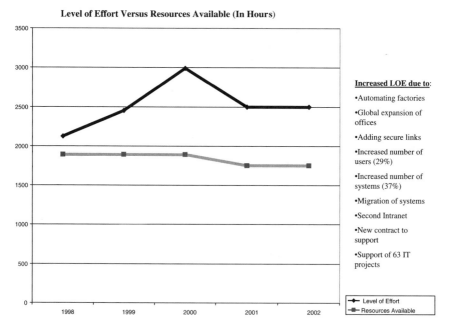

Figure 9.18   The LOE versus the hours available to do the work.

Generally, when management decides to cut costs, they lay off employees as the easiest method. They also usually direct each manager to cut a certain percentage of staff, say, 20%. However, although this may be the easiest way, it is not the best way; sometimes it would be cheaper to keep some of the staff, because their loss causes delays costing millions of dollars worth of production, sales, etc. As we all know, executive management often takes a short-term, "what's in it for me now" approach to managing their parts of the business.

Metrics management can help the ISSO plead the case to not cut 20% of staff. One word of caution: The ISSO should do this objectively and based on providing effective and efficient service and support to the IWC departments. It should never, ever be based on keeping a large staff and bureaucracy for the sake of status, power, ego, or other nonbusiness reasons.

Along with the chart shown in Figure 9.19, the ISSO would include information relative to the impact of both IWC's directed layoff numbers and those of the ISSO. This must be objectively done based on a business rationale. This information would include the following, identified as increasing the level of risks to information and information systems:

- *Contingency planning*: Contingency, emergency, and disaster recovery testing and plan updates will be delayed. The result will be any-

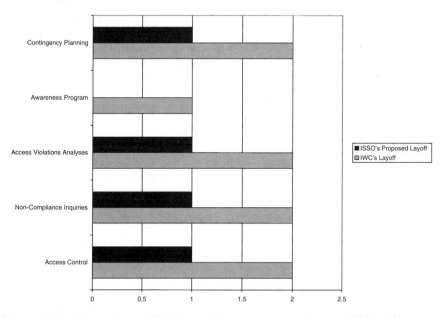

Figure 9.19 Comparison of IWC executive management requested layoff versus a counterproposal by the ISSO.

thing from no impact to not being able to effectively and efficiently deal with an emergency.

- *Awareness program*: Employees may not be aware of their responsibilities, thus leaving the systems open to potential attack or an increase in the potential of the loss of sensitive information.
- *Access violations analyses*: There will be delays of between 48 and 72 hours in the analyses of audit records. Thus, an attack against IWC systems would not be known for at least 48–72 hours. During that period, information could be stolen. However, something like a denial of service attack would be known when it was successful. The opportunity to identify the initial attempts at these attacks over a period of time would be lost, and with it the chance to mount defenses before the attacks were successful. The result will be systems, possibly production systems, that are down for an unknown period of time.
- *Noncompliance inquiries*: The average time it would take to complete an inquiry would increase by more than 2 weeks. Thus, no action to adjudicate the alleged infraction would be possible until the report was delivered to management. Furthermore, the alleged infraction may have called for the revocation of system privileges of the employee or employees who are the subject of the inquiry. Thus, their ability to be productive employees during that time would be negated.
- *Access control*: It is assumed that the number of new employees hired would be drastically reduced, and that could mitigate some of the level of effort expended by the access controllers. However, employees requiring changes in privilege would have those access changes delayed an additional 48–72 hours from the present average of 8–12 hours. This may adversely affect their productivity. To allow departments to do their own employees' privilege changes was evaluated under a previous project and found to not be realistic: The information to which the employees needed access did not belong to that department; most often it belonged to another information owner. These information owners did not want others to access their information without their approval. In addition, this change would just a transferring of costs and would not save IWC any additional resources.

The foregoing is a small example of how metric management techniques can be used when the need for budget cuts occurs. The example provides some insight into how metric management techniques help mitigate the risks of budget and staff downsizing when such downsizing will hurt the CIAPP and IWC. Metric management techniques can help the ISSO make a case to executive management. Furthermore, if the ISSO, supported by the metric management approach, has been periodically briefing management of the CIAPP and ISSO's projects and level of effort, the ISSO will have gained the confidence of management as a reliable manager who gets the job done as efficiently and effectively as possible.

PROJECT MANAGEMENT

As previously discussed, there are two basic types of work performed by the ISSO and staff: (1) level of effort (LOE) and (2) projects. We have discussed LOE and have provided some examples of process and metrics flowcharts relative to LOE.

It has been stated several times, but bears repeating: Projects are established where some tasks related to the CIAPP and/or InfoSec functions must be completed but they are not ongoing tasks. It is imperative that the ISSO be intimately familiar with and experienced in project management—as well as time management.

Remember that whether or not some task should be a project depends on whether it has the following:

- A stated objective (generally in one clear, concise and complete sentence);
- A beginning date;
- An ending date;
- Specific tasks to be performed to successfully meet that objective;
- A project leader; and
- Specific personnel to complete each task and the time period when the task will be completed.

Let's assume that the CIO sent a memo to the ISSO based on a conversation that the CIO had with the Director of IT. It seems that they had a meeting and during the meeting the discussion turned to IT projects related to their projects of upgrading systems, such as hardware, software, and their general maintenance. The CIAPP policy called for such upgrades and maintenance efforts to ensure that the information environment is maintained in compliance with the requirements set forth in the CIAPP. The Director stated that the IT staff didn't know if that was always the case when they made changes to systems. Consequently, the Director suggested that members of the ISSO's organization be part of the IT project teams with responsibility for determining whether the changes kept IWC's information environment secure. The CIO agreed and sent the ISSO a letter to that effect. When the ISSO received the memo, the ISSO discussed the matter with the Senior Systems Security Engineer. It was decided that a project be developed in order to establish a process and function to comply with the request from the CIO and Director of IT.

As an ISSO, you should be able to identify several issues that the ISSO must resolve apart from initiating this project. First, the Director of IT and the ISSO should be working closely together, and by doing so, they could have dealt with this matter without involving their boss, the CIO. In addition, the fact that the CIO sent a memo to the ISSO, instead of calling or meeting personally with the ISSO, indicates that the communication and working relationship between the CIO and ISSO must be improved. The ISSO must take action to immediately begin improving the communication and relationship with the Director and CIO.

That aside, using Figure 9.20 as an example, let's develop a project and fill in the blanks for major portions of the chart:

- SUBJECT: The project name: Security Test & Evaluation Function Development
- RESPONSIBILITY: The name of the project leader: John Doe, InfoSec Senior Systems Security Engineer.
- ACTION ITEM: What is to be accomplished: IT requires ISSO support to ensure that information and systems protection are integrated into IT systems' integration, maintenance, and update processes.

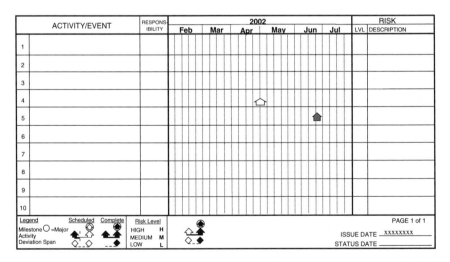

Figure 9.20 A basic project management chart that can be used to track CIAPP and InfoSec functional projects.

- REFERENCES: What caused this project to be initiated. For example: "See memo to ISSO from CIO, dated November 2, 2002."
- OBJECTIVE(S): State the objective of the project: Maintain a secure information environment.
- RISK/STATUS: State the risk of not meeting the objective(s) of this project: Because of limited staffing and multiple customer projects being supported, this project may experience delays as higher priority LOE and projects take precedence.
- ACTIVITY/EVENT: State the tasks to be performed, such as "Meet with IT project leads."
- RESPONSIBILITY: Identify the person responsible for each task. In this case, it is the Senior Systems Security Engineer, John Doe.
- CALENDAR: The calendar could be a year-long, monthly, quarterly or 6-month calendar with vertical lines identifying individual weeks. Using the 6-month calendar, the Project Lead and assigned project team members would decide what tasks had to be accomplished to meet the objective. The arrows and diamonds identified in the legend would be used to mark the beginning and ending dates of each task. The arrows are filled in when the task is started and when the task is completed; the diamonds are used to show deviations from the original dates.
- RISK—LVL: In this space, each task is associated with the potential risk that it may be delayed or cost more than allocated in the budget for the task. Using "High," "Medium" or "Low" or "H," "M" or "L," the Project Lead, in concert with the person responsible for the task, assigns a level of risk.
- RISK—DESCRIPTION: A short description of the risk is stated in this block. If it requires a detailed explanation, that explanation is attached to the project plan. In this block the Project Lead, who is also responsible for ensuring that the project plan is updated weekly, states "See Attachment 1."
- ISSUE DATE: The date the project began and the chart initiated goes in this block.
- STATUS DATE: The most current project chart date is placed here. This is important because anyone looking at the project chart will know how current the project chart is.

Other types of charts can also be developed to show project costs in terms of labor, materials, and the like. A good, automated project plan software program is well worth the costs for managing projects.

In the case of project charts, the ISSO uses them to brief management relative to the ongoing work of the InfoSec organization and states of the CIAPP. The ISSO receives weekly updates on Friday morning in a meeting with all the ISSO's project leaders, where each project lead is given 5 minutes to explain the status of the project—for example, "The project is still on schedule" or "Task #2 will be delayed because the person assigned the task is out sick for a week; however, it is expected that the project completion date will not be delayed because of it."

The ISSO holds an expanded staff meeting the last Friday of each month. All assigned InfoSec personnel attend these meetings, which last 2 to 3 hours. At these meetings, 1 hour is taken for all project leads and InfoSec functional leads to brief the status of their LOE and projects to the entire staff. The ISSO does this so that everyone in the organization knows what is going on—a vital communications tool. Also during this time, other matters are briefed and discussed, such as the latest risk management techniques, conferences, and training available.

QUESTIONS TO CONSIDER

Based on what you have read, consider the following questions and how you would reply to them:

- Do you use formal metrics management techniques?
- If not, why not?
- If so, are they used to brief management?
- Are each of your InfoSec functions documented not only in work instructions but also in process flowcharts?
- Do you use similar charts to document the InfoSec functional LOE?
- What other charts would you develop for each of the ISSO functions?
- Do you have at least one metrics chart to track costs of each InfoSec function?
- How would you use metrics management charts to justify your budget requests?
- How would you use metrics management charts to justify the number of your staff?
- How many charts, by function and description, would you want to use as an ISSO?

SUMMARY

Metrics management techniques will provide a process for the ISSO to support InfoSec- and CIAPP-related decisions. The ISSO should understand the following points:

- Metrics management is an excellent method to track InfoSec functions related to LOE, costs, use of resources, etc.
- The information can be analyzed, and results of the analyses can be used to:

Identify areas where efficiency improvements are necessary;

Determine effectiveness of InfoSec functional goals;

Provide input for performance reviews of the InfoSec staff (a more objective approach than subjective performance reviews of today's ISSOs); as well as

Indicate where InfoSec service and support to IWC requires improvement, meets its goals, etc.

10

Annual Reevaluation and Future Plans

Read not to contradict and confute, nor to believe and take for granted, nor to find talk and discourse, but to weigh and consider.—Francis Bacon[1]

CHAPTER OBJECTIVE

This chapter, "Annual Reevaluation and Future Plans," describes the process that can be used each year to determine the successes and failures of the InfoSec organization and CIAPP, and a methodology that can be used to correct the failures and plan for the upcoming years.

INTRODUCTION

The information environment of IWC is very dynamic and must be so in order for IWC to successfully compete in the fast-paced widget business in the global marketplace. Consequently, the world of the ISSO must also be very dynamic. The IWC ISSO must constantly be looking at where the IWC business is going and modify the CIAPP and InfoSec organization accordingly. The ISSO cannot sit back and think that the CIAPP is in place, the InfoSec organization is established, and everything is running smoothly—even when you think it is.

As IWC's ISSO you must be working everyday to provide effective and efficient service and support to IWC in the future. You must project ahead and look at potential new threats to IWC's information and systems and begin now to mitigate those future threats, such as cellular phones with installed digital cameras. The IWC ISSO, like all ISSOs, must establish proactive processes, as today's corporations depend too much on

---

[1]Francis Bacon (1561–1626), English philosopher, lawyer, and statesman. *Essays* "Of Studies" (1625)—*Encarta Book of Quotations* © & (P) 1999, Microsoft Corporation. All rights reserved. Developed for Microsoft by Bloomsbury Publishing Plc.

information and information systems to have those systems fail because the ISSO did not see the threat coming. *Today's ISSOs must be proactive and not constantly reactive.* Proactive processes are prepared to mitigate threats before they can occur—and it is cheaper than being reactive.

The ISSO must also reevaluate the CIAPP and have processes in place to constantly update it. In addition, all InfoSec functions must be reevaluated and updated as the need arises, but at least annually. The ISSO should lead an annual year-end review and analysis of the CIAPP and InfoSec functions. This is done so that the ISSOs can have some assurance that they are operating in the most effective and efficient way possible and needed changes are in place.

ONE-YEAR REVIEW

IWC's fiscal year and calendar year both end on December 31st. The ISSO decides that the beginning of the fourth quarter (October) is a good time to start planning for the coming year and begin evaluating the current year.

In order to plan for the coming year, the ISSO must first determine how successful the CIAPP and the InfoSec staff have been for this past year. Of interest would be:

- What was accomplished?
- What was planned but never completed, and why?
- What was planned but never started, and why?
- What was successful, and why?
- What wasn't successful, and why?
- What processes are current?
- What processes require updating?
- If a process was outdated, why was it not updated as needed?
- Is the InfoSec organization operating within budget?
- If not, why not?
- What budget is required for the coming year, as well as 2 or 3 years from now?
- If more budget is required, why?
- If more budget is needed, are there other measures that can be taken to minimize the need for a larger budget? (Remember that as an ISSO, you get paid for results and not the size of your InfoSec staff or the size of your budget.)

Level-of-Effort Activities

The ISSO has tasked each InfoSec functional lead to form a project team with selected members of the InfoSec functional staff and evaluate the processes used for completing their assigned LOE function. Of course, if the InfoSec function was a one-person job, that person would conduct the review by him- or herself and ask for input as needed from other staff members and the ISSO. Remember that the level-of-effort (LOE) activities are those activities or functions that are the day-to-day InfoSec tasks performed by the InfoSec staff. These activities are those identified as the ISSO responsibilities previously discussed and include:

- Access control;
- Awareness program;
- Noncompliance inquiries; and
- Security tests and evaluations program, etc.

This is to be accomplished by each functional team sitting down together to determine:

- What worked;
- What didn't work;
- Why it worked (process may be useful for other functions);
- Why it didn't work;
- How much time they spent doing each task, sub-task on the average;
- How the job might be done better;
- How the processes might be changed, why, and identified potential savings;
- Which forms, if any, should be modified or eliminated; and
- Other considerations.

The ISSO directed that any recommended changes be quantified in time and/or cost savings, as applicable. If the changes could not be quantified, the staff members would have a difficult time changing the process. The ISSO reasoned that with few exceptions, process changes that did not save time or money were probably not worth making, as nonquantified changes cost money with usually no return value.

The ISSO directed that all members of each function support their functional lead in this endeavor and provide a briefing to be held the first week in November as part of the ISSO's expanded staff meeting where all InfoSec staff attended. During that briefing, the functional processes would be discussed and modifications approved where necessary. If the modifications could not be accomplished within 30 days, a formal project plan would have to be developed and briefed at that November meeting.

Projects

During the first week of October, the ISSO will also begin the evaluation of the CIAPP for the past year. The ISSO, in concert with the InfoSec staff, will review the projects that were begun this year, as well as those projects that were begun last year and completed this year.

The ISSO will determine the following:

- Did each project accomplish its objective?
- Was the project completed in accordance with the project plan?
- For those projects not completed on time, what was the cause of not meeting the completion date?
- For those projects completed ahead of schedule, why was it completed ahead of schedule? (The ISSO wants this information because it may be due to poor project planning which must be corrected, or it may be due to a unique approach that could be used on other projects.)
- What was the cost of each project?
- Were the projected benefits of the projects realized and if not, why not?

The ISSO will, in concert with the InfoSec staff, analyze all the projects, and based on that evaluation, modify the process used for initiating, determining costs, determining resource allocations, and determining schedules for all new projects.

Also of importance is feedback from IWC employees: their evaluation of service and support provided to them by the ISSO and InfoSec staff. The employees' opinions as to what improvements can be made in the CIAPP to minimize costs and provide the necessary level of information environment protection are also important. The ISSO and staff developed a survey to be sent out to all departments. The feedback received will also be incorporated into the year-end evaluation–analysis. Some ISSOs may not want to take this survey approach, because they may be reluctant to receive criticism and complaints from non-InfoSec professionals about how the ISSO and InfoSec staff can better do their jobs. However, such feedback is important and should be welcomed and considered at all times.

Once the analysis is complete, the ISSO and staff members will determine what new projects will be required for the following year. Those projects, once identified, will be assigned to the applicable member of the staff as the project lead. The staff members will then be given 30 days to complete a draft project plan. That plan will identify the specific objective to be accomplished, all tasks, milestones, resources required, etc.

During the staff meeting held during the first week of November, all the project leads will present their project plans to the ISSO and the staff. The project plans will be evaluated and discussed by the ISSO and the staff. Any recommended changes to the project plans will be cause for actions to be taken to change the plans as appropriate. In addition, the overall project plan process will be discussed and modified as needed.

It is the responsibility of the ISSO to ensure that adequate resources are allocated for the completion of the projects as planned. Where several members of the InfoSec staff are assigned to lead or support multiple projects, the ISSO will prioritize the projects and then allow the project lead and project support staff to work out the details. Where conflicts in work arise, the matter will be discussed with the ISSO, who will make the final decision based on the input of all those concerned and the proper allocation of resources.

This approach follows the management philosophy of having decisions made at the lowest possible level where the required information on which to base a decision is known. It also meets the ISSO's philosophy of trusting your professional InfoSec staff and treating them as part of the professional InfoSec team.

INFOSEC STRATEGIC, TACTICAL, AND ANNUAL PLANS

Once the ISSO has been briefed on the above LOE and projects, the results will be mapped against the InfoSec Strategic, Tactical, and Annual Plans. The LOE and project results could be identified as some of the specific building blocks of each of the plans.

The InfoSec Annual Plan's goals should have been accomplished. If so, the ISSO then identifies the links between the successful accomplishment of those goals with the IWC Annual Business Plan and the IWC and InfoSec Strategic and Tactical Plans as appropriate.

If a direct link between the accomplishments of the InfoSec staff and the goals of the plan cannot be shown, the ISSO must question why the specific projects or LOE identified were ever done in the first place. There may be a very valid reason; however, this should always be questioned, as any resource allocations which cannot be directly linked back to accomplishment of stated goals are probably misallocations. They are an added cost burden on the InfoSec budget as well as an additional overhead cost to IWC.

LINKING INFOSEC ACCOMPLISHMENTS TO IWC GOALS

The ISSO believes that the initial reasons for the IWC CIAPP and IWC's reasons for establishing the ISSO position have not changed, but a reverification and validation would probably be a good idea. To be sure that the CIAPP and the ISSO's accomplishments are meeting their stated purpose, the ISSO decided on the following course of action:

- Using a link analysis methodology, the ISSO maps all the LOE and project results to all applicable InfoSec and IWC plans; and

- The ISSO develops a formal presentation to be given to IWC executive management in which the CIAPP status is briefed (assuming that the ISSO's boss agrees).

The results of the link analysis (Figure 10.1a and 10.1b) disclosed that overall CIAPP goals, LOE, projects, and objectives were, with some minor setbacks and exceptions over the year, meeting the needs of IWC.

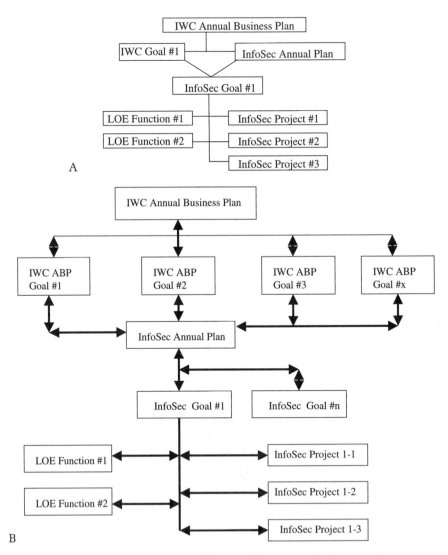

Figure 10.1   A and B are examples of linking the InfoSec LOE and projects support to the CIAPP and IWC's goals.

The ISSO discussed the matter with the CIO. The CIO agreed that a briefing would be a good idea, especially since this is the end of the first year of the formal CIAPP under the ISSO. The executive management would want to know:

- What was accomplished;
- The cost of the CIAPP;
- The status of the overall protection of the IWC information environment; and
- What else was needed to ensure a secure information environment.

The CIO provides several recommendations:

- The briefing should take no longer than 15 minutes and allow 15 minutes for questions;
- The ISSO should not use any technical jargon but speak in business terms of costs, benefits, and competitive advantage, and give the IWC management some sense of assurance that the information and systems are being protected as needed;
- The briefing charts should be clear, concise, and more of a graphical presentation than text—another reason for "management by metrics";
- The briefing should be given professionally and objectively; it should not be used as a soapbox for requesting additional resources or to show how great a job the ISSO is doing;
- All briefing charts should be provided in a package for each member of the audience with supporting detailed charts; and
- At least 5 of the 15 minutes should be used to brief on next year's projects, goals, their costs, and how they would benefit IWC.

The ISSO had not been prepared to present the new year's plans and projects as part of the briefing. However, it appeared that the necessary information would be available based on the previous briefings and discussions with the InfoSec staff.

The ISSO suggested a briefing to be held the first week of December. The CIO agreed to set it up. The ISSO's rationale for a meeting in December was that the InfoSec staff's LOE and project input would be available on or about the first week of November, and that would provide sufficient time to develop the briefing.

The ISSO wanted to ensure that the briefing accomplished its goals, and that could be jeopardized, not by the material, but by the manner and format used. The ISSO had heard of several briefers having their messages ignored because the format, fonts, colors, or whatever was used to present the facts was not liked by one or more of the executive management.

The ISSO knew that such trivia should not be a prime concern of executive management, but the ISSO also knew that such things did occur.

To ensure that the InfoSec briefing was successful, the proper format would be the first item of business.

The ISSO stopped by the desks of several of the key executive managers' secretaries, who provided insight as to the correct format, font size, and color of slides to use. At the same time, the ISSO was given some valuable tips from several of the secretaries as to how to present the material in a manner that the executives preferred. (Note: Although throughout this book the ISSO actions are discussed, some may be delegated by the ISSO, such as this task to the ISSO secretary or administrative assistant.)

The ISSO long ago learned that the secretaries of the executive managers had great insight into what worked with their bosses and what didn't. The ISSO's respect for them and informal assistance to them over the year had made them close allies. Now, that friendship would be able to help ensure a successful briefing format.

As part of this briefing, the ISSO developed an annual report for each IWC department vice president based on the metrics charts used throughout most of the year. That annual report contained some narrative and analyses supported by metrics charts showing the status of each department's compliance with the CIAPP and the security of their information environment. It included an Executive Summary in the front of the report and recommendations for improvements that could be made in the future, as well as the benefits of the recommended improvement versus the potential costs and cost savings.

METRICS ANALYSIS

As part of the year-end review, the ISSO did a complete analysis of the metrics charts that had been developed and used throughout the first year of the CIAPP.

The ISSO noted that the charts had grown to more than 47 separate metrics charts. The ISSO was concerned that some of the charts had outlived their usefulness, while others continued to be of value, and possibly some new charts were needed.

The analysis of the metrics charts indicated that several of the charts had been necessary to track particular problem areas. However, some of the problems appeared to have been resolved and the metrics charts, for the previous 4 months, had supported that view.

Some metrics charts were developed and briefed periodically to management because some managers were interested in periodically knowing the amount of LOE being used to support some specific tasks. The ISSO decided to identify those charts to the managers who were interested in the information and gain their approval to eliminate those charts, as it appeared the information provided had met their needs. If not, it might

	Chart Identification				
Purpose					
	Chart #1	Chart #2	Chart #3	Chart #4	Etc.
Cost	X				
Schedule	X		X	X	
Brief Mgt.		X		X	
Brief Cust.			X		X
LOE Drvrs.		X		X	
Etc.					X

Figure 10.2 An example of a matrix chart to be used to evaluate metrics charts, based on the charts' purposes.

be possible to provide that information to management on an annual or semiannual basis instead of the current monthly or quarterly report. The final decision should be made by the ISSO's customer.

The ISSO took all the metrics charts and identified them by their objectives—in other words, their purpose for being developed and used. Those would also be linked to specific areas that support the IWC CIAPP and InfoSec organizational plans. The ISSO wanted to be sure that the metrics used to help manage the CIAPP and the InfoSec organization met the needs of the CIAPP, of management, and of the InfoSec organization.

The ISSO knew that metrics charts tend to increase and seem to sometimes take on a life of their own. The ISSO was concerned that the time it took to track specific LOEs and projects using metrics was sometimes not cost-effective. By identifying the charts against their purpose in a matrix, the ISSO found that it was easy to analyze the metrics charts and their purpose (Figure 10.2).

PLANNING FOR NEXT YEAR

The ISSO had received the input from the InfoSec staff at the November meetings. Based on that input, the ISSO was prepared to write next year's InfoSec Annual Plan and update the InfoSec Strategic and Tactical Plans. However, in order to accomplish those tasks, the IWC Plans must be received. After all, the InfoSec Plans had to support the IWC Plans.

The ISSO knew that the draft IWC Plans would not be available until January. Therefore, the ISSO drafted the InfoSec Annual Plan and updated the InfoSec Strategic and Tactical Plans based on information gathered through discussions with various levels of management involved in developing the IWC Annual Plan and updating the IWC Tactical and Strategic Plans.

The ISSO implemented the InfoSec Plans January 1st, without waiting for the draft IWC Plans. The ISSO did so in order to begin the much-needed LOE modifications and projects that were time-dependent. If they were not started right after the first of the year, their schedules might have to be slipped. The ISSO could not afford to do that and took the risk that the information gathered to date was accurate, and that any changes at the IWC level would only cause minor adjustments to the InfoSec schedules—if any.

As part of the ISSO and InfoSec staff year-end analyses, a flowchart was developed (Figure 10.3) which would be used for briefings and also would let InfoSec staff see how their jobs supported IWC.

The ISSO and staff also took all their risk management reports for the year and evaluated what was accomplished to correct CIAPP deficiencies and determine what needed to be done in the coming year to correct other deficiencies (Figure 10.4). These then were linked through a vulnerabilities-projects flowchart to identify "Strategic Direction: CIAPP Projects to Address Vulnerabilities."

After completion of all the executive management briefing charts, and 1 week prior to briefing IWC executive management, the ISSO gave the briefing and with additional analysis of the CIAPP and InfoSec functional accomplishments to the InfoSec staff. The 1-week interval was to ensure that the briefing was accurate and that the charts said what needed to be

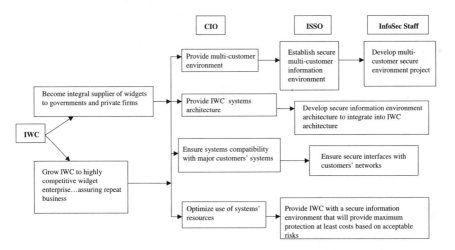

Figure 10.3 An example of how corporate goals' InfoSec support can be visually linked to provide a simple view of InfoSec service and support functions.

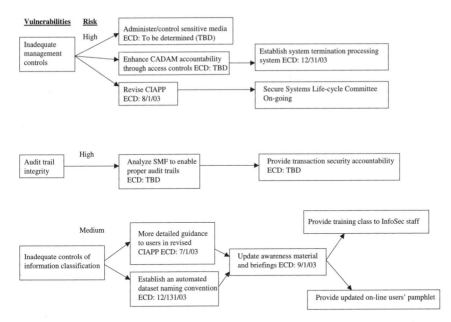

Figure 10.4   An example of how vulnerabilities identified throughout the year by risk management methods, such as risk analyses and risk assessments, can be visually linked to provide a simple view of work accomplished or needed to provide a more secure IWC information environment.

said. The InfoSec staff could evaluate the briefing and provide an avenue for constructive criticism. After all, the ISSO wanted, as a side issue, to show executive management the outstanding job done by the InfoSec staff during the past year, without saying so. In other words, let the briefing speak for that.

The CIO was invited to attend the ISSO's "expanded staff meeting" so that the CIO would not have any surprises at the executive management briefing. In addition, the ISSO wanted the CIO to attend to say a few words after the briefing, thanking the InfoSec staff for their fine work over the past year. The ISSO believed that such visibility of InfoSec staff to executive management would also boost morale, as they would see that their hard work was appreciated.

Upon the completion of the successful briefing, the ISSO scheduled another expanded staff meeting to be held on a Friday before the holidays and scheduled to last all day. At that expanded staff meeting, the ISSO had a catered lunch brought in as a special measure of thanks to the InfoSec staff. After all, if the InfoSec staff was not successful, the ISSO could not be successful.

QUESTIONS TO CONSIDER

Based on what you have read, consider the following questions and, as an ISSO, how you would reply to them:

- Do you have a process in place to conduct a formal year-end analysis of your CIAPP and InfoSec functions?
- If not, why not?
- If so, does it include cost–benefit analyses?
- Do you provide a "state-of-InfoSec" report of the corporate information environment at year's end?
- If so, is it briefed to executive management?
- Are "subreports" provided to each department head addressing specifically the status of the protection of their information environment?
- Do you involve your InfoSec staff in the year-end reviews, analyses, and planning?
- Do you reward your InfoSec staff for a job well done at year's end—by more than words?
- How would you go about conducting and improving on the process described in this chapter?

SUMMARY

Evaluations and analyses of the entire CIAPP and InfoSec organization help maintain a proactive and current protected-information environment. The ISSO should remember the following points:

- It is a good idea to evaluate the entire CIAPP and InfoSec functions on an annual basis.
- The evaluation should include all projects and LOEs.
- Changes should be made where value is added in terms of cost decreases, productivity gains, or time savings.
- Executive management should receive a clear, concise, business-oriented briefing on the state of the CIAPP and IWC's current protected information environment on at least an annual basis.
- Metrics charts should be evaluated at least annually, then eliminated or modified as necessary.
- Link analysis methodologies are useful in determining the success of an InfoSec Program.

11

High-Technology Crimes Investigative Support

It was a common saying of Myson that men ought not to investigate things from words, but words from things; for that things are not made for the sake of words, but words for things.—Diogenes Laërtius[1]

CHAPTER OBJECTIVE

This chapter, "High-Technology Crimes Investigative Support," discusses the duties and responsibilities of an ISSO when it comes to providing service and support for deterring high-technology crimes, conducting noncompliance inquiries, assisting with computer forensics support, and dealing with law enforcement.

INTRODUCTION

Not long after the ISSO took over the job as the IWC ISSO, a meeting was held between the ISSO and the IWC Director of Security. At that time, an agreement was reached as to the ISSO's duties and responsibilities and those of the Director of Security. The Director of Security agreed that the ISSO's duties and responsibilities would conflict with those of the Security Department if the ISSO conducted any type of investigation. The Director of Security and the ISSO reached a compromise and agreed that any infractions of the CIAPP could be looked at by the ISSO as long as it related to noncompliance with the CIAPP, such as violation of automated information protection.

    They both agreed:

---

[1]Diogenes Laërtius (lived 3rd century?), Greek historian and biographer. *Lives of the Philosophers* "Myson" (3rd century?)—*Encarta® Book of Quotations*, © & (P) 1999, Microsoft Corporation. All rights reserved. Developed for Microsoft by Bloomsbury Publishing Plc.

- To differentiate between an investigation and the ISSO's inquiries by having the ISSO call that function "noncompliance inquiries" (NCI) and focusing on the CIAPP infractions;
- An information copy of each NCI was to be forwarded to the Director of Security;
- The ISSO would provide technical and forensics support to the Security staff, when requested;
- The Director of Security was the IWC focal point for law enforcement liaison activities, and any need to contact a law enforcement agency must be approved by the Director of Security, as well as others such as the IWC Public Relations staff and the IWC legal staff;
- In the event the ISSO or members of the ISSO's staff were contacted for any requests by outside agencies for investigative assistance, that request must be coordinated with the Director of Security and others at IWC;
- The ISSO's staff would provide in-house computer forensics training to the Security staff twice a year;
- The Security staff would provide in-house training in assets protection and basic investigative techniques, such as how to conduct an interview, to the InfoSec staff twice a year; and
- The Security staff would provide budget for computer forensics software to be used in support of Security investigations, on an as-needed basis.

After completion of the discussion by the ISSO, the Director of Security knew that the ISSO and the InfoSec organization under the CIO were where they should be. The complicated job and headaches of the ISSO relative to NCIs and the entire CIAPP matter was something that the Director did not want to be responsible for.

DUTIES AND RESPONSIBILITIES OF AN ISSO IN DETERRING HIGH-TECHNOLOGY CRIMES

Although investigations at IWC are the purview of the Security staff, the ISSO and Director of Security both knew that many such investigations, or NCIs, are high-technology-based, such as those involving microprocessors (computers). Therefore, the ISSO's staff would be active in supporting Security's anticrime program as part of Security's assets protection program for IWC. They both knew that the entire IWC assets protection program would be best served, that is, more effectively and efficiently accomplished, if the ISSO and the InfoSec functions reported to the Director of Security instead of to the CIO.

However, at IWC, as at many corporations, the Director of Security really did not want that responsibility, and politically, it was a difficult sell to executive management. Furthermore, the ISSO position that now reports to the CIO who reports to the CEO would be downgraded, as the ISSO would report to the Director of Security, who reports to the Vice President, Human Resources, who reports to Corporate Office Executive Vice President, who reports to the CEO. The position would also mean less prestige, less money, and the inability to exercise management authority at a sufficiently high level.

However, the Director and ISSO agreed that a high-technology crime prevention program should be established at IWC as part of the IWC's total assets protection program that is led by the Director of Security. Therefore, the Director and ISSO decided to establish a project to provide such a program and ensure that it interfaced with the CIAPP. It was also agreed that a long-term goal would be to integrate the crime prevention, CIAPP, and IWC physical assets protection policies into an overall IWC Assets Protection Program under the authority of both the Director and ISSO using a matrix management approach.

The Director and ISSO agreed that the ISSO's approach to the CIAPP and related InfoSec functions was adaptable to the development of a high-technology crime prevention program. After that initial baseline was developed by the ISSO, the Director would integrate antitheft, antifraud, and other crime-related policies, procedures, and processes into the program and baseline it as part of the IWC assets protection program under the authority of the Director of Security.

They both agreed that the basic goal on which to build the IWC high-technology crime prevention program (HTCPP) is the development of a comprehensive high-technology crime prevention environment at least cost and impact to IWC.

The Director and ISSO decided to categorize HTCPP investigations and NCIs so that they could more easily be analyzed and placed in a common database for analyses such as trends or vulnerabilities of processes that allow such incidents to occur. The ISSO agreed that the ISSO's organization would maintain the database, but the security staff would have input and read access. However, modifications, maintenance, upgrades, and deletions would be controlled by the ISSO to ensure that the integrity of the database was maintained. The initial categories agreed to by the Director and ISSO were:

- Violations of laws (required by law to be reported to government investigative agency);
- Unauthorized access;
- Computer fraud;
- Actions against users;
- Actions against systems;
- Interruption of services;
- Tampering;

- Misuse of information;
- Theft of services;
- Other crimes where computers were used:

    Money laundering

    Copyright violations

    Intellectual property thefts

    Mail fraud

    Wire fraud

    Pornography

- Other crimes
- Violators

    Internal

    External

It was further agreed that these categories would be expanded based on analyses of investigations and noncompliance inquiries conducted to date.

ASSISTING WITH COMPUTER FORENSICS SUPPORT

Businesses, public agencies, and individuals increasingly rely on a wide range of computers, often linked together into networks, to accomplish their missions. Because computers have become ubiquitous, they are often a highly productive source of evidence and intelligence that may be obtained by properly trained and equipped InfoSec and investigative professionals. Equipping the specialists to be able to competently search IWC systems is essential. In many cases, a suspect will use a computer to plan the crime, keep diaries or records of acts in furtherance of a conspiracy, or communicate with confederates about details via electronic mail. In other schemes the computer will play a more central role, perhaps serving as the vehicle for an unauthorized intrusion into a larger system from which valuable files or other information is downloaded or tampered.

Surprisingly, even many sophisticated criminals who are highly computer literate remain unaware of the many software utilities available that allow evidence to be scavenged from various storage media, including hard drives, random access memory, and other locations in the operating system environments such as file slack, swap, and temporary files. Therefore, every investigation of crimes and unauthorized activities should now assume that some effort will be invested in examining computers and computer records to locate relevant evidence that will prove or disprove allegations or suspicions of wrongdoing.

Whether computers are themselves used as the tool to commit other crimes or merely contain documents, files, or messages discussing the scheme or plans, computers can provide a wealth of useful information if properly exploited. A major barrier to obtaining this potentially valuable evidence is the relative lack of knowledge of many corporate and law enforcement investigators concerning high-technology—computer technology. This lack of familiarity and experience hampers the computer forensics specialists' ability to conduct effective searches. When the crime scene itself is a computer or a network, or when the evidence related to the illegal or unauthorized activities is stored on a computer, there is no substitute for the use of "computer forensics" to gather relevant evidence.

Webster's Dictionary defines forensics as "belonging to, used in, or suitable to courts of judicature or to public discussion and debate."[2] Thus, *computer forensics* is a term that we define as describing *the application of legally sufficient methods and protocols and techniques to gather, analyze, and preserve computer information relevant to a matter under investigation.* Operationally, computer forensics encompasses using appropriate software tools and protocols to efficiently search the contents of magnetic and other storage media and identify relevant evidence in files, fragments of files, and deleted files, as well as file slack and swap space.

The ISSO and InfoSec Non-Compliance Inquires (NCI) specialist assigned as the security support focal point provided a computer forensics awareness briefing to the IWC security staff. The briefing gave an introduction to computer forensics and also discussed the support the ISSO staff would give the security staff. The ISSO agreed to support the IWC security staff by providing high-technology-related forensic services.[3]

DEALING WITH LAW ENFORCEMENT

There is a great lack of communication between ISSO professionals and law enforcement agencies. Neither profession seems to know what the other does, or how they can assist each other. The ISSO works primarily in the internal world of the corporation. Therefore, ISSOs usually are ignorant of what investigations are being conducted by law enforcement agencies, even in the cities where the corporation has facilities.

This lack of communication means that the ISSO, and more often than not the Director of Security, is not aware of local high-technology crime investigations that law enforcement are conducting. Thus, the ISSO is unaware of some high-technology crime techniques which would be useful to know about when developing internal defenses and controls to protect the corporation against such attacks.

---

[2] *Merriam-Webster's Collegiate Dictionary.* G.&C. Merriam Company, 1973.
[3] Supplemental information concerning one approach to retrieving and preserving electronic evidence can be found at the author's web site: http://www.shockwavewriters.com. Click on Books, this book, and then Chapter 11.

When to Call for Help—and Whom

If you or one of your staff is conducting an NCI or supporting a security staff member conducting an investigation, there is more than one person who can be of assistance. These include:

- Victims,
- Witnesses,
- Consultants,
- Vendors,
- Suspects, and
- Law enforcement officers.

What if a high-technology crime is perpetrated at IWC and the law requires a law enforcement agency to be contacted? What if management decides that they want the perpetrator caught and prosecuted? They will file a complaint with the appropriate law enforcement agency and support criminal prosecution of the offender. Even though this is primarily a Secretary Department matter, often the ISSO has an important role to play. Therefore, the ISSO should be aware of the processes involved. Some of the things to consider are:

- Does IWC have a company policy as to when or when not to call an outside law enforcement agency?
- Are Legal staff involved?
- Are Human Resources personnel involved?
- Are Public Relations personnel involved?
- Is budget available to support the investigation and prosecution?
- Is the question "Can IWC stand the bad publicity?" considered in making the decision?
- Is executive management prepared for the required commitment?
- Is reporting required by law?
- If yes, should it be reported?
- If not, should it be reported?

When deciding whether or not to call law enforcement, one should also consider:

- Costs versus benefits;
- Extent of loss;
- Probability of identifying and successfully prosecuting the suspect;
- Potential lawsuits that will follow if someone is identified (whether or not he or she is successfully prosecuted); and
- Time in supporting the criminal justice process: investigation through prosecution.

There are some advantages to calling law enforcement, who can:

- Perform acts that are illegal if done by citizens;
- Obtain search warrants to recover property;
- Gain access to related information; and
- Protect victims under some instances.

Some of the disadvantages of calling law enforcement for help include:

- Control over the incident is lost;
- It is probably costly and time-consuming; and
- The company must be willing to cooperate in prosecution where the case may receive high visibility from news media, stockholders, and others.

If you decide to call in a law enforcement agency, IWC management must also decide which one to call and why—national, state, or local. No matter which one is called, IWC management must also be prepared to help them for an extended period of time. Initially, the ISSO in concert with the Director of Security should[4]:

- Prepare a briefing for investigators;
- Ensure that executive management and legal staff director attend;
- Be sure of their facts;
- Brief in clear, concise, and nontechnical terms;
- Identify the loss, the basis for the amount, and the process used to determine that amount;
- Gather all related evidence;
- Know the related laws;
- Describe action taken to date;
- Explain the real-world impact of the alleged crime;
- Identify and determine if any victims will cooperate;
- Explain what assistance they can provide.

If the incident is to be handled internally:

- What is the objective?
- What is the plan to accomplish that objective?
- What expertise is available to help?
- What is the cost?
- What are the consequences?
- What can be done to be sure it doesn't happen again?

---

[4] See http://www.shockwavewriters.com; Articles; ShockwaveWriter for a detailed case scenario related to calling law enforcement for help, entitled, "There's Been a Computer Crime! Call the Sheriff?"

QUESTIONS TO CONSIDER

Based on what you have read, consider the following questions and how you would reply to them:

- Do you think the ISSO's responsibilities should include conducting any type of investigation or inquiry?
- If so, why?
- If not, why not?
- Do you think it is the job and professional responsibility of an ISSO and staff to support internal and external investigations by providing forensics support?
- If so, what limitations would you set on that support?
- As an ISSO, do you have a policy, plan, processes, and procedures in place as to when and how you would support an internal or external investigation?
- If so, are they current?
- Have they been coordinated with applicable internal customers, such as auditors and security staff?

SUMMARY

Usually, a security department's staff is not trained to conduct high-technology investigations where technical evidence and forensic expertise are needed as an integral part of solving the crime. The ISSO and staff are in the best position to support the Security Department or an outside law enforcement agency in conducting their investigations. An agreement should be worked out between the Director of Security and the ISSO as to who has what authority for investigations relevant to violations of corporate policies as well as those that would also be a criminal offense.

Corporations must have current policies detailing when an outside law enforcement agency should be called and when a matter identified as a violation of law, criminal or civil, should be investigated internally. It is absolutely mandatory that such decision *not* be made by the ISSO, but by executive management supported by the Legal staff, Public Relations staff, and Human Resources staff. If a law enforcement agency is contacted, the corporation must be prepared for usually many months of support to the investigative agency as well as bad publicity.

High-technology crime investigations and NCIs are based on basic investigative techniques and answering the questions of who, how, where, when, why, and what.

High-technology criminals are beginning to install more sophisticated security systems, including encryption systems. Such devices will require very sophisticated devices and expertise to access them. Some have focused on methods of destroying evidence if law enforcement or investigators tamper with the system.

The challenges to high-technology crime investigators and computer forensics specialists are many and quickly increasing. Only through constant training will investigators and ISSO staff members have any hope at all of keeping up with these changes, including searching media for evidence.

Keys to successful searches: know the technology, have a plan, use common sense, and use a specialist who is an expert in the technology and accompanying software to be searched.

12

InfoSec in the Interest
of National Security

The security needs of a nation-state must be balanced with the inherent human rights and basic freedoms of its citizens.—Dr. Gerald L. Kovacich

CHAPTER OBJECTIVE

This chapter identifies and explains InfoSec requirements, specifically those related to information systems, in the national security environment of a government-related corporation, such as a government contractor. This chapter also discusses the philosophy and processes that can be adapted to InfoSec programs in the world of business.[1]

INTRODUCTION

One may wonder why national security should be discussed in the context of InfoSec. There are several reasons for this, as noted below:

National security obviously affects government agencies; however, it also affects individuals and businesses of every size and type. This also includes other nation-states, and thus foreign governments, as well as foreign businesses and citizens from other nations. It also affects global corporations such as IWC.

In today's global marketplace and global information environment, what happens in one nation often affects what happens in other nations. In this age of information warfare, one has many examples of national

---

[1] The reader who does not work for a company or university with government contracts may want to skip this chapter. However, many of the requirements set forth by various government agencies for the protection of their (the government's) information and InfoSec can cost-effectively be applied to the protection of nongovernment information. Also, one never knows whom they may be working for from time to time. Thus, the information presented in this chapter may provide some future value.

security affecting other nations and businesses: the defacing of government and business Web sites and denial of service attacks between the Chinese in mainland China and those on Taiwan; the Israeli—Arab incidents; and the Serb—NATO incidents, just to name a few.

If national security is affected, businesses are affected. One can look to World War II and see the bombing of industrial plants—commercial businesses—by the Allied and Axis powers. In any incident, police action, or war where a nation's security is adversely affected, the businesses of that nation are also adversely affected. Therefore, it is obvious that in any conflicts between nations where at least one of the nations is information dependent, attacks will be made against telecommunications systems, Web sites, Internet accesses, and the like. These are for the most part non-government systems.

Furthermore, in today's global, competitive marketplace, economic power is being emphasized more than military power. Therefore, in order for an adversary to weaken a nation, the adversary would undoubtedly attack the economic might of a nation—its economic might is derived from its businesses. So, virus attacks, denial of service attacks, theft of sensitive information, placing misinformation on corporate networks, and such are very likely to be used.

In every modern nation and especially information-based nations of the world, corporations are under contract to research, design, develop, and produce weapons that can be used for the protection of the nation-state. In today's modern, information-based nations, there are literally thousands of universities and corporations under contract to government agencies. In the U.S., there are over 800,000 industry personnel with security clearance working in over 11,000 contractor facilities. There are over 11 million classified documents, most of which reside on computers.[2] These businesses may exist solely to develop products for government agencies, or they may be producing products for government agencies and also products for commercial use. They may be accomplishing these projects using the same information systems and application programs, and even the same information. Corporations carry out many of the current government-sponsored research projects under contract. These not only can and will be used to assist government agencies, but also eventually can be used by businesses. The research into information-based defensive weapons is of such a nature.

A cyber-attack on a corporation can also be viewed as an attack against national security. Nations are preparing to attack other nations' information infrastructures, which are generally private businesses.

The modern world is rapidly becoming one integrated supply chain. Corporations for government agencies, other corporations that may be involved in the defense industry or for commercial businesses and cus-

---

[2] See http://www.dss.mil/sec/index.htm.

tomers are producing products. Some of these may even be of a foreign nature. This inter-relationship means that what may happen to one corporation or nation, may adversely impact other corporations on a global scale. And since these modern corporations are information dependent and information based, InfoSec plays an important role. One just has to look at the devastating earthquake in Kobe, Japan, and its affect on worldwide supply of chips, to see this global dependency.

NATIONAL SECURITY CLASSIFIED INFORMATION

When one thinks of information valuation in the national security arena, one has just as difficult a time determining its value as is the case in the corporate world. However, there is no doubt that the value of information of national security interest is obviously much greater than that of any corporation. If a corporation's information is not adequately protected and defended, the corporation may go out of business. However, if the same thing were to happen to a nation's national security information, the nation may cease to exist except as part of another nation.

National security classified information is one of the most important categories of information, and it must be safeguarded by all in the interest of national security. It is mentioned here briefly because the process used to place a value on that information goes through more stringent analysis than personal, private, and business information.

In the United States, as an example, national security classified information is generally divided into three basic categories: *confidential*: loss of this information can cause damage to national security; *secret*: loss of this information can cause serious damage to national security; and *top secret*: loss of this information can cause grave damage to national security.

There is also national security information that is not classified, like that stated above, but requires some lesser degree of controls and protection because it has value, though less value. These include:

- For Official Use Only;
- Unclassified But Sensitive Information; and
- Unclassified Information.

There is also a category of classified information that is considered *black* or *compartmented*. Such information is further protected by not only requiring a security clearance and the need-to-know, but also often an additional background investigation and special briefing. Such information is often termed Special Access Required information, Special Access Program information, and Sensitive Compartmented information. In these compartments, InfoSec must include some of the most stringent processes, as this information can truly be considered the "crown jewels" of a nation.

InfoSec Requirements in the National Security Arena

There are many similarities between the InfoSec requirements in the corporate world and those in the world of national security as practiced by government agencies and defense industry-related corporations. Of course, such things as initial and recurring background investigations of employees are more stringent, as well as physical security requirements and the implementation of the need-to-know principle. This section will concentrate on those related directly to information and information systems protection and defense requirements. The information systems are sometimes called automated information systems (AIS).

In the case of a defense-industry-related corporation, the InfoSec requirements are incorporated into the contract between the government agency and the contractor. A defense-industry-related corporation would then include such InfoSec requirements in contracts with subcontractors, associated contractors, team members, etc., where those businesses will also be handling government information. This is logical, as it does no good to provide InfoSec in one corporation while another uses the same information and is not required to do likewise.

The main emphasis of InfoSec deals with compromise of national security information. Unless there is a state of war, information that is destroyed or inappropriately modified may be reconstructed, though this may take a great deal of time. However, the compromise of national security information may make the product being developed of little use, since the adversary has the information and can build similar products or products of a defensive nature. The worst-case scenario is when a compromise occurs and no one knows that it has occurred. Time, money, and other resources are expended to develop products that will be of little use if they are needed since, as noted earlier, using the compromised information the adversary has developed defensive systems against those products. The InfoSec requirements are implemented so that:

- National security information is protected from compromise that would allow an adversary to compete in building similar systems, developing countermeasures, or delaying operational use of the systems.
- The compromise or delays in product development would be accomplished through manmade, hostile acts of:

  Espionage through authorized or unauthorized accesses to information, such as theft; and

Sabotage through fire (destruction), water (destruction), or software (e.g., destruction, theft, manipulation) using such malicious codes as Trojan horses, viruses, and logic bombs.

- InfoSec in a national security environment must also protect and defend against natural acts such as fire, water, earthquakes, and windstorms.

It is the responsibility of the InfoSec specialists to understand the national security requirements, especially those specified in the contract. The InfoSec specialists must provide an InfoSec program for the defense-industry-related corporation that includes increasing awareness of the need for an effective InfoSec program in the government environment, and that also provides basic guidance and understanding necessary for the development of the InfoSec program in that environment.

The fundamental national InfoSec requirements are as follows:

- *InfoSec policy*: the set of laws, rules, and practices that regulate how a defense industry-related corporation manages, protects, defends, and distributes national security information.
- *Accountability*: individual and information accountability is the key to protecting, defending, and controlling any system that processes, stores, and transmits national security information on behalf of individuals or groups of individuals.
- *Assurance*: guarantees or provides confidence that the InfoSec policy has been implemented correctly and the InfoSec elements of the system accurately mediate and enforce that policy.
- *Documentation*: development documentation records how a system is structured and what it is supposed to do, and also gives the background information upon which the design is founded. Control documentation records the resources used in developing and implementing a system that will process, store, and transmit national security information.

InfoSec Objective in the National Security Environment

The overall objective of InfoSec in the national security environment is to prevent unauthorized access to classified information during or resulting from information processing and prevent unauthorized manipulation that could result in national security information being compromised. This is done by:

- protecting and defending information stored, processed, and transmitted by an automated information system (AIS);

- preventing unauthorized access, modification, damage, destruction, or denial of service; and
- providing assurances of:

  compliance with government and contractual obligations and agreements;

  confidentiality of private, sensitive, and classified information;

  integrity of information and related processes;

  availability, when required, of information; and

  use for authorized business and by authorized personnel only of information and AIS; and

- identification and elimination of fraud, waste, and abuse.

RESPONSIBILITIES

The responsibilities for compliance with the AIS security requirements in the world of national security are similar to those of the corporate world. Management is responsible for ensuring compliance with InfoSec requirements, policies, and procedures, as well as ensuring the reporting of violations. All employees are of course responsible for understanding their responsibilities, as well as complying with InfoSec policies, procedures, contract requirements, and the like, and reporting violations to management. However, in this case, the seriousness of the information, and the implications of its loss or compromise, requires that violations be immediately reported and inquiries conducted. The disciplinary action taken against violators is usually more severe.

COLLECTIVE INFOSEC CONTROLS

The InfoSec controls that must be considered for any national security environment include:

- Individual accountability;
- Physical controls;
- System controls;
- System stability;
- Data continuity;
- Least privilege[3];

---

[3] *Least privilege* means that the user or program can only access the information needed and no more. Furthermore, the user does not have any authority that is not absolutely necessary to perform the work assigned—for example, a user might not be allowed to add, delete, or modify databases or information.

- Communications security; and
- National security information controls.

These controls are based on the contractual and noncontractual requirements and generally established national security principles. The InfoSec program that includes the objectives and controls noted above is usually approved by the government security officer responsible for the security of the corporation's contractual efforts. In fact, each system that is considered for use to process, store, display, and transmit national-security-related information must be approved by the government's security officer (GSO) for the contract. The entire effort often has a name designated for it by the government customer, and it is also called a program instead of a contract, for example, Widget Program.

GOVERNMENT CUSTOMER APPROVAL PROCESS

The government customer must approve each AIS prior to authorizing its use to process, store, or transmit national security information. In order to gain that approval, the government customer usually requests:

- Identification of the AIS;
- Physical location;
- Mode of operation (also called by the U.S. government agencies "security profiles" and "levels of concern");
- Level of national security information to be processed;
- Equipment information:

  Size and type of internal memory and storage medium;

  Components where national security information is retained;

  Disconnect methods used to separate various components, such as printers;

  Switching devices to disable equipment; and

  Block diagram of hardware with links;

- Software information to include the types of operating system(s) and firmware; application programs, vendor's name, and version numbers; and
- Communications devices:

  Configuration;

  Interfaces;

  Identification;

  Points of encryption;

  Remote devices; and

  Protection procedures.

AIS MODES OF OPERATION

There are a number of modes of operation that can be used to process, transmit, and store various types of national security information. The mode used is authorized by the government customer based on the authorized variations in the AIS InfoSec environment. It is based on the personal security clearances of the users and national security information access needs, for example, Secret clearance held by the users and their need to use that information to accomplish the contractual tasks assigned. It is also based on the automated and manual information protection and defense controls that will be used.

The modes of operation that are used generally fall into four distinct categories:

- *Dedicated*: the users all have a personal clearance equal to the highest level of national security information being processed, stored, and transmitted by the AIS, and a need-to-know (NTK) for all the information on that AIS.
- *Systems high*: all the users have a personal clearance, but not a NTK for all the information on the AIS. The users must be separately identified and controlled. This is generally done through passwords, identification devices, and add-on software packages.
- *Partitioned*: all users have a personal clearance for the highest level of national security information processed, but have not necessarily had a special briefing and NTK for all the information on the AIS. The general controls include a separate identity and password for each user, possibly a special briefing and NTK. The AIS is partitioned, to include possibly two or more CPUs in the same "box," using the same communications links.
- *Multilevel*: this mode permits concurrent processing of various, separate national security-related, multicontractual programs' information. This level is the highest, the most costly, and the least flexible of the security modes and is seldom used. Users on these AIS may or may not have a personal security clearance or NTK for all the information on the AIS. Thus, someone with no national security background check or clearance can use the system containing national security information. This is possible because the system is so secure that it prevents the user from accessing national security information of a higher level than the user is cleared to access.

THE APPOINTMENT OF THE DEFENSE INDUSTRY-RELATED CORPORATION'S FOCAL POINT FOR INFOSEC

Gaining approval to process, store, display, and transmit national security information usually requires the approval of the government customer security officer. As with any such process, documentation is required on which to base that approval. The types, format, and specific requirements will vary depending on the customer and the classification of the information, such as Top Secret, Secret, or Confidential.

This InfoSec-related document usually requires that the defense-industry-related corporation (in this case, the ISSO) appoint a focal point with the responsibility for ensuring the national security information is protected in accordance with the contract and applicable related laws, regulations, and other provisions as specified by the government customer.

The responsibilities of the IWC ISSO[4] include:

* Directing the InfoSec program for the contract;
* Ensuring that the personal clearance and NTK of users is in place and enforced;
* Ensuring that the users receive national security briefings and training;
* Ensuring audit trails are in place and audit records reviewed in a timely manner;
* Ensuring the AIS is operating as approved by the government customer;
* Ensuring that any InfoSec-related problems are promptly handled; and
* Designating InfoSec custodians for each AIS who are responsible for the day-to-day InfoSec program for the specified AIS.

DOCUMENTING AND GAINING GOVERNMENT CUSTOMER APPROVAL FOR PROCESSING, STORING, AND TRANSMITTING NATIONAL SECURITY INFORMATION

As mentioned earlier, many government customers require that they approve individual AIS or groups of similar AISs that will be used to process, store, display, and transmit national security information.

---

[4] The individual appointed may have a title other than InfoSec, depending on the government customer, nation-state, or defense-industry-related corporation. That person may be known as the Corporate InfoSec Officer, the Corporate Information Security Officer, the Widget Program InfoSec Officer, etc. Furthermore, the need for documentation, type, etc., will vary not only by nation but also by government agencies within a nation.

However, this approval may be delegated to the corporate InfoSec leader, in this case, the IWC ISSO.

The approval is considered after reviewing the AIS InfoSec-related documentation in a format that they specify and which is usually stated in the contract. The documentation requirement can be very detailed or it can be general in nature, depending on the AIS and the government customer's requirements. The government customers using the government-approved document for that AIS written by the defense-industry-related corporation may then periodically inspect the AIS. Regardless of the format, what is of primary importance is that the InfoSec-related issues be addressed and documented. The following is an example describing the various InfoSec-related issues that may be addressed in documentation:

- *Identification*: Identify the specific AIS or AISs (if they are all identical, e.g. desktop computers, local area networks with workstations). This would include the make, model, serial number, physical location, and mode of operation of each AIS.

- *Summary of System Usage*: This section would include the level of national security information to be processed; any local and remote capabilities; hours of national security information processing; and the percentage of information on the AIS that is considered national security, classified information.

- *AIS Hardware*: The specific hardware must be identified and include a floor plan, schematic, disconnect methods if networked, and any switching devices for disabling the AIS.

- *AIS Software*: The name, type, and versions of the software and how they are safeguarded to ensure that they were not replaced with another version; this includes protection and defense software such as those used for access control or intrusion detection.

- *Communications*: This section would include the identification of the equipment and transmission lines, disconnect methods, configurations and interfaces, remote devices, protection procedures, and physical controls on the lines.

- *Personnel*: Their InfoSec responsibilities, controls to restrict access, visitor and maintenance personnel controls.

- *Physical Controls*: This section would include a description of the physical safeguards and characteristics, including any computer facilities and remote areas.

- *General Access Controls*: Described here would be how passwords were used, logon and logoff procedures, and how users with various national security clearances and NTK were segregated.

- *AIS Operations*: This section would describe how systems were started, used, and shut down, including how they were reconfigured if used at different times for different government programs.

- *Information Storage, Protection Controls*: This section would be used to describe how information was controlled, handled, marked, stored (using what type of accountability system), and declassified (e.g., the process used to downgrade information, such as from Secret to Restricted); and how the information will be destroyed when required. This section deals not only with the hard copies coming off the systems but also the electronic media used as storage devices.
- *Audit Trails and Records*: This section would be used to describe the various types of manual and automated audit trail programs and records that would be used. Included here would be samples of each, as well as their analysis processes.
- *Emergency Plan*: This section would describe the procedures to be used in the event of any emergency, including a security violation, system crash, or other emergencies that may be possible depending on the information environment.

Remember, the level of description and details documented would be based on the national security requirements as specified in the contract.

QUESTIONS TO CONSIDER

Based on what you have read, consider the following questions and how you would reply to them:

- Does your corporation have government contracts?
- Do you have responsibility for an InfoSec program for the government information and/or systems used on the government contracts?
- If not, why not?
- Are you in communication with the government customers' security focal point to ensure that you are meeting the customers' security needs?
- Have you been delegated customer-approval authority to approve systems processing government-agency customer information?
- If so, what are the pros and cons of such a responsibility?
- Are the InfoSec programs used for your government customers always meeting the contractual requirements?
- Do your government customers conduct compliance inspection of your systems, processes, documentation, and the like?
- If deficiencies were noted, do you not only fix the problems, but also install processes so that they will not happen again?
- What are you doing to assist in attracting new government customers?
- If nothing, why not?
- If you could help attract new government customers, how would you go about doing it?

SUMMARY

Thousands of universities, as well as large and small corporations, have government contracts. These contracts vary from research and development contracts to production contracts. Most of them rely heavily on information systems and the use of national security information. These corporations are targets of attacks by other corporations, as well as by a nation's adversaries. This includes some of its "allies" (who are allies in a military sense but adversaries in an economic sense) who also want to gain that competitive edge in economic and military development. Furthermore, they want to do so without paying the high costs of research and development. It is cheaper to steal the information than to develop it on one's own.

A defense-industry-related corporation whose systems will process, store, display, and transmit national security information has a responsibility not only to the corporation, but also to the nation and its citizens. How well the corporation implements an InfoSec program that will be used to safeguard the national security information has a direct bearing on the security of the nation.

Although the loss of national security information would have more serious consequences than would follow the loss of corporate sensitive information, the InfoSec-related requirements, and the processes implemented to meet those requirements, really are not that much different from those of a corporation's InfoSec program.

Establishing an InfoSec focal point, establishing InfoSec controls, and documenting how systems will operate and how information and systems will be protected is always a good practice—regardless of the type of sensitive information processed, stored, and transmitted.

Section III

The Global, Professional, and Personal Challenges of an ISSO

In the first two sections of this book, you have been introduced to the internal and external world of the ISSO. The third and last section of this book discusses the major challenges for the ISSO, now and into the future. The most challenging threat to the ISSO—and a growing threat—is that of information warfare, including terrorism. Although various types of information warfare have been around since someone first used the term *information*, because of high technology that threat is rapidly growing. Therefore, Section III begins with an introduction and overview of information warfare (IW).

The IW chapter is followed by a chapter on the ISSO and responsibilities related to ethical conduct. This new chapter was considered important since ethics and being an ISSO professional go hand-in-hand, while at the same time, ethical conduct throughout many societies, cultures, governments, and corporations is on the decline.

The next two chapters, "ISSO Career Development" and "How to Market Yourself as an ISSO," discuss the education, training, and experience needed to qualify for a position as an ISSO, as well as how to "interview by portfolio" to gain the ISSO position you've been looking for.

As part of that career progression, there comes a point where an experienced ISSO decides that working for oneself is more rewarding than working for others. Thus, the chapter "So, Are you Ready to Become an InfoSec Consultant?" is provided. This chapter describes how to determine whether InfoSec consulting is right for you and, if so, how one goes about getting started.

The final chapter of this book looks into the future and discusses the challenges and risks the ISSO will face in this 21st century.

13

The Related World of Information Warfare, Information Operations, and Information Assurance

War does not determine who is right—only who is left.—Bertrand Russell

CHAPTER OBJECTIVE

This chapter, "The Related World of Information Warfare, Information Operations, and Information Assurance," describes an old, yet new type of warfare. Terms such as information warfare, information assurance, and information operations will be discussed; as well as their impact on business.

INTRODUCTION

The Cold War has ended, but it has been replaced by the continuance of older wars by other methods. These wars involve unprecedented use of high technology as tools to assist in conducting information warfare (IW). IW encompasses electronic warfare, techno-terrorist activities, and even economic espionage. It includes attacks against governments' and businesses' networks using malicious codes. While ISSOs may look at attacks against their corporate systems as "some hacker," it may in fact be a probe of the corporate InfoSec defenses by a competitor, possibly even a competitor from a foreign nation-state. It may be for the purpose of stealing corporate trade secrets to share with its domestic businesses, or even a prelude to an all-out attack against the corporations and government agencies of a nation-state.

As we have seen from the attacks on the World Trade Center, and as can be seen throughout history, hostile groups or nation-states will attack the corporations of their nation-state adversaries. The Allies in World War

II bombed the cities and factories of their enemies. The targets included commercial businesses such as the oil refining plants and the ball bearing plants of Germany. That was because the adversaries relied on such plants to prosecute the war. Today, the nation-states target more information-based "factories" such as telecommunications corporations and computer networks. They do so for the very same reason: Such "plants" help an adversary prosecute their wars—wars of business competition, or wars of nation-states—using information warfare tactics. What if you worked for IWC—would such attacks apply to IWC? Of course they would. If not directly, what about collateral damage? If major telecommunications links were not available because of an IW attack, would IWC be able to conduct its online business transactions, communicate via e-mail, and the like? The answer is no, they would not. IWC would be the victim of an IW attack even if it was not the intended, direct target of the attack. As an ISSO, what are your responsibilities relative to direct and indirect attacks?

It is imperative that as an ISSO, you understand basic concepts related to IW and also expand the focus of your attention beyond defending against "some hacker." The IW attacks may use hacker techniques as a ruse, but they may also be using very sophisticated attack techniques that you never thought possible. Such tactics, such as malicious code as an offensive IW weapon, are considered weapons of mass destruction by nation-states that are very dependent on information and information-based systems.

As global competition increases, governments are becoming more actively involved in gathering information about the companies of foreign countries. The terrorists of the future are using technology not only to communicate among themselves, but also to commit high-technology crimes to fund their activities. They are beginning to look at the potential for using high technology against their enemies. As their level of sophistication increases, so do the threats to the nation-state's government agencies and businesses.

These threats will challenge the ISSO more than ever before. The threats from teenage hackers, company employees, and phreakers are nothing compared to what may come in the future. These information warfare warriors aren't "script kiddies" but individuals with doctorates in computer science who may have reverse-engineered IBM mainframe computer systems in the past. They are backed by financial support from foreign governments. They are conducting and will continue to conduct sophisticated attacks using these new weapons of mass information and information systems destruction against companies' and government agencies' systems.

Wars have been fought ever since there were human beings around who did not agree with one another. These conflicts continue to this day with no end in sight. The use of information in warfare is nothing new.

Those that had the best information the fastest and were able to act on it the soonest were usually the victors in battle.

Is it any wonder, now that we are in the Information Age, that we should also have information warfare? No, that is certainly not surprising—or at least it shouldn't be. Since we now look at almost everything on a global scale, it should also not be surprising that information warfare is viewed on a global scale. Information warfare is today's much-talked-about type of warfare. A search of the Internet in just one language (English) on the topic using Google.com disclosed 472,000 hits. Information warfare is becoming an integral part of warfare of all types in the modern era. One can argue that information warfare has existed in all generations of warfare and included spying, observation balloons, breaking enemy codes, and many other functions and activities. True, information warfare is as old as humanity, but many aspects of how it is being applied in our information-dependent, information-based world are new.

INTRODUCTION TO GLOBAL INFORMATION WARFARE[1]

In the early 1990s several people in the U.S. Department of Defense (DoD) articulated a unique form of warfare termed *Information Warfare*, or IW. The Chinese say they were developing IW concepts in the late 1980s. Who's correct? Does it matter? As the areas embraced by IW have been developed over the centuries and millennia, these have been a normal part of human activities from mankind's beginning. What's unique about IW is that it's the first instantiation of trying to tie together all the areas that make up the information environment (IE). The IE runs through every part of your country, organization, and personal life. At the present time there is no cookbook recipe to do the extremely complex task of bringing together all the areas. IW is both art and science.

What is IW? IW basically is a coherent and synchronized blending of physical and virtual actions to have countries, organizations, and individuals perform, or not perform, actions so that your goals and objectives are attained and maintained, while simultaneously preventing competitors from doing the same to you. Clearly this embraces much more than attacking computers with malicious code. The litmus test is this: If information is used to perpetrate an act that was done to influence another to take or not take actions beneficial to the attacker, then it can be considered IW.

The definition is intentionally broad, embracing organizational levels, people, and capabilities. There are also many areas of IW (See Figure 13.1).

---

[1] The majority of the information provided in this chapter was excerpted from Chapter 1 of the book *Global Information Warfare: How Businesses, Governments and Others Achieve Objectives and Attain Competitive Advantages*; published by Auerbach Publications, a CRC Press Company, 2002; co-authored by Gerald L. Kovacich, Perry Luzwick, and Andy Jones, and reprinted with permission of the publisher.

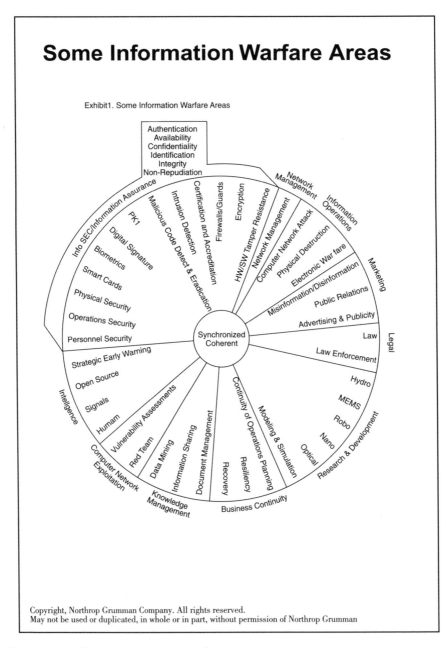

Figure 13.1   Many information warfare areas.

It allows room for governments, cartels, corporate, hacktivists, terrorists, other groups, and individuals to have a part. It is up to each enlightened enterprise to tailor the definition to fit its needs. This should not be a definition of convenience, to "check the box."

You are asked, and many times forced by government and businesses, to depend on the Internet. The Internet that is home to hackers, crackers, phreakers, hacktivists, script kiddies, industrial espionage, and information warriors. The Internet that is home to worms, Trojan horses, software bugs, hardware glitches, distributed denial of service (DDOS) attacks, and viruses. All this, and the Internet is only a portion of the areas that IW addresses. Although the Internet touches many critical infrastructures, and these in turn affect the many information environments (IE) with which you interface, most of the IW areas were around before the Internet.

As "competition" is analogous to "enemy" or "adversary," other business-military analogies can be made with profit, shareholder value, competitive edge, and industry rank to achieve brand recognition, customer loyalty, exerting power, influence, and market share. A business leader or military leader must train and equip forces; gather intelligence; assemble, deploy, and employ forces at decisive places and times; sustain them; form coalitions with other businesses and nation-states; and be successful. There are many physical and virtual world parallels, as can be seen in this news item: "Cisco to use SNA as *weapon* against *competition*. . . . Cisco believes its experience in melding SNA and IP internetworks can be used as a *weapon* in the company's *battle* with Lucent and Nortel for *leadership* in converging voice, video, and data over IP networks."[2]

Purists will focus on warfare as a state of affairs that must be declared by a government and can only be conducted by a government. Microsoft attacking Netscape, guerrilla warfare, economic warfare (one country forcing another country to spend itself into bankruptcy, as the United States did to the Soviet Union), or a company adjusting prices to damage its competition (e.g., taking a long time horizon to use volume and time to adjust prices downward). "Conflict" or "that's business" doesn't carry the same sound of ultimate struggle as referring to business as "war." Clausewitz stated, "War is an extension of politics." By analogy, since business is the implementation of a country's laws, economic policy, and values, business is an extension of politics.

In a free market economy, competition is central to business strategy to win customers and market share. Competition, like war, is a struggle for a winning position. The marketplace can then be referred to analogously as a battlefield with winners and losers. It follows that business is analogous to war. Therefore, using military phraseology in a business context is appropriate. In fact, one just has to remember September 11, 2001, and New York's World Trade Centers to see that in today's world, warfare is

---

[2] *Network World*, August 10, 1998.

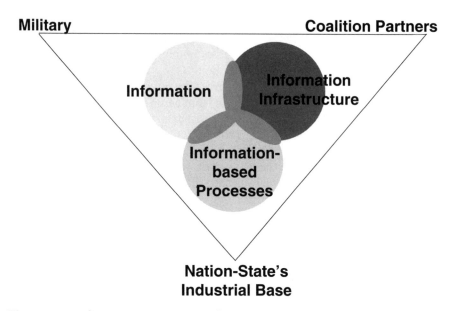

Figure 13.2   The major components of an information environment (IE).

waged on many levels by various adversaries against various targets. These targets may be nation-states, their governments, groups, businesses, or individuals. The tools will be any that can be applied for attackers to successfully attain their goals.

Information moves across information infrastructures in support of information-based processes. Information infrastructure is the media within which we store, process, display, and transmit information. Examples are people, computers, fiber optic cable, lasers, telephones, and satellites. Examples of information-based processes are the established ways to obtain and exchange information. This includes people to people (e.g., telephone conversations and office meetings), electronic commerce/electronic data interchange (EC/EDI), data mining, batch processing, and surfing the Web. Attacking (i.e., denying, altering, or destroying) one or more of the IE's components can result in the loss of tens of millions of dollars in profit and degraded national security, and can be more effective than physical destruction. Degrade or destroy any one of the components and, like a three-legged stool, the IE will eventually collapse.[3] The combination of military coalition partners, and a nation-state's industrial base may be such a stool. (See Figure 13.2.)

---

[3] "What's a Pound of Your Information Worth? Constructs for Collaboration and Consistency," Perry Luzwick, American Bar Association, Standing Committee on Law and National Security, National Security Law Report, August 1999.

For every minute information systems are not up and fully running, revenues, profits, and shareholder value are being lost. The last thing a general counsel needs is a lawsuit from unhappy shareholders who are suing for millions because the corporation did not follow best practices to protect information. One problem is that commercial off-the-shelf (COTS) hardware and software is very difficult to protect. Another concern is that firewalls, intrusion detection devices, and passwords are not enough. The state of the art in IA is against script kiddies and moderately skilled hackers. What about the competition, drug cartels, and hostile nation-states who are significantly better funded? There isn't a firewall or intrusion detection device on the market that cannot be penetrated or bypassed. Password dictionaries can cover almost any entire language, and there are very specific dictionaries (e.g., sports, *Star Trek*, or historic dates and events).

IEs exist internal and external to an organization. An IE is tailorable so it can support many actors. The example below involves a corporation, its customers, and the government. Another IE may be a military, its allies and coalition partners, and the government (see Figure 13.3). Whatever makes up a specific IE, the important fact remains that if its elements aren't protected and secured, the consequences can range from irritants to catastrophes.

All organizations have employees. These employees deliver products, services, and processes to customers. To keep the organization running, suppliers deliver products, services, and processes. Financial stakeholders—venture capitalists, banks, stockholders, and others—provide capital. The public has a positive, neutral, or negative view of the

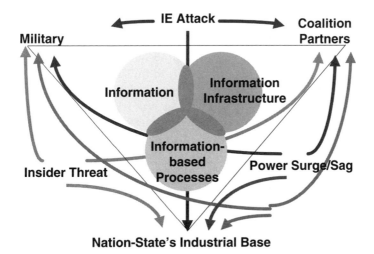

Figure 13.3 An enterprise IE.

organization. Strategic teaming partners provide physical, financial, cerebral, and other capabilities. Every entity with which the organization is linked has its own IE. IEs are connected to, and interdependent upon, other IEs. (See Figure 13.4.)

IW TERMS OF REFERENCE

IW cuts across national borders, educational background, and cultural views. To ensure a consistent understanding during this discussion, working definitions of IW and many supporting terms will be offered. This does not preclude national interpretations and certainly does not attempt to rationalize, harmonize, and normalize definitions. Common terms of reference (TOR) permit a shared understanding, as well as a point of departure for applying the TOR within specific organizations.

There are as many definitions of IW and related topics as there are people. It's reminiscent of three blind men describing an elephant by touching the animal's various parts. One blind man said, "An elephant is a reptile and is thin and long" as he was touching the tail. Touching the tusks, another blind man said, "An elephant is like a big fish with its smooth and pointed body." The third blind man said, "An elephant resembles a large leaf with a hole in the middle" because he was touching the ears. None of them could extrapolate their interpretations to a real elephant. Similarly, what one sees is not necessarily what one gets. "Quesque c'est?" will be mispronounced if one does not have a basic understanding of French diction. So, too, is it with terms used to describe various practices in the information realm.

In some cases, more terminology only detracts. "Cyber" is too limiting. It's as if, rather than push through difficult points to achieve philosophical insights and technical understanding, people create terms to differentiate themselves without knowing what they are doing.

Information and knowledge are now in vogue. We are in the Information Age, and rapidly transitioning into the Knowledge Age. Acquiring the right data, deriving good information, and applying it to make sound decisions to positively affect the bottom line is essential. Search engines have made finding information on the Internet very simple. Witness during the past 15 years the explosion of terminology related to the protection of information and using information for national security purposes. The most important point is to understand the meaning of these terms and what the different functions can—and cannot—do in order to make an informed decision whether or not to commit resources (i.e., people, money, and time).

Many countries have developed definitions. IW, information assurance, information operations, information superiority, and other constructs popular in the U.S. military are part of the Revolution in Military

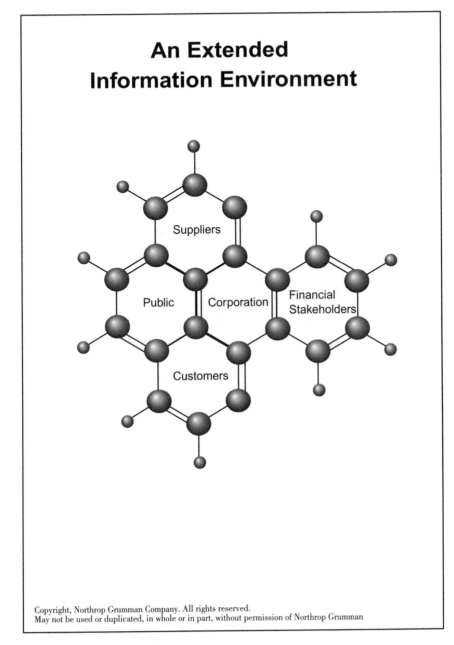

**An Extended
Information Environment**

Suppliers

Public   Corporation   Financial
Stakeholders

Customers

Figure 13.4   An extended IE.

Affairs (RMA) and Revolution in Security Affairs (RSA). Government organizations and businesses have developed additional terms, and some do
not agree with the national version. So there can be a point of departure
for this discussion, definitions accepted by many are put forth. In some
cases, working definitions will be used. The following definitions are from
the U.S. Department of Defense Dictionary of Military and Associated
Terms[4]:

- *Command and Control Warfare (C2W):* The integrated use of operations security, military deception, psychological operations, electronic warfare, and physical destruction, mutually supported by
  intelligence, to deny information to, influence, degrade, or destroy
  adversary command and control capabilities, while protecting
  friendly command and control capabilities against such actions.
  Command and control warfare is an application of information
  warfare in military operations and is a subset of information warfare.
  Command and control warfare applies across the range of military
  operations and all levels of conflict. Also called C2W. C2W is both
  offensive and defensive.
- *Defense in depth:* The siting of mutually supporting defense positions
  designed to absorb and progressively weaken attack, prevent initial
  observations of the whole position by the enemy, and to allow the
  commander to maneuver the reserve.
- *Information assurance (IA):* Information operations that protect and
  defend information and information systems by ensuring their availability, integrity, authentication, confidentiality, and nonrepudiation.
  This includes providing for restoration of information systems by
  incorporating protection, detection, and reaction capabilities.
- *Information environment:* The aggregate of individuals, organizations, or systems that collect, process, or disseminate information;
  also included is the information itself.
- *Information warfare (IW):* Information operations conducted during
  time of crisis or conflict to achieve or promote specific objectives over
  a specific adversary or adversaries.

Let's expand on this because of the definition of IW. What is IW? It's
more than computer network attack (CNA) and defense (CND). That much
everyone agrees on. But what else is encompassed by it? Heated debates
go on today about what IW should embrace and accomplish. IW is an
umbrella concept embracing many disciplines. IW is most effective when
performed in a synchronized and coherent fashion. That is why knowledge management (KM) complements it so well. All components of an

---

[4] *Department of Defense Dictionary of Military and Associated Terms*, April 12, 2001.

organization, as well as across the enterprise, need to be included in an IW action plan.

The good news is IW embraces the marketing, public relations, counterintelligence, and other functions you now perform. IW is not these functions renamed. They continue to be run by the subject matter experts. IW is the coherent application and synchronized approach of these functions. What is needed are experts who, by analogy, are conductors of the orchestra. They know where the expertise resides within the organization, understand what the functions can and cannot do, and bring them to bear for optimum performance. At present only the military in a few countries comes close to understanding the relationships and functions of linking the physical domain with the virtual realm, and has begun policy development and allocation of resources. The equivalent does not exist in industry—yet.

The purpose of IW is to control or influence a decision-maker's actions. An area of control can be directly manipulated, whereas an area of influence can only be indirectly manipulated. Control and influence are the essence of power. From a business perspective, sector and industry leading market share and profit are the results of proper IW execution.

What would make a decision-maker act or not act? Perhaps false or misleading information, an analysis of open source information, documents mysteriously acquired, or intelligence from an employee hired away from the competition. IW at the corporate level manifests itself in marketing, public relations, legal, research and development, manufacturing, and other functions. With the introduction of commercial high-resolution satellite photography, some companies have altered their delivery and shipment schedules, including using empty rail cars and semi-tractor trailers to mask inventory, production capability, and customer quantities. IW is a full spectrum of capabilities. Ingredients are carefully selected and tailored to each case.

IW can be conducted without using physical destruction. Military psychological operations (PSYOPS) and commercial advertising both heavily depend on psychology and sociology, the study of individual and group behavior. The implications of this insight are enormous. Businesses engage in IW all the time, or is it that only the effective ones do?

IW enables direct and indirect attacks from anywhere around the world in a matter of seconds. Physical proximity to a target is not necessary. How is this possible? Because we have made conscious and unconscious decisions to have speed and connectivity without complementary security. In Sun Tzu's and Genghis Khan's eras, physical, personnel, and operational security were all that was needed for protection. Today we have fiber optics, satellites, personal digital assistants (PDAs), infrared and laser communications, interactive cable television, mobile phones, and a host of other technology marvels that allow us in a few seconds to reach anywhere. Now in seconds our information can be intercepted, modified, manipulated, and stolen.

No simple sentence or paragraph effectively describes IW. There are broad and narrow interpretations within national and international government, business, and academic communities, and some even totally reject the notion of IW. The overall view of IW must be expansive. Information is everywhere. We find information, for example, in mass media such as radio, television, and newspapers, at World Wide Web (WWW, or Web) sites, in communications systems, and in computer networks and systems. Any and all may be subjected to attack via Offensive IW (OIW). It follows that all these areas must be defended with Defensive IW (DIW):

- *Offensive IW* can make a government, society/nation, or business bend to the will of the attacker. Attacks can be very large, devastating, and noticed, such as economic or social disruption or breakdown, and denial of critical infrastructure (e.g., power, transportation, communications, and finance) capabilities. They can also be small, low key, and unassuming, such as a request for publications and telephone calls (as the basis for social engineering). Businesses do not have the deep pockets of a government, but that does not restrict them from engaging in IW. A business wants to deny the competition orders, customers, and information about its research and development (R&D). Industrial espionage has its share of illegal activities: theft, monitoring communications, and denying use of servers to conduct electronic commerce. Governments engage in psychological operations (with the subsets of mis-/disinformation, propaganda using leaflets, television, and radio broadcasts). Businesses must identify when disinformation is being used to lure customers away and have the means to counter it. Of course, that's starting from a position of weakness. What is a proactive, defensive IW approach to counter the attack? Inoculate the customers, suppliers, business partners, and others in the IE.
- *Defensive IW* is the ability to protect and defend the IE. Defense does not imply reactive. Measures can be taken to forewarn of attacks and to preposition physical and virtual forces. Examples of virtual forces are software and brainpower. The acme of skill is to present a posture to prevent a competitor from attacking and to achieve victory without having to attack. Perception management is as important as demonstrable physical and virtual capabilities.

Information operations (IO) as described below is included in IW: Actions taken to affect adversary information and information systems while defending one's own information and information systems. Also called IO.

- *Defensive IO*: The integration and coordination of policies and procedures, operations, personnel, and technology to protect and defend information and information systems. Defensive information operations are conducted through information assurance, physical security, operations security, counter-deception, counter-psychological operations, counterintelligence, electronic warfare, and special information operations. Defensive information operations ensure timely, accurate, and relevant information access while denying adversaries the opportunity to exploit friendly information and information systems for their own purposes.
- *Offensive IO*: The integrated use of assigned and supporting capabilities and activities, mutually supported by intelligence, to affect adversary decision makers to achieve or promote specific objectives. These capabilities and activities include, but are not limited to, operations security, military deception, psychological operations, electronic warfare, physical attack and/or destruction, and special information operations, and could also include computer network attack.
- *Information superiority*: The degree of dominance in the information domain, which permits the conduct of operations without effective opposition. Information superiority is the relative state of influence and control of the IE between two or more actors. Some argue the opposite of "superiority" is "inferiority." This is not the case. All actors have equal access to open source information. Restricted, sensitive, and classified information can be acquired through overt or covert operations. Having the data, information, and knowledge is not the key to attaining and maintaining information superiority. What is done with the information and the speed at which it is done is the gold nugget. Information sharing, automation, cross platform information sharing, automating processes (such as air traffic control; sales-manufacturing/production-inventory-transportation; and military intelligence-platform maneuver-weapons selection and release-battle damage assessment) are essential in order to have execution cycles faster than those of the competition.
- *Operations Security*: A process of identifying critical information and subsequently analyzing friendly actions attendant to military operations and other activities to: (a) identify those actions that can be observed by adversary intelligence systems; (b) determine indicators that hostile intelligence systems might obtain that could be interpreted or pieced together to derive critical information in time to be useful to adversaries; and (c) select and execute measures that eliminate or reduce to an acceptable level the vulnerabilities of friendly actions to adversary exploitation. Also called OPSEC.

In addition to the above definitions, U.S. National Security Telecommunications and Information Systems Security Committee (NSTISSC)

4009, National Information Systems Security (INFOSEC) Glossary[5] offers the following:

- *Attack*: Type of incident involving the intentional act of attempting to bypass one or more security controls.
- *Confidentiality*: Assurance that information is not disclosed to unauthorized persons, processes, or devices.
- *Critical Infrastructure*: Those physical and cyber-based systems essential to the minimum operations of the economy and government.
- *Integrity*: Quality of an IS reflecting the logical correctness and reliability of the operating system; the logical completeness of the hardware and software implementing the protection mechanisms; and the consistency of data structures and occurrence of the stored data. Note that, in a formal security mode, integrity is interpreted more narrowly to mean protection of unauthorized modification or destruction of information.
- *Nonrepudiation*: Assurance the sender of the data is provided with proof of delivery and the recipient is provided with proof of the sender's identity, so neither can later deny having processed the data.
- *OPSEC*: Process of denying information to potential adversaries about capabilities and/or intentions by identifying, controlling, and protecting unclassified generic activities.
- *Probe*: Type of incident involving an attempt to gather information about an IS for the apparent purpose of circumventing its security controls.

INFORMATION WARFARE IS A POWERFUL APPROACH FOR ATTAINING AND MAINTAINING A COMPETITIVE ADVANTAGE

The purpose of a business is to create value for its shareholders, and the purpose of a government is to provide for the common good. From a business viewpoint, being effective and efficient in current markets and opening new lines of business is key to sustained revenue generation and profits. At the same time, the business may be the target of an IW attack (see Figure 13.5). From a national security perspective, we should expect the military, intelligence community, and law enforcement to develop and use capabilities in order to maintain sovereignty, create and sustain peace and economic prosperity, and ensure public safety from criminals and monopolies. Neither entity can survive by insulating itself. They must

---

[5] National Security Telecommunications and Information Systems Security Committee Publication 4009, September 2000.

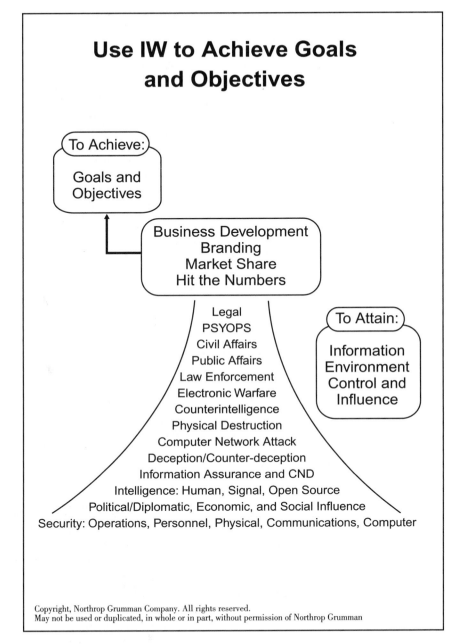

Figure 13.5 How to use IW to achieve goals and objectives.

embrace, within their value system, whatever it takes to go beyond surviving in order to "thrive."

The complexity interwoven across government, industry, and society presents a daunting challenge for IW. It is in the best interest of any government, business, and other organization to take prudent action to defend against information warfare attacks and to be able to launch them.

The advanced cracker breaks into online shopping exchanges, manipulates orders, steals merchandise, plunders credit card numbers—the modern day pirate, highway robber, and Wild West outlaw. Those who would be part of the online shopping population come to expect this malicious behavior and are dissuaded from shopping online. The result: "dotcoms" go out of business, venture capitalists withdraw support and are reluctant to back new startups, and, in the very near future, insurance either will not be written or the premiums will be too high and there will be lawsuits. It appears IW is tailor-made to handle such a situation.

Espionage, disinformation, physical destruction (normally permitted by law only for the military and law enforcement), and other actions are a means to an end. IW is a higher level, cerebral activity. The target can be a population (the national will or a specific political, religious, or ethnic group), a despot, a general, or anyone in an organization. How, then, should IW be applied to industry? After all, isn't war a declaration of Congress, Parliament, or other government entity? If a business is destroyed by an act of war or terrorism, it will not be remunerated by insurance. Is this a misnomer? By no means!

Since business is war, the principles of war normally associated with the military ought to be applied. These are not rigid, and their application is tailored to each use. Objective, offensive, mass, economy of force, unity of leadership, maneuver, security, surprise, and simplicity are generally recognized principles that will benefit any organization. Applying the principles to coherent and synchronized IW will produce a positive return on investment (ROI).

In the IT world, determining ROI is considered the Holy Grail. The problem for quantitative metrics for IW is orders of magnitude more difficult because of the many disciplines, organizational levels, and the sheer scope involved. Some prefer it that way because it allows them to hide behind classified information and black magic. If IW is to be successful, metrics are necessary. Existing traditional measures are a good start (e.g., How many probes did our intrusion detection system pick up?), but are not sufficiently expansive and precise. What is the value of a database? What is the value of that database after it has been successfully data mined? Since quantitative metrics still need to be developed, qualitative ones will need to be used.

Information warfare is an embracing approach, customizable to produce positive results in any organization, and tailorable to meet the demands of the marketplace. By balancing tried and true capabilities with leading-edge technologies and concepts, IW remains fresh and a useful approach for achieving goals and objectives on the way to attaining and maintaining a competitive advantage.

QUESTIONS TO CONSIDER

Based on what you have read, consider the following questions and how you would reply to them:

- As an ISSO, do you think you have a role to play in IW?
- What do you think is the role of an ISSO in the "IT battlefield"?
- Does your CIAPP or related documents consider IW attacks?
- Do your plans consider what must be done to avoid collateral damage in the event of IW attacks against others?
- Can your systems determine whether attacks against it were IW attacks?
- Do you believe offensive IW is a good way to defend against IW attacks, for example, tracing the attacker back to his or her systems and unleashing malicious code against the attacker?
- Do you believe that some of the IW philosophies should be incorporated into your CIAPP, such as OPSEC, information operations?
- If not, why not?

SUMMARY

Information warfare is an embracing concept that brings to bear all the resources of a nation-state or business organization in a coherent and synchronized manner to control the information environment and to attain and maintain a competitive advantage, and to gain power and influence. Judicious use of IW, when coupled with knowledge management and Network Centric Business, leads to reduced or avoided costs, increased revenues, more satisfied customers, and greater profits and national security. Governments and businesses can use IW offensively and defensively in the physical and virtual domains. Counters to IW do not have to be in kind; they can be no, low, or high technology; and they can be asymmetric. Not conducting IW will result in a reduced market presence and lower national security. Although the name may change over the years, IW will evolve from its nascent stage and become mainstream in 20 years.

IW occurs when, in the physical and virtual domains, you attack your competition or they attack you. IW is about synchronized and coherent relationships and capabilities. As previously discussed, central to IW are those physical and virtual capabilities to control the IE.

14

The ISSO and Ethical Conduct

Ethics is not a policing function. It's about creating the kind of climate in which people are encouraged to make the right decisions in the first place.[1]—Kent Kresa

CHAPTER OBJECTIVE

This chapter will discuss the issue of ethics and the ISSO; its importance to the profession; examples of codes of ethics of security and related professions; and the impact of ethics on compliance with the Corporate Information Assets Protection Program (CIAPP).[2]

INTRODUCTION

We hear a lot about ethics these days when it seems everyone is out for themselves, from the executives of major corporations to a secretary in a small company office who perpetrates a fraud. One thing that makes a professional a true professional is ethical conduct. That is especially a requirement for an ISSO.

When you think of ethics and ethical behavior, what comes to mind? For some it means "doing the right thing." But what is the "right" thing to do? For some, it is anything that they can get away with and not violate laws. In fact, some narrowly define being ethical as doing anything as long as it does not violate laws. However, ethics and morality go hand-and-hand but what is moral? For example, communists believe that whatever furthers the advance of communism is moral and acting in a manner that does not further communism is immoral.

Remember that we talked earlier in this book about committing crimes and committing crimes takes opportunity, motive, and rationaliza-

---

[1]Kent Kresa is Chairman of the Board and CEO of Northrop Grumman Corporation.
[2]This chapter is a modified excerpt from a similar chapter related to the corporate security manager in the book *The Manager's Handbook for Corporate Security*, published by Butterworth–Heinemann, 2003, and written by Dr. Kovacich and Mr. Edward Halibozek.

tion. The same applies to ethical behavior. You can use opportunity, motive, and rationalization to do the "right" thing or to not do what is right.

eth·ics [éthiks] noun

1. study of morality's effect on conduct: the study of moral standards and how they affect conduct (takes a singular verb); Also called moral philosophy; 2. code of morality: a system of moral principles governing the appropriate conduct for an individual or group (takes a plural verb) [15th century. Via Old French ethiques from, ultimately, Greek ēthikē, from ēthikos "ethical" (see ethic).][3]

If you find someone's wallet, you have the opportunity to keep it. Suppose the motive is that you do not have a job and you have a family to support. You can rationalize it by saying that the money can buy much-needed food for the family, and besides, the person must be well off based on the number of gold and platinum credit cards in the wallet. Let's say that you just found the money and there is absolutely no evidence indicating to whom it belonged. Would it then be ok to keep it? The answer in both cases is no. Why? It does not belong to you. Therefore, even if it were not against the law to keep the money, it would be still unethical. However, sometimes the process is that you turn it over to the local police and if, after a set period of time, no one claims the money, it is yours. That would be ethical because you followed the locally established processes. What about illegally copying software in violation of copyright laws? Isn't that also unethical?

The interesting thing about ethics is that it may also depend on your culture. For example, the businessperson who gives gifts to a procurement officer in a corporation that he or she wants to do business with may be breaking the law in some countries, but such gifts are expected in others. Is it wrong to accept the gifts in those countries where that is a tradition? No. Of course, if it violated a law or company policy, it would also be unethical because violating a law is in itself unethical. Add to all this the moral issues, knowing what is right and what is wrong, considering what you were taught growing up, and all this brought together and integrated in each of us with our culture, working environment, and the like. The philosophy of morals and ethics has been the subject of study and discussions for centuries. We surely will not provide the definitive answers here. However, we must understand the basics of ethics because it does have an impact on protecting corporate assets.

---

[3]*Encarta World English Dictionary,* © & (P) 1999, Microsoft Corporation. All rights reserved. Developed for Microsoft by Bloomsbury Publishing Plc.

mor·al [máwrəl] adjective

1. involving right and wrong: relating to issues of right and wrong and to how individuals should behave; 2. derived from personal conscience: based on what somebody's conscience suggests is right or wrong, rather than on what the law says should be done; 3. in terms of natural justice: regarded in terms of what is known to be right or just, as opposed to what is officially or outwardly declared to be right or just; a moral victory; 4. encouraging goodness and respectability: giving guidance on how to behave decently and honorably; 5. good by accepted standards: good or right, when judged by the standards of the average person or society at large; 6. telling right from wrong: able to distinguish right from wrong and to make decisions based on that knowledge; 7. based on conviction: based on an inner conviction, in the absence of physical proof.

noun (plural mor·als)

1. valuable lesson in behavior: a conclusion about how to behave or proceed drawn from a story or event; 2. final sentence of story giving advice: a short, precise rule, usually written in a rather literary style as the conclusion to a story, used to help people remember the best or most sensible way to behave

plural noun mor·als

standards of behavior: principles of right and wrong as they govern standards of general or sexual behavior

[14th century. From Latin moralis, from mor-, stem of mos "custom," in plural "morals" (source of English morale and morose).][4]

Ethical behavior is expected of everyone who works in a corporation. Few if any corporations or any type of business or government agency want to be seen as doing anything unethical.

Some people believe that if it is not against the law, it is ethical. Often it seems that corporations that walk a fine line between legal and illegal behavior use a great deal of rationalization to justify their actions. However, in most circumstances, the ethical question remains: Yes, it is legal, but is it the ethical thing to do?

If you see someone in your corporation doing something that violates corporate policy, should you report that person to management? This is probably an employee's most difficult ethical dilemma. In some nation-states, it is better to not report anyone, even committing a serious crime, because many children were brought up to not be a "squealer," a "fink," a "snitch." In some societies, that is almost as bad, if not worse, as committing the offense that is being reported.

---

[4] *Encarta World English Dictionary,* © & (P) 1999, Microsoft Corporation. All rights reserved. Developed for Microsoft by Bloomsbury Publishing Plc.

Because of the amount of unethical behavior within some corporations and nation-states, there are processes by which one, sometimes called a *whistleblower*, can receive financial rewards for identifying illegal or unethical behavior. However, as much as corporations like to say that they have an ethics program within their corporation, when an employee comes forth and reports illegal activities, it seems that, more often than not, he or she is the subject of harassment, receives no promotions, and is made to feel unwanted in the corporation. Management looks upon that person as one who could not be trusted. Ironic, isn't it? A person reports someone's unethical behavior in accordance with the corporate policy. That person, instead of being considered an honest and loyal employee, is considered to be untrustworthy. There are many examples of such conduct within the corporations of the United States and other nation-states. Suffice it to say that corporate management can tout an ethics program, but one that truly works as stated in the brochures is another matter.

CODES OF ETHICS

Most, if not all, professional associations have a Code of Ethics. They are all about the same in that one must do what is right and report what is wrong. As an ISSO professional, you must behave in a professional manner at all times and therefore, comply with the professional code of ethics.

It is quite possible that members of associations with a code of ethics have actually never read the code of ethics, even though as an ISSO professional and member of one or more security-related associations, you are required to comply with the associations' codes of ethics. In fact, it can even be considered unethical not to have ever read the codes of ethics for the various associations to which you as an ISSO professional belong.

What does that say about you and your professionalism? One may counter by saying that he or she always acts in an ethical manner and doesn't have to read any codes of ethics. This "know-it-all" attitude is a symptom of possibly a more serious matter: the idea that one has no more to learn about an InfoSec-related topic. That is not only impossible but will end up costing the corporation in terms of effectiveness and efficiency. How? Because the ISSO who is not continuously learning and applying new and better techniques does not take advantage of new (and possibly better and cheaper) ways of protecting assets.

Now is a good time to take the opportunity to read some codes of ethics from security-related professional associations. Please take the time to read, understand, and apply the codes of ethics that follow.

American Society for Industrial Security[5]

Aware that the quality of professional security activity ultimately depends upon the willingness of practitioners to observe special standards of conduct and to manifest good faith in professional relationships, the American Society for Industrial Security adopts the following Code of Ethics and mandates its conscientious observance as a binding condition of membership in or affiliation with the Society:

Code of Ethics

I.   A member shall perform professional duties in accordance with the law and the highest moral principles.
II.   A member shall observe the precepts of truthfulness, honesty, and integrity.
III. A member shall be faithful and diligent in discharging professional responsibilities.
IV.   A member shall be competent in discharging professional responsibilities.
V.   A member shall safeguard confidential information and exercise due care to prevent its improper disclosure.
VI.   A member shall not maliciously injure the professional reputation or practice of colleagues, clients, or employers.

Article I

A member shall perform professional duties in accordance with the law and the highest moral principles.

Ethical Considerations

I-1 A member shall abide by the law of the land in which the services are rendered and perform all duties in an honorable manner.

I-2 A member shall not knowingly become associated in responsibility for work with colleagues who do not conform to the law and these ethical standards.

I-3 A member shall be just and respect the rights of others in performing professional responsibilities.

Article II

A member shall observe the precepts of truthfulness, honesty, and integrity.

---

[5] See http://www.asisonline.org/codeofethics.html

Ethical Considerations

II-1 A member shall disclose all relevant information to those having the right to know.

II-2 A right to know is a legally enforceable claim or demand by a person for disclosure of information by a member. Such a right does not depend upon prior knowledge by the person of the existence of the information to be disclosed.

II-3 A member shall not knowingly release misleading information nor encourage or otherwise participate in the release of such information.

Article III

A member shall be faithful and diligent in discharging professional responsibilities.

Ethical Considerations

III-1 A member is faithful when fair and steadfast in adherence to promises and commitments.

III-2 A member is diligent when employing best efforts in an assignment.

III-3 A member shall not act in matters involving conflicts of interest without appropriate disclosure and approval.

III-4 A member shall represent services or products fairly and truthfully.

Article IV

A member shall be competent in discharging professional responsibilities.

Ethical Considerations

IV-1 A member is competent who possesses and applies the skills and knowledge required for the task.

IV-2 A member shall not accept a task beyond the member's competence nor shall competence be claimed when not possessed.

Article V

A member shall safeguard confidential information and exercise due care to prevent its improper disclosure.

Ethical Considerations

V-1 Confidential information is nonpublic information, the disclosure of which is restricted.

V-2 Due care requires that the professional must not knowingly reveal confidential information, or use a confidence to the disadvantage of the principal or to the advantage of the member or a third person, unless the principal consents after full disclosure of all the facts. This confidentiality continues after the business relationship between the member and his principal has terminated.

V-3 A member who receives information and has not agreed to be bound by confidentiality is not bound from disclosing it. A member is not bound by confidential disclosures made of acts or omissions which constitute a violation of the law.

V-4 Confidential disclosures made by a principal to a member are not recognized by law as privileged in a legal proceeding. The member may be required to testify in a legal proceeding to the information received in confidence from his principal over the objection of his principal's counsel.

V-5 A member shall not disclose confidential information for personal gain without appropriate authorization.

Article VI

A member shall not maliciously injure the professional reputation or practice of colleagues, clients, or employers.

Ethical Considerations

VI-1 A member shall not comment falsely and with malice concerning a colleague's competence, performance, or professional capabilities.

VI-2 A member who knows, or has reasonable grounds to believe, that another member has failed to conform to the Society's Code of Ethics shall present such information to the Ethical Standards Committee in accordance with Article VIII of the Society's bylaws.

Information Systems Security Association[6]

The primary goal of the Information Systems Security Association, Inc. (ISSA) is to promote management practices that will ensure the confidentiality, integrity, and availability of organizational information resources. To achieve this goal, members of the Association must reflect the highest standards of ethical conduct and technical competence. Therefore, ISSA has established the following Code of Ethics and requires its observance as a prerequisite and continuation of membership and affiliation with the Association.

As an applicant for membership and as a member of ISSA, I have in the past and will in the future:

- Perform all professional activities and duties in accordance with the law and the highest ethical principles;

---

[6] See http://www.issa-intl.org/codefethics.html

- Promote good information security concepts and practices;
- Maintain the confidentiality of all proprietary or otherwise sensitive information encountered in the course of professional activities;
- Discharge professional responsibilities with diligence and honesty;
- Refrain from any activities which might constitute a conflict of interest or otherwise damage the reputation of employers, the information security profession, or the Association; and
- Not intentionally injure or impugn the professional reputation or practice of colleagues, clients, or employers.

High Technology Crime Investigation Association[7]

I will support the objectives and purposes of the HTCIA, as stated in Article II of the Association Bylaws. I agree to respect the confidential nature of any sensitive information, procedures, or techniques that I become aware of because of my involvement with the HTCIA. I will not disclose such confidential material to anyone who is not a member in good standing of the HTCIA without the written permission from the HTCIA Board of Directors.

Association of Certified Fraud Examiners[8]

All Certified Fraud Examiners must meet the rigorous criteria for admission to the Association of Certified Fraud Examiners. Thereafter, they must exemplify the highest moral and ethical standards and must agree to abide by the bylaws of the Association and the Certified Fraud Examiner Code of Professional Ethics. . . .

- A Certified Fraud Examiner shall, at all times, demonstrate a commitment to professionalism and diligence in the performance of his or her duties.
- A Certified Fraud Examiner shall not engage in any illegal or unethical conduct, or any activity which would constitute a conflict of interest.
- A Certified Fraud Examiner shall, at all times, exhibit the highest level of integrity in the performance of all professional assignments and will accept only assignments for which there is reasonable expectation that the assignment will be completed with professional competence.
- A Certified Fraud Examiner will comply with lawful orders of the courts and will testify to matters truthfully and without bias or prejudice.
- A Certified Fraud Examiner, in conducting examinations, will obtain evidence or other documentation to establish a reasonable basis for any opinion rendered. No opinion shall be expressed regarding the guilt or innocence of any person or party.

---

[7] See http://www.htcia.org/searchframeset.htm
[8] See http://www.cfenet.com/about/codeethics.asp

- A Certified Fraud Examiner shall not reveal any confidential information obtained during a professional engagement without proper authorization.
- A Certified Fraud Examiner will reveal all material matters discovered during the course of an examination which, if omitted, could cause a distortion of the facts.
- A Certified Fraud Examiner shall continually strive to increase the competence and effectiveness of professional services performed under his or her direction.

CORPORATE ETHICS, STANDARDS OF CONDUCT, BUSINESS PRACTICES, AND CORPORATE VALUES

Many corporations in many countries of the world today concern themselves with ethics, standards of conduct, business practices, and values. What does all that mean? Basically, it still means that one must know the difference between right and wrong, acceptable conduct versus unacceptable conduct. In today's world, corporations are successfully sued because of the unethical conduct of their employees. Therefore, if for no other reason than loss of revenue, such matters are a serious concern of corporate management.

There are corporate policies and awareness training sessions given to employees and often special training given to management. This is because it seems that it is mostly management that is involved in the unethical conduct. For example, management may direct their employees to act in an unethical manner by taking a shortcut in a manufacturing process such as a quality check in order to get the product out the door faster.

ISSO professionals in corporations are often involved in following up on ethics matters that have been reported by managers or employees, either directly or through a corporate ethics hotline, for example, noncompliance with the CIAPP. The ethics hotline provides a communications medium to obtain reports of unethical behavior. It should never be used to try to identify the caller if that caller did not leave any information relative to his or her identity. In fact, to do so would be unethical in itself, and once word got out of such conduct by management, the chances of obtaining further information concerning unethical behavior would be almost zero. If that did occur, that manager seeking the identity of the caller should be the subject of an ethics inquiry. One should never dwell so much on the messenger as the message. After all, isn't that the objective of the ethics program and ethics hotline? It is amazing how many managers in corporations focus on identifying the caller instead of acting on the information the caller provided. That alone tells a great deal about the ethics of some managers.

One often hears about managers "shooting the messenger." Any manager who verbally or otherwise attacks the messenger is "not getting the message." So, what does this have to do with the ISSO and professionalism? As an employee of a corporation, you have probably been on one end or the other—or both—of such incidents. Think about it. No one likes to receive bad news, and finding out through some ethics channel that some assets were stolen, someone was not complying with the assets protection policies, and that this person was a senior executive, may cause management to "shoot the messenger."

As an ISSO professional, you have a professional responsibility not to allow the shooting of messengers. Instead, you must direct management efforts to the identified problem. If you are requested or directed to do all you can to identify the anonymous reporter of ethics violations, you should explain that such conduct is in violation of the corporate ethics policy and therefore, the request or demand itself is unethical. Unfortunately, it may cost you your merit raise, a less than favorable performance review, and the like, but that is a price that you must be willing to pay. It is a matter of principle—your professional integrity—and that means a matter of ethical conduct.

IMPACT OF ETHICS ON THE CORPORATE INFORMATION ASSETS PROTECTION PROGRAM (CIAPP)

There is a direct and, one hopes, obvious relationship between ethical conduct and all that it implies and the CIAPP. Remember, if everyone followed the rules, you would not have a job. If the vast majority of corporate employees followed the rules, you would have less work. Although you will never become obsolete in the world of corporate information and information systems assets protection, wouldn't it be nice to at least get your workload down to the lowest possible level? You would then require less staff, and by having less staff, you would have fewer staff problems to deal with.

Think of it. Less work, less staff, less of a budget to justify, and fewer complaints from employees about how the CIAPP is adversely affecting their work. You could work a regular 8-hour day, weekends off, no nighttime telephone calls, less stress. Ah, wouldn't life be grand? All that you must do is get everyone to always be ethical. In doing so, they would comply with the CIAPP by protecting the company's assets as if the assets were their own. Yes, if only.... However, that is the goal. That is what everyone in the corporation should have as a baseline goal—follow ethical and business standards of conduct by following a code of ethics.

QUESTIONS TO CONSIDER

Based on what you have read, consider the following questions and how you would reply to them:

- Does your company have an ethics program?
- Are you and your staff actively involved in the ethics program?
- Do you support the ethics program by conducting inquiries into non-compliance with the CIAPP or company ethics policies?
- Does your corporation have an ethics hotline?
- Do you discuss ethical behavior with your staff?
- If not, why not?
- If so, what do you discuss and how often?
- Do you use the corporate ethics program to support following the CIAPP?
- If so, do you try to get management to view a CIAPP noncompliance issue as also an ethics issue?

SUMMARY

ISSO professionals must be extremely honest people of high integrity. After all, they know the vulnerabilities of the corporate information and information systems assets as well as the protection mechanisms. That is very valuable information. ISSOs must conduct themselves in an ethical manner at all times. If they belong to a professional, security-related association, they must also adhere to the association's code of conduct.

ISSO professionals must also do their best to encourage all corporate employees, led by executive management, to act in an ethical manner when doing their work at the corporation. The CIAPP will benefit through fewer information thefts, damage, unauthorized modification, and CIAPP violations and will provide for a corporate information assets protection environment that is better overall.

15

ISSO Career Development

A man must serve his time to every trade Save censure—critics all are ready made.[1]—Lord Byron

CHAPTER OBJECTIVE

The ISSO professionals of the 21st century must possess many skills that differ from those possessed by some current and past ISSO professionals. In this chapter, the discussion will center on what are the necessary skills that an ISSO and professional InfoSec staff should possess to be successful; as well as how to establish and maintain an InfoSec career development program.[2]

INTRODUCTION

If you have read this book from the Foreword on to this chapter, you already have some idea of the changes that have occurred over the years in the duties and responsibilities of the ISSO professional. They include a working environment that involves increasing amounts of:

- Complexity;
- Rapidity of change;
- Technology dependence;
- Technology drivenness;
- Sophistication of the workforce;
- Competitiveness in the business world;

---

[1] *Encarta Book of Quotations*, © & (P) 1999, Microsoft Corporation. All rights reserved. Developed for Microsoft by Bloomsbury Publishing Plc.; Lord Byron (1788–1824), English poet. "English Bards and Scotch Reviewers" (1809).

[2] Some of the information noted in this chapter was excerpted from another Butterworth–Heinemann book, *The Manager's Handbook for Corporate Security: How to Develop and Manage a Successful Assets Protection Program*, published in 2003, and co-authored by Gerald L. Kovacich and Edward P. Halibozek.

- Instant communications;
- Information available to more people than ever before;
- Incidents of corporate fraud, waste, and abuse;
- Threats to, and vulnerabilities of, corporate information-related assets; and
- Competition for high-level InfoSec positions.

Since this 21st-century environment means more competition for InfoSec positions, those that want to succeed in this career field must gain *more experience* and have *more education* than ever before—or at least more than other InfoSec professionals they are competing against.

The corporate culture, InfoSec duties, responsibilities, and positions vary almost as much as the number of corporations. Many outsource much of their InfoSec service and support functions while others find it more cost-effective to use employees. No matter what type of corporation—business or government agency for that matter—that you work for, the main goal is still to protect the information and information systems assets of the company (or government agency). Corporations want to hire ISSO and InfoSec professionals who can do that successfully at *least impact to cost and schedules.*

pro·fes·sion·al [prō féshən'l, prō féshnəl, prə féshən'l] adjective

very competent: showing a high degree of skill or competence

noun (*plural* pro·fes·sion·als)

member of profession: somebody whose occupation requires extensive education or specialized training

somebody very competent: somebody who shows a high degree of skill or competence[3]

For those who got into the ISSO profession as a retirement job, well, this is probably not a career for you but just that, a retirement job. The first question one should ask oneself is "Why am I in InfoSec?" This is an important question because it helps determine whether you want to be the best possible ISSO professional the world has even seen; or whether this is just a job and it is too late in life to change careers.

If you consider yourself an ISSO professional and want to be the world's best, then you need a career development program. So read on. If not, skip this chapter and enjoy your "retirement job."

---

[3] *Encarta® World English Dictionary* © & (P) 1999 Microsoft Corporation. All rights reserved. Developed for Microsoft by Bloomsbury Publishing Plc.

THE ISSO'S CAREER DEVELOPMENT PROGRAM

Some questions you may want to ask yourself about an InfoSec career:

- What InfoSec-related career do I want to get into?
- Why?
- What are the qualifications (education and experience) for the entry level, and other security positions?
- What are the positions (specialization) within that profession?
- Are there any that I would like to specialize in?
- Why?
- What are the other positions within the InfoSec profession that I may want to specialize in?
- Can I list them in order of priority, including their education and experience requirements?

The ISSO profession should be researched to obtain the answers to the above questions by:

- Interviewing various ISSO professionals in different types of businesses, nonprofit entities, and government agencies;
- Researching the ISSO profession and its various specialties through the Internet;
- Discussing the profession with representatives from the American Society for Industrial Security (ASIS); High Technology Crime Investigation Association (HTCIA); Association of Certified Fraud Examiners (ACFE); Information Systems Security Association (ISSA); and various training institutes and universities that teach InfoSec-related courses; and
- Reading job descriptions for ISSO positions in the trade journals and newspapers and through interviews with recruiters.

Based on this research, you as an ISSO professional can establish a career development plan beginning at a high level with subsections for education and experience for each position. Let's consider an example. The IWC ISSO knew that one cannot plan for today's job now but one must look at trends in the world, business, high technology, crime, InfoSec, and general security in order to *prepare now for tomorrow's InfoSec job*. The ISSO wanted to work up the InfoSec professional ladder and have experience and education in as many specialties as possible. The ISSO thought that such an approach would be interesting and would provide a chance to learn as much about InfoSec as possible. Also, the ISSO would become most knowledgeable about the various aspects of the profession and also gain a competitive advantage over others when applying for InfoSec positions. However, the ISSO also set two limits:

- Experiences and education must be relevant to eventually becoming an ISSO.
- Time learning through education, training, and gaining experiences must be scheduled so that the intermediary milestones and ultimate goal could be met.

The ISSO also included the goal of supervisory and management experience as well as experience in the worlds of finance, marketing, sales, accounting, investigations, communications, technology, international travel, and human resources. The ISSO, at age 20, set a goal of gradually gaining increased responsibility, experience, and education in security jobs that would prepare the ISSO for a highly paid ISSO position in an international corporation.

Based on the ISSO's research, the ISSO came up with the idea of a "four parallel lines" approach to career development (See Figure 15.1). The ISSO reasoned that there were four main items that should be integrated into the career development plan:

- Money—How much do I want and when to meet my goals?
- Position—What InfoSec positions pay me the money I want to meet my goals based on my timeline of goals?
- Education—What are the education requirements for each position I want to get?
- Experience—What are the experience requirements for each position I want to get?

The ISSO's goal was to be the most qualified person for each position in the ISSO's career development plan. The ISSO knew that one could

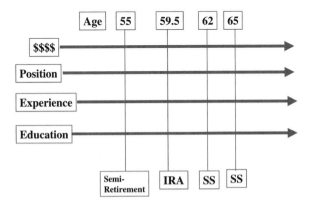

Figure 15.1 The four parallel lines approach to career development from the beginning including Individual Retirement Account (IRA) funds and Social Security funds (SS).

not plan for other events such as office politics and any issues related to hiring based on gender or ethnic origin. Other than those issues and in spite of any of those issues, the ISSO wanted to be the best of the best—always.

The ISSO looked at the various corporate InfoSec-related positions and trends indicating what future positions' qualifications might be, and began documenting the education and experience required for each position and their pay range. The ISSO also decided that working in a variety of businesses in various locations would broaden the ISSO's background and would be an additional asset to any firm. The ISSO's goal was to quit working for a corporation as their ISSO at age 55. At age 55, the ISSO would start an InfoSec consulting business and run that until age 62 or 65. At that time, the ISSO would retire with Social Security and other investments as additional incomes.

Also during the ISSO's research, the ISSO found that to be the best ISSO professional required one to have knowledge, education, and experience in areas other than InfoSec, including:

- Business
- Investigations
- Technology
- Dealing with people
- Communications skills
- Management
- Writing
- Project planning
- Public speaking
- Major foreign language or languages

First, and foremost, the ISSO knew that today and into the distant future, the consummate ISSO professional must be technologically savvy. The 21st-century ISSO professional must of course know how to use and protect information technology. ISSO professionals will find themselves working with professionals from many other disciplines to develop and implement methods and InfoSec processes. To be effective, the ISSO professional must possess facilitator skills, team-building skills, and process management skills—and of course also time management skills. The continued emphasis from the business and financial community on cost-effectiveness will drive the ISSO professional to become a more highly skilled generalist as opposed to a specialist, as one climbs the InfoSec career ladder. In addition, financial and accounting skills are a great benefit.

The ISSO also continued to update the career development plan, including preparing now for owning and managing an InfoSec-consulting firm after leaving IWC. In addition, the ISSO knew that learning and gaining new ISSO-related experiences was a lifelong process, as the working environment continues to change too fast to let anyone safely remain complacent with a know-it-all attitude.

ESTABLISHING AND MANAGING AN INFOSEC CAREER DEVELOPMENT PROGRAM

The IWC ISSO knew that as the ISSO, there was an additional responsibility: to be a mentor to the IWC InfoSec staff and help them in their careers. This would include a career development plan for each staff member for progressing within the InfoSec Department.

If a staff member wanted mentoring or some assistance in developing a career development plan that was not limited to working at IWC, the ISSO would assist in that also, but only based on a staff member's request. The ISSO reasoned that the career plan for progressing inside the InfoSec Department and IWC was a benefit to the InfoSec Department and IWC; whereas a career development plan that included working outside of IWC was a personal matter.

The ISSO discussed the career development program with the InfoSec managers and subsequently at staff meetings with all InfoSec personnel. One InfoSec manager stated that career development was the individual's responsibility, and InfoSec managers had enough to do. The ISSO explained that each InfoSec manager would also be involved with the ISSO in his or her own career development plan. The ISSO explained that one cannot sit idly by without continuing to learn. For example, the InfoSec professional must continue to learn about high technology to provide more efficient and effective protection, as well as continue to meet the future needs of IWC. No training, within or outside of IWC, would be approved unless it was part of an individual's career development plan. The ISSO further advised that if the manager wanted to attend an InfoSec conference every year or periodically, it must be part of the manager's career development plan. Also, as part of the InfoSec managers' career development plan, there would be milestones and tasks related to mentoring staff members. After all, the ISSO stated, managers manage through people, and the more education and experience a staff member received, the better for all concerned. After all, isn't that why IWC pays college tuition for salaried employees?

The ISSO advised that career development for staff members would include, as mandatory, gaining all education and experience that could be gained during regular business hours. Also, the InfoSec staff member, without being coerced, must decide to also use personal time. After all, the plan benefited the staff member as well as IWC. Any staff member who did not want to participate at all would be explained the benefits on an individual basis.

The ISSO reasoned that those who did not want to participate considered themselves to be employed in a job, not professionals in the InfoSec profession. The ISSO would view such individuals as valuable employees as long as they did their job to the best of their ability. However, it would be difficult to consider them for promotions and merit raises or other bonuses if they only did their 8-hour job while others took on more tasks and responsibilities, exerted extra effort to learn and gain additional security knowledge, and grew in the profession. The promotions, merit raises, and bonuses would obviously be given to them as a priority. This would also be explained to any employee who did not want to participate. If the person still insisted on not participating, the employee would be asked to state that in writing, and then would be allowed to not participate. This was done to ensure that the employee could not later deny opting out of the program, especially after being passed over for a bonus or promotion. This process was agreed to by the Human Resources Department and the IWC CIO.

The career development plan was developed as follows:

- Each employee was interviewed by the ISSO and the employee's security manager.
- Each employee completed a form noting his or her education in a list of both college/university courses taken and technical courses taken, for example at conferences.
- The manager's career plan for them, such as future jobs leading to promotions, was noted and compared to those noted by the employees. Where there was a conflict, a mutually agreeable compromise was worked out.
- The education and experience future needs of the employees were identified at the meeting. Based on the needs assessment, education and training courses and ways of gaining additional experience were identified.
- The career development goals for the first year were identified and agreed to by the employee, InfoSec manager, and ISSO.
- The goals were incorporated into the employee's performance goals for the year, thus committing the managers and the InfoSec staff member to supporting the successful completion of the goals.

The ISSO also explained to the security staff that career development meant learning in formal and informal ways. Matrix charts were used to support the employees' career development program (see Figures 15.2 and 15.3). The ISSO provided the following examples:

- Courses at colleges and universities;
- Courses at technical schools;
- Courses at conferences and workshops;

Management Topics	Current Knowledge	Learning Priority
Time Management		
Project Management		
Communicating with Others		
Managing People		
Planning		
Directing		
Controlling		
Budgeting		
Managerial Finance		
Managerial Accounting		
Marketing		

Figure 15.2   Example of a table to be used to determine current ISSO management strengths and weaknesses, and to identify training needs.

Technical Topics	Current Knowledge	Learning Priority
InfoSec Policies & Procs.		
Sys. Authorization & Access Control		
Systems Security		
Risk Assessment		
Communications Security		
Physical/Environmental Security		
Security Awareness & Training		
Contingency Planning		
Disaster Recovery		
Application Security		

Figure 15.3   Example of a table to be used to determine current ISSO technical strengths and weaknesses, and to identify training needs.

- Reading books, magazines, and trade journals, such as security-related associations' magazines;
- Networking with peers, for example, learning how they solved some of their asset protection problems;

- Studying for certifications, such as Certified Protection Professional (CPP), Certified Fraud Examiner (CFE), Certified Information Systems Security Professional (CISSP), Certified Information Systems Auditor (CISA);
- Volunteering at senior centers and other centers for children and adults; and
- Reading online (Internet).

Experiences would be gained by providing opportunities for employees to become involved in projects and tasks in order to gain experience in other aspects of the InfoSec profession.

Whether you want to become an ISSO, or are an ISSO now, you should have a career development plan. That plan is similar to any other project plan. That is, it has a stated objectives, milestones, and starting and ending dates. The starting time is now and the ending date is the date of your planned retirement. Remember, it is never too early, or too late, to begin planning your ISSO career and developing the career plan which will challenge you to reach your full potential. The sooner you start, the more likely you are to succeed in meeting your goals and objectives before your retirement. After all, once you're retired, you don't want to spend your time thinking what might have been!

Assume that you enjoy the profession of InfoSec and being an ISSO. That is your chosen profession—your career. Therefore, you should strive to be the best ISSO in the business, and the one most eligible to fill any ISSO position. That takes hard work and dedication.

So, let's put together an ISSO career development plan outline. You can add the specifics as they apply to you. Also, let's assume you are new to the field and you're starting with no InfoSec experience whatsoever.

The basic categories which are the foundations for your career development are (1) the basic categories that make up the ISSO profession; (2) education and training required for each position; (3) experience needed for each position; and (4) certifications.

For the person putting together his or her personal career development program or plan, it is important to know the basic positions available within the ISSO career field. The job family provides a gradual progression through an ISSO career beginning with little or no education and experience. The job family emphasizes the technical career development. The management career field generally follows the common management job family; therefore, it is not addressed here. In addition, in most corporations the InfoSec management position(s) within the corporation are very limited—actually limited to one! Career growth is likely to be achieved by changing corporations or government agencies.

An ISSO or InfoSec job family was previously provided. The titles, functional descriptions, and qualifications are based on actual ISSO job families found in several InfoSec organizations of international corporations.[4] They should be used as part of your career development plan outline. Note especially the position description and job qualifications for each position.

EDUCATION

There are two different approaches which most ISSOs have used:

- They began with a technical education such as a degree or degrees in computer science, mathematics, or telecommunications. Because of their degree, or probably some related InfoSec experience, they were chosen or volunteered to be the company's ISSO.
- They began with a general degree such as business, security, criminal justice, or liberal arts and eventually, somehow, found themselves in the ISSO position. And once in that position, they liked it and decided to stay in the ISSO profession.

In today's environment, a college degree with a major in computer science or telecommunications is one of the best ways to start an ISSO career. An alternative is to major in InfoSec. As colleges and universities see the demand for such subjects, they will offer InfoSec courses and programs. As the need for InfoSec grows, more universities and colleges will begin to offer majors in InfoSec.

An alternative to a college or university is a technical school that offers InfoSec-related specialized programs in various aspects of the computer and telecommunications functions. This training usually offers hands-on experience and may provide a faster avenue into the ISSO profession. Also, many colleges and universities offer certificates in a specialized ISSO-related field such as local area networks and telecommunications. These courses can also be applied to the degree program, but check the college or university to be sure. Those who choose the technical training path should still pursue a college degree that will enhance promotion opportunities in the ISSO profession.

Education, whether technical or academic, provides the future ISSO with an opportunity for an ISSO position. You notice that I said *opportunity* for a position. In today's business environment the certifications or degree will only get you a possible interview. As you probably have already discovered, there is growing competition for these positions. As the profession grows in importance, that competition is expected to increase.

---

[4]Detailed job descriptions and responsibilities will be found in Chapter 7, "Establishing a CIAPP and InfoSec Organization."

In today's marketplace, the need for experience coupled with advanced degrees and certifications has increased. It has increased to the point where all your education, experience, and certifications only get you through the first resume filtering process. *It is the interview that will get you the job.*

CONFERENCES AND TRAINING

To prepare yourself for an ISSO position, try to complement your education with as much training as possible. There are numerous associations, consultants, and companies which provide training classes, workshops, and conferences covering the entire field of InfoSec. None are very cheap—though of course that is relative—but they do provide opportunities to gain firsthand knowledge on the many InfoSec topics.

These InfoSec topics range from the administrative, nontechnical aspects of InfoSec to the technical. One can find many of these conference and their agendas by looking online at related associations' Web sites, such as those of the Information Systems Security Association (ISSA) or the MIS Training Institute (MISTI).

These training courses and workshops also give you the opportunity to find out what works and what does not work. This will come in handy some day when you become an ISSO. You won't have to learn the hard way—by experience. Don't concern yourself with the "not-invented-here" syndrome. Learn from the mistakes of others and apply what will work for you, your career, and your InfoSec program!

Remember, it's not where you get your information or methodology, it's whether or not you successfully apply it. Your company is interested in results. So, *be results-oriented!*

Before attending any conference or workshop, which provides a choice of courses on various topics, you should know what up-to-date information you are lacking. Then be sure to attend those courses. Also, be sure to ask questions. The purpose of the courses is to exchange information and learn from each other.

To determine what InfoSec courses and knowledge areas you should concentrate on while at the conferences, or what training you require, use the matrices previously shown in Figures 15.2 and 15.3. Rate your experience/knowledge using either a scale from 1 to 5, or "high," "medium," or "low." Be honest and objective, because if you are not, you are only cheating yourself. After you complete that section, sequentially number the training you need in a priority order. Obviously, the lower your current knowledge rating, the higher you should rank the type of training needed, and vice versa.

NETWORKING

While at the conference or training course, be sure to get a copy of the list of participants, which is normally available.

Using the list of participants, you should make it a point to identify and seek out those who work in the government agency or business that you would like to target for employment. For example, some ISSOs like to work in the banking and finance business, others in manufacturing, some in aerospace, and some in accounting firms.

During the breaks, find these people. It won't be that difficult: Everyone is given a badge to wear that normally contains his or her name and the business or government agency that he or she works for. Also, conference lunch tables are often identified by type of business. Go through the crowds, find the person, introduce yourself, and ask your questions. You will find that you may not be the only one puzzled by a new technology or how to apply InfoSec to a particular system configuration.

Many attendees are strangers on the first day of these events but become professional friends by the time the conference ends. Then it is a matter of continuous networking (keeping in touch by e-mail, fax, or telephone) and discussing what is going on in the profession, in industry, or whatever.

A word of caution: If you find someone who is not interested in discussing InfoSec with you or wants you to pay for providing that information to you (yes, it does happen on occasion), don't feel bad. Don't be embarrassed or discouraged. Go find others more professional. Like any other profession, the ISSO profession has some *un*-professionals.

During each session, sit with someone you have not met before and learn what he or she does, what company he or she works for, etc. With each break and at each luncheon or dinner, try to meet someone new. Remember your objective is to meet people who will share InfoSec information with you, people whom you can contact at a later date to find out about job opportunities, how to fix a particular problem, etc.

When you attend these conferences, training sessions, and association meetings, be sure to bring plenty of business cards, and don't be shy. Ask people for their cards. If you don't have a card, get some printed, even if you only have your name, home address, telephone number, fax number, and e-mail address on it. Often you can get 500 business cards for as little as $30 or print your own, professionally! A small investment when you consider that the person with your card may some day call you and tell you of a great new ISSO position in some company—one that was made for you.

If you hand out your card and someone asks you what you do, be honest. If you are unemployed, employed in a non-ISSO position, or a student, just say so. Tell the person you really enjoy the ISSO profession and are trying very hard to get started in it. You may be surprised at the response and how people will try to help you.

One of the greatest benefits of conferences, and attending chapter meetings of InfoSec-related associations, is the opportunity to network with those in the profession. This is the best way to find out what the ISSOs in government agencies and businesses are doing in the InfoSec arena. They are also some of the best sources of information as to what ISSO positions are open at which company or government agency.

You must remember that few of the ISSO positions are advertised in the newspapers. Those that are advertised are usually because the company did not want to hire an employment firm to find a person to fill the position, or because the position called for $100,000 worth of experience but they wanted to pay $25,000.

If you are new to the ISSO profession, you may have to apply for such a position and hope that although you don't have all the experience and education they desire, you're the best candidate that has applied for the position. There is nothing wrong with "buying in" to the position by accepting the lower salary. It's a start, and once you have two or three years of experience, you have a better opportunity to get a better ISSO position and command a higher salary. Who knows, your company may give you a counteroffer if you have done a great job for them.

Another great tool for networking is the Internet. By obtaining the names and e-mail addresses of people you meet at conferences, association meetings, etc., you can begin a dialogue with those in the profession.

THE INTERNET

A rapidly growing source of InfoSec information is the Internet. There are many groups out on the Internet that discuss both general and specific InfoSec issues. There are many government sites, business sites, sites managed by InfoSec product suppliers, and even easy-to-find hacker sites.

All the Internet sites provide information that can help you learn about InfoSec positions, problems, solutions to those problems, techniques for breaking into systems, etc. All this information is available just by doing an Internet search.

If you do not have Internet access, subscribing to an Internet service provider should be your number one goal. It is almost impossible to be an ISSO professional today without having an Internet account and Internet address for e-mail.

You will probably find that your major problem is not finding useful InfoSec information on the Internet, but keeping up with all of it. Don't feel bad—no one can! Using your completed self-evaluation knowledge charts (Figures 15.2 and 15.3, above), you can concentrate your information search in those areas where you are the weakest. Then, if you have time, you can research and review the other InfoSec documents.

A good way of ensuring that you do the research and review is to:

- Set up your Internet Web sites through the use of your Internet browser's "bookmarks" or "favorites." That way, you won't have to continually search for the sites that have the best information relative to your InfoSec needs.
- Set up a specific time each day when you can and do commit at least 1 hour to reading and learning from the material in your personal library, textbooks, Internet sites, etc.

In order to be successful, you must of course have self-discipline and good study habits. You will find that the rewards of new InfoSec knowledge gained through such study habits, as well as successfully applying those newly learned techniques, will be well worth your efforts.

USING TRADE JOURNALS AND MAGAZINES FOR TRAINING

Other overlooked and usually free sources of information are the technology trade journals and magazines. Such journals and magazines contain articles about the latest technologies or problems with this or that software; and more and more contain InfoSec-related articles. All this information will help you stay abreast of the technology and the related security issues.

Trade journals related to data communications, telecommunications, InfoSec, disaster recovery/contingency planning, information news, etc., are especially useful. Many of those journals can now be found on the Internet, making the search and the training convenient and, best of all, costing nothing but your time.

You must stay up-to-date on these changes. Once mainframe computer experience and access control software experience was needed. Now, you read about TCP/IP, UNIX, Web pages, etc. If you stay in this profession, be prepared to learn the rest of your professional life.

If you don't keep current in the technology, the technology will probably make you *obsolete* in less than 5 years.

EXPERIENCE

Many of the people filling ISSO positions today did not start out to be ISSOs. For many, the ISSO position did not exist when they began their journey in InfoSec.

As with any person entering any profession for the first time, the challenges are many. How does one become an ISSO if the company or government agency wants a person with experience? The inexperienced candidates seem to never have the chance to gain that experience— the typical "Catch-22" situation. However, isn't that the same for all professions?

There are far too many excellent books on the market, books that specifically address the issues of job hunting and how to gain experience, for this author to deal with the subject in any great level of detail in this book. Suffice it to say that the reader can find many of these types of books at the local library, online through the Internet, and at the local bookstore. The important point is to get several of these books and articles, and use them to your advantage.

The best approach to take is to get experience anywhere and in any way you can. Many people fall into the trap of thinking that they can only gain the InfoSec experience they need by being employed in the profession by some company or government agency. If you can do that, that's great! However, what if you can't?

There are several other ways to gain related experience. There are many schools, ranging from elementary schools, to universities, to senior associations, that may need some type of help which is information systems-related. So, volunteer!

You can volunteer to help them with their computer needs. Sometimes the help needed may be as simple as helping to load new software on a microcomputer, or installing a new piece of computer hardware.

While you are doing your volunteer work, also volunteer to set up some access controls and audit trails. Maybe you can even volunteer to periodically review the audit trails for them to be sure that the systems aren't being abused or used for unauthorized purposes.

The main point is that it is a win–win situation. They get the help they need, while you gain the experience you need. You may be surprised to learn that many small companies would also greatly appreciate your volunteered assistance.

You can find such work by contacting various charitable organizations, or by discussing it with members of your church, city council members, local chamber of commerce, business associations, etc. Who knows, you may find that your volunteer work leads to consulting work or a permanent position.

So, volunteer! You'll not only be helping yourself, but maybe more importantly, others in need, your community, and your chosen profession.

CERTIFICATIONS

What is meant by certification? For our purposes, certification means that based on your experience, education, and successful passing of a test, generally given by some InfoSec or related association, you have basic knowledge and ability that meet the criteria for certifying you as a professional or expert in a particular field.

Using the word *expert* may not be the right thing to do, because in the InfoSec business, technology and systems vulnerabilities change rapidly, making it impossible for anyone to be an expert. So, let's say that by being certified, you are considered to have *expertise* in the particular field.

There are several certifications that are directly related to the position of an ISSO. A professional ISSO should have the basic knowledge in some, if not all, of these ISSO-related certifications. There are several associations that certify professionals in InfoSec-related professions. Some certifications are widely acknowledged throughout industry, while others are not—their sponsors may have developed them as a get-rich-quick scheme. These may look good on paper but are really meaningless. No certification is worth anything without being accepted by the ISSO profession, then by related professions, and most importantly, by executive management—for example, the Certified Public Accountant (CPA) is widely recognized throughout industry.

ASSOCIATIONS[5]

As a ISSO and security professional, it is more than likely you will be involved with professional security associations. These associations differ in specific focus but all have one common purpose: to enhance and improve the profession of security. Whether private, corporate, institutional, commercial, industrial, government, or any other type of security organization, these associations seek to advance the cause of the profession. Members are asked to support the associations' efforts to seek a higher degree of professionalism and recognition of the security discipline. Some of these associations will work with local colleges and universities in an effort to build curriculum consistent with contemporary issues in InfoSec. Together, they assist in the preparation and development of future InfoSec professionals, experts who are capable of dealing with new and more complicated InfoSec issues.

Association membership may be a general membership, as is the case with the American Society for Industrial Security (ASIS), the largest professional security association in the world. Membership may also be very specific to a type of industry, such as the security committee within the Aerospace Industries Association (AIA). Within AIA, security profession-

---

[5] We do not imply an endorsement of these or any other associations. The ones selected are ones that we have been members of and therefore, can speak about based on our experiences. However, we are not indicating that they are better than any others; quite frankly, we don't know. We simply offer them as examples.

als from aerospace companies work together for the benefit of the entire industry. Common challenges, issues, practices, and objectives are addressed by the membership, who are usually senior security managers of member companies.

Suppose you are the IWC ISSO. An essential part of representing IWC's InfoSec-related programs, such as CIAPP, within the professional InfoSec community is to ensure you understand how your company chooses to represent itself to the external world at large. How does it want to be perceived? You are an advocate for IWC, and how you deal with external organizations must be consistent with IWC's expectations and values. For example, company management may believe it is important for its management team to take a leading role in associations, thereby being better positioned to influence policy development or implementation. With this in mind, you should seek officer or director positions within any association you are part of. On the other hand, if your company does not advocate such activities, you may find yourself without the necessary support, both time and money, should you be in a leadership role. In fact, it may be perceived that you are not spending sufficient time on company matters and too much time on outside activities. This can be a difficult line to walk if you don't take the time to learn what company expectations are in this area. One way to consider this issue is to discuss it with your boss as part of your career development plan.

InfoSec-related associations can play an important role in the career of an ISSO professional. Associations often provide professional training and certification in a variety of InfoSec and related disciplines. Furthermore, they serve as a forum where ISSO professionals can meet and discuss current issues and problems and share lessons learned.

There are many InfoSec-related associations in the world today. However, one must be careful, as some have been established for the purpose of making money. Some may even offer certifications that may look good but are not recognized within the professional community.

There are at least five InfoSec-related associations[6] that have been around for many years and also are considered to be very professional organizations:

- The American Society for Industrial Security (ASIS);
- The Association of Certified Fraud Examiners (ACFE);
- The Information Systems Security Association (ISSA);
- The Information Systems Audits and Controls Association (ISACA); and
- The High Technology Crime Investigation Association (HTCIA).

---

[6] Information about each association noted is quoted from the association's Web site.

ISSO PROFESSIONALS—WHAT YOU CAN DO TO HELP OTHERS

> Give a man a fish and he will eat for a day. Teach a man to fish and he will eat for the rest of his life.[7]—Chinese proverb

Those of you who have spent a few decades in the ISSO or InfoSec profession have learned quite a bit about how to do your jobs. Some things you learned easily and some things you unfortunately had to learn the hard way.

Looking back on your careers, as long or as short as they may be, did you, or do you, have a mentor, someone to help you learn InfoSec? Did you have someone to rely on—a kind of InfoSec father or grandfather figure to guide you? If you did, you are one of the few but lucky ones.

Many of you in the ISSO profession probably learned the hard way—by trial and error, without a mentor. Wouldn't it have been nice for someone to have been there to answer your questions and to guide you around those bad learning experiences? Yes, experience is a great teacher, but there is the easy way, with help from another, and the hard way, on your own.

Those of you who have years of InfoSec and ISSO experience should be ISSO professionals. As part of calling oneself a professional, one should also be doing things to give back to the profession. It is important that we all help each other and work together to make this honorable and necessary profession one where we can help each other and learn from each other. Doing so will make it so much easier in furthering our cause of *protecting information assets as effectively (good) and efficiently (cheap) as possible so as not to adversely affect our employers' costs and schedules.*

In many corporations, the culture is such that those of you in the ISSO profession are as well liked as the auditor or a tax collector. We must all strive to change this attitude and help each other to do so. It is our professional responsibility to get people to understand that we in the ISSO profession are an integral part of corporate business, and we do assist in making a difference by helping our corporations gain and maintain that competitive advantage.

> Some men see things as they are and ask, "why?" I dream things that never were and ask, "why not?"[8]—Robert Francis Kennedy

As part of your career development plan, you should add tasks such as mentoring, lecturing, writing, teaching, and being an active participant

---

[7] From http://www.quoteland.com/topic.asp?CATEGORY_ID=140
[8] From: http://www.quoteland.com/author.asp?AUTHOR_ID=324 NB: This quote is a paraphrase of a similar quote by G. B. Shaw.

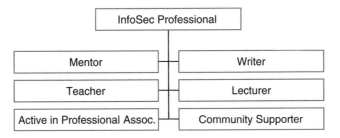

Figure 15.4   What helps makes an InfoSec specialist a professional.

in our professional associations. You may say that you have enough to do and you don't have any time for such things. Well, make the time. You owe it to yourself and the rest of those in the profession.

If you are wondering what is in it for you, other than more work, remember that such tasks also assist in providing you with visibility to others. That visibility will be helpful when someone is looking for the best ISSO professional he or she can hire. Also, if you decide to eventually go on your own and become a consultant, you will have a track record of contacts and visibility, and you will be well thought of. After all, you are a published author, international lecturer, experienced, educated, certified, so obviously you must know more than other consultants who are competing with you and don't have your track record. So, there is a great benefit to you and your own career development (see Figure 15.4).

Another thing you can do is share your knowledge through such methods as[9]:

- Writing InfoSec-related articles,
- Conducting InfoSec-related lectures, or
- Writing books on InfoSec-related topics.

Educational Institutions

In many nation-states of the world, colleges and universities are beginning to recognize the need for providing formal education curriculum and courses that address the needs of security professionals. There are also trade schools and community service programs where your expertise may be useful. For example, you may volunteer to give some training to seniors at a senior center on how best to avoid fraudsters, identify theft, and such.

---

[9]Detailed information on how to get started in lecturing and writing can be found on the author's Web site: http://www.shockwavewriters.com. Click on Books, this book, and this chapter.

As an ISSO professional, you should seek out colleges and universities in your area, and if you have the necessary qualifications, you should consider teaching a course or two part-time, usually in their evening programs. As with lectures, writing, and active membership in security-related associations, teaching is part of being an ISSO professional. There are many benefits to teaching InfoSec-related courses at the local community colleges or universities. Among them are:

- Recognition;
- Supporting the community—always a big corporate public relations goal;
- Having students provide research for future articles, lectures, and books;
- Practicing public speaking for conference lectures and vice versa;
- Giving something back to the profession by helping others along; and
- Learning new security methods, concepts, ideas, and the like.

Mentoring

Being an ISSO professional, as was previously mentioned, requires one to be a mentor, to help others learn and be better at their jobs of assets protection. Being a mentor requires patience and a true desire to help others along their security career paths. It also has its own rewards. Unless you try it, you won't know the satisfaction and the good feeling that come with helping others learn and develop as security specialists.

Why should others have to learn the hard way as many of us have in the past? Shouldn't we all be working together as advocates for a profession that offers job satisfaction and is a much-needed profession within government agencies and corporations in today's hostile world in which we all live, work, and play? To do otherwise is not professional.

men·tor [mén tàwr, méntər] *noun* (*plural* men·tors)

experienced adviser and supporter: somebody, usually older and more experienced, who provides advice and support to, and watches over and fosters the progress of, a younger, less experienced person

transitive verb (*past* men·tored, *past participle* men·tored, *present participle* men·tor·ing, *3rd person present singular* men·tors)

be a mentor to somebody: to act as a mentor to somebody, especially a junior colleague

[Mid-18th century. Via French from, ultimately, Greek *Mentōr* (see Mentor).][10]

---

[10] *Encarta World English Dictionary*, © & (P) 1999, Microsoft Corporation. All rights reserved. Developed for Microsoft by Bloomsbury Publishing Plc.

QUESTIONS TO CONSIDER

Based on what you have read, consider the following questions and how you would reply to them:

* Do you consider yourself as having a career or a job?
* If a career, do you have a career development plan?
* Is it in writing and as a project plan?
* If not, why not?
* If you do have a career development plan, does your boss support it?
* As an ISSO professional, do you believe you have some responsibilities towards your staff when it comes to career planning?
* Do you support career planning by your staff?
* If so, how?
* As a professional, do you believe in giving something back to the profession?
* If you do, how do you do that?
* If not, can you really consider yourself as an ISSO professional, and if so, why?

SUMMARY

As an InfoSec professional or ISSO professional, one should always plan for a career and, as an ISSO, also help the InfoSec staff plan theirs:

* ISSO career development planning helps ensure that the ISSO has an opportunity for a successful career.
* Career development planning requires an understanding of ISSO positions and the education, training, experience, and certifications needed for each.
* Education and training can be gotten from many sources such as trade journals, universities, conferences, and technical schools.
* Experience can be gained by volunteering to assist others in InfoSec and information systems functions.
* The information provided in this chapter will not only help you on your ISSO career path, but eventually, it can be used for helping members of your staff on their path to career development.

16

How to Market Yourself as an ISSO

*Work is a responsibility most adults assume, a burden at times, a com-
plication, but also a challenge that, like children, requires enormous
energy and that holds the potential for qualitative, as well as quantitative, rewards.*—Melinda M. Marshall[1]

CHAPTER OBJECTIVE

The objective of this chapter, "How to Market Yourself as an ISSO," is
to provide the person seeking to be an ISSO, or a current ISSO, a unique
approach to assist in obtaining a desired ISSO position, and how to
develop a personal ISSO portfolio for use during the job interview process.

INTRODUCTION

Throughout the first 15 chapters of this book, you have been able to
develop your own perspective on the ISSO profession, and you have
learned some techniques that can help you succeed in that profession.
Once you have your career plan in place and have begun to focus on the
next InfoSec function that you want to perform in the ISSO profession,
you must begin to plan on getting that next position.

Sometimes an ISSO professional will have some conflicts when it
comes to seeking out a new position instead of staying "loyal company
employee." There should not be any such conflict, because that should
have been resolved in your career development project plan.

If you are happy doing what you are doing and would like to do
the same thing for the rest of your life in the same company, then do it.
However, one word of caution—in today's corporate world, no position

---

[1] *The Columbia World of Quotations.* 1996 (http://www.bartleby.com/66/2/38002.html);
Melinda M. Marshall (20th century), U.S. writer and editor. *Good Enough Mothers*,
introduction (1993).

seems to last forever, and it appears that today's corporations do not want their employees to stay forever. So, it is always better to be prepared by having a backup plan in the event you are notified that your services are no longer wanted.

Also remember that it is easier to find a job if you already have a job. So, the best time to find out your worth as an ISSO is to look for advancement opportunities or lateral opportunities to other InfoSec positions while you are still employed. If nothing else, the employment interviews will keep you in practice and help you fine-tune your interview skills and your personal portfolio.

INTERVIEWING FOR THE ISSO POSITION

Congratulations! Your resume has finally made it through the filtering process and you are being asked to appear for an interview. You will probably find that ISSO positions are very competitive, with talented ISSO professionals competing against you for each of those positions. So, you must be prepared. As with most job interviews these days, you will probably be subjected to a series of interviews consisting of members of the human resources department, information systems organization, auditors, and security personnel.

Don't be nervous, but this interview is what will put you back on the road to ISSO job hunting or offer you the challenges of the new ISSO position. So, you must be prepared!

There are many books on the market telling you how to interview for a position. They offer advice on everything from how to dress to how to answer the "mother of all interview questions"—*What are your salary expectations?*

It is not the purpose of this book to help you answer those common interview questions. It is assumed that you will have read those books, and that you have prepared and practiced for the upcoming interview. The purpose of this chapter is to show you how you can separate yourself from your ISSO competition.

You have probably already interviewed more times than you care to admit. In all those interviews, you probably, like your peers, walked in wearing dark, conservative business attire, neatly groomed, and prepared to answer any question thrown at you. The question is, *What separated you from your competitors?* What was it that would make the interviewers remember you and choose you above the rest?

You probably answered most questions in the most politically correct way, e.g., *What is your major weakness?* Answer: *My major weakness is that I have very little patience for those who don't live up to their commitments. When someone agrees to complete a project by a specific date, I expect that date to be met unless the project leader comes to me in* advance of the deadline and explains the reason why that date can't be met. I believe in a team effort and each of us as vital members of that team must work together to provide the service and support needed to assist the company in meeting its goals.

Will that answer to that question be considered a weakness or strength by the interviewers? Probably a strength, but that is how the game is played.

Many interviewees have "been there and done that" but still didn't get the position. Why? Maybe because our answers "float" in the interview room air. They hang there mingling with those of the other candidates before us and will be mingling again with the candidates that come after us.

The only real, lasting evidence of the interview is what was written down by the interviewers and what impressions you, the prospective ISSO, left in their minds! Many of the interviewers are "screeners," human resource people who have no clue as to what InfoSec is all about. They are there because we do teaming today. We operate by consensus. So, getting selected may be much more difficult.

So, you need one thing—one thing that will leave a lasting impression on the interviewers. One thing that will show them you have the talents, the *applied* education (that's education that you gained in college and other places, and something that you can actually use in the business world!), the experience, *and* the game plan. You've done it! You've been successful in building an InfoSec program before, and you will be successful again. You can prove that you can do it because you have your ISSO portfolio!

The next question that the reader may ask is, "What the heck is my ISSO portfolio?" You probably have seen movies where the models show up at the model studio or movie studio and present a folder containing photographs of themselves in various poses. No, sorry—your photo will probably not help you get the ISSO position—but think about it. They took with them to their interview physical evidence in the form of photographs, meant to *prove* that he or she was the best person for the position.

What you must do is develop your own portfolio to take with you, and leave with the interviewers—*proof* that you've been there, done that. You are the best person for the position. It's all there in the portfolio.

Your ISSO portfolio is something you should begin building as soon as you begin your first ISSO job or before. It should contain an index and identified sections that include letters of reference, letters of appreciation, copies of award certificates, project plans, metric charts you use for measuring the success of your InfoSec programs, and, probably most important, your InfoSec philosophy and InfoSec plan outline that you will implement as soon as you are hired.

The InfoSec plan is probably the most important document in your portfolio and should be the first page after your index. All the other documents are just proof that what you plan to do, you've done before.

In the case of someone who has never been an ISSO, the prospective ISSO can build his or her InfoSec plan and InfoSec portfolio from the information provided in this book. Build it for IWC.

The next question that may arise is, "If I never worked there, how do I know what I should do if I get hired?" Again, go back to doing some research. Remember that if you really want this job, you have to work at least as hard to get it as you will once you do get it.

Your first stop should be the Internet. Find out about the company. Some information that you should know is:

- When was it started?
- What are its products?
- How is the company stock doing?
- Where are their offices located, etc.?

You should also stop by the company and pick up an application, any company brochures available, their benefits pamphlets, etc.

You should study the information, complete the application, and place it in your portfolio. After all, if they decided to hire you, you'd have to fill one out anyway. You should go into the interview knowing as much if not more about the company as the people interviewing you. This is invaluable, especially if you are interviewing for a senior-level position. These interviews will undoubtedly include the members of executive management. Your ability to talk about their company in business terms with an understanding of the company will undoubtedly impress them and indicate that you are business-oriented.

All your answers to the interviewers' questions should be directed to something in your portfolio. For example, if they ask you how you would deal with downsizing in your department and what impact that would have on your ability to adequately protect the company's information and its related systems, how would you answer? You should be able to direct them to a process chart, a metric, something that indicates that you have done it before, or that you have a business-oriented approach to dealing with the issue.

If you have not done it before, write down how you could, and would, perform these functions, assess the InfoSec program, etc.

The portfolio can work for any new ISSO in any company. The following is a sample portfolio outline, which can be used as a guide by a new or experienced ISSO. In this case, it is the ISSO applying for the IWC ISSO position. It's up to you to fill in the details. Many of the ideas of what to put in your InfoSec portfolio will be found in this book.

You will note that the prospective ISSO applying for the IWC position has done the research necessary to tailor an InfoSec program for IWC. The beauty of building this type of portfolio is that it seems specific, and yet it's generic.

The ISSO also practiced interviewing skills. The ISSO knew that the resume or personal contacts got one the interview, but the interview got one the job. Before any interviews and during the IWC interview, the ISSO knew that one must do the following:

- Learn all one can about the potential employer.
- Read and learn from books, magazines, and the like about interviews and proper clothing to wear.
- Prepare answers to typical questions that will be asked, and practice answering them without seeming as though the answers were rehearsed.
- Develop and maintain an updated work portfolio.
- During the interview always refer to "we" or "us" instead of "I" and "you" as much as possible, so it seems as if you already have the job and are just briefing fellow employees.
- Refer interviewers to your portfolio in answering their questions.

The IWC ISSO established the career development plan as a formal project plan with an objective, goals, milestones, and tasks. The project plan helped the ISSO focus on the career progression, and also that focus made it easier not to get sidetracked and waste time on matters that did not lend themselves to meeting the project plan milestones. The ISSO continually updated the plan. At the end of each calendar year, the ISSO would analyze the progress in meeting the plan goals and objective. Regardless of whether the plan progressed ahead of schedule or behind schedule, the reasons for the change were noted and lessons learned. Then the updated plan would be used for the next year.

Over the years, the ISSO developed a portfolio. In the portfolio, the ISSO maintained a plan that would be continually updated and used during all interviews with extra copies available for the interviewers, and the ISSO successfully used it for IWC.

When others went through the interview process answering the interviewers' questions, their responses were lost in the air like smoke; however, the ISSO's thoughts, experience, education, plan for a CIAPP, and other information relevant to meeting IWC's needs were down on paper and could be referred to by the interviewers. This portfolio also indicated a person who was organized and came in with an action plan. Furthermore, since the ISSO researched IWC prior to being interviewed, the ISSO was intimately familiar with the corporation and even offered some information about IWC that was new to some of the interviewers.

SAMPLE ISSO PORTFOLIO OUTLINE

The following is a sample outline for an ISSO position. You can use it to build your own, personal portfolio. Even if you don't have all the experience needed, you can still explain how you would do the job if given the chance.

- Table of Contents
- Introduction
- The ISSO Position and IWC Values
- InfoSec Strategic Objective
- InfoSec Tactical Objectives
- InfoSec Transition Plan and the Future
- Why I'm the Right ISSO for the IWC Position
- Examples of a Proven ISSO Record Which Will Meet IWC's Expectations and Needs

I. Introduction

- *Purpose*: To tell you about me, my InfoSec-related education and experience, and how I can establish and lead an InfoSec program for IWC based on a cost-effective philosophy providing InfoSec services and support to our internal and external customers. (*Note*: Remember, a good technique to use during the interview is to use "we" and "our" in your discussions. This will help the interviewers look at you as a IWC team member. Approach it as if you already worked at IWC and you were in a IWC meeting discussing InfoSec issues.)
- *Objective*: To convince you that I am the most qualified—and best— person for the position of ISSO for IWC, and to show how we can establish a business-oriented InfoSec program for IWC.

II. The Position and IWC Values

- Customers:

  Meet our customers' reasonable expectations.

  Show by examples that we are the best in the industry in meeting any of their InfoSec needs.

- IWC:

  Establish and manage an InfoSec program that supports business needs and requirements.

  Strive for an InfoSec program that adds value to IWC products and services.

- IWC Suppliers:

  Advise them so they can develop quality InfoSec products that meet IWC needs at a reasonable price.

  Assist them in understanding our InfoSec needs.

  Direct them to only bring InfoSec products that can be integrated into the IWC InfoSec program, cost-effectively, with minimal maintenance.

- Quality:

  Establish and manage an InfoSec program that provides quality service and support to its internal and external customers.

  Provide that quality service and support with least impact to cost and schedules.

- Integrity:

  Follow the rules, both the spirit and the intent.

  Always be honest.

  Demonstrate ethical conduct at all times.

- Leadership:

  Set the example.

  Help others along.

III. Strategic Objective

Build a comprehensive InfoSec environment that supports the IWC's business needs at least cost, least impact to schedules, and minimum risks to IWC's business, information, and systems.

IV. Tactical Objectives

- Define detailed milestones for IWC's comprehensive InfoSec environment identified as the IWC strategic objective.
- Describe the current IWC InfoSec environment.
- Identify the difference between 1 and 2.
- Establish the Master Project and Schedule to meet the strategic, tactical, and annual objectives as integral parts of IWC's business plans.

V. Transition Plan and the Future

First Month

- Week 1:

  1. Begin transition meetings with management to discuss expectations, goals, objectives, and budget.

2. Begin familiarization with IWC processes and how systems are being used at IWC by all key departments.
3. Begin review of IWC policies and procedures which relate to InfoSec.
4. Establish appointments to meet with applicable department heads to discuss their ideas related to InfoSec, and how it may help or hinder their operations.

- Week 2:

  1. One-on-one meetings with each department head.
  2. In-depth interviews with peers in InfoSec-related organizations.
  3. Begin defining the InfoSec level of effort required.

- Week 3:

  1. Coordinate personnel and organizational issues with HR staff.
  2. Coordinate with internal customers.

- Week 4:

  1. Finalize InfoSec plans, to include strategic, tactical, and annual.
  2. Begin recruitment and hiring as applicable.
  3. Continue coordination meetings with applicable peers and executive management.

- Rest of the Year:

  Develop, implement, and manage InfoSec projects.

  Develop InfoSec metrics and manage the InfoSec program.

  Continue working InfoSec issues with the IWC InfoSec team.

  Continue evaluating potential InfoSec cost reductions based on cost–risk assessment methodology.

- At year-end, analyze successes and failures; validate goals and objectives; and plan projects for the next year.
- Continue to evaluate various InfoSec program processes; make changes where necessary to keep it a fresh, active, and viable program.
- Next Year—2004

  Continue and refine from first-year goals.

  Increase/enhance skills of organization/staff.

  Ensure that IWC's InfoSec program becomes an integrated, value-added program.

VI. Why I'm the Right ISSO for the IWC Position

This section includes the highlights of your resume; a copy of the resume should also be inserted in this section. Remember, don't use a boilerplate resume. Tailor it for the IWC job based on the "advertised" IWC job description.

- A bachelor's degree in InfoSec, which shows that I have the educational background to understand the academic and technical aspects of the profession.
- An MBA, which shows that I have the business and management background to understand IWC from a business perspective.
- Experience in supporting and providing services and support to similar customers.
- Enjoy the trust and confidence of other professional ISSOs in both government agencies and business environments.
- Detailed knowledge of all InfoSec-related federal and state laws and regulations. (*Note*: The ISSO should identify all federal and state laws that apply.)
- A detailed knowledge of information systems, their threats, vulnerabilities, and associated risks.
- Always enjoyed the trust and confidence of corporate management wherever I have been employed.
- A proven InfoSec plan is already prepared, tailored for IWC and ready for implementation.
- Previous experience in coordinating related activities with local District Attorney, FBI, local police, and Secret Service.
- Experienced in InfoSec and management leadership roles, such as government standards, committees, and working groups.

VII. Examples of a Proven ISSO Record Which Will Meet IWC's Expectations and Needs

- Functional Costs Averages (In this section, list all the information related to past budget, tracking, etc.)
- Project Management (In this section, list samples of project management tracking, e.g., Gantt charts.)
- Metrics Management (In this section, list the metrics you have developed or would use to manage InfoSec functions.)

QUESTIONS TO CONSIDER

Based on what you have read, consider the following questions and how you would reply to them:

- Do you critique your job interviews and note how you thought you came across to the interviewers?

- Do you write down the questions that were asked and who, by position, such as Human Resources person or IT technical person, asked each question?
- Do you practice your interview techniques and answering the most common questions that interviewers ask?
- Do you practice interviewing, such as having friends ask you job interview questions and critique your response, including body language?
- Do you practice your interview techniques in front of a mirror so you can see yourself as others see you?
- Do you have an "interview portfolio"?
- If so, have you practiced using it so that you become adept at using it during interviews?
- Do you research the corporations where you are scheduled for interviews so that you are intimately familiar with the corporation and tailor your interview specifically to that corporation?

SUMMARY

The resume and job application may get you the interview, but the interview will get you the job. Remember the following points:

- Before being interviewed for IWC's ISSO position, learn all you can about IWC.
- Read books about how to prepare and dress for interviews.
- Prepare answers for the questions you will probably be asked, and practice the interview process so your answers come across naturally, and not as memorized, rehearsed answers.
- Develop an ISSO portfolio to be used during the interview.
- During the interview, refer the interviewers to the portfolio.
- During the interview, use "we" and "our" as if you already worked at IWC and were giving an in-house briefing to corporate management.

17

So, Are You Ready to Become an InfoSec Consultant?

If you wish to succeed, consult three old people.—Chinese Proverb

CHAPTER OBJECTIVE

This chapter, "So, Are you Ready to Become an InfoSec Consultant?" describes determining whether InfoSec consulting is right for you, an InfoSec consultant's business plan, and running an international InfoSec consulting business.

INTRODUCTION

Information systems security (InfoSec) is a very challenging profession, and these days it commands a good salary, of course depending on one's education and experience. In fact managers of InfoSec programs in New York City command salaries of $350,000 or more, while those of London ISSOs are in at least the £80,000–100,000 range. Even for such expensive cities as New York City and London, that's not bad. Add to that the free or minimal-cost benefits that are provided and other compensations such as bonuses, and one can see that the profession has come a long way.

However, there is a price to be paid. The price is constantly keeping up with high technology, new protection products, new malicious codes, attack techniques, and defenses, and also putting in many long days. However, these should be the fun, challenging parts of the job. The part that may not be so much fun are the people problems that arise when you are an ISSO. Then there are the management meetings, performance reviews, and such that have nothing to do with InfoSec but have to do with being part of a corporation.

No, managing a successful CIAPP or InfoSec organization is not a "9 to 5" job. If you are a conscientious and dedicated professional it can consume your life. So, when one looks at the salary and benefits compared with the number of hours one works, job pressures, stress, time to commute to and from work, and lack of personal time, maybe that salary is not worth it. Add to all that the fact that you are not really your own boss. In fact, you may work for one of those bosses that one thought only existed in bad movies. You know the type—a boss who demands everything, takes credit for what you do, and blames you when things are not going right. There once was a boss who said with pride, "I don't get stress, I give it." Needless to say, the person was not a joy to work with!

Some like the big city and the challenge of this type of job. Others don't see a way out and feel trapped. After all, their lifestyle has caught up with or even surpassed their salary. For those with more of a personal career plan, the sacrifice of working as an ISSO in a demanding position may serve them well. Those professionals may take such jobs for just a short period of time, such as 3 to 5 years. Their purpose is to build up experience and credentials for going out on their own as InfoSec consultants.

To be in any type of profession working for oneself takes a special type of personality to succeed. After all, there is no one to continue to pay you when you are on vacation, no benefits that you don't have to pay for, and if you decide to just hang around the office and not work, you won't get paid for that, either. There is no safety net, no paid time off when sick. No work—no pay. For the independent consultant, the old saying " time is money" is certainly true. In addition, there is a constant need to maintain contacts (potential customers) and keep up with high technology, and of course there is the almost constant travel.

Some InfoSec technicians and managers may have the connections and believe that they are well thought of as InfoSec professionals, called upon to lecture at conferences, assist clients with their InfoSec needs, and the like. However, those that do so as a member of a large firm such as a large accounting–consulting firm believe that it is they who are the ones that draw clients to them for help, when in fact it is usually not that at all. It is usually the large corporate name that brings these clients to the InfoSec person.

Some InfoSec managers and technicians don't realize this fact. Then when they decide to go out on their own as InfoSec consultants, they find that what they thought was a great client base on which to build their business trade turns out to be the client base of their former employer, and they aren't switching to your firm. Furthermore, there are legal and ethical matters relating to "stealing" clients away from a former employer. When the shock of this fact hits them, they find themselves scrambling for clients.

Some advice for those who may be ready to take the InfoSec consulting plunge: Be sure that you objectively inventory your skills and potential client base, and also have at least 2 years of your current salary (including funds for equivalent benefits) safely in the bank. That emergency fund will provide a year or more of income as you grow your business. If nothing else, it will provide a good emergency fund for some lean times or for the times when you will want to take a break for a week or two and go on vacation. After all, you have to pay for your own days off now. Oh, and don't forget insurances such as "errors and omissions," also known as professional liability insurance, general liability, and workman's compensation. Some clients require proof of some or all of these policies before you set foot in the door.

With all that said, if you have the education, experience, business sense, and personality to handle being out on your own, it does offer its own rewards. These rewards include setting your own schedule and hours; being your own boss; vacationing whenever you like; doing it your way— but wait a minute, that's not completely true. Your hours will be set by your workload and your clients. You will be able to do the work pretty much your way, but only doing the work that meets the clients' needs. And vacations can be cut short by an urgent client need. You really can't afford to postpone an urgent client request, as you risk losing the client to a competitor. Payments from clients may be slow in coming and they may be shocked by their bill for services rendered, causing you to negotiate or get your lawyer to negotiate for you. That means additional costs if you can't get your lawyer's costs ported over to the clients. However, one thing is certain: When such issues arise, you may eventually get your money, but you will probably never do business with that client again. How many clients can you afford to lose?

So, being an InfoSec consultant looks great on paper and it may do your ego good, but after a while the real world takes over. It's a tough life and not for the faint at heart. So, before you think about it, be sure you have a good business plan and one that is done objectively. Also, be sure you can support yourself and your family without work for extended periods of time. Yes, it sounds great, but maybe that salary, working conditions, and boss weren't all that bad?

However, you have successfully worked your career plan and have developed the education and experience skills over the years that have given you the confidence to think about going out on your own as an InfoSec consultant. You have had articles published in magazines, have lectured internationally, and have developed a reputation as a professional ISSO. So, you think you are about ready for this career move. If so, you need a plan.

YA GOTTA HAVE A PLAN

If you decide to become an independent InfoSec consultant, the first thing you should do is develop a business plan—before you resign from your current job. Developing the plan may ultimately make you decide that you don't or can't make it as an independent InfoSec consultant. There are many sample business plans available in books and as software programs that can help you get started. Regardless of how you proceed to develop your InfoSec business consulting plan, you must be objective. If you are to assume anything, assume the worst. That way, you will be prepared for the worst-case scenario and will be able to successfully deal with it. Your plan should be looked at as a project plan and, as a minimum, should address the following:

- Your business goals and objectives;
- Why you want to start this business;
- Your education and experience skills and whether they will fit your consulting business—be realistic;
- How much money you will need to begin;
- How much money you have;
- How you will get the money you don't have but need;
- How you will financially survive when business is slow;
- If you have a family or significant other, whether they will support you;
- If not, whether you might have to decide your relationship–business priorities;
- Whether you are willing to travel the majority of your time—after all, you must go to clients and not them to you;
- What steps you will take to begin the business and the costs for each line item or task;
- Whether you will incorporate your business;
- Whether you know the marketplace—your competitors;
- Whether you offer better services at lower prices;
- Your competitors' strengths and weaknesses;
- Your strengths and weaknesses;
- A complete competitive analysis;
- A complete market scope;
- Whether you have a logo and business motto, and if so, what they are and why;
- Whether you should get a lawyer to assist you;
- Whether you will have copyrighted material, trademarks, and/or trade secrets and, if so, how you will handle those processes;
- Whether you have standard invoices, proposals, confidentiality agreements, contracts, billing and general business processes and forms in place and ready for use;
- Whether you have trusted InfoSec specialists available to support your contracts as subcontractors (after all, you can't be experienced in everything);
- How you will obtain business;
- How much you will charge for what work; and

- Whether you are aware of the laws and regulations that affect you doing business.

These are but a few of the many questions that you should answer before making the plunge into the InfoSec consulting services business. Remember also the guiding principles that you should employ:

- Confidentiality;
- Objectivity;
- Professionalism;
- Respect;
- Integrity;
- Honesty;
- Quality;
- Efficiency; and
- Client focus ("we").

GETTING STARTED

Once you have your business plan in place and have decided to become an independent InfoSec consultant, your plan should provide you with a step-by-step approach to getting started.[1] Let's break down the InfoSec consulting business into sections (see Figure 17.1):

- Engagement setup
- Engagement process
- Assessment services
- Advisory services
- Security implementation
- Augmentation
- Legal issues
- International aspects

Engagement Setup

To begin, you need an "entry into the business" strategy. You must have established and continue to refine your information network (trusted contacts within your business arena who can tell you what is going on where, etc.). You must also use other sources to find your potential customers—

---

[1] Some of the information provided in this chapter was provided by Steve Lutz, President, WaySecure, a very successful international security consultant and InfoSec specialist for decades.

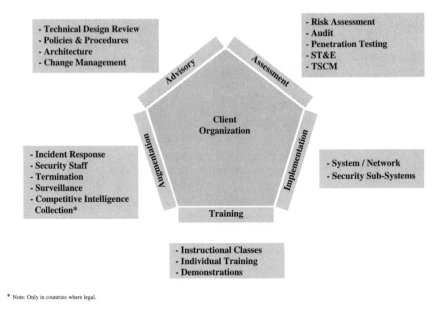

- Technical Design Review
- Policies & Procedures
- Architecture
- Change Management

- Risk Assessment
- Audit
- Penetration Testing
- ST&E
- TSCM

Advisory

Assessment

Client
Organization

Augmentation

Implementation

- Incident Response
- Security Staff
- Termination
- Surveillance
- Competitive Intelligence
  Collection*

- System / Network
- Security Sub-Systems

Training

- Instructional Classes
- Individual Training
- Demonstrations

* Note: Only in countries where legal.

Figure 17.1   An example of InfoSec consulting components.[2]

or clients, as some like to call them. Such other sources include referrals, marketing through brochures, pamphlets, lectures, books, articles, and your business Web site. It also includes "cold calling" of potential customers and explaining to them what services you offer.

Once you have made contact with a potential client, you must clearly and precisely communicate your services; you must "find their pain" and explain how you can help solve their problems. Try to make this a question-and-answer session where a dialogue takes place. You should also use the opportunity to explain your experience by citing examples of your past services to clients, without providing specific names, of course.

Assuming the meeting went well and they ask you for a proposal, you should provide one in the most expeditious manner possible and be sure that you understand: Each client requires a different approach depending on the size of the client—small, medium, or large organization—as the scale, tactics, and strategy will vary with each. In the proposal you should be precise, include a project schedule with logistics requirements, roles, and responsibilities (for both you and your client), and address liability issues. Other matters to consider are:

- Understand who you are dealing with and be sure to get to the right level of authority to make decisions that affect your work;

- Identify their needs as specifically as possible;
- Understand their budget (size and cycle);
- Get the "big picture";
- Be sure you have a clear understanding of their expectations and your deliverables, before leaving the potential client;
- Determine any time factors that they want to consider; and
- If needed, exchange encryption keys so correspondence can be done in private.

As part of your engagement setup, you should have a specific written proposal prepared, as well as one in the standard format you have developed. Both should be on your notebook computer so that they can be modified immediately to fit the situation. If you believe your specific written proposal is just right for your potential client, be sure to have several hard copies available to present to the potential client. The proposal, as a minimum, should include:

- Proposal Structure
- Work to Be Performed
- Project Schedule
- Timing and Fees
- Roles and Responsibilities
- Assumptions and Caveats
- Legal Issues

Engagement Process

Once you begin, remember to document everything to include:

- Time and dates;
- Whom you spoke to;
- What was said;
- Any action items resulting from the conversations;
- Task you completed and their time and date;
- Notable events that occurred; and
- All other matters that can be used to support your activities, position, time spent, and the like.

More than one consultant has found that they performed work based on conversations with a client's employee, and then found that the client balked in making payments for that work, since they considered it unauthorized—the person had no authority to direct a consultant to perform that function. It is imperative that you and the client both have a clear understanding of what is agreed to, when it will be accomplished, proof that it was accomplished, and the fees relative to completing the work. Notes help when discussing the work performed, and especially in dealing with the billing process. An excellent technique to use during the engagement management process is to monitor the progress of the engagement on a daily basis. Constantly communicate with the client the progress (or lack of it) and delineate why there are delays. If there are delays due to a fault on the part of the client, inform the client of the impact to the engagement and give choices such as:

- Ask for additional funding,
- Abbreviate certain tasks, or
- Eliminate certain tasks.

This technique helps avoid unpleasant surprises and misunderstandings. It's a "we" mentality. You approach your counterpart project manager and say "Joe, we've got a problem. The project is behind because of this, this, and this. How do you think we can fix this?" If the project is screwed up, Joe has just as much to lose politically as you do monetarily. If there is a debate as to why things aren't going well, the events are fresh in everyone's minds and it's easy to sort out and correct or compensate. A common mistake is to wait until near the end of the engagement when things are way behind schedule and inform the client, thinking that somehow everything might work out. This will end up in a best-case scenario as souring the client relationship and worst-case, in court arguing over who did what when.

If there are delays due to your own performance or lack of planning, work extra hours and accept the loss. Do whatever you have to do to meet the objectives of the proposal, and don't complain about it. Make careful notes as to why you miscalculated or undermanaged the engagement, and use that knowledge when writing your next proposal.

Assessment Services

You may want to break your services into various groups. One group may be "assessment services." This should have been decided as part of your business plan. These services include such things as penetration testing and security tests and evaluations of software, systems, and it may include supporting documentation analyses. Also included may be technical security countermeasures (TSCM), audits, and risk assessments.

Advisory Services

Advisory services, also previously considered as part of your business plan, include the following:

- Technical design review;
- Policies, procedures, and guidelines;
- Security change management;
- Systems and network security; and
- Security architecture.

Security Implementation

The services to be considered, based on your expertise, of course, include ensuring that products to be installed on systems don't make the systems and networks more vulnerable and any security software meets the needs of the business and operates as advertised. Again, be sure to document everything.

Augmentation

Augmentation services may include such things as termination surveillance and assisting in client investigations of employees, such as computer forensic services. You may also be requested to respond to incidents. If so, this should be addressed in your contract, and also the billing for such responses—which often seem to happen after midnight.

Legal Issues

Legal issues may arise as to your authority in conducting or assisting in high-technology crime investigations; as well as issues related to your contract. It is imperative, to avoid legal problems later, that all matters be clearly and concisely stated in the contract. The worst thing you would want is conflicts in contract interpretations, delayed payments, or refusal to pay what you billed the client, not to mention the problem of your reputation, which will follow you (good and bad) from client to client.

Above all, *never* begin an engagement without a signed contract. Make certain that the person signing it has the legal right to do so for the organization (usually an officer or director).

International Aspects

More and more InfoSec consultants are working all over the world and with foreign clients. In dealing with such clients, it is important to:

- Avoid slang, colloquial terms;
- Learn as much of the foreign language and culture as possible;
- Make positive comments on the food and architecture;
- Use local hand gestures and volume of speech;
- Understand the foreign governments where you will be working;
- Understand the latest terrorist threats in the region;
- Explain InfoSec terms in local context;
- Don't complain about their country or culture or brag about yours; and
- Avoid political discussions or, if you are dragged into a conversation, remain neutral.

QUESTIONS TO CONSIDER

Based on what you have read, consider the following questions and how you would reply to them:

- Do you want to be an independent InfoSec consultant?
- If so, what are its pros and cons for you?
- Do you believe you have the education, experience, and reputation necessary to be a successful InfoSec consultant?
- If so, can you list them in detail?
- Do you plan on becoming an InfoSec consultant in the future?
- If so, should you begin planning today?
- If so, what would be your business plan?
- Do you have the financial resources to get started?
- If not, how will you get these resources?
- What services would you offer?
- Why do you think you could succeed?

SUMMARY

Being an independent InfoSec consultant is not for everyone. One must not only have the education and experience in the InfoSec profession to be successful, but also the required personality, self-discipline, and confidence. The bottom line is that it's not really better being an independent consultant, just different. New headaches replace old ones, and different benefits arise. The real change is in lifestyle and sources of stress. The new boss is the client, and some can be better or worse than your old boss. The good part is that you only have to deal with a bad "boss" for the duration of the engagement.

Some ISSOs working for corporations believe that they can succeed but have not conducted sufficient, objective analysis to validate their beliefs. Before beginning a career change from a corporate ISSO to an independent InfoSec consultant, you should develop a detailed business plan and supporting project plan. In doing so, you may find that being a consultant is not something you can do. It is better to find that out before making the career change than afterwards.

18

21st-Century Challenges for the ISSO

Man has a limited biological capacity for change. When this capacity is overwhelmed, it is in "future shock."—Alvin Toffler[1]

CHAPTER OBJECTIVE

The objective of this chapter, "21st-Century Challenges for the ISSO," is to look into the future and discuss the challenges to the ISSO and the risks to information systems and information as we begin the 21st century.

INTRODUCTION

In the beginning of this book, we looked at the past world of the ISSO professional. We then transitioned to today's InfoSec world; that of the global marketplace; and the corporate world of the ISSO and InfoSec staff. We will conclude this book with an overview of the possible future working environment of the ISSO professional and what the ISSO professional must do today to prepare to address tomorrow's information and information systems assets protection issues.[2]

As we look at the past, the present, and their trends, we can project those trends to provide some reasonable, at least short-term, visions of the future working environment of the ISSO professional.

As we progress through the 21st century, the ISSO will face many challenges—many brought on by high technology, but not all of them. Let's look into the possible future. We'll begin by taking the broad view and narrowing it down to the narrower, InfoSec-focused outlook, in the following order:

---

[1] Alvin Toffler (1928–), U.S. writer. *Future Shock* (1970). Taken from *Microsoft Encarta World English Dictionary*.
[2] Some of the material in this chapter was excerpted from other books written by Dr. Kovacich and is reproduced with permission of the publisher, Butterworth–Heinemann.

- Nation-states
- Societies
- High technology
- Global competition
- The future of the ISSO professional
- Managing an InfoSec department in the future

Keep in mind that changes cause conflicts and destabilize information environments (IE). Therefore, the more things change, the more risks there are to IE assets. Since we are now globally connected, any change anywhere has a likelihood of adversely affecting an ISSO's IE.

NATION-STATES—WILL THEY LAST?

When we look back from the times of the caveman up to today, we often fail to realize that the entity we call the nation-state has a very short history of only several hundred years. Some, such as Davidson and Rees-Moog, believe

> Something new is coming. Just as farming societies differed in kind from hunting-and-gathering bands, and industrial societies differed radically from feudal or yeoman agricultural systems, so the New World to come will mark a radical departure from anything seen before. . . .[3]

Davidson and Rees-Moog, among others, believe that the "sovereign individual" will rise out of the nation-states. If what they say is true, then we all probably can agree that the nation-states will not go quietly. Just as individuals fight for survival, so will the nation-states. There are many rather recent examples such as the former Yugoslavia, the former Union of Soviet Socialist Republics, and Indonesia (East Timor and other conflicts for independence from this republic).

There will be those citizens, including ISSO professionals, whose patriotism and "love of country" will support the nation-states over their citizens. They will join with those in the government who do not want to lose power, as well as those corporations who find the power of the nation-states to be an effective and important ally in the competitive world of global business. Many, if not most, of these changes have been brought about by technology, and of course that includes the Internet.

> The real issue is control. The Internet is too widespread to be easily dominated by any single government. By creating a seamless global-economic

---

[3] Davidson and Rees-Moog, authors of *The Sovereign Individual: Mastering the Transition to the Information Age*, published by Simon & Schuster, New York, 1999.

zone, anti-sovereign and unregulatable, the Internet calls into question the very idea of a nation-state. —John Perry Barlow.[4]

The global changes will continue to affect, in a positive and negative manner, the interactions of nation-states, as well as their very existence.

Nation-states will be torn apart with ever-increasing chaos and rapid disintegration into factions. These factions try to build a "world consensus" in their favor to force governments to allow more freedom, as well as dissolving portions of these nation-states into smaller nation-states. The nation-states will justify their controls, government policies, etc. As was previously stated, the breakups of the Soviet Union and the old Yugoslavia are just two examples of what other nation-states may have to look forward to in the 21st century.

The economic domino effect that continues to take place throughout the world, for example, recession in Asia affects the Americas and Europe, validates the interlinking and interdependencies of nation-states. These dependencies will play a more crucial role in the global order. Economic espionage—the theft of information—will continue to grow in support of a nation-state's objective of becoming an economic power. The increasingly more sophisticated and more dangerous threats will offer the ISSO professionals some of their greatest challenges. Netspionage (network enabled espionage) is a relatively recent type of espionage and grows as global networks expand.

Asia's economic woes will ebb and flow. They will lessen and the Asian nation-states will gain renewed strength as the dominant, economic region of the world, which will be led by China. The financial and intellectual resources of Singapore (Chinese), the intellectual resources and technology of Taiwan (Chinese), integrated with the cheap labor and natural resources of mainland China, including the financial power of Hong Kong, will ensure the domination of "Chinese" as an Asian and global economic power that even today reaches beyond national borders. For example, it has been reported that in Indonesia alone, the Chinese make up only about 4% of the population but control more than 70% of Indonesia's wealth. Thus, the Chinese in Indonesia became a scapegoat for the Indonesian economic woes. Such ethnic violence due to religion and race will continue to grow on a global basis. Factions, ethnic groups, and religious groups will increase their presence and conflicts throughout the world, replacing some of the conflicts between nation-states as the world's biggest challenges. With more than 90% of the populations of Indonesia, Malaysia, and Brunei being Muslims, not to mention the Middle East, they offer, as we have already observed, a growing terrorist faction as a very real threat. These terrorists will expand their targets to include major

---

[4] John Perry Barlow, "Thinking Locally, Acting Globally," *Time* magazine, January 15, 1996, p. 57.

foreign corporations with the goal of damaging their adversaries' economic stability.

ISSOs must understand these terrorists' threats. Although many are now relegated to blowing up people and facilities—which include IEs—they are also beginning to look at targeting networks. What global networks does your corporation rely on? What will you do when a terrorist takes them out?

For an ISSO in a corporation with a global presence, the protection of the IE and its assets takes on a more critical role in helping the corporation compete in the global marketplace. Your corporation's IE assets may be at greater risk because of what happens in another part of the world. And with the ability of factions, groups, and nation-states to attack your corporate IE assets from anywhere in the world in a nanosecond, the challenges to the ISSO professionals will dramatically increase.

It is expected that the majority of nation-states' citizens will want the priority and the limited resources of law enforcement agencies to be spent on protecting the citizens from violent crimes such as terrorism. This will require more and more corporations to take care of themselves, especially in matters of white-collar crime, such as fraud against the corporation. As IE assets protection becomes more high-technology-based, the use of IE assets protection specialists will be called upon by corporate management. There will be an increased demand for IE assets protection specialists—consultants who can provide these services. IE assets protection consultants will be required to understand the global risks, including the risks posed by fraudsters, terrorists, hackers, Netspionage agents, and the like. This will increase the ability of InfoSec specialists to ply their trade. The focus will change from narrowingly focusing on technology solutions and more on holistic solutions, including eliminating the motive and rationale for attacks on systems.

Governments will continue to use Industrial Age legislative processes in vain attempts to "control" citizens of nation-states, including those portions of the Internet that affect their nation. They will continue to fail, although some small successes may occur here and there. The issue of privacy (or the lack thereof) will continue to be discussed on one hand, while other government agencies heighten their monitoring activities, for example, of the Internet. Unfortunately, privacy issues will continue to run contrary to the needs of businesses and government agencies; thus they will be given no more than lip service, so that businesses can grow uninhibited by personal privacy issues of the individual. At the same time, governments can maintain their power and control.

Such things as the United States' Homeland Security bureaucracy and Critical Information Infrastructure Protection bureaucracies are examples of using Industrial Age methods to solve Information Age problems. Such methods are too slow and will not work in the Information Age. Political appointees and not security professionals run them. Therefore, the

ISSO can expect little in the way of government support for protecting corporate IW assets. As for such agencies as the FBI, well, they never were much help and now with the emphasis on terrorism, they will not be of any future help.

The ISSO professionals must help maintain the privacy of individuals if the citizens of the world are to maintain or increase their chances for opportunity and freedom.

SOCIETIES

The people of all the nation-states who have high-technology communications access—Internet, cellular telephones, faxes, satellite television, cable television—will become more sophisticated. They will have ever-increasing, massive amounts of information at their disposal, allowing them to become more knowledgeable on global matters. They also will become more aware of those throughout the world who have similar and different views.

The Internet and other high-technology tools provide massive, personal communications pipelines that will provide the means for people to communicate globally as never before. Such massive one-on-one communications will be a driving force that will affect governments, businesses, and societies to such an extent that the governments and businesses will develop extremely sophisticated techniques to influence these Internet communicators on a global scale—or attempt to deny them access to information.

Societies will become more sophisticated as they become more educated and knowledgeable about the world in which we live. High technology such as the Internet will also be the driver in helping people become better educated, often replacing today's Industrial Age school systems. Already, colleges and universities are offering courses and degrees through Internet access. This will allow individuals to obtain degrees from universities and colleges located in different nation-states of the world.

The Internet as a global learning center will not come without challenges from those in the educational systems and their unions who see such endeavors as a threat to their power and their bureaucracies. However, their delaying tactics will be just that, delaying the inevitable. ISSO professionals will be able to enroll in courses and learn from the best in their profession no matter where that professor may reside. Specialized, technology-related institutes will take on a more legitimate role as an educational institution and dominate the educational institutions of today.

The InfoSec professionals will be able to obtain degrees from the best colleges, universities, and institutes of the world. Furthermore, they will be able to take these courses based on *their* schedule. Papers will be transmitted via e-mail, and tests will be conducted through secure channels where the students' identification will be confirmed. Education of tomorrow not only will be different, but will be a required, lifelong endeavor. For those in the InfoSec profession and other professions, there will be less emphasis on where you received your education, and more on what you know and can apply to further business and protect IE assets. There are already signs of this, as those who can implement and maintain high-technology devices are sought out by corporations, regardless of their college degree or lack thereof.

THE FUTURE OF HIGH TECHNOLOGY

As the global marketplace continues to change and becomes more dependent upon technology, the need for corporate IE assets protection will become greater and more complicated. It is obvious that the technological trend to make microprocessors. and everything that they are used for, smaller, more powerful, and cheaper will continue. This coupled with the ever-increasing bandwidth, multimedia, and personal communications systems will provide for a microportability only dreamed of and shown in science fiction movies. Furthermore, the wireless age coupled with the integration of devices into one device—for example, combining Internet access, telephone, database, digital photography, and television—will offer new challenges to ISSO professionals.

The need to have such devices in order to work, shop, and access information will require that everyone be guaranteed such a system as an inherent right as a citizen of an Information Age nation-state. Without such devices, the government will be "depriving" the citizens of everything from due process to the right to work. The Internet, which seemed a novelty not so long ago, will be in truth one of the mainstream methods of working and communicating.

The development of more sophisticated systems that are able to understand and react to normal human speech will become commonplace. This technology will be a major breakthrough that will allow previously computer illiterate individuals to use the power of the computers, networks, and the Internet to work, play, and communicate. This will allow people who could either not afford a computer or could not learn how to use one to become better-educated and valuable members of societies with less effort. Voice recognition security will become a major necessity to protect assets in the voice recognition environment. ISSO professionals must begin now to learn all they can about biometrics, nanotechnology, wireless systems, and such high technology to be prepared to address such issues as voice recognition access to IE assets in the future.

Enhanced technology will continue to support the drive to global telemedicine, where the best specialists in the world will be in a position to medically assist anyone, anywhere, at any time. However, with this enhanced use of the Internet will come telemedicine murders. These will be accomplished by changing medical test results or the automated dosages of prescription drugs, and denying telemedicine services. Security and law enforcement specialists will be involved in conducting murder investigations where the crime scene will be the Internet.

The future will also bring us biological computers. For example, it is rumored that some are even looking at using electrically charged amoebas or other methods that can allow a direct interface with the human brain. Such incredibly advanced computers could perhaps store the entire history of the human race on a single chip. Who will determine what is contained in that history? What are the social ramifications of such dramatic extensions to personal information access? What happens if a criminal or a terrorist embeds a virus, logic bomb, or other malicious software in a computer extension attached to your brain? What input do ISSO professionals currently have in this research? None. However, for InfoSec, for example, access criteria, will be a major issue. How does one ensure the integrity of the hardware, software, firmware, and information that is to be embedded for access by the brain? ISSO professionals may require a degree in some field of medicine in order to successfully perform their asset protection duties vis-à-vis telemedicine.

The "wireless age" is already upon us, and with it the increased use of technology allowing mobile electronic communications from any place on earth to anywhere. As the growth of wireless networks continues worldwide, it will bring with it more threats from sophisticated, international criminals. Such threats will include an increased use of jamming techniques as a denial of service, to commit electronic extortion or to harm a competitor's ability to perform electronic commerce on the Internet. As more forms of public communication come to rely on the Internet, we expect that more sophisticated eavesdropping techniques will rise, which will allow Internet miscreants, business adversaries, and government agencies to invade personal privacy to their respective ends. The increasing use of the many Internet telephone and video teleconference systems which are vulnerable to eavesdropping will make this more common.

Encryption will continue to become more sophisticated while the issue of key management overhead costs, prohibitions on exporting of effective encryption methods, will continue to be debated on a global scale. Nation-states' security agencies will require and continue to obtain access to encrypted communications via "key escrow." (No, the issue is not dead. It has "gone covert" because of the bad publicity and concerns that have been voiced over this concept.) Also, "backdoors" will be used, but on a massive scale. There have already been attempts to outlaw all encryption that does not meet a nation's "standards." That of course was impossible to enforce; however, the basic issue is still alive and well. For indications of software backdoors, just look at the software vendors who have contracts with the National Security Agency of the United States and other high-technology-dependent nation-states.

Do you trust your government to have "backdoor" access to your corporation's sensitive and vital networks and information without your control or knowledge? How do you know what the government agents and bureaucrats are doing with that information? Government employees are human, and there are those who betray their countries. Can you place alarms on such systems without the knowledge of the vendors who may be cooperating with the government by placing backdoors in their vendor-provided products? Furthermore, if there are backdoors, they are also vulnerable to attack by competitors and other governments. Is it any wonder why some government agencies of nation-states don't use Microsoft's operating systems? Maybe they don't feel comfortable with Microsoft's employees working so closely with the U.S. National Security Agency staff. Does anyone really believe that there are no backdoors in today's software?

Other nation-states with less sophisticated technology will request that technology in order to allow Internet communications to transit their nation. Others will prohibit any encryption under the banner of "national security interests." Their concern, and excuse, will be the use of encryption by factions whose purpose is to bring down the current government, or to attack corporations.

These vulnerabilities will be exploited by other nation-states and Internet miscreants, who will become more sophisticated in decrypting communications as computers become more and more sophisticated and as massive chaining of computers is used to break encrypted messages. Also, they will be usable to find and exploit the government-required, vendor-provided backdoors. As an ISSO professional, are you aware of other techniques such as steganography? If not, you should be, as their use will increase in the future.

Copyright violations on the Internet will continue unabated with more and more information being made available on a massive scale. The "software police" and others will be so overwhelmed that they will only attempt to investigate and prosecute those cases that provide good public relations for the agency and are major violations. These issues will continue to be a concern of only a few of the most mature Information Age nation-states. Other nation-states, including some members of the European Union, East European nation-states, and other nation-states, such as those in Asia, South America, and Africa, will provide only token assistance. This will be done in order to rapidly and cheaply bring their nation-states into the Information Age through the use of "free" copyrighted information. As an ISSO for a corporation that has copyright issues, what are you doing to protect the copyrighted corporate assets?

Political factions and "pressure groups" with common causes, such as "Save the Whales," will become more active in denying the use of the

Internet and Web sites of those businesses or government agencies whose actions are opposed by the factions.

Information warfare will play an increased role in 21st-century warfare. Civilized nation-states today have little tolerance for violence, human death, and suffering. The use of computers and networks to fight the information wars of the future will become more common as they offer a cheap, rapid, and powerful "weapon of mass destruction."

Electronic and computer weapons to destroy an adversary's information infrastructure, and thus its economic power, will take on more importance. The use of the Internet by military forces and techno-terrorists will continue to increase as a nation's adversaries become more dependent on information systems and the Internet for their political and economic power.

Electronic commerce is already on the Internet, and the Internet is too large for corporations and Internet miscreants to ignore. Billions of dollars' worth of transactions will be conducted each year. To have electronic commerce, one must have sellers, customers, and infrastructure to transfer goods, services, and money *securely*. Security will continue to be enhanced, thus providing reasonable, cheap, simple transaction security. This will happen exponentially and cause a rapid expansion of electronic commerce through the Internet.

Perry Luzwick[5] of Northrop Grumman's Corporation's Information Technology Group has pointed out:

New technologies have affected competitive advantage by:

- Leveraging existing strategies or efforts
- Enabling new and unexpected strategic uses of existing technology
- Providing new capabilities
- Neutralizing or mitigating the effects of competitors' capabilities and strategies
- Providing or denying the element of surprise

The enactment of international laws will lag behind high technology and international crimes, making it extremely difficult to identify, apprehend, and prosecute global criminals across national boundaries. Some successes will of course occur, as in the international fight against child pornography. However, the more sophisticated, financially based, Internet-based miscreants will grow in number because ISSO professionals lack the capabilities to protect against them and law enforcement professionals lack the capabilities to investigate and apprehend them.

---

[5] Perry Luzwick is the Director, Information Assurance Architectures at Northrop Grumman Information Technology, a Northrop Grumman company, and coauthor of the book *Global Information Warfare*, published with Andy Jones and Dr. Kovacich by Auerbach Publishers, 2002.

GLOBAL COMPETITION

As economics plays an ever-increasing major role in the world of nation-states, it will become the dominant weapon that nation-states will use to project their power and influence. Economic power will replace military power in that regard, as the United States continues over at least the next decade or more to be the most militarily powerful nation-state in the world, with China vying for that status.

> NEW YORK (CNN/Money)—The United States will impose a 30 percent tariff on steel imports over the next three years in an effort to give the nation's beleaguered steel industry breathing space to recover, the Bush administration announced Tuesday.[6]

Economic power will lead to more economic warfare, including anything from trade wars using tariffs to factional battles in the World Trade Organization (WTO) arena, as nation-states argue that others are not complying with the WTO agreements.

Increased global competition among nation-states will lead to more nation-states supporting their corporations, both national and international, more strongly than ever before. Furthermore, because of the dependencies of modern nation-states and the corporations on information and information systems, such systems will become more of a target and also a weapon in the trade and economic wars.

> The EU move came in a letter from its ambassador to the World Trade Organization, Carlo Trojan, to his U.S. counterpart in Geneva, Linnet Deily. It followed statements from U.S. officials rejecting EU calls for compensation, which the EU, supported by Japan and some other countries hit by the U.S. measures, argues is provided for in the WTO's Safeguards Agreement. [7]

At the same time, global corporations will help by having more and more influence in the nation-states where they are located. They will also become more of a stabilizing force, as business abhors conflicts and uncertainties. Such events are bad for business. Therefore, as nation-states over time have less influence, global corporations will continue to expand their influence and in some ways take the place of nation-states, in particular the smaller nation-states. We already see instances of that where the corporations have more power, influence, and assets (including money) than some of today's Third World nation-states. These corporations are providing more and more for the welfare of some nation-states' citizens than

---

[6]http://money.cnn.com/2002/03/05/economy/steel/index.htm, March 5, 2002.
[7]http://money.cnn.com/2002/03/15/news/international/eu_steel.reut/index.htm, March 15, 2002.

do the governments of these nation-states, including housing, medical services, and recreational sites.

Businesses will continue to expand their use of outsourcing InfoSec functions and the use of consultants to meet their IE asset protection and investigative needs. In the realm of large, multinational corporate enterprises, the cost of employing sophisticated "private InfoSec" services to ensure that businesses' IE assets are protected will be seen as merely a cost of doing business. However, small and medium-size organizations will be significantly challenged to provide adequate IE assets protection—yet a failure to do so may well subject them to ruinous losses. Furthermore, such small and medium businesses are being linked to major, global corporations as their suppliers and subcontractors. One wonders if there will be anyone who will be affordable and available to protect the small businesses that are some of the major "weak links" in the IEs of major corporations.

As high technology continues in its sophistication, power, and miniaturization, there will be no way of protecting sensitive corporate information unless it is retained only in hard copy and not stored on any computer system. Corporations will try to gain a competitive advantage by making better products faster than the competition.

One of the strategies that will be adopted more and more by corporations is one of *knowledge management* (KM). According to Mr. Perry Luzwick:

> Knowledge management (KM), the development and integration of technologies, processes, and cultural changes, provides a means for well-informed, rapid decision making via collaborative information and knowledge sharing by varied and dispersed organizations and individuals. KM tenets include support for organizational processes; tailored content delivery; information sharing and reuse; capturing tacit knowledge as part of the work process; situational awareness of information and knowledge assets; and valuation. KM enables an organization to be more agile, flexible, and proactive. The approach is ideal for integrating intelligence (e.g., economic and open source) and security (e.g., physical, personnel, and operations). Organizations can use KM to both gain competitive advantage and also protect their Information Environment (IE).

The corporations will begin to look more and more at some of the military strategies of warfare for providing the competitive advantage in their "global business wars." As stated earlier in this book, among these strategies is one based on the *OODA loop* (Observe–Orient–Decide–Act). The idea (attributed to Colonel John R. Boyd, United States Air Force) is that the corporation (in this case) that can be the quickest to move through this loop gains a competitive advantage. Furthermore, the advantage is created because the competitor becomes more confused and uncertain over events, and that may influence the competitor's judgment and decisions.

In his document *Patterns of Conflict*, Boyd concluded that operating inside an opponent's OODA loop generates "uncertainty, doubt, mistrust, confusion, disorder, fear, panic, and chaos." How you can use this technique and also defend against it may very well mean the difference between profit and loss for your corporation.

THE FUTURE ROLE OF ISSO PROFESSIONALS

The ISSO professionals of the future will face many more challenges than is now the case—although for some that is hard to believe, as they battle under increased stress and pressure to protect corporate IE assets. As noted earlier, the world will continue to be an unsafe place, there will be more competition, and technology will support and also adversely affect corporations and the protection of the corporate assets.

The ISSO professional of the future should:

- Have a formal education including at least associate degrees and bachelor's degrees in computer science, criminal justice, business, sociology, government and politics, and psychology, and at least one master's degree (MBA in international business);
- Have certifications in all aspects of security and security-related fields, such as CPP, CFE, CISSP, CISA;
- Understand the world, changes in nation-states' relationships, different societies and cultures, and their impact on IE assets protection philosophies, strategies, and the like;
- Understand the global marketplace and competitors;
- Understand your corporation, its history, products, marketing strategies, processes; and plans;
- Understand how to establish and manage the most effective and efficient assets protection program that protects IE assets at least cost, at an acceptable level of risk, with least impact to corporate costs and schedules consistent with sound business and assets protection practices; and
- Understand the world and role of the ISSO professional in the future.

MANAGING A CIAPP AND CORPORATE INFOSEC ORGANIZATION IN THE FUTURE

The ISSO professional responsible for establishing and managing a CIAPP and corporate InfoSec organization in the future must do so using the philosophies stated throughout this book if he or she is to have an effective and efficient CIAPP. The ISSO professional must take every opportunity to use technology where it will support the CIAPP; however, the ISSO must also consider the human element and changes in world affairs.

The ISSO professional must be constantly learning and applying new techniques and processes, at the same time being a leader in the community, corporation, to the InfoSec staff, and in the professional associations.

The individuals who take on this challenge and apply cost-effective techniques will gain personal and professional rewards and will be able to say that they are truly ISSO professionals.

One of the key elements is the ability of the ISSO professional to be flexible, react, and change when needed to support the corporations' IE assets protection needs—cost-effectively.

OTHER CONSIDERATIONS

When a government agency or corporate computer system is attacked, the response to such an attack will be based on the attacker. Will the attacker be a hacker, phreaker, cracker, or just someone breaking in for fun? Will the attacker be an employee of a business competitor, in the case of an attack on a business system, or will it be a terrorist, or a government agency-sponsored attack for economic reasons? Will the attacker be a foreign soldier attacking the system as a prelude to war?

These questions require serious consideration when information systems are being attacked, because the answers dictate the response. Would we attack a country because of what a terrorist or economic spy did to a business or government system?

To complicate the matter, what if the terrorist was in a third country but only made it look like he/she was coming from your potential adversary? How do you know?

The key to the future is in information systems security for defense and information warfare weapons. As with nuclear weapons used as a form of deterrent, in the future, information weapons systems will be the basis of the information warfare deterrent.

Each nation must begin now to prepare for 21st-century warfare by establishing a program to ensure the protection of information assets in the 21st century.

Remember, it is bad enough to be attacked, but it is worse to be attacked and not know it until it is too late!

QUESTIONS TO CONSIDER

Based on what you have read, consider the following questions and how you would reply to them:

- Have you looked at the world in which your corporation does business?
- If so, what are the specific threats that you see which affect your IE assets protection functions now and in the future?
- Does your corporation have facilities in other nation-states?
- If so, what processes do you have in place to protect the IE assets in those nation-states?
- Do you follow political and social trends in the nation-states where your corporation does business?
- If so, do you have processes in place to analyze those trends for impact on the protection of your corporation's IE assets?
- Do you look at the future of high technology and analyze what protection mechanisms must also be ready for integration into those products when your corporation buys them?
- Are you aware of the vulnerabilities of the networks that are integrated or in some way attached to your corporation's networks?
- What can you do to ensure that vulnerabilities of the networks of others interfacing with your corporation's networks do not adversely affect your IE?
- Do you understand the culture and languages of those nation-states where your corporation has facilities?
- Do you understand the global marketplace and use that knowledge in developing your CIAPP?

SUMMARY

Our present world will continue to be one of military, economic, and business wars that will affect the ability of global corporations to compete and succeed in the global marketplace. Changes will continue to occur rapidly and probably exponentially, as high technology, technology driven by the microprocessor, is the driver for IE assets protection changes and challenges.

The world remains in a constant state of change—some changes that are for the better and some that are not. All of these changes affect the ISSO professionals in their objective of successfully protecting corporate IE assets. The ISSO professionals of tomorrow must be more educated, experienced in all aspects of the world, technologically literate, and flexible in meeting the needs of the corporation.

The ISSO professional of tomorrow also has great opportunities to make more of a positive difference in the world, community, corporation, and profession. For those of you in the ISSO profession, enjoy the exciting ride that awaits you in the future.

There are four basic ISSO challenges for the 21st century:

- The continued increase and globalization of the Internet and its connections to the businesses' and government agencies' intranets (electronic commerce);
- The increasing threats of Netspionage espionage;
- The increasing potential and threats of high-technology-oriented terrorists (techno-terrorists); and
- The concern and potential threats of information warfare.

Boni, a highly skilled, professional ISSO, said of the ISSO's 21st century challenges:

ISSOs will likely end up in the line of fire in a future type of information warfare (e.g. banking, telecommunications, power grids, transportation, etc.). They *will* be the combatants in such conflicts and their systems at risk to the hostilities of the time.

ISSO roles therefore will only grow in importance, so new entrants to this fascinating career field will find they are embarked upon a lifelong voyage of growth, learning and discovery.

There will be long periods of boring repetition punctuated by moments of adrenaline rush as they face off with a techno-criminal or hostile competitor bent on destruction of the organization's competitive stature. At that moment in time, they will learn if their protection mechanisms are up to the challenges of the 21st century.

They are part of the future "thin blue line," the close alliance of the ISSOs in the organizations and society's protective institutions (law enforcement, national defense) against the rising forces of techno-anarchy and destruction.

Welcome to the front lines!

Index